Petty Tyranny and Soulless Discipline?

Petty Tyranny and Soulless Discipline?

Patients, policy and practice in public mental hospitals in England, 1918–1930

Claire Hilton

UCLPRESS

First published in 2025 by
UCL Press
University College London
Gower Street
London WC1E 6BT

Available to download free: www.uclpress.co.uk

A CIP catalogue record for this book is available from The British Library.

ISBN: 978-1-80008-859-7 (Hbk)
ISBN: 978-1-80008-860-3 (Pbk)
ISBN: 978-1-80008-861-0 (PDF)
ISBN: 978-1-80008-862-7 (epub)
DOI: https://doi.org/10.14324/111.9781800088610

Printed and bound by CPI Group (UK) Ltd, Croydon, CR0 4YY

In memoriam

Professor David James Jolley (1944–2024)

An inspiring, learned and kind colleague, mentor and friend who worked incessantly to improve the lives of mentally ill older people.

The memory of a righteous man shall be for a blessing (Proverbs 10:7)

Contents

List of figures

List of tables

List of abbreviations

BMJ	*British Medical Journal*
BoC	Board of Control
GMC	General Medical Council
GNC	General Nursing Council
GPI	General paralysis of the insane (brain syphilis)
HC	House of Commons
HL	House of Lords
JMS	*Journal of Mental Science*
LCC	London County Council
MACA	Mental After Care Association
med sup	medical superintendent
MoH	Ministry of Health
MPA	Medico-Psychological Association
MRC	Medical Research Council
NAWU	National Asylum Workers' Union
NCLR	National Council for Lunacy Reform (later, NSLR)
NCMH	National Council for Mental Hygiene
NHS	National Health Service
NSLR	National Society for Lunacy Reform (earlier, NCLR)
RMPA	Royal Medico-Psychological Association
Sub-Com	Sub-Committee
TLA	The London Archives
TNA	The National Archives, Kew
WL	Wellcome Library
WW1	World War One

Note on pre-decimal currency

I have used the notation '£ s d' for 'pounds, shillings and pence'.
For 'shillings and pence' I have used the forward slash e.g. 1 shilling and 6 pence is 1/6d
12d =1/- (today, 5p)
20/- = £1

Preface

During the First World War, patients' care in the civilian 'lunatic asylums' in England was often disturbingly inadequate. Post-war, national schemes for social and welfare improvements aimed to make the country 'fit for heroes'. Might the patients also begin to fare better?

Despite initial post-war optimism, the austerity and traumas of four years of war, plus the devastating Spanish influenza pandemic, were soon followed by economic turmoil, high rates of poverty and unemployment, and public unrest. Overall, the poorest in the population benefitted least from 'progress', and among them were mental hospital patients. Much was known about what to do to improve patients' lives, but achieving it was another matter. Many mental hospital leaders – including doctors, nurses, lawyers and people in local and national government – were resigned to providing a rigid, custodial and impersonal regime. Others took a more liberal stance and sought to create flexible, humane and individual-focussed care. Across the country, patients' experiences were far from uniform.

Some people recoil when I mention the theme of this book, on the assumption that the historical findings must be universally horrific and that we inevitably do better today. Although clinical and scientific research over the last century has benefited many patients, the overall picture is not quite so rosy. In addition to the eerie resonance of prolonged austerity and pandemics which led into both the 1920s and 2020s, mental healthcare echoes, including of institutional culture, attitudes and priorities, reverberate a century on.

This book narrates and explains how the mental healthcare system impacted on the lives of patients a century ago, how and why steps were taken to make changes, and what happened. It will have done its job if it also stimulates creative consideration about how services might be improved today.

Foreword

Claire Hilton has performed a significant public service in writing this book. She operates authoritatively in two different modes of experience when describing and analysing mental healthcare in England in the 1920s: history and clinical practice.

The historical account is chastening and properly rooted in the available sources. Dr Hilton documents with clarity, insight and proportionality the significant weaknesses of 1920s policy and operation in relation to the care of people called in stigmatising fashion 'pauper lunatics'.

To balance the record of institutional defensiveness, and consequential strategic failure, Dr Hilton is careful also to focus on 'history from below', accounts of the lived experience of patients and families caught within the too often routine 'animalistic' standards of care.

The author is also excellent in utilising her clinical background to explore the challenges associated with the development of mental healthcare. She describes how new clinical ideas from Europe and North America, such as linking biological, psychological and environmental factors to account for mental symptoms, were slow to permeate mental hospitals in England. This was in part because of a prevailing culture of authority, self-interest and deference. It was also because of unreasonable workloads on clinicians, isolation from general hospitals and (encouragingly) a healthy scepticism protecting patients from misleading research and unproven interventions. The respect for a combination of diverse motives of actors is a continuing theme in the book.

Despite the historical focus on the 1920s, to read this book is not to enter another world. Rather, it is to feel, a century after the events described, that there are some eerie and disturbing modern similarities. This is not to suggest that the language of 'herding', 'trotting' and 'keepers' has endured, or that surgeons any longer routinely write that 'the bones of maniacs are frequently fragile' in the context of allegations of physical abuse to patients. Nor is it to suggest the continuation of inadequate diets, or the use of patients as substitute, unpaid labour for unpleasant tasks which need to be done. But, the continuation of a top-down, insensitive, hierarchical approach to regulation, the rejection of complaints to protect the reputation of hospitals, and the deficit of kindness and compassion in patient care are familiar themes to those engaged in contemporary healthcare practice. I was particularly struck by the denial of sanitary products to menstruating women in mental healthcare, an issue still complained about in contemporary Ombudsman investigations.

Despite the 'silent pain' of so many patients in the 1920s and the appalling, patronising, generalised contempt so many experienced, one leaves this exemplary writing heartened. This is for three reasons. First, because of the force of rigorous scholarship and research in locating issues in their proper historical context. Second, because the citation of many examples of individual good practice even in dark times is testimony to instances of fundamental integrity. Third, because Dr Hilton's mapping (without focus on individual blame) of the elements of reform necessary to protect vulnerable individuals and their human rights in England in the twenty-first century is illustrative of the possibilities open to policy makers, notwithstanding the complexities and previous failures associated with mental healthcare.

Rob Behrens
Parliamentary and Health Service Ombudsman 2017–24

Acknowledgements

Numerous people have contributed to this book directly and indirectly over many years, through their patience, encouragement and guidance, and by helping me to develop good clinical and historical practices. Recently, I have bombarded some of them with long tirades of historical narrative accompanied by my anger and joy at what I have found while researching and writing about the mental hospitals a century ago. I am very grateful for their valuable insights, suggestions, enthusiasm and support. Those colleagues and friends include Gordon Bates, Nicol Ferrier, Clare Groves, John Hall, Louise Hide, Margaret Shepherd, Jane Whittaker, Susan Yadin and Sarah Marks, my mentor at Birkbeck, University of London.

Archivists and librarians, particularly at the National Archives, London Archives and Wellcome Collection, each of which I visited numerous times, have good humouredly answered endless questions and retrieved countless books and papers. The London Archives allowed me access to documents from Colney Hatch Mental Hospital in the 1920s which are usually closed to researchers under the 100-year rule to ensure confidentiality of personal data. Without the London Archives' agreement, this book would have lacked much detail concerning the lives of patients and staff in the second half of the decade.

Invitations to speak at academic seminars, including at the Royal Society of Medicine, the Manchester Medical Society and the Royal College of Psychiatrists, have helped shape my ideas, as has the sharp literary eye of Fiona Watson, the College librarian, who edits the Library, Archives and History blogs. Two anonymous reviewers offered valuable feedback following submission of the book proposal, and one of them then read the entire manuscript, giving advice which has added polish to the final text. Pat Gordon-Smith, Elliot Beck, Ruth Massey, Laura Glover and the production team at UCL Press have been meticulous and a pleasure to work with. I am also very grateful to UCL Press for giving me a fee waiver regarding costs of open access publication.

My husband Michael has coped with my long periods of social hibernation while researching and writing, and has accompanied me on visits to former mental hospitals and to find graves of patients from the distant past, sometimes in the most inclement weather. Our three sons Samuel, Jacob and Benjamin all took on tasks which I found daunting: designing the timeline, doing statistical analysis and creating the bespoke map.

Reuven Silverman kindly forwarded my email to Sir Rob Behrens asking him if he would write the foreword. Rob's enthusiasm for the project is much appreciated. Lastly, I must mention my colleague David Jolley. He died in May 2024, but even after being told of his prognosis a year prior to that, he asked to read the manuscript and provided feedback. This book is dedicated to him for his inspiration and endless encouragement throughout my psychiatry and history careers.

1
Introduction: historical context and methodological considerations

In November 1918, within days of the Armistice marking the end of the First World War, Prime Minister David Lloyd George took to the stage of the Grand Theatre, Wolverhampton and declared his intention to 'make Britain a fit country for heroes to live in'.[1] Despite high expectations for a better world, turning inspiring words into reality was much harder. Initially post-war, food prices fell and rationing ceased, the economy flourished and unemployment was lower than feared. There were moves to challenge deep-rooted social and gender inequalities. The Labour Party and trades unions were increasingly active and the Representation of the People Act 1918 gave many women the franchise, although not yet on the same footing as men.[2] Historian Pat Thane argued that the success of wartime state controls increased support for socialist approaches to the welfare of the population, leading to more state involvement in directing economic and social matters.[3]

A Ministry of Health was established in the wake of the lethal influenza pandemic of 1918–19. Many plans for prompt and wide-ranging Poor Law, health and welfare reform did not become reality, although some changes did take place. One of these was the Housing and Town Planning Act 1919, which offered generous subsidies to local authorities to build according to local need and to charge reasonable rents. However, in many places, the new housing provided homes for low-paid white-collar and skilled workers, and was not allocated to the poorest in the population. Overall, the most disadvantaged benefited least from changes aligned with 'progress'.[4]

Policies and implementation pointing away from the needs of the poorest people were ominous for mentally unwell patients living in the network of publicly funded county and borough lunatic asylums. Those people were officially designated 'pauper lunatics' – a derogatory and stigmatising term ascribed to them because their inpatient stay under the Lunacy Act 1890 was funded through the Poor Law. The pauper label, associated with a sense of un-deservingness, was unlikely to generate public sympathy or policy priority in their favour.

Rationale and aims of this study

In 1920, around 120,000 'insane' patients were detained under the Lunacy Act 1890. The vast majority were pauper lunatics housed mainly in the publicly funded county and borough asylums, with some also in the workhouses. Around 14,000 were private patients, and about 800 were classed as 'criminal lunatics', most of whom were detained in Broadmoor State Criminal Asylum, with a few scattered in the county and borough asylums. Of the pauper lunatics, about 30,000 were in asylums with 500 to 1,000 beds; 20,000 were in asylums with 1,000 to 2,000 beds; and a further 20,000 were in asylums with over 2,000 beds.[5] These public asylums and the people in them are at the heart of this book. Others who had the means to pay privately for their care are peripheral to the main theme, but I draw on their experiences when that contributes to discussion on the broader provision of services and processes of reform. This book is also mainly about England: while the Lunacy Act 1890 applied to both England and Wales, regarding the national population and the number of mental hospitals, Wales comprised only about seven per cent of the total.

This study seeks to explain how stagnation and change in the public mental hospital system affected patients. It brings together problem, policy and political components. As John Kingdon argued in his 'Multiple Streams Framework', all of these are required to enable change in public policy, and they are shaped by various interest groups, societal attitudes and understanding, and other forces inside and outside officialdom.[6] It also seeks to encourage readers to contemplate the complexity of providing mental health services today. Reflecting on the past has the potential to contribute to shaping the future, by stimulating questions and encouraging consideration of novel solutions. In healthcare, this can generate perspectives beyond those conventionally adopted by twenty-first-century clinical, management and policy leaders. Most of the then-and-now parallels, apart from the obvious ones of prolonged austerity and a post-pandemic environment, became apparent to me while researching and writing this book. They linked into my ongoing interest regarding dilemmas in mental health services today. Current issues have helped shape the questions asked about the 1920s, but the research has remained within the bounds of academic historical methodology, drawing conclusions which are grounded in the context of the past.

Although one finds other eras with then-and-now parallels regarding health and social welfare, they are particularly apparent when considering the 1920s and 2020s. The First World War (WW1) and the Spanish influenza pandemic preceded the 1920s, and over a decade of National Health Service (NHS) and social welfare austerity, combined with Covid-19 (and the consequences of Brexit), are shaping the 2020s. Both decades are associated with social unrest and a cash-strapped public economy, with the realities of mental healthcare provision falling short of recognised best practice, and reports from inside officialdom offering reassurance while those from other sources are less convincing about the adequacy of care provided.[7] Both eras feature mental health service red tape, tight top-down regulations, and defensive professional and management cultures.[8] The culture which existed in the 1920s gradually became more flexible, but mainly after the Second World War. However, as sociologist Graham Scambler noted, since then there have been other gradual changes linked with various ideologies, including shifts from 'welfare state capitalism' to harsher 'financial capitalism', and a 'fracturing of society', including a recasting of concepts of personal responsibility. These have contributed to moving towards the current crisis in welfare and healthcare and a more rigid culture of institutional working.[9]

Regarding the term 'care' as it applies to patients, I have followed the definition used by the Royal Commission on Lunacy and Mental Disorder 1924–6: 'all the factors involved in the environment and treatment of patients', including the legal and administrative mechanisms through which it was delivered.[10] Providing high-quality care for mentally unwell people is a 'wicked' problem, the adjective 'wicked' being used to conjure up images of mischievous and sometimes malevolent challenges. Typically, wicked problems are ill formulated, and information is confusing: individuals, groups and decision makers hold conflicting values; ramifications are baffling; and 'solutions' may not cure the problem.[11] 'Wicked' seems to be an apt description for the challenges faced within mental health services in both the 1920s and 2020s. Only an unsolvable, wicked problem in the 1920s would have been granted a Royal Commission, and that on Lunacy and Mental Disorder minuted one million words of evidence in an attempt to begin to understand the issues and propose remedies.

Setting the context: from the Victorian legacy to the impact of shell shock

By the beginning of the Victorian era, conditions for mentally unwell patients in English lunatic asylums were a public concern. In the 1840s the Alleged Lunatics' Friend Society, an organisation of former patients, began to campaign for improvements.[12] Around the same time, the Association of Medical Officers of Asylums and Hospitals for the Insane (later, Medico-Psychological Association, MPA; granted royal charter 1926, RMPA; today, Royal College of Psychiatrists) was a new venture. In the 1840s it comprised only a few dozen doctors[13] and it had little public or political influence when social reformer Anthony Ashley-Cooper, Lord Shaftesbury, championed the Lunacy and County Asylums Acts through Parliament in 1845.

The County Asylums Act mandated each county to build and maintain a public lunatic asylum. These aimed to provide support and treatment for mentally unwell people to recover their mental equilibrium. They were well built, usually situated in rural areas, often on hillsides to catch the fresh air and sunshine, all aiming to provide an environment which would promote good health. Since they sought, and were funded (through local taxation), to provide better treatment than that available in general hospitals (also called 'infirmaries' and located in workhouses), statutory funding for treating people with mental disorders in those institutions was withdrawn – other than for short-term crisis situations.[14] Alongside the new network of publicly funded asylums serving the majority of the population, a variety of other mental institutions developed. They included 'licenced houses' and 'registered hospitals', some of which were funded through charitable foundations, but more usually they served private patients and were funded through their fees.

Successive Lunacy Acts since 1828 required asylums with more than a hundred patients to have a 'resident medical officer'.[15] These medical officers had initially trained as any other doctor, only then making further career choices post-qualification, usually either to enter general practice or to specialise in a discipline such as surgery or psychiatry. According to social scientist and historian Kathleen Jones, doctors were appointed as superintendents of the asylums 'because they were professional men of some public standing, not because they possessed some new and exclusive technology'.[16] Their appointment, however, established the 'medical superintendent' in an asylum leadership role.

The Lunacy Act 1845 provided a workable balance between medical and legal approaches to insanity and its treatment.[17] Later in the nineteenth century there was a shift towards legal dominance over medical principles. This shift culminated in the Lunacy Act 1890, applicable to England and Wales. It remained in force for 70 years, amended by the Mental Treatment Act 1930 and finally repealed by the Mental Health Act 1959.

The Lunacy Act 1890 was largely drawn up by lawyers, with relatively little influence from the medical profession. Lawyers at that time held higher public status and were more influential than doctors, associated with law having been an established profession for centuries, in contrast to medicine only achieving full professional status with the Medical Registration Act of 1858.[18] A key principle of the Lunacy Act was 'habeas corpus': a person can only be detained by legal means. That brought magistrates to the fore in deciding whether a lunatic or person of 'unsound mind' should be admitted to an institution. In line with the funding decisions taken in 1845, the 1890 Act only permitted local authority expenditure on pauper lunatics in asylums.[19] Thus, while a person able to pay privately could seek early treatment for a mental disorder, for the majority of the population the Lunacy Act denied them such recourse because they had to wait until they were sufficiently ill to be legally detainable.[20] This went against medical teaching, which emphasised the benefits of obtaining treatment early in the course of an illness to prevent worsening and hopefully to reverse it, and regarded social class and wealth as an inappropriate means of determining access to treatment. According to the MPA, the 1890 Act was 'framed more to protect society [from wrongful detention] and safeguard the liberty of the subject than to treat and cure the patient'.[21] In Kathleen Jones' opinion, '[f]rom a medical point of view, the Lunacy Act of 1890 was out of date before it was passed', and according to historian Edgar Jones, the Act so dominated medical practice that it reduced many psychiatrists to 'little more than custodians of the bizarre or unruly'.[22]

The quest for lunacy law reform began before WW1. Inspired by medical arguments, more liberal legislation in Scotland and more flexible approaches to treatment in Germany, bills were introduced to Parliament in 1900, 1903 and 1905.[23] They sought to remove the compulsory certification requirement but failed to do so. Some members of the MPA blamed this on a lack of interest in Parliament and the failure of the medical profession to push its points sufficiently.[24] The quest, however, continued, and in 1914, two weeks before war was declared, Earl Russell addressed the House of Lords on Lunacy Act reform.[25] A report from an MPA committee discussing the same subject was published shortly after the onset of war.[26] The war then halted any intention of taking the matter forward.

Victorian legislation shaped the treatment available for mental disorders and laid the ground rules for many aspects of asylum organisation and practice. It established the Lunacy Commission, the central government body which had responsibility for overseeing and regulating the public asylums and other mental institutions. The Lunacy Commission was renamed the Board of Control in 1913. Being affiliated to the Home Office indicated the primacy of its quasi-judicial functions to ensure that the institutions followed the legalities, rather than focussing on the humanity of the care provided. The Board's deeply embedded pattern of regulatory priorities continued even after it shifted from under the authority of the Home Office to that of the Ministry of Health in 1920.[27] In the words of Dr Edwin Goodall, medical superintendent of Cardiff City Mental Hospital into the 1920s, the dominating legalistic conceptions of insanity and provision of care created the impression that 'merely an alien is being dealt with, and not a sick man'.[28]

Public, political and medical interest in the causes and treatment of mental disorders increased during WW1 in the context of 'shell shock' – the mental trauma suffered by servicemen, particularly soldiers fighting in the trenches. Concerns also arose about the standard of care being provided for civilian patients in the asylums. During the war, conscientious objectors and those exempt from military service were employed in the asylums to cover for permanent staff serving in the forces. Unaccustomed to the regimes of these institutions, some were shocked by the low standards they encountered, and were unafraid to publicly state their views on the subject.[29] One of them was Dr Montagu Lomax, a retired GP. While on the staff of the Lancashire County Asylum at Prestwich, he observed patients being punished, drugged and purged, and that they lacked potentially beneficial employment, amusement and exercise. Missing from their treatment was tact, kindness, sympathy and patience. Leaving the mental hospital service in 1919, Dr Lomax blew the whistle.[30]

Also during the war, 24 of the 97 public county and borough asylums – around twenty-three thousand beds – were vacated and repurposed as military hospitals. Some civilian patients became very distressed when they were moved out. One medical superintendent described the patients departing from his asylum: '[T]he whole gamut of emotion was exhibited by the patients on leaving, ranging from acute distress and misery, through gay indifference, to maniacal fury and indignation ...

I did not realise the strong mutual attachment till it was severed.'[31] The asylums were by no means ideal and the dependence which they created for their patients probably contributed to their sense of both attachment and abandonment. However, patients' distress upon leaving suggests that meaningful human relationships and a sense of security also existed within them. Some of these patients were moved to workhouses and others were discharged, but the majority were accommodated in alternative, already overcrowded mental institutions.[32] Overcrowding, inadequate diet and a lack of fuel and heating contributed to an escalating number of deaths in the asylums. In 1918, deaths from tuberculosis reached 30 times the rate suffered among civilians in the community.[33] In 1919, a *Times* editorial asked: 'Have we been sending some of our lunatics into the Army and starving the others?'[34]

Treating shell-shocked servicemen had the potential to influence the provision of psychiatric care for civilian mentally unwell patients. As physician Grafton Elliot Smith and psychologist Tom Hatherley Pear argued in 1917, lessons from shell shock would be 'truly beneficial' if mentally unwell civilians were provided with care of the same standard as that which had 'proved such a blessing to the war-stricken soldier'.[35] That care included psychological understanding, staff gaining patients' confidence, and taking an individualised and eclectic approach to treatment.[36] In recognition of their war service, mentally unwell servicemen were also granted privileges which civilian patients did not have, including better food and higher quality hospital clothes. Regarding such basic items as privileges indicated official awareness that provision for civilian patients was substandard. In addition to the contrast between care for civilians and that provided for servicemen, Dr Smith and Mr Pear queried whether the humanity shown to mentally unwell soldiers was 'merely temporary' and 'limited to the duration of the war, and to be restricted to the army'.[37]

Soldiers' privileges related to the legal framework under which they were admitted to mental institutions. Early in the war there was concern that they might have to be treated under the Lunacy Act. The public considered it inappropriate for men mentally traumatised in the service of their country to be automatically given the denigrating epithet of pauper lunatic. The Army Act 1881, however, provided a loophole to delegate responsibility for funding their treatment to the new wartime Ministry of Pensions, thus avoiding the pauper taint.[38] In their post-war review of the asylums requisitioned for military use, psychiatrists Edward Marriott Cooke and Charles Hubert Bond advocated that the 'pauper lunatic' term should be abolished so that all patients would be treated on an equal footing.[39]

Post-war, soldier-patient privileges gradually disappeared from the public mental hospitals.[40] With little acknowledgement of their wartime service and despite policy rhetoric, soldiers lived cheek-by-jowl with the 'ordinary' lunatics.[41] In an appeal for funds in 1924, the Ex-Services Welfare Society (today, Combat Stress) stated that there were over five thousand patients in the public asylums for whom '[w]ar broke their reason. They were brought home. And because they had nothing, having given ALL, they were put away in Asylums, to live under pauper conditions.'[42] While advocating primarily for ex-servicemen, the Society took a broader stance: 'Our agitation, therefore, if agitation it be, is to rouse in the minds of the public a permanent and not merely a fitful and evanescent interest in the welfare of those suffering from mental disorders.'[43] As Dr Smith and Mr Pear had feared, higher standards of care for soldier patients were temporary, and were not extended to civilian patients in the asylums. Nevertheless, the legacy of WW1 and shell shock were among the factors which helped to stimulate the development of ideas within psychiatry as a medical discipline. Historian Michael Robinson, for example, linked wartime learning with the development of psychiatric outpatient clinics and the reform of lunacy law to allow more flexible approaches to treatment.[44]

Despite wartime concerns about psychologically traumatised servicemen (and a few servicewomen) which drove mental healthcare higher up the welfare agenda, post-war there were several priorities competing for attention – education, housing, poverty, unemployment and physical healthcare among them. Not all issues could be dealt with at once and, as circumstances changed, the salience of each rose and fell. Post-war, many liberal ideas emerged, or re-emerged. Among them was the impetus for asylums to adopt the more positive sounding designation of 'mental hospital'. However, there was little indication of change of approach from custodial to more hospital-like therapeutic models of care to match the name change. Given widely held stereotypical ideas that mentally unwell people were dangerous to themselves and/or others, many medical and non-medical leaders were psychologically more comfortable with the safety provided by the status quo of custodial care, rather than face the perceived risks of instigating change. As psychologist Tali Sharot explained in 2024, familiarity with, or habituation to, an environment and culture is a survival strategy, enabling people to notice anything unusual, out of place or potentially dangerous.[45] Changing routines can therefore disrupt psychological security, even in the face of evidence that the fears are disproportionate to the reality, or that change overall may be beneficial and reduce risks.

In any era, such instinctive psychological mechanisms can impact on planning and implementing new ways of treating patients with mental disorders.

Despite sluggish implementation of new ideas in mental healthcare in the UK, psychiatrists were keen to learn. Other knowledge, such as on biological aspects of mental disorders and the new psychologies, came from further afield. High-profile voices included those of Emil Kraepelin in Germany, Sigmund Freud and Julius Wagner-Jauregg in Austria, and Adolph Meyer in the USA. Their observations, theories and innovations had the potential to influence UK psychiatry, but most of them remained peripheral to the workings of the public mental hospitals or were adopted only hesitantly. The disastrous state of affairs at the end of WW1, particularly the high death rate in the public mental hospitals, arguably necessitated urgent improvement.[46] However, overall, the period from the Armistice in 1918 until the introduction of the Mental Treatment Act 1930 (a period of a little beyond the decade, so also referred to as the 'long 1920s') saw only pockets of change.

Methodological considerations

Historians of psychiatry Volker Hess and Benoît Majerus refer to psychiatry as a 'practical science that aspires to provide medical help to mentally ill people – in whatever form'.[47] However, because it is shaped by many contextual factors, a multi-dimensional approach is needed to understand its history. This requires reaching beyond the scientific and clinical elements of the care provided. It needs to incorporate the experiences of patients and staff inside the institutions. It also needs to include the attitudes, expectations and actions of those beyond the institutions' walls: the general public, central and local government, voluntary organisations, and various professional groups and individuals. The panoply of ideas and actors all interact through an assortment of alliances and antagonisms.

The picture is of wicked issues, graduations, variations and nuanced shades of grey, rather than a duality of black and white. For example, while care and control in mental healthcare have frequently been perceived as opposites, historian Janet Weston noted that 'control is not always simply harmful, any more than care is always harmless'.[48] Two other historians, Louise Hide and Joanna Bourke, added dimensions related to individual interpretation: '[T]he same behaviours and attitudes are conceptualised differently depending on the cultural context and perspective of the individual.'[49] In a broader context, other illustrations of the beneficial coexistence of care and control include vehicle safety belts, speed limits and road safety laws; or, in the healthcare framework, sedating a physically ill distressed patient, or one in intensive care, as the only way to undertake life-saving procedures.

In 2015, insights from a series of discussions between historians, clinicians and policy makers concerning the history of mental health services in modern England, pointed to the need for historians and others not to perpetuate 'single-issue mythologies'.[50] Too often, the historiography of psychiatry has emphasised a narrow track rather than exploring a diversity of factors. Broadly labelled anti-psychiatry historical analyses, such as those of Michel Foucault and Andrew Scull, brazenly attack biological psychiatry and emphasise that themes of coercive practices and scandalous happenings are due to institutional medical authority.[51] Concluding at that point does not encourage exploration of broader influences on psychiatric practice – for example, of the ways in which the profession was subject to external factors, including lunacy law; public attitudes and expectations concerning mentally unwell people; and government leadership, including decision making regarding public expenditure.

Historian of psychiatry Andrew Scull noted that making history takes place on many levels, including those of the original actors and of historians. Regarding historians, he wrote that one has to consider 'the preferences, prejudices, and predilections of those of us who write it, the ways in which our own biases and blindnesses, selective attention and inattention, shape still further the history we collectively make'.[52] Aspects of historians' personal lives may influence their perspectives, and some adopt theoretical models to guide their analysis.[53] Some find social construction theories useful, while others consider that they may 'blind us from considering alternatives'.[54] We cannot entirely avoid our own personal or theory-based interpretations, but we must recognise these agendas. They otherwise risk distracting us from our quest to analyse data as objectively as possible, such as by letting us place too much weight on a single individual, institution or event, or drawing simplistic, hasty or sensationalist conclusions.

Regarding the original actors, sources indicate their various agendas and the subjectivity of their accounts. If eyewitnesses always told the same story, multiple versions would not be reported across various media: aspects of memory, including forgetting, misremembering and nostalgia, all shape the subject we are trying to understand.[55] The methodology of oral history deliberately introduces subjectivity into a narrative, but it is recognised as giving invaluable insights into the lives of individuals, and how they comprehended the happenings they experienced and witnessed.[56] People write with different intentions, such as to complain, to praise, to reassure, for self-reflection or to fulfil administrative requirements. Some differences in reporting are inevitable and unintentional, but sources are not neutral and deliberate distortions may also occur.

There are other potential biases of source material. Historian Jack Pressman noted psychiatry's 'cautionary tales' – events in healthcare which should never occur. Cautionary tales teach us to be wary of relying on simplistic values and are vital to promote consideration about past actions and to learn from them with a view to preventing recurrence.[57] However, cautionary tales become problematic if one extrapolates from them and considers them as representative of the whole. This is particularly challenging with healthcare history: controversial, difficult or scandalous issues and problems which need solving are likely to occupy a disproportionate amount of space in archived records, and if they reach wider audiences via the media, they may well be remembered more than acceptable happenings which pass unnoticed. Researchers must therefore obtain data from a range of observers and collate them, and '[i]f trends consistently emerge from a variety of sources, the researcher may place a high degree of confidence in their reality'.[58] Taking a variety of sources and looking at them in an open-minded way, triangulating findings with other data and looking for patterns, continuities and consistencies, contradictions and discontinuities, should help researchers draw justified conclusions.[59]

To untangle the numerous threads and weave them into a cohesive whole to create an informed analysis of what was happening regarding provision for mentally unwell people, historians need to look both inside and outside the mental hospitals. Contrasting with many traditional histories of psychiatry, often written to give a 'macro' view, this study delves into the 'micro', especially relating to the lives of patients. Neurologist Oliver Sacks wrote: 'I was always conscious … there were always *two* books, potentially, demanded by every clinical experience' – one which offered objective descriptions of 'disorders, mechanisms and syndromes', and the other which was 'existential and personal, and empathic entering into patient's experiences and worlds'.[60] Ideally, if we are to understand patients' experiences, their views and insights and their encounters with the people who 'judged them, or cared for them', we must pay attention to their own words.[61] Historian Roy Porter called this history 'from below'.[62] Patients' narratives, as historian Alice Brumby wrote in her analysis of mentally disturbed WW1 ex-servicemen, 'can provide a colourful and original insight' into their worlds and are vital to our understanding of how they responded to being in an institution.[63] She also cautioned us about the reliability of such narratives, referring to the 'complications associated with analysing the testimony of those who were certified "insane" and reported to be suffering from various delusions'. On the other hand, their narratives are 'too important to simply ignore'.[64] I would argue that similar caution needs to be extended beyond accounts compiled by patients and into other sources. Given the emotive nature of the subject of mental disorders and their treatment, patient-created sources are probably no more slanted than any other. All are shaped by the message the author wants to convey and the nature of the expected readership. Many present competing agendas, and they may be one-sided, expressed to defend ideals or deflect blame, or they may articulate unfounded or contradictory generalisations. Such documentation arose from staff, social commentators, campaigners for lunacy reform, people in the echelons of government, recipients of care and their advocates, and others.

Regarding the complexity of documenting and understanding individual experiences, the National Survivor User Network (a service-user-led charity that connects and gives voice to people with experience of mental health issues) states: 'There is no one unified narrative around what it means to experience long-term mental distress. [The Network] was set up to gather and hold these diverse narratives and represent them in an authentic, safe and powerful way.'[65] It is with similar objectives that I endeavour to convey individual experiences related to the institutions. Various challenges come with this, such as insufficient written sources from patients in the inter-war years to allow a comprehensive approach from their perspective, as Jane Freebody found in her study of work and occupation in the mental hospitals.[66] The same is true in this study. Nevertheless, I have made every effort to identify and use as many first-person narratives as possible. I have drawn on Gail Hornstein's bibliography and Roy Porter's anthology of first-person narratives.[67] Further important evidence about the 1920s is available in the testimonies given by patients and former patients to committees of investigation into mental hospital practices: transcripts of their oral testimonies are available for both the Ministry of Health's Committee on Administration of Public Mental Hospitals (Cobb Inquiry) and the Royal Commission on Lunacy and Mental Disorder.[68]

Diaries written for self-perusal are probably the most reliable sources of personal reflection. Some inpatients were known to have kept diaries,[69] but none have been identified during the course of this study. Letters composed by inpatients are reported to be more vivid than accounts written later. Some surface as serendipitous findings in case notes or committee minutes, although uncovering unsent letters written by patients and withheld by the institution is disturbing in terms of patients' agency. Allan Beveridge analysed such unsent letters written between 1873 and 1908 at the Royal Edinburgh Asylum. He identified diverse attitudes and experiences, from speaking warmly about the asylum and its staff, to complaining of coercive and harsh regimes.[70] While such letters provide insights into patients' lived experience, they were shaped by the writer-recipient relationship and fear that they might be intercepted and read by staff, so, as with other sources, they cannot be entirely objective. When, in the 1950s, psychologist Robert Sommer and psychiatrist Humphry Osmond studied patients' autobiographical narratives of their experiences of mental illness and treatment, they noted that while some had axes to grind, the 'axes are manifestly of different sizes and shapes'. Sommer and Osmond urged their colleagues to pay more attention to patients' written narratives: '[W]hat other source of information is so uncontaminated by our professional influence? It is easy for us to become extremely ignorant of things that go on under our noses.'[71]

Compiling reminiscences after discharge gave time for reflection and shaping according to the author's needs and intentions. For some patients, a personal search for meaning was important, to help them make sense of their illnesses and treatments. Others took a more outward focus, such as Mary Riggall, who aimed to educate the public about mental illness and hospitals, and James Scott, who wrote to encourage better care.[72] Stigma did not silence past generations of patients, although some sought anonymity in the process.

There is also the challenge of interpreting accounts written anonymously, particularly by patients and staff fearful of backlash from others of higher rank inside their institution, or former patients cautious of revealing too much of their personal history which might leave them open to stigmatisation. There were also more formal traditions of anonymity, such as editorials and leading articles in newspapers and magazines for a general readership, and in medical professional journals including the *British Medical Journal*, *Lancet* and *Journal of Mental Science*. Anonymity raises issues of reliability and accuracy, but to discard those sources would leave many voices unheard, both from within and outside the establishment. Some recent evidence also points to anonymity encouraging honesty on personal mental health matters.[73]

There is little guidance on using anonymous sources as they relate to the history of psychiatry.[74] However, the need to deal with various levels of evidence is recognised in other disciplines, including both law and medicine.[75] Anonymous voices may not be ideal evidence, but they may be the best available. In this study they provide valuable personal opinions and reflections on experiences encountered, and I have used them to add those dimensions. Their anonymity may, at some points in the book, create a sense of vagueness – 'someone' describing 'something', 'somewhere'. Other issues of anonymity are discussed as they arise in the book.

To make this study as bottom-up and person-centred as possible, and to capture narratives about patients and those people looking after them, I have drawn in depth on the archive of Colney Hatch Mental Hospital (opened as the Second Middlesex County Pauper Lunatic Asylum in 1851; from 1937 to 1993 known as Friern Hospital) (Figure 1.1). On the edge of the North London suburbs, by the 1920s it was the largest London County Council mental hospital, with around two and a half thousand beds. Although not totally self-sufficient, it had a farm and many facilities of a village.

To achieve the fullest possible exploration of the lives of individual patients, it seems logical for a historian to delve into their medical notes. However, historians have different views on the value of doing so. Hazel Morrison advised that, when cautiously approached, they may reveal a 'wealth of meaning',[76] while Liana Glew pointed to their tendency to represent bureaucracy and ableism and to silence individual patients' narratives. Nevertheless, Glew also acknowledged that they contain traces of individual patients' voices, their 'desires, drives, and wholeness', and the processes by which those were fulfilled or denied.[77]

Many important historical and ethnographical studies have stemmed from cautious analysis of individual people or institutions. Erving Goffman's authoritative 1950s study *Asylums*, on the working of 'total institutions' such as mental hospitals, was built on case-based ethnographic observations and narratives.[78] Some historical institutional case-based studies have produced deep insights, such as Louise Hide's on gender and class in asylums,[79] and Stephen Cherry's on the Norfolk Lunatic Asylum.[80] Janet Weston's in-depth study of Miss Alexander's story concludes, cautiously, that the findings have 'opened up for consideration some of the complex issues that surround welfare and citizenship, vulnerability and dependence, care and control, history writing and the law. These are issues that connect past, present, and future, and should concern us all'.[81] Hasty over-generalisations from a particular narrative

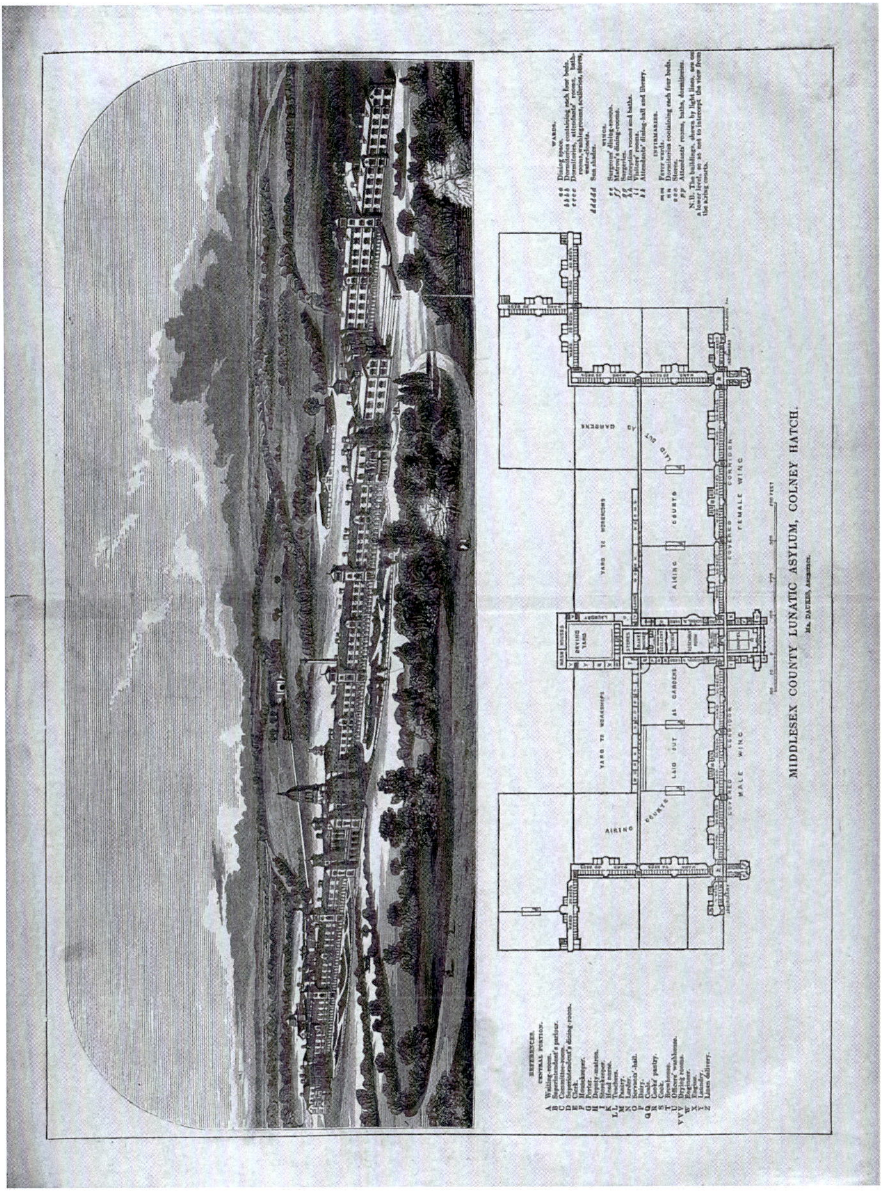

Figure 1.1 A bird's eye view of Middlesex County Lunatic Asylum, Colney Hatch with floor plan and key, showing separate male and female wings, circa 1850. Wood engraving by Laing after Daukes. Source: Wellcome Collection. Licence: Attribution 4.0 International (CC BY 4.0).

may be rash, but case study research can provide important hooks which are meaningful for readers and have the potential to open doors for further consideration, of both past and present.

There are biases and risks associated with any methodology, and these need to be acknowledged. In this study I have heeded Ludmilla Jordanova's warning that 'untempered localism will lead to anecdotal history'.[82] To address the issue of drawing misleading conclusions from specific instances, I have used evidence from other sources to triangulate with and support case study illustrations of both place and person. Archival and published findings about Colney Hatch have been used as stepping stones into a range of additional sources relating to other institutions across England, Scotland and Wales (Figure 1.2). A similar triangulation approach has been taken to individual narratives. In this way, some unusual personal accounts have been included because individual people are the building blocks of this study, and ignoring them would perpetuate the injustices of those who failed to listen to them in the 1920s.

Like personal accounts, official reports also require cautious analysis. In some years, when workforce and economic climates permitted, the Board of Control published descriptive summaries of its mental hospital inspection findings and recommendations in its annual reports. However, official inspections could be contrived, 'window dressed' and superficial, if not farcical, and they shaped the observations and the reports.[83] Even when inspections were made without warning, official-looking strangers alighting at the train station or booking into a hotel for an early start the following day could foster rumours of an imminent inspection and give staff some time for preparation.[84] Even after arriving at the hospital porter's lodge, a formal greeting by the medical superintendent could delay the inspectors' tour. The Lunacy Act required inspectors to 'see every patient therein, so as to give everyone, as far as possible, full opportunity of complaint'.[85] In the inspectors' view, they accomplished this by gathering patients and staff together, so they could 'see' everyone, and asking each group if anyone wanted to speak to them, thus providing 'opportunity'. In a culture where patients were considered inherently unreliable, and patients and staff were fearful of those more senior than themselves in the institution, the words of those further up the hierarchy were heard over and above those at its base. There was little scope for honest feedback from either patients or frontline staff.[86]

There is also a need to be mindful of how official and personal documents have survived to the present day. In officialdom, rules and bureaucracy accompany subjective and objective judgement about what

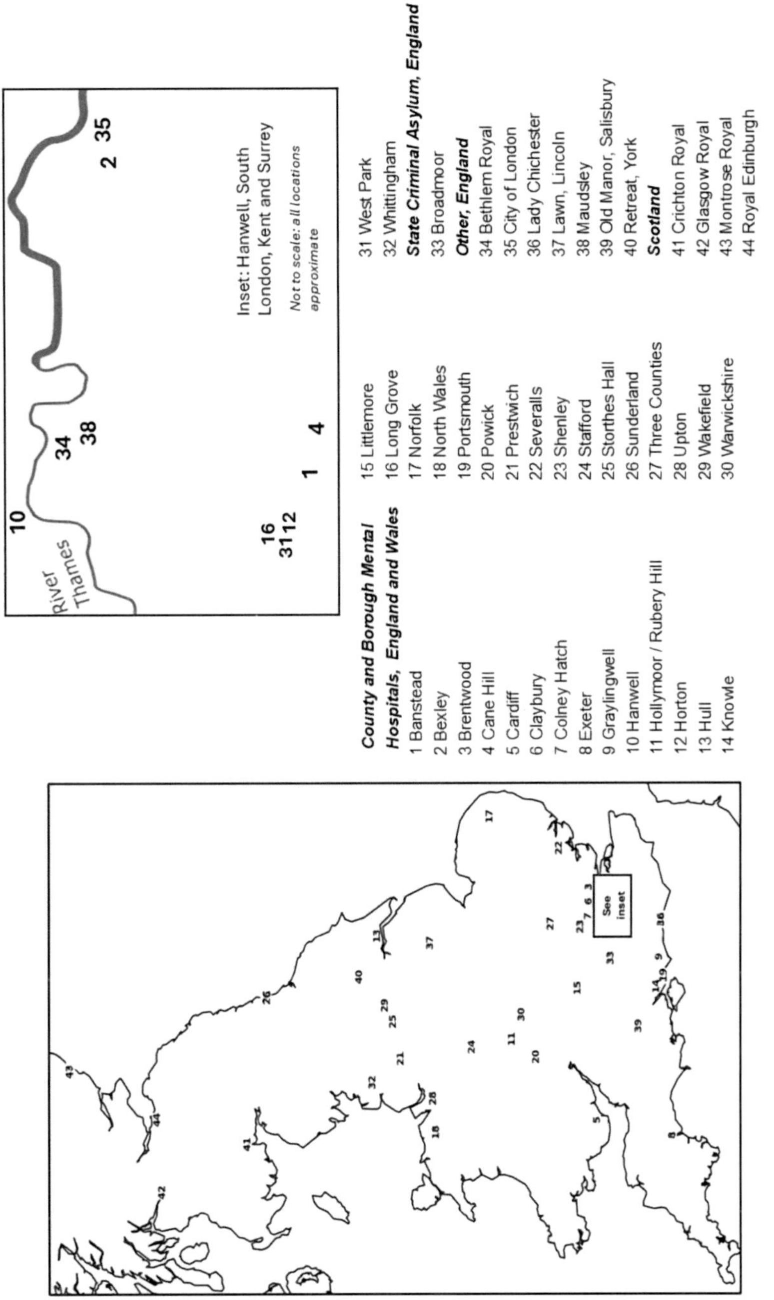

Figure 1.2 Map of England, Scotland and Wales showing key mental institutions referred to in this book. Design: Benjamin Hilton.

is recorded, kept and destroyed. Board of Control correspondence was generally destroyed once dealt with, but other records were retained during the organisation's lifetime, based on criteria estimating their usefulness as reference points when looking for precedents to inform future decisions.[87] Within the mental hospitals, large swathes of records were compiled and stored – in part because they proved the institution's compliance concerning collecting the data demanded of them by the Lunacy Act and Board of Control. Later, when the institutions closed, records could be destroyed haphazardly: at Claybury Mental Hospital, many were deliberately incinerated.[88] Elsewhere, however, many survived, including those from Colney Hatch Mental Hospital which today occupy 80 linear metres of shelf space at the London Archives. Records under a century old which contain patients' personal information are usually closed to researchers, so I am grateful to the London Archives for permission to explore the Colney Hatch collection across the whole of the 1920s on condition of maintaining the anonymity of patients. Balancing this with the way patients were deprived of much of their personal identity during their stay, to leave them nameless would perpetuate this disdainful aspect of the way many were treated. For most, I have used their first name to engender a sense of empathy and identification with them, to emphasise that each was a human being whose experience in the institution this study seeks to understand.

The changing language

Language associated with mental illness, patients and the institutions providing care has changed over the years. Upbeat new terminology may be introduced in an attempt to reduce stigma and create, or reinstate, more positive attitudes. However, as mental hospital medical superintendent Dr Robert Turnbull declared in 1922: 'The mere changing of the name to mental hospital is an unworthy subterfuge and will not deceive the public.'[89] Reginald Sorensen MP agreed, explaining that 'If you delete the word "mental" and put in another word' it too will acquire stigma; 'The whole thing depends on an alteration in the public mind.'[90] The least demeaning language might temporarily alleviate stigma, but whether that shift would permeate and persist long enough to ensure improvements in standards of care was a different matter. A century on, this resonates with Dr Niall Boyce's comment that, 'we too often fall into the trap of thinking that a change in wording will automatically be followed by radical reconceptualization.'[91]

New language may not change ideas, but obsolete terms tend to retain their acquired derogatory, rather than their original, meanings. This has implications when considering the best language to use to convey the meanings of words as they were used in their historical context. In the 1920s, changes in relevant language were initially adopted informally, such as shifting from 'lunatic' to 'patient', 'asylum' to 'mental hospital', and 'pauper' to 'rate-aided'. Only at the end of the decade, with new legislation, were these terms officially confirmed. However, throughout the 1920s, the out-going and in-coming words were used together in single narratives, including in government documentation.

On another dimension relating to terminology, the history of psychiatry has been 'beset by a sterile battle over the reality of mental illness', as historian Mathew Thomson explained.[92] This study does not tackle those epistemological issues. Instead, it is concerned with the concepts and terminology as used and understood in the 1920s, to describe the conditions suffered by people admitted to mental hospitals. They include mental illness, disease, distress and disorder, lunacy, insanity and unsound mind. 'Mental illness' in particular was more acceptable than 'insanity' or 'lunacy'.[93] However, for some, 'mental' was a menacing term, despite being part of the concept of 'mental hygiene', meaning the way in which people 'could respond normally to the calls made upon them by daily life' and maintain their mental equilibrium.[94] 'Mental' could also be ambiguous, and examples from the popular press amply illustrate the confusion which could occur between mental illness (which this book is primarily about), defined as usually occurring from adolescence onwards, and mental deficiency (today, learning or intellectual disability), usually apparent in infancy or early childhood.[95]

Sometimes, out-going language indicated the speaker's underlying prejudices. This was apparent in the minutes of the Royal Commission, where the older and newer terms were accompanied by different adjectives. Using corpus linguistic methodology to look at occurrence of nouns and adjectives in combination, a person might be described as an 'alleged lunatic', but not an 'alleged patient' – 'alleged' implying a suspected misdemeanour or criminal activity, with implications of blame and punishment. Similarly, adjectives such as 'pauper', 'dangerous' and 'criminal' were commonly used to describe lunatics, but rarely to describe patients.[96] More demeaning words, such as 'asylum' and 'lunatic', were also used by patients when emphasising the feelings engendered in them by negative aspects of their treatment, but not when describing positive experiences. Sometimes, including in official circles, people used abandoned, far outdated and officially obsolete language, stemming from the 'madhouse' era before the mandatory asylum-building years of the mid-nineteenth century. This gave the impression that the speaker held far outmoded attitudes towards patients and institutions. Their language included words like 'keepers', rather than the more acceptable alternatives of 'attendants' or, preferably, 'nurses'. The word 'keepers', as used for animals in zoos or stock in shops, suggested safe custody and control, without restoration of health.[97] It is difficult to imagine that words such as 'inmate', 'keeper' and 'madhouse', used by educated politicians, policy makers and other leaders in the 1920s, reflected anything other than disparaging and dismissive attitudes towards those people they had an obligation to help. When, in 1926, Board of Control inspectors wrote about Colney Hatch's 'inmates', a term more commonly applied to prisons and workhouses, it suggested a demeaning and laissez faire attitude to the standards of care therein.[98] These observations support the need to use terminology, as far as possible, as it appears in the original sources: choice of words carries the meaning expressed by the creator.

In contrast to terminology which has become derogatory, other vocabulary is used in a respectful manner a century on but cannot be assumed to carry static meanings. For one, the word 'diagnosis' in psychiatry in 1920s England tended to be synonymous with the most prominent clinical symptom at the time of initial assessment,[99] while today it incorporates various aspects of symptoms, including their type, degree and course over time. Another example which illustrates change of meaning concerns Dr Edward Anderson's research on depression in 'later life', which he defined as over 40 years of age – hardly considered 'later life' today.[100] A further example appears in Board of Control minutes, referring to nurses 'sleeping with patients', but without the colloquial connotations of today, instead meaning that nurses had bedrooms adjacent to the wards so that they would be available to assist in the event of a night-time emergency.[101] At the Worcester State Hospital in the USA, a five-year-old patient was described as 'homicidal and suicidal'.[102] It is hard to imagine 'homicidal and suicidal' being used to describe a young child today, however disturbed their behaviour.

Structuring the book

Theories, ideas and plans regarding making improvements to the mental hospitals and facilitating access to treatment passed through the hands of many protagonists, with diverse professional, lay, political and policy-making interests. Too often they were at odds and out of step with one another, with recommendations open to interpretation and resulting in reluctant implementation, if at all. These disjointed streams of stagnation, innovation and implementation flowed at different rates bound to

CONTEXT		MENTAL HOSPITAL LANDMARKS
Armistice, 11 Nov 1918		
Influenza pandemic Sex Disqualification (Removal) Act Housing and Town Planning Act Nurses Registration Act and GNC		Report: asylum deaths due to infectious diseases Mental After Care Association, 40 years old
League of Nations	1920	Ministry of Health (Miscellaneous Provisions) Bill National Council for Lunacy Reform
First public telephone box in UK Economic crisis and cuts in public spending		Montagu Lomax, *The Experiences of an Asylum Doctor*
Insulin used to treat diabetes BBC begins radio broadcasts		National Council for Mental Hygiene, in UK Inquiry: Administration of Public Mental Hospitals Malaria inoculation to treat GPI, in UK
Two Conservative governments and one Labour, Oct 1922–Nov 1924		Maudsley Hospital opens to civilian patients
		Mr Harnett awarded £25,000 damages for wrongful detention under Lunacy Act
	1925	Royal Commission on Lunacy and Mental Disorder 1924–6
General Strike Television demonstrated		Medico-Psychological Association receives Royal Charter Emil Kraepelin, 70th birthday
First automatic traffic lights in UK		Henderson and Gillespie, *Text-Book,* first edition Henry Cotton at RMPA annual conference
Representation of the People (Equal Franchise) Act		
Local Government Act Wall Street Crash; start of Great Depression		
	1930	First International Congress on Mental Hygiene Mental Treatment Act

Figure 1.3 Timeline: mental hospital landmarks in the context of other events across the long 1920s. Design: Samuel Hilton.

political, cultural and societal forces inside and outside the system of mental healthcare. This has led me to write this book thematically rather than chronologically. A timeline illustrates the key mental health landmarks in England alongside other occurrences, which, although not discussed in this chapter, appear elsewhere in the book (Figure 1.3).

When considering the history of psychiatry, the period investigated in this book is of very short duration, but that gives scope to dig deep and find the complex interactions which culminated in the care provided for patients. Clearly demarcated, however, are the start and end points, beginning with the cessation of WW1 hostilities and ending with the passing of the Mental Treatment Act 1930. The new Act was a landmark which permitted more liberal approaches to psychiatric treatment and created more options for people seeking help with mental problems. Unfortunately, it came into force at a time of profound world uncertainty with the start of the Great Depression, associated with rising unemployment, poverty and social unrest in many countries, and contemporaneous with increasing far-right political activism.

Following on from this introduction, chapter two addresses the attitudes and understanding of the public which influenced the lives of people suffering from mental disorders and their help-seeking behaviours at times of mental distress. Each patient deemed to require mental hospital admission brought their knowledge, understanding and expectations from the community into an institution. Community understanding also influenced provision of support to patients, their relatives and friends, and attitudes of staff and the elected local councillors who had decision-making authority for the neighbourhood, including the running of the mental hospital. Wider still, members of the public without specialist knowledge were involved in national political and policy arenas. For these reasons, the chapter looks at public understanding in the broadest sense, and the route to mental hospital admission which patients and their families would likely encounter.

The third chapter looks primarily at the lives of patients inside the mental hospitals. Drawing on patients' own words wherever possible, the chapter explores their experiences. These include their interactions with staff; freedoms and restrictions; their ward companions, environment and activities; and issues of privacy, dignity and personal possessions. Keeping in touch with the outside world, convalescence, discharge and after-care, and how death was dealt with in the social context of the institution are also explored. The chapter is largely descriptive, setting the scene for the following three chapters which are more analytical and explain and contextualise what influenced patients' lives, how and why. The question is raised whether it was all 'petty tyranny and soulless discipline', as the medical correspondent of the *Times* referred to it in 1921,[103] and as incorporated into the title of this book.

Chapter four approaches the particular challenges faced in the mental hospitals concerning biological and psychological theories and their potential to shape treatment. No medications were available to alter the long-term course of psychiatric disorders, but some medications were used, and allegedly misused, in situations perceived as crises. The theory of 'focal sepsis' and the success of treating general paralysis of the insane (GPI – syphilis affecting the brain) by inoculation with malarial parasites helped to keep infective causes of mental disorder on the research agenda. The chapter also explores developments in the fields of heredity and eugenics. Eugenics did not lead to biological interventions for patients in mental hospitals in the UK, such as sterilisation, but it is bound up with attitudes to mental disorders and the people suffering from them, which influenced the quality of the care patients received.

Chapter five explores the roles, responsibilities and actions of people (mainly above the ranks of the staff in daily contact with the patients) who shaped life within the hospital walls, and how others, outside the hierarchy, impacted on it. The mental hospitals faced new challenges post-war such as being obligated to re-employ recently demobbed soldiers, including those with disabilities. This required a shift from the expectation that individual staff would fit the institution's needs, towards showing some flexibility towards the needs of employees. The chapter is broadly structured according to the leadership hierarchy, starting at the top, with the Ministry of Health and Board of Control, then the local authorities, Boards of Guardians and lay 'visiting committees'. Each mental hospital visiting committee was appointed from among elected local councillors and its management decisions directly affected both patients and staff. Doctors and nurses also faced skirmishes within and beyond their own professional groups. In addition, a long-running challenge which illustrates the complexity of making changes is given attention: crossing the gender line within the usually gender-segregated institutions, including employing women nurses to care for disturbed male patients, and having women doctors working across both 'sides' of the institution.

Forthright advocates sought to liberalise and humanise practices inside the mental hospitals and provide treatment without compulsion whenever possible. Chapter six looks at this, and the drawn-out and frustrating process of repeatedly having to re-tread steps on the path to reform. The protagonists and their opponents spanned many sectors of the population, from multiple backgrounds and social classes, including grass-roots campaigners, patients and whistleblowers, government ministers and peers in the House of Lords. Eventually the court case of Mr William Harnett triggered the appointment of the Royal Commission on Lunacy and Mental Disorder. By the end of the decade, little change had materialised in the mental hospitals, but the Commission's report authorised more liberal, patient-centred approaches, even if they required greater expenditure, and it paved the way for the Mental Treatment Act 1930.

The public mental hospital system a century ago was far from perfect. Aspects of it were inhumane and disrespectful towards both patients and frontline staff. The science of the time led up blind and dangerous alleyways, lunacy law was outdated, funding was insufficient, and an autocratic leadership was unreflective about how it contributed to the deficiencies. Today, NHS mental healthcare, serving the majority of the population, is also far from ideal. In many respects things have improved, but not all. The epilogue draws together some of the lessons from the past and considers whether they may have anything to teach us a century on.

Notes

1 Lloyd George, Speech, 23 Nov 1918.
2 Representation of the People Act 1918; Representation of the People (Equal Franchise) Act 1928.
3 Thane, *Divided Kingdom*, 68, 86.
4 Thane, *Divided Kingdom*, 68–74, 86, 108.
5 BoC, *Annual Report for 1920*, 4.
6 Kingdon, *Agendas, Alternatives and Public Policy*.
7 MoH, *Report of the Committee on Administration* (Cobb Report); Woolnough, Challenge and change; Monbiot, Covid deaths are on the rise again; *Lancet*, Editorial.
8 Brown, Asylums: what are the basic facts?, 147; Smyth, Red tape.
9 Scambler, Liberal ideology.
10 Royal Commission on Lunacy and Mental Disorder, *Report*, 94–5, para. 182.
11 Churchman, Guest editorial: wicked problems; Rittel and Webber, Dilemmas in a general theory of planning.
12 Hervey, Advocacy or folly, 245.
13 Bewley, *Madness to Mental Illness*, 15–16.
14 BoC, *Annual Report for 1925*, 51–2.
15 Winslow, *Manual of Lunacy*, 15; Lunacy Act 1845; Lunacy Act 1890, s. 276(1).
16 Jones, *Asylums and After*, 69.
17 Hubbard, Risk and confinement, 123.
18 Jones, *Mental Health and Social Policy*, 10.
19 Lunacy Act 1890, s. 238.
20 Voluntary Mental Treatment Bill, *Hansard*, 22 Jul 1914.
21 Medico-Psychological Association, Report of English Lunacy Legislation Sub-Committee, 44.
22 Jones, *Mental Health and Social Policy*, 93; Jones et al., The Maudsley Hospital, 362.

23 Medico-Psychological Association, Report of English Lunacy Legislation Sub-Committee, 49; Anon., Lunacy Acts Amendment (London) Bill 1903; Lunacy Act Amendment (London) Bill, *Hansard*, 5 Apr 1905.
24 Medico-Psychological Association, Report of English Lunacy Legislation Sub-Committee, 49.
25 Voluntary Mental Treatment Bill, *Hansard*, 22 Jul 1914.
26 Medico-Psychological Association, Report of the Committee on the Status of British Psychiatry, 667–74; Medico-Psychological Association, Report of English Lunacy Legislation Sub-Committee, 36–44.
27 BoC, *Annual Report for 1920*, 1.
28 Medico-Psychological Association, Memorandum of the evidence, 519.
29 Parley, *Life in a Madhouse*.
30 Lomax, *The Experiences of an Asylum Doctor.*
31 Thomson, A descriptive record, 123.
32 Cooke and Bond, *History of the Asylum War Hospitals*, 1; BoC, *Annual Report for 1916*, 2.
33 Hilton, *Civilian Lunatic Asylums*, 215.
34 Anon., Lunacy during the war.
35 Smith and Pear, *Shell Shock and its Lessons*, 108, 25.
36 Smith and Pear, *Shell Shock and its Lessons*, 74.
37 Smith and Pear, *Shell Shock and its Lessons*, xv.
38 Mental Treatment Bill, *Hansard*, 17 May 1915.
39 Cooke and Bond, *History of the Asylum War Hospitals*, 29.
40 Farquharson, Health and hierarchy, 80.
41 Brumby, 'A painful and disagreeable position', 37.
42 Ex-Services Welfare Society Fundraising leaflet, Armistice Day 1924, TNA PIN 15/2499.
43 Thompson and Howard, Ex-service mental patients.
44 Robinson, 'Definitely wrong', 91.
45 Sharot and Gledhill, 'Just because we are used to something, doesn't make it OK'.
46 Crammer, Extraordinary deaths.
47 Hess and Majerus, Writing the history, 143.
48 Weston, *Looking after Miss Alexander*, 20.
49 Hide and Bourke, Cultures of harm, 684.
50 Turner et al., The history of mental health services, 599.
51 Foucault, *Madness and Civilization*; Scull, *Desperate Remedies*; Scull, *Madhouse*; Szasz, *The Myth of Mental Illness.*
52 Scull, *Madhouse*, 274.
53 Hess and Majerus, Writing the history.
54 Jordanova, The social construction of medical knowledge, 361; Jane Whittaker, A difficult case to manage: Looking back to look forward in the care of people with eating disorders. draft manuscript, 2023.
55 Wynter et al., Marking time.
56 Calabria, Exploration of the function of nostalgia.
57 Pressman, *Psychosurgery*, 17.
58 Sommer and Osmond, Autobiographies, 660.
59 Noble and Heale, Triangulation in research.
60 Sacks, *Awakenings*, xxxvi; Morrison, Conversing with the psychiatrist, 18.
61 Porter (ed.), *The Faber Book of Madness*, xiv.
62 Porter, The patient's view.
63 Brumby, 'A painful and disagreeable position', 49.
64 Brumby, 'A painful and disagreeable position', 39.
65 National Survivor User Network, Our mission, 2024.
66 Freebody, *Work and Occupation,* 44.
67 Hornstein, *Bibliography*; Porter (ed.), *The Faber Book of Madness*.
68 Cobb Inquiry, Committee on Administration of Public Mental Hospitals 1922, TNA MH 58/219–20; Royal Commission on Lunacy and Mental Disorder, *Minutes*.
69 National Society for Lunacy Law Reform, *Report* 1931, 9, WL SA/EUG/D142.
70 Beveridge, Life in the asylum.
71 Sommer and Osmond, Autobiographies, 649.
72 Riggall, *Reminiscences of a Stay in a Mental Hospital*, 23; Scott, *Sane in Asylum Walls*, 26.
73 Warner et al., Importance of anonymity.

74 Millard and Wallis (eds), *Sources in the History of Psychiatry*.
75 Burns et al., The levels of evidence.
76 Morrison, Conversing with the psychiatrist, 32.
77 Glew, Documenting insanity, 26.
78 Goffman, *Asylums*.
79 Hide, *Gender and Class in English Asylums*.
80 Cherry, *Mental Health Care in Modern England*.
81 Weston, *Looking after Miss Alexander*, 136.
82 Jordanova, The social construction of medical knowledge, 361.
83 See Holocaust Memorial Day Trust, 23 Jun 1944; Evidence to Cobb Inquiry, Rev JJ Brownhill, q. 2,427, TNA MH 58/220.
84 Royal Commission on Lunacy and Mental Disorder, *Report*, 8, para. 19; Hilton, *Improving Psychiatric Care*, 187–8; MoH minutes, CMO, Secretary, 11 Oct 1921, TNA MH 58/222.
85 Lunacy Act 1890, ss. 169, 187, 188.
86 Wilberforce, *The Autobiography of a Pioneer Woman Doctor*, 131–2; Warmark, *Guilty but Insane*, 186.
87 Destruction of papers, records and documents 1889–1938, TNA MH 51/723.
88 Archivist, London Borough of Redbridge, email, 2017.
89 BoC, *Conference on Lunacy Administration*, 80.
90 House of Commons, *Standing Committee A*, 20.
91 Niall Boyce, Twitter/X, 26 Sept 2023.
92 Thomson, *The Problem of Mental Deficiency*, 9.
93 Advert, *Daily Telegraph*, 21 Sept 1914, WL SA/MAC/G.3/7.
94 Anon., Mental hygiene.
95 Newspapers, journals and periodicals: correspondence on mis-statements 1925–47, TNA MH 51/530.
96 Royal Commission on Lunacy and Mental Disorder, *Minutes*, Analysis of patient* and lunatic* samples using #LancsBox software.
97 Anon., Dancing in asylums.
98 BoC, *Annual Report for 1926*, Part 2, 135, Colney Hatch Mental Hospital, 17 Jul 1925.
99 Anon., Medico-Psychological Association, *JMS* 1906, 820.
100 Anderson, Prognosis of the depressions of later life, 559.
101 BoC minutes, 6 Jan 1926, 8, TNA MH 50/54.
102 Ackerly, Worcester State Hospital.
103 Our Medical Correspondent, Asylum horrors.

2

Outside to inside: public experience and understanding, and into the mental hospital

An appalling incident occurred in 1924 when 16 adult male patients from a mental hospital were processed by four uniformed staff members through a busy town centre, to a matinée performance at the local picture house:

> As the matinée was mainly a show for children, the patients had the discomfiture of listening to children shouting to each other to look at the loonies. When the show was over there was actually a gathering of children at the door to see the unfortunate patients march out again and back to the institution.

Some well-meaning person had donated the tickets, and the mental hospital had accepted them on behalf of the patients, but taking adults to a children's performance resulted in public ridicule.[1] The donor may not have known the ages of the people resident in the institution – whether pre-school or school-age children or adults – or the nature of the conditions which had led to them being there. It is also unclear why the hospital accepted the tickets, how it decided who should attend and whether it had any inkling of the likely public response to the patients. Among the various issues was the degree of public understanding about people with mental illness and what was then called mental deficiency, and their abilities and needs. By the 1920s, the difference was recognised legally, in medical and educational circles, in welfare policy and among charitable organisations, such as the Central Association for Mental Welfare which supported mentally deficient people, and the Mental After Care Association (MACA; today, Together for Mental Wellbeing) which worked with mentally ill people. For the wider population, the situation was less clear: the language of mental deficiency and illness was confusing, and magazines such as *John Bull*, written for a public readership, conflated the two.[2]

The differences had another significance in the public eye: when they were distinguished, mental illness carried more stigma than mental deficiency. Mentally deficient people were more likely to attract sympathy associated with the need for protection, and mental illness was associated with stereotypes of dangerousness requiring removal to an institution. The Lunacy Act 1890 initially included both mental deficiency and mental illness, but from 1913 the Mental Deficiency Act provided separate legislation for the former, while the Lunacy Act remained in force for the latter. The Lunacy Act stipulated compulsory 'certification' for admission to mental hospitals – a feature which the public perceived as intensely stigmatising and more ominous than a prison sentence: prison sentences usually incorporated a release date, and lunacy certification did not.[3]

Fears of wrongful detention and infringement of personal liberty loomed large on the public agenda. Public concern that a doctor or magistrate might certify a person erroneously when they were sane was reinforced by legal cases, autobiographical accounts and novels.[4] Former patient Rachel Grant-Smith wrote that the legal protections did not go far enough. Although a magistrate was obliged to sign the 'order for reception' to a mental hospital, there was no formality of the patient 'being brought into the presence of his judge before being sentenced'.[5] The sick person was therefore at a disadvantage, compared to a criminal.

The popular press also made generalisations about psychiatrists, tending to portray them as malevolent and ignorant of the conditions from which their patients suffered. A popular literary magazine in 1922 published the views of Paul Elgood, a former asylum attendant, probably writing under a pseudonym. He wrote: 'The question of where madness begins is a baffling problem. Doctors know as much about the subject – that is a real analytic knowledge – as a pig does of a holiday.'[6] By contrast, physicians and surgeons who treated people with physical disorders were generally regarded more positively, as knowledgeable and benevolent. Given the science and technology which influenced treatment of all patients, neither generalisation was realistic.

Regarding benevolence and malevolence, Henry Devine, the medical superintendent of Portsmouth Mental Hospital, told delegates at a conference in 1922 that when a new patient was admitted to his hospital, '[their] friends sometimes say to me, "Do you treat them kindly?" That is a nice thing to be asked! Of course we treat them kindly ... [How otherwise] can we gain the confidence of the public which is so eminently desirable?'[7] Dr Devine may have run an exemplary mental hospital, or he may have been unaware of harmful practices taking place within it, but his words do not point towards malevolence.

Societal values which stressed self-reliance, moral earnestness and individual responsibility could deter people from seeking help for mental problems.[8] A sense of blame and personal failure directed towards sufferers also hindered provision of services, which the public often viewed as a grudged expenditure.[9] Disparaging attitudes might also undermine rehabilitation and regaining employment post-discharge.[10] The rural locations of many mental hospitals contributed to distancing the public from them, both physically and metaphorically, and generated suspicion and speculation.

Ideas that had been germinating before WW1 stopped in their tracks in 1914, but began to regrow post-war – a time of 'uninhibited passion for new ideas on all topics'.[11] Alongside material, scientific and cultural change, the war raised poignant questions about human worth and the understanding of the mind, human nature and behaviours.[12] The theories of Sigmund Freud and concerns about shell-shocked soldiers contributed to bringing the understanding of mental disturbance towards the forefront of public interest.[13] Greater public awareness had the potential to exert pressure on policy makers, politicians and psychiatrists to make changes to allow early treatment and 'after-care', and to improve mental hospital standards to match the level of care that had been provided for the soldiers.

It is necessary to be as clear as possible about who is meant by the sweeping term 'the public'. Historian Vicky Long emphasised that 'the public' is not a single entity – there are multiple 'sub-public' groups, with no one group representative of the whole.[14] While recognising that 'the public' is far from a unitary concept, this book uses the term to refer to people who were neither patients nor the professionals working with them – at that time, mainly doctors and nurses. In the 1920s, in the context of mental disorders, influential sub-public groups included politicians and civil servants. Many other people undertook public 'citizen' roles as magistrates and elected local councillors. Some councillors were appointed to the lay 'visiting committees' which managed every mental hospital in conjunction with the institution's professional leadership, making decisions that directly affected patients and staff. Other members of the public took on voluntary roles working with, and campaigning for, people with mental disorders and for Lunacy Act reform.

Members of the public interacted with, and influenced the lives of, mentally unwell people, from the time their symptoms first appeared, and through the various sorts of care they received before, during and after mental hospital admission. The public could be involved on many levels, from responding as individuals to a distressed person's needs, to having roles in government shaping laws and national policy. Public knowledge and understanding were thus crucial to patients' experiences. With that in mind, this chapter aims to explore publicly held ideas about mental disorders and mental hospitals, and how people acquired their information. The chapter then moves through the help-seeking and administrative processes which a mentally distressed person would likely encounter leading up to certification under the Lunacy Act, and those first few days in the mental hospital following admission – a time when their public perceptions might be challenged or upheld.

Informing the public

Stereotypes and fears abounded. In the early 1920s, Middlesex County Council planned to build two mental institutions in rural Hertfordshire. One would be for people with mental illness, the other for mental defectives, and each would have two thousand beds. Local people objected to the Council purchasing Porters Park – a large estate near Radlett – for this purpose. They said that it was an 'outrage to dump 4,000 lunatics in one of the most beautiful spots in Hertfordshire, and one of the finest residential districts near London'. Residents feared depreciation of property values and suggested that a location closer to London and the population to be served would be more appropriate.[15] Given that the well-publicised government inquiry into the Administration of Public Mental Hospitals (Cobb Inquiry) in 1922 had recommended that institutions should not exceed a thousand beds, they had some grounds for their protest.[16] Local people did not want existing place names to be given to the institutions, and they proposed that patients should not be allowed to use their railway station in Radlett. Instead, patients would use Napsbury Station, which was merely a platform located between the slow lines and without a shelter, about three miles to the north and close to another Middlesex mental institution. They also did not want disruption to their golf club, and, fearful of the behaviour of people who would be moved into the area, they requested that 'lunatics and mental defectives should be kept off the roads'.[17] It was a heated and prolonged dispute lasting several years which the authorities finally won, although the institutions had fewer beds than originally proposed.[18]

Numerous sources of information shaped public understanding about mental disorders, the people who suffered from them, and mental institutions more broadly. There were books on psychology, psychiatry and institutions written specifically for a lay readership; memoirs, novels, newspapers and periodicals; and *Hansard*, the published transcript of parliamentary debates. Patient-authored accounts and other lay perspectives support and triangulate with happenings raised in official sources.[19] In addition, individual psychiatrists, such as John Lord, medical superintendent of Horton Mental Hospital near Epsom, recognised the need to improve public understanding, and attempted to do so.

Books for a general readership on psychology, psychiatry and the institutions

Towards the end of WW1, Elliot Smith and Tom Pear wrote *Shell Shock and its Lessons*. Shell shock was not a new phenomenon, they said, but an example of 'nervous breakdown' which people had experienced before the war, and it would 'not disappear miraculously with the coming of peace'.[20] They noted that public attitudes played a 'great part in the causation of the prevalent dread of treatment for mental disorder', and that the 'practical Englishman' asks: 'What about the financial aspect?'[21] They explained:

> The cost per day of repairing a motor car is usually distinctly higher than the daily charge for garaging it in its broken-down state. Yet we gladly pay the higher charge for the simple reasons that a motor car in its garage is of no use to us, and that the daily charge for housing the car would amount to a colossal figure if paid for many years. Cannot we apply the same reasoning to the case of the mentally disordered human being?[22]

Given the timing, they also took a bold step by comparing psychiatric care in England to that in Germany, asking: 'Can we be content to treat our sufferers with less sympathy, insight and common-sense than Germany?'[23] At that time, suggesting that German humanity could be greater than that of the British was like showing a red rag to a bull.

Lionel Weatherly, a psychiatrist, and Montagu Lomax, a retired GP who undertook asylum work during WW1, both wrote for a public readership, taking a fiercely reformist agenda.[24] Like Elliot Smith and Tom Pear, Dr Weatherly also advocated learning from psychiatric practice in Germany.[25] Public outrage about poor standards of care described in

Dr Lomax's book, *The Experiences of an Asylum Doctor* (1921), prompted the Ministry of Health to appoint a committee of inquiry. The book also fed into public campaigns for asylum improvements and into the Royal Commission on Lunacy and Mental Disorder (1924–6), all of which received much attention in newspapers and periodicals written for a broad readership.

Memoirs

Mary Riggall, a patient discharged from a mental hospital in 1919, wrote a book about her experiences. Her motivation for writing these reminiscences, both positive and negative, came from her desire to better inform the public about life as a patient:

> I have often wished I could do something, or write something, that would make people try to brighten the lives of those unfortunate folk, who, through no fault of their own, are doomed to live, cut off from their friends and the outside world. No one could possibly explain the monotony of such a life. It has to be experienced to be believed.[26]

Rachel Grant-Smith, James Scott and 'Warmark' (Stephen George Penny) also wrote about their time in mental hospitals in England.[27] In the USA, Clifford Beers' book, *A Mind that Found Itself* (1908), detailed his mental illness and experiences at the hands of psychiatrists, relatives, friends and acquaintances.[28] A Mr Davidson published his memoir regarding his experiences in England and Australia. Despite being in different types of institutions, on three continents, and published over two decades, these authors' accounts suggest commonalities across the English-speaking Western world. They correlate with material in other sources and appear sufficiently true to life to draw on illustratively in this study.

It is clear that stigma did not silence past generations of patients, although some sought anonymity when writing about their experiences. Regarding Mary Riggall, my recent correspondence with the company which published her book, Arthur H Stockwell, has failed to give any pointers as to whether she wrote under her own name, or details of where she lived, which might have given clues as to the hospital where she was treated.[29]

Novels

Popular novels about mental disturbance and its treatment were another influential source of public information. They tended to feature the wrongful detention of a sane person, and kindnesses and misguided practices of psychiatrists and others involved in leading institutions and treating patients, as well as the roles of relatives and 'friends', both loyal and disloyal to the patient. Melissa Dickson, whose academic research focusses on the interactions between creative literature, science and medicine, regards literature as a valid source for informing historical research. It gives artistic expression to the workings of the mind, and reflects on and imaginatively illustrates psychiatry. In the course of evaluating creative literature, she advises that historians should also consider the evidence and resources used by the author when constructing the text.[30]

Mrs Victor Rickard's novel *Cathy Rossiter*, which details Cathy's experiences in a private mental institution, has many parallels with the memoir of a former patient, 'Oxonian', which was published in the *English Review*, a magazine of literature and social commentary.[31] This suggests that the two authors communicated, or perhaps Mrs Rickard was also 'Oxonian', or that the happenings described in both works were commonplace. Both the memoir and the novel conveyed many unfavourable, and a few favourable, aspects of mental hospital care. *Cathy Rossiter* described the utter despair of patients, at least in part due to not being believed or understood by those in authority, as well as their environment and treatment. It also illustrated the stigma of mental illness. As Cathy heard from a fellow patient: 'Once the stigma of lunacy is branded upon any living soul … no one will listen to you; … you and I are outcasts.'[32] This echoed Rachel Grant-Smith's experience: 'Once tainted with a certificate of madness, every statement made by the so-called lunatic can be characterized as a further sign of his or her unsoundness of mind.'[33]

Another novel, *Christina Alberta's Father* by HG Wells,[34] tells the story of Mr Preemby, a retired laundryman and widower who believed himself to be Sargon, the ancient king of Sumeria, returned to restore harmony to a disordered post-WW1 world. The story was said to have emerged during an after-dinner discussion between Wells and the founder of analytical psychology, Carl Jung.[35] Its themes overlap with those in *Cathy Rossiter*. Wells' novel incorporated the social-cultural milieu of the time, public anxieties about mental illness and wrongful detention in a mental hospital, and issues of heredity, stigma, family loyalty, the kindness of strangers, variable standards of care behind closed doors, and the dilemma facing doctors trying to determine where eccentricity ends and insanity begins. Later, Jung praised the book, giving his view on Mr Preemby's state of mind and emphasising its psychodynamic underpinning: 'Some kind of Sargon, in various disguises, is hiding in everyone [*sic*] of us. The fact that he cannot get out of the subconscious and is unable to develop himself is often the case of severe psychic disturbances.'[36]

Unsurprisingly, the Board of Control (the central government authority which oversaw the mental institutions) deplored Wells' attitude.[37] Psychiatrist Robert Cole accepted that novels indicated public concern for the 'welfare of the insane', but he regarded *Christina Alberta's Father* as biased, particularly against psychiatrists, and considered that its 'destructive criticism' was of little value in shaping the future.[38] By contrast, the National Society for Lunacy Reform (NSLR, a campaign group; in the early 1920s, the National Council for Lunacy Reform (NCLR)) supported the novelists' approach. It regarded negative publicity as essential to educate the public, who had the power to influence change through local and central government:

> The public conscience needs to be stirred. If the public only knew the truth, there would be a wave of indignation throughout the country, which would compel the authorities to change their ways ... the battle is to be fought on the floor of the House of Commons. Members must be bombarded.[39]

In contrast to historical happenings which tend to be forgotten with time, emotive messages in creative literature may remain long in people's consciousness and be cited by subsequent generations. Charles Reade's *Hard Cash*,[40] a novel published in 1863, focussed on one man's wrongful detention and his harsh, sometimes brutal, experiences in a private asylum. Half a century later, an anonymous former patient wrote in a London weekly newspaper that Reade had exposed 'the most fiendish cruelties which at that time were practised upon the insane' and that 'similar atrocities' continued.[41] In 1927, Earl Russell referred to *Hard Cash* during a House of Lords debate on wrongful mental hospital detention, implying that his audience knew the book.[42] *Cathy Rossiter* also lingered long in the public imagination, and *Mrs Dalloway*, Virginia Woolf's 1925 novel about inter-war social life, shell shock and unhelpful psychiatrists, remains in print.[43]

Insights from newspapers, periodicals and *Hansard*

In addition to publishing reports about standards of psychiatric care, campaigns for improvement and the nightmare of wrongful detention,[44] national and local newspapers contributed to feeding the public a diet of reports on criminal trials and other legal scenarios associated with psychiatrists and people with mental disorders. The press relayed psychiatric evidence, transformed by journalists into language suitable for a lay readership.[45] This had ramifications for public understanding, such as on the reliability of psychiatrists and their evidence, the nature of mental illness and abnormal or dangerous behaviours, and the use of capital punishment. It also had the potential to influence decision making by juries. The press sometimes also threw professional tensions between doctors and lawyers into the public arena.[46] These might concern life-and-death decisions, but were also apparent in less contentious circumstances and could ridicule psychiatrists. At a trial in 1920, Mr Justice Darling triggered laughter in court when he chastised psychiatrist Sir Robert Armstrong-Jones, who did not agree with a particular legal rule. The judge referred to the teachings of Freud, saying that his name would be better spelt with 'an "a" instead of an "e"', and that: 'We take the law of England from the King's Bench, and not from Harley-street; from the House of Lords and not from Wimpole-street or any other street.'[47] Excessive reporting could also cause harm in other ways: coroners in the 1920s pointed out that over-reporting of suicide methods was unsafe due to the 'power of suggestion' for those at risk. Coroners therefore suggested that they should have discretion 'to forbid the publication of the evidence in cases of suicide, which can be of no possible service to anyone, is a source of pain and injury to friends and relations, and at the same time of danger to the community'.[48]

Since the late nineteenth century psychiatric evidence had contributed to the increasing proportion of people tried for murder who had been found insane and spared the death sentence – then the mandatory penalty for that crime. This was associated with an increase in pre-trial assessments by psychiatrists and other medical specialists, and a greater acceptance by the legal profession that their evidence was scientific and objective.[49] That view had also surfaced during WW1 with professional evidence given at courts martial on the effect of trench warfare in inducing shell shock, thus sparing some soldiers the firing squad for desertion or cowardice.[50]

Reporting crimes committed by people when mentally disturbed could also influence, and give insight into, mental illness-related stigma. That the Infanticide Act 1922 abolished the death penalty for a mother who killed her infant while of unsound mind after childbirth suggests a degree of sympathy towards women in that predicament. Around the same time there was also public consternation concerning two widely reported murder trials – those of Henry Julius Jacoby, who was hanged, and Ronald True, who was admitted to Broadmoor State Criminal Asylum. Mr Justice McCardie presided over both trials. The contrasting verdicts raised questions as to whether the difference was one of wealth rather than sanity, with True being able to buy his reprieve and Jacoby not.[51] Public disquiet around their sentencing contributed to the Government appointing a committee to consider practice and procedure relating to criminal trials where the plea of insanity was raised as a defence. The committee comprised legal and Home Office experts only, with no medical members.[52]

Despite the fact that most mentally unwell people were neither criminal nor dangerous, reports that such people perpetrated violent crimes raised the public's concern about potential risks to themselves. This reinforced opinion that mentally unwell people should be detained, with the primary objective being to safeguard the public 'against the menace to its comfort and security which such persons constitute'.[53] In 1925, in light of the concern about risks posed by mentally unwell people and in the context of overcrowded mental hospitals and vacant beds in workhouses, *Hansard* reported that Harry Day MP asked the Minister of Health 'whether, in view of the danger to the inmates of Poor-Law institutions, he will consider the advisability of new mental hospitals being built, instead of lunatics being housed with normal old people'. Sir Kingsley Wood, answering on behalf of the Minister, reinforced negative stereotypes but reassured Mr Day, by replying that lunatics and normal old people would not be housed together.[54] In contrast, in Scotland and in the Belgian city of Geel, people with similar conditions to these 'lunatics' could be found living successfully in households with families,[55] suggesting that in England risks were perceived in a climate of disproportionate public fear.

Hansard provides other insights into lay understandings and attitudes regarding mental disorders. There were occasions when parliamentarians demonstrated disturbingly low levels of knowledge and understanding when expounding on statements as if they were established fact and assuming that others in the House would concur. David Logan MP, for example, advocated for segregating mentally disturbed people since, for newly admitted patients, after 'one, two or three days, cases that otherwise would have gone home have become insane owing to the cases they meet with inside ... The same thing happens in the case of smallpox.'[56] He did not mention mental hospital staff, who did not 'catch' insanity. He also declared that his infection model of mental disorder 'cannot be disputed' – a conversation stopper, derailing any challenges to his comment by implying that anyone who thought otherwise was mistaken. In a similar way, Lord Buckmaster, a Liberal peer and lawyer by profession, asserted: 'Everyone knows that insanity may, roughly, be divided into three or four classes' – a position which was out of step with scientific and clinical paradigms. 'Everyone knows' implied that those who thought differently were ignorant, yet his words – 'three or four' – simultaneously reveal his own uncertainty. When, in the same debate, the Bishop of Worcester addressed the House of Lords on the subject of mental hospitals, he spoke of them as 'great and glorious institutions', and that he had ministered 'in the great chapels of these mental hospitals … [talking] to the patients as if they were an ordinary congregation'.[57] His 'great and glorious' suggests a lack of awareness or a denial of recent disturbing publicity about the institutions, and 'as if' implied the stereotype of mental illness as encompassing every facet of a person's mind. It seems unlikely that he would have used his 'as if' clause in a similar manner in the context of speaking to people hospitalised with physical disorders.[58]

Psychiatrists' attempts to educate the public

Some psychiatrists, such as John Lord, were enthusiastic about educating the public to help dispel erroneous notions. Concepts of 'demoniacal possession' still existed 'in a shadowy form unconsciously' and, according to psychiatrist Charles Read, they created fear and ostracism of mentally unwell individuals.[59] The term 'lunacy', meaning a disease caused by the moon, was also archaic and incompatible with modern ideas.[60] Dr Lord noted that patients' friends and relatives were 'suspicious, over-anxious, querulous and imbued with wrong notions', such as that it was a disgrace to be mentally unwell.[61] He proposed appointing voluntary or paid social workers to the staff of mental hospitals. Their tasks would include bringing the public into closer touch with the institutions, thereby improving understanding and public relations. Social workers would also address public audiences at seminars, and Dr Lord was certain that 'the public would listen and have confidence in what they said'.[62]

Dr Lord urged some caution with public education measures, to avoid the community becoming 'hypochondriacal and neurasthenical' due to knowledge increasing personal introspection. Information needed to be clear, with 'the simple facts of mind and mental disorders' aligned to biological understanding, rather than more philosophical arguments which 'may be confused with ethics, morality and religion about which the public … are prone at all times to take up unhealthy and bizarre notions'.[63] Correcting erroneous notions was also considered likely to help dispel stigma. That, however, has been a topic of long-term debate: it might be part of the solution, but on the evidence of stigma continuing, it is by no means the whole answer.[64]

Following publication of the Royal Commission's report (1926), its chairman, Hugh Pattison Macmillan, reflected on public opinion: 'I cannot see why a person whose misfortune it is to be ill in mind should suffer a stigma, and the person who is ill in his appendix incurs no such stigma.'[65] Macmillan echoed Weatherly's words that ridding the public mind 'of the idea that mental disease is any more of a stigma on the family, than consumption, syphilis, cancer, small-pox, spotted fever or many other diseases' was vital to reform.[66] Towards the end of the long 1920s, the Minister of Health, Arthur Greenwood, told the Commons that insanity is 'a disease like other diseases, though with distinctive symptoms of its own, and … can be ministered to no less effectively than a body diseased'. It should be thought of 'as a visitation of Providence, not as something indecent, about which we ought not to talk in public, but as something in the same category as other forms of human ailment'.[67] Around the same time, the Board of Control bemoaned that the 'old conception of insanity dies hard and its traces are still persistent … [It is] still too widely prevalent, that the occurrence of any kind of mental disorder can only be regarded as a mysterious visitation about which the less said the better.'[68]

In contrast to Dr Lord's advice on educating the public, stimulating interest and welcoming their involvement, some psychiatrists were scathing of any attempt to educate the public about their field of expertise. Psychiatrist Gilbert Mould wrote in a London weekly newspaper that 'the ignorance of the general public about insanity is so profound, that one might as well discuss the fourth dimension of space with an agricultural labourer'.[69] Historian Stephen Soanes pointed out that Dr Lord may have been more optimistic than some of his colleagues because of his recent wartime experiences. Dr Lord retained the leadership of Horton hospital when it was requisitioned for military purposes, which may have given him a positive outlook regarding relations with the public and expanding the reach of the institution into the community. That contrasted, for example, with Dr Lomax's contemporaneous experiences, working as an assistant medical officer in a poorly run, under-resourced wartime civilian asylum.[70] Soanes' interpretation suggests subtle and personal ways in which the war may have influenced developments in the mental hospitals over the ensuing years.

New ways of understanding mental experience

Freud's treatises, *The Interpretation of Dreams* and *The Psychopathology of Everyday Life,* appeared in English shortly before WW1.[71] By the end of the war, some of his doctrines were raising eyebrows, especially those concerning sexual drive and child development, and some people regarded them as potential threats to morality and decency.[72] In 1919, an anonymous author explained in the *Athenaeum*, a London-based literary magazine:

> Freud's views have won a large measure of acceptance in England as a result of the war. Five years ago he was to most of us simply the founder of the fantastic and perverted theory that every nervous disorder, every dream, and indeed every kind of mental activity had a direct reference to the sexual instincts. To-day we have learned that the really important part of his theory is not the relation of conscious mental activity to one particular instinct, but its relation to the instincts generally. We have learned to accept his theory of the repression of painful thoughts and desires into the unconscious, and their reappearance in a distorted form in dreams, in trivial misquotations and lapses of memory, or in the definite symptoms of nervous disorder.[73]

In an attempt to understand human mental experiences, some people turned to psychoanalytic concepts, and others to psychic or paranormal phenomena – happenings which appear to be contrary to physical laws and suggest the possibility of mental activity existing apart from the body – such as telepathy and trance states.[74] Social commentator and novelist Gerald Langston Day was convinced that his wife 'was cured of insanity by psychic methods when orthodox treatment had proved futile'.[75]

As with investigations into psychoanalysis to shed light on the workings of the mind, aiming to understand the occult – including spiritualism, fortune-telling, theosophy, animal magnetism and astrology – was a serious pursuit. Leading academics and intellectuals from a range of disciplines, many affiliated to the Society for Psychical Research, investigated these phenomena.[76] In his study of psychoanalysis in Britain in the inter-war years, Graham Richards attributed interest in these fields to a flourishing popular counterculture seeking to 'reconnect with the non-rational and ancestral' as a response to the 'escalating success of materialist science'.[77]

Freud's psychoanalytical ideas were received enthusiastically by lay people – more so than by members of the medical profession, few of whom found them convincing. According to Richards, for the public: 'To be able to speak Freudish marked one as modern in the same way as being able to refer to electrons, endocrines or the "fourth dimension"'. As well as being fashionable, Freudish (and Jungish, Adlerian and Kleinish, relating respectively to concepts of Carl Jung, Alfred Adler and Melanie Klein) provided ways of expressing mental function and distress untainted by the legacy of lunacy and asylums.[78]

Despite complex concepts and controversy, psychoanalysis enjoyed popular success and cultural influence. Some of its concepts, such as ego, projection and repression, became assimilated into everyday parlance.[79] In Agatha Christie's 1926 novel *The Murder of Roger Ackroyd*, when her fictional detective, Hercule Poirot, referred to the 'psychology of a crime', police inspector Raglan replied: 'you've been bitten with all this psycho-analysis stuff?'[80] Fascination with dreams and how they express desires and fears also influenced new media: the macabre, sinister and morbid silent film *The Cabinet of Dr Caligari* 'aroused passionate discussions' on the subject and helped popularise psychoanalytic ideas.[81]

Many people sought a better understanding of the workings of the mind and the brain, both when functioning well and when disturbed. Regardless of the balance of facts and fictions, and huge uncertainties, ideas sparked interest and provoked debate, questions and further investigation. Openness to debate about the mind, brain, consciousness and various psychoanalytical concepts, and seeking to understand and repair an individual's psychological dysfunction, stood in stark contrast to the regimented processes and often untherapeutic custodial methods employed in many of the large public mental hospitals.

Preventing insanity: enhancing public mental health

The Lunacy Act 1890 influenced concepts of insanity and many of the practicalities around preventing and treating it. Dr Lord explained in 1923 that, unlike for physical disorders:

> It is not the onset of disease which makes him a 'patient' but an act under the law. It is not the cessation of disease which occasions his ceasing to be a 'patient' but the failure to find sufficient cause for detention ... There is undoubtedly a legal aspect, and an important

one too; the liberty of the subject cannot lightly be tampered with, but the medical aspect of insanity, its prevention, its cure, should be the basis of the law on lunacy.[82]

Kathleen Jones echoed this in her 1993 book *Asylums and After*: 'From the legal point of view, [the Lunacy Act] was very nearly perfect. From the medical and social viewpoint, it was to hamper the progress of the mental health movement for nearly seventy years.'[83]

When the Board of Control declared that there had been a decrease in insanity during WW1, it meant fewer people admitted to asylums.[84] The Board's narrow definition, based on admission and discharge data, was neither representative of the weight of mental distress and suffering in the community nor indicative that there were likely to be people who might benefit from early treatment or a preventative course of action. Despite a lack of community data, the Board wanted to 'foster and encourage by all means in our power' a more 'healthy outlook of the general public'.[85] This aligned with objectives of the up-and-coming 'mental hygiene' movement which had grown from Clifford Beers' memoir and subsequent campaign in the USA.[86] In collaboration with psychologist Dr William James and the internationally renowned – although sometimes controversial – psychiatrist Dr Adolf Meyer,[87] Beers founded the National Committee for Mental Hygiene there in 1909. The Committee aimed to prevent mental disorders, promote mental health and improve standards of care.

Psychiatrist Helen Boyle, who founded and led the charitable Lady Chichester Hospital in Hove, Sussex, which was dedicated to treating women suffering from early mental disorders, visited the USA shortly after WW1 and met Clifford Beers. Inspired by his model, upon her return she enlisted influential psychiatrist colleagues and others, including Sir Courtauld Thomson, a businessman and philanthropist, to embrace a mental hygiene approach in the UK.[88] Making mental hygiene international aligned with Beers' personal ambitions, with the USA striving for internationalism after WW1, with the aims of the new League of Nations, and with a widespread desire to create a better world. According to historian Mathew Thomson, WW1 'was seen by many to have stemmed from a European mental malaise, antagonised by the anxieties of prewar national animosity'. Thus, mental hygiene protagonists aligned good mental health with international cooperation, with the potential to keep aggressive drives for war at bay.[89]

The National Council for Mental Hygiene (NCMH) was created in England in 1922. Dr Lord was involved, and Mr Beers attended the inaugural meeting while on a European tour spreading the gospel of mental hygiene.[90] Others at the inaugural meeting included 'clergy, lunacy officials, members of various societies interested in the welfare of the mentally afflicted and deficient', and medical and legal professionals. The NCMH's aims differed from those of the USA movement, and those of other countries, but fitted UK needs and priorities. It sought to work collaboratively across various professional groups and with lay people to achieve its goals, which included encouraging research, improving institutional standards, and promoting public education and good mental health for the whole population.[91] To do this well would require psychiatrists learning from other fields of public health, such as education campaigns concerning tuberculosis.[92]

Psychiatrist David Kennedy Henderson, medical superintendent at Glasgow Royal Mental Hospital, Gartnavel, adopted a broader perspective on mental hygiene: better social conditions were needed to alleviate poverty, unemployment and poor housing, and to achieve good mental and physical health.[93] Scotland's General Board of Control (the equivalent to the Board of Control for England and Wales), in keeping with Henderson's arguments concerning alleviation of poverty, found that fewer 'persons suffering from senile insanity of mild types' were admitted into their asylums when the Old Age Pension was raised.[94] This was likely to have been associated with the pension contributing to household income taking pressure off family members who were supporting the older person. A Labour Party hospital policy statement concurred regarding the effects of poverty: fewer hospital beds for all conditions would be needed if there was a forward-looking social policy, including a national minimum wage, abolishing all slums and providing better housing.[95] The latter was government policy – part of the vision to provide 'homes fit for heroes'. However, amid an economic crisis with rising unemployment, high interest rates and falling exports, savage cuts in public expenditure in 1922 (the 'Geddes Axe', named after the committee chaired by Sir Eric Geddes) relegated the building of homes and other social welfare initiatives to the back-burner.[96]

The Board of Control for England and Wales tended to follow innovations from individuals and organisations, rather than take initiatives itself. It took a greater interest in outpatient clinics after the NCMH set out its prevention-focussed goals. There was recognition that outpatient clinics accessible to the whole population were required for early treatment to help avoid deterioration into insanity, synonymous with Lunacy Act certification and admission. Not providing them was contrary to general medical principles, which recommended treating ailments early in the hope of reversing them. Clinics were few and far between due to the Lunacy Act restricting public expenditure on services other than for mental hospital inpatients.[97] However, some charitably funded non-statutory or 'voluntary' hospitals, such as teaching hospitals, usually located in major cities, provided them for 'early nervous and minor mental disorders', for people who could not afford to pay.[98]

The Board of Control reviewed outpatient facilities in 1925. In addition to those in the voluntary hospitals, it reported on a clinic established by Professor Bevan-Lewis 30 years earlier at the West Riding Mental Hospital, Wakefield. The hospital was close to the town, so the site was accessible to the local population and to those from the surrounding area travelling to the town by train. The clinic was located in a room at the entrance to the hospital, and in the 1920s the hospital's medical superintendent, John Gilmour, commented that patients who attended appeared to lose 'asylum fear', and were not opposed to admission if inpatient treatment was recommended.[99] The Wakefield model, along with an outpatient clinic at Oxford's Radcliffe Infirmary in conjunction with the Littlemore Mental Hospital, demonstrated what might be achieved in terms of the public accepting psychiatric treatment when the local authorities supported a more outward-facing approach. The Earl of Onslow, Parliamentary Secretary to the Ministry of Health, commented on the Oxford clinic in 1923:

> No difference is made between nervous and mental patients. They all wait in the same hall for treatment, and they are all treated without difference or distinction. It has been found that patients and their friends are much more ready to come to a clinic of this kind than to a separate mental hospital, and altogether the results have been justified.[100]

The Board was enthusiastic about creating outpatient clinics in general rather than mental hospitals, despite the successful schemes at Wakefield and at the Maudsley, London – a publicly funded mental hospital established by an Act of Parliament and offering treatment without certification.[101] Opening to civilian patients in 1923 after a period as a military hospital, in 1925 the Maudsley exceeded expectations by treating over a thousand outpatients, but the Board and the Earl of Onslow concurred that public beliefs about mental hospitals might deter attendance. The Board therefore advised collaboration between mental and general hospitals to establish clinics, as in Oxford, arguing that mental and physical illness had no clear demarcation between them, so '[t]reatment of mental disorder should approximate as near as possible to the treatment of physical disorders'.[102] Dr Lord also sought to establish clinics, envisaging them as part of a linked-up continuum of provision, from early treatment through to admission and after-care, making mental hospitals rehabilitative, medical and humanitarian community-centred institutions.[103] Soanes described Lord's idealised picture as a 'strategic professional response to a crisis of public confidence in mental hospitals'.[104] If so, that was positive, as it indicated that professionals were hearing the public voice. Dr Lord's initiatives, however, did not become widespread in the 1920s.

Pioneering charitable bodies, such as the Lady Chichester Hospital and MACA, undertook preventative work. Teaching hospital outpatient departments referred patients to MACA, which demonstrated the benefits of early intervention for poorer people who 'by timely care and removal to pleasant and sympathetic surroundings have frequently made good recoveries of their mental balance without certification'.[105] In 1928, most of the 97 people admitted to a MACA home for early treatment returned to their own homes and occupations.[106] Such pilot schemes concurred with medical opinion and that of the NCMH, demonstrated what could be achieved, subsidised the public sector and inspired the Royal Commission and the Government towards introducing measures to help avoid admission.[107] Lacking statutory funding, however, MACA had limited resources, and in the 1920s its interventions were numerically a drop in the ocean.

The route to mental hospital admission under the Lunacy Act 1890

Twenty-eight-year-old Annie C was admitted to Worcester County and City Mental Hospital, Powick in 1921. Her parents described her as of 'weak intellect since birth'. Over a period of six months prior to her admission, she had experienced 'delusions' and had become socially disruptive and increasingly dependent on her parents. Employment demands may have made it difficult for the family to support Annie at home, and neither specialist advice nor community support were available to help them. Annie's hospital admission papers and other clinical records did not mention violence, but successive generations of her family believed it had been a major problem. When I discussed Annie's story with her great-great-niece, it appeared that allegations of violent behaviours evolved later. This may shed light on aspects of stigma and public understanding. First, Annie's parents may have felt guilty about not supporting her at home and exaggerations may have drawn sympathy from other people regarding their predicament. Second, accounts of violence may have reflected stereotypical beliefs about how people in asylums were thought to behave.[108]

Annie C's story highlights the lack of community support, and families' attempts to do their best to care for relatives for as long as possible. For a physical ailment, a patient could seek help in the casualty or outpatient department of the local general hospital or workhouse infirmary. Based on that premise, if help was needed for a mental condition, some patients and their relatives went directly to a mental hospital. However, if they did, they were turned away, with instructions to go to their local workhouse infirmary, or to apply to the 'relieving officer' – a Poor Law Board of Guardians official – to seek certification.[109] These routes could add to patients' distress and be risky in crisis situations. When Annie K, a former patient of Colney Hatch Mental Hospital, was 'depressed and suicidal' her sister took her back there. Colney Hatch, however, obeyed the rules and insisted that she first had to go to the workhouse infirmary near her home to be certified under the Lunacy Act. That necessitated a 20-mile round trip back to Whitechapel before she could be admitted to Colney Hatch.[110] This was not an isolated occurrence. Such incidents contributed to discussion among psychiatrists and in policy-making circles as to whether certification was necessary at all when a patient sought admission themselves.

If a relieving officer was called to the home of someone who was mentally very disturbed, they would most likely take the person to the workhouse. A police constable or parish overseer could do likewise if the person was found in a public place. The Guardians operated the local workhouse, which the Lunacy Act stipulated had to provide shelter for an 'alleged lunatic' in an emergency, for their own welfare or for 'public safety'.[111] The Lunacy Act permitted the workhouses to provide assessment and treatment for up to 17 days, but even the Royal Commission was baffled by the legal complexities of them doing that.[112]

In England, 'mental observation wards' arose around the beginning of the twentieth century and were established in many of the larger workhouses in their infirmary wings.[113] Colin Cowan, in his historical analysis of mental observation wards, contextualised them as part of a system of emergency healthcare then developing, with parallel facilities being established in fever hospitals, children's hospitals, prisons and elsewhere.[114] The mental observation wards also kept mentally disturbed patients separate from other patients in the institution, at least in part reflecting, and perhaps reinforcing, public fear of 'catching' insanity from

Figure 2.1 Miss Ethel Vickers (far left), MACA Annual General Meeting, the Mansion House, London, 1927. Reproduced with permission from Together for Mental Wellbeing.

them.[115] In addition, according to Miss Ethel Vickers (Figure 2.1), who ran MACA and who channelled the opinions of former inpatients into official circles, patients suffering from recurrent mental disorders would rather avoid going to mental observation wards, preferring instead to return directly to a mental hospital if they required treatment.[116]

The quality of the mental observation ward environment and its medical and nursing care varied. London-based public health physician Sir Allan Daley noted in 1929 that in some, 'equipment, staffing and organisation were of a deplorably low standard'.[117] Mental observation wards did not employ specialist psychiatrists. Instead, the workhouse infirmary's general medical officers oversaw patients' initial care, treatment and certification.[118] Consequently, the psychiatrists who would take over their care in the mental hospital had no say as to the appropriateness of their admission – a situation which would have been untenable for physicians or surgeons practising in the infirmaries.

The workhouse catchment area was much smaller than that covered by a county mental hospital. With workhouses relatively local to people's homes, they had the potential to provide prompt attention which mental hospitals, often miles away, were unable to do. Observation wards also had the potential to prevent unnecessary mental hospital admission, providing breathing space between a crisis and a decision being taken that certification was the best option. Some patients might recover promptly, such as from fevers, alcohol intoxication, arsenic poisoning or other toxins, and could be discharged.[119] Observation wards could also provide a very short-term half-way house, as former patient JSC thought was needed:

> It is terrible to send a young person to wake up in a lunatic asylum, to be branded for life for that which is often the fault of others, or a mere nervous disturbance which may be all over in ten days. That in itself is enough to cause a permanent deterioration of the brain. There should be certainly a half-way house between the asylum and a patient's own home.[120]

HG Wells provided a glimpse of a mental observation ward in *Christina Alberta's Father*. The atmosphere was hardly welcoming, and could add to a patient's distress:

> A heartless great dingy room it was, with green-grey distempered walls discoloured in patches, lit by a few bare lights ... The floor was of polished bare boards. Far off was a table set against the wall with two or three torn and crumpled magazines thereon, and at the end an empty fire-place ... There was a foul smell in the air, faint and yet indescribably offensive, a faecal smell mixed with a heavy soapy odour.
>
> ... Two men were jammed behind the table against the wall and one, a fleshy lout with a shining pink skin and curling red hair on his bare chest, was making violent gestures, hammering the table with a freckled fist, talking in a voice that rose and sank and occasionally broke into curses while the other, a sallow-complexioned, cadaverous individual, seemed to be sunken in profound despair.[121]

Despite the environment and company, Wells also described the staff's empathy and understanding towards the new arrival – in this case Mr Preemby, who believed he was Sargon:

> A small bright-eyed man in a grey suit came and looked at Sargon. For some moments they regarded each other in silence. 'Well?' said the man in the grey suit.
>
> 'My name is Sargon. I do not know why I have been brought here. Is this a hospital? I understand it is. I am not ill.'
>
> 'You may be ill without knowing it.'
>
> 'No.'
>
> 'We just want to have you here for a bit to have a look at you.'
>
> Sargon shrugged his shoulders.[122]

A mentally unwell person's route to mental hospital was rarely straightforward in terms of symptoms, legalities and practicalities. Assessment for certification under the Lunacy Act, involving a doctor and magistrate, generally took place on the observation ward. Often, doctors had difficulty deciding whether a person was sane or insane: it 'is one of the most difficult matters that doctors have to decide', as Earl Russell summarised for the House of Lords in a debate on voluntary admission.[123] Psychiatrist Sir James Crichton-Browne referred to 'half mad' people:

> The out-and-out lunatic can be controlled and his injurious influence circumscribed, but the half mad is practically unrestrained and free to go about broadcasting trouble and perplexity ... there is nothing to be done but to put up with it as best they may ... These half-mads are a public as well as a domestic nuisance.[124]

Despite the unsympathetic tone, James Crichton-Browne at least recognised the difficulties faced by families who knew that their relative was mentally unwell and needed psychiatric help but had no option other than to wait until the person deteriorated to crisis point.

Certification to a public mental hospital automatically designated the mentally unwell person a 'pauper lunatic'. This was a legal technicality, due to the costs of care in the mental hospitals being means tested, with variable contributions made by the Poor Law Guardians. Thus someone who was self-supporting before becoming mentally disturbed was suddenly labelled a pauper, although in the ordinary sense of the word the person was not a pauper at all.[125] This humiliating designation probably contributed to deterring people from seeking help and hoping a crisis would never be reached.[126]

The need to abolish the 'pauper lunatic' term became more pressing during WW1 in the light of public opinion which wanted soldiers, mentally traumatised in the service of their country, to be spared the derogatory epithet.[127] Curiously, if someone was physically ill and required treatment in the workhouse infirmary, officially he too was briefly designated a pauper, but to all intents and purposes the label was ignored.[128] That was likely to have been associated with his illness being explained in acceptable, medico-scientific terms, having the 'pauper' word uncontaminated by the 'lunatic' part of the couplet, and because his stay would probably have been of short duration with recovery (or death) within sight. In contrast, once certified under the Lunacy Act, detention was for an indeterminate duration, and public conceptions of mental disorders plus admission to a mysterious, inscrutable institution usually outside the immediate vicinity contributed to the weight of stigma. Of all these factors, the one which a patient's family might be able to alter was the pauper lunatic label: some sought to have their family member upgraded from pauper to private lists, going to great lengths to accomplish this and despite the financial cost to themselves.[129]

In Scotland, mental observation wards functioned differently from those in England, as lunacy legislation differed north and south of the border. To the north, the Lunacy Act (Scotland) 1857 was still in force. It was more flexible and provided greater scope for innovation than the Lunacy Act 1890 to the south. In Scotland, mental observation wards developed under specialist psychiatric leadership in hospitals attached to poorhouses (the Scottish equivalent of workhouses). This meant that mentally unwell patients in those wards were treated as any other hospitalised individual – by specialists with expertise in their type of ailment.

Psychiatrist John Carswell introduced the first of this type of observation ward in Glasgow in 1887.[130] When found to reduce asylum admissions, the model was replicated. By the 1920s, patients could remain in these observation wards for up to six months without certification. The General Board of Control for Scotland reported that in 1925 over half of the patients were discharged either improved or recovered, with only around one-third requiring transfer to an asylum.[131] In England, without the flexible use of observation wards, the rate was two-thirds. To give an idea of the magnitude of the operation, in London alone around four thousand people were transferred from observation wards to mental hospitals each year.[132]

Preventing unnecessary mental hospital admissions in Scotland also had the benefit of avoiding capital expenditure on building more mental hospitals.[133] However, Edinburgh professor of psychiatry George Robertson, an innovator in psychiatric care, wrote to the *Times*. While bewildered by the inflexibility of the English legislation, he acknowledged that even the Scottish Lunacy Act could hinder progressive practices: in Scotland, central government funding was only provided for certified patients, and, human nature 'being what it is ... it encourages the certification of the patient as a lunatic for the sake of the Government grant, rather than treatment without certification'.[134]

In a 1987 study of mental health policy in Scotland, Anne Keane noted that observation wards staffed by psychiatrists created a bridgehead between the local general hospitals and their linked mental institution. They also added to evidence that it was feasible to treat mentally unwell patients on a voluntary basis without formal certification, and they created a model for the future development of general hospital psychiatric wards and outpatient departments. Although only a small part of the total institutional provision, in Scotland their importance was out of proportion to their size,[135] and with exchanges of knowledge across the border, they also influenced developments in England and Wales.

From the observation ward and into the mental hospital

Mental hospitals' walled and gated estates, as with rurally located stately homes, schools for the wealthy and other establishments, sent a message to the public that what went on inside was nothing to do with them and, unless on official business, they should keep their distance physically and metaphorically. For the population residing in the 28 metropolitan boroughs comprising the County of London, nine large mental hospitals were located semi-rurally around its periphery. Banstead, Bexley, Cane Hill, Horton, Long Grove and West Park were to the south of the Thames, with Hanwell, Colney Hatch and Claybury to the north. Colney Hatch admitted patients from across the entire London County Council (LCC) area, as far afield as Leyton in the east, Kensington in the west, Streatham to the south, and Hampstead to the north. Most came via the mental observation wards, with others transferred in, such as from Broadmoor, prisons, long-stay wards of workhouses, mental deficiency institutions, and private mental facilities when families could no longer afford the fees.

Many extremely unwell people passed through the mental hospitals' gates, often entering what they and their families perceived as a place of last resort.[136] Upon arrival, the gate porter could be suspicious, unfriendly or unhelpful.[137] Often he would need to unlock the gate, and the new arrival would be taken along the drive to the main building – or possibly, in the most up-to-date institutions, to a separate building which housed a 'reception' or 'admission' ward. Whether or not in a separate building, admission wards were often better staffed than the rest of the institution. They aimed to provide new patients with an environment of hope and recovery, sheltering 'recent cases from the possibly adverse effect of association with confirmed mental disorder'.[138]

The new architectural preference was for a system of detached 'villas' which could serve different purposes, such as for admission and convalescence. Despite being built for specific purposes, as Soanes argued in his 2011 study of convalescence in public mental hospitals in the inter-war years, intention did not necessarily match usage.[139] Neither did other ideals match reality. Erving Goffman, the Canadian-born sociologist and anthropologist, described undignified, rather than respectful, mental hospital admission processes which induced a sense of humiliation and shame, a 'mortification of the self', and placed a patient's needs secondary to those of the institution.[140] Although Goffman based his analysis on mental hospitals in the USA in the 1950s, it rings true for those in 1920s England. The experience of a new patient in a gender-segregated environment, with uniformed staff, and patients displaying strange behaviours associated with their mental condition, could be frightening. The staff might also be unpleasant. Former patient Mrs M spoke about this in her evidence to the Royal Commission, describing what happened to her when waiting to be allocated a bed. Unfortunately, we know nothing more about Mrs M's identity as the Commission considered it in the best interests of former patients to shield their identity with anonymity. Mrs M said:

> While I was sitting in the dormitory on my arrival there was a woman named H; she was in bed and had got most lovely hair falling all over her shoulders; and she was quite lost; and she was calling out for her husband and her child, and the nurses said 'Just hark at that beast H; let us put her in the pads,' and they took her out of bed and put her in the padded cell, and put me in that bed. It was very distressing to have this poor woman calling out for her husband and her child, and then to hear her being dragged out and put away somewhere. 'Let us put this beast H. in the pads:' You do not hear those terms in a general hospital, do you?[141]

The admission procedure often included a bath and handing over personal possessions which the authorities deemed unnecessary for their stay. Former patient 'Oxonian' wrote:

> No sooner was I in the bath than a wooden-faced woman with a notebook came and stood over me, the young attendant meanwhile drawing the shabby curtains that cut off the little ante-room where I had undressed. A horrible examination for bruises was the next ignominy of the 'lunatic' programme, and at that, terror took definite shape. In vain I pointed out that the discolorations on my back had the square outline of plasters; and that my ankles were scarred through sitting too close to the fire throughout the endless winter we had just left behind. The woman commented aloud and with apparent gusto on my 'bruises,' and chronicled them all. A sickening, writhing sense of impotent indignation mingled with my fear as I took the towel and stepped between the curtains to dress myself again. Then all sensation was obliterated for a moment by a violent shock. My clothes were gone.[142]

Once dressed in hospital clothes, the admission process continued. It included a physical examination, which often took place in the main dormitory with little privacy, although 'a custom which is growing' was to use a 'clinical room' attached to the ward.[143] Time, privacy and respect for the patient were needed if staff were to let them tell their own story so that they felt understood as a human being rather than a mere organic entity. Some practitioners recognised this need and achieved it,[144] but recognition was not universal. Mrs M described her encounter with the doctor:

> he was in a very old brown overcoat; he kept his bowler hat on; he had a little short cigarette in his mouth, and he kept walking in and out of the room muttering 'Telephone, telephone.' What he said to me I do not know, and I kept thinking who on earth can this man be? He asked me a few questions when he could contain himself and sit down; and then he got up again and muttered 'Telephone.'[145]

At Colney Hatch, when relatives accompanied patients to the hospital, they provided much of the patient's background history and social information. Sometimes, though, the doctors found it 'difficult to ascertain the whole truth, or, indeed, any of the truth' from them.[146] Particularly challenging was obtaining information about a family history of mental disorders. The inter-war years were the heyday of eugenics. National eugenics societies, established in many countries, promoted ideas of selective breeding and control of reproduction to improve the hereditary health of the population. Admitting to a family history of mental disorder could be perceived as tainting all its members, which was problematic because, in historian Marius Turda's words, 'improvement of the nation's health began with the wise choice of a spouse'.[147]

Dr Edward Younger, a former mental hospital doctor who later became senior physician at the charity-run Finsbury Dispensary, explained that relatives would use their knowledge as they thought best:

> It is a common experience of the asylum medical officer, when taking a patient's history from a relative who may himself have neurosis writ large on his forehead, to find that person deny strenuously all knowledge of a history of insanity in the family, only for the doctor to discover later from a more truthful informant (probably a 'friend' and not a relative) an altogether opposite state of affairs. The doggedness with which the members of some neurotic families will deny the heredity of insanity to the [medical] psychologist is only equalled by the readiness with which they divulge it, and the assiduity with which they hunt for records of it, when their relation has got into the hands of the police instead of into those of the asylum officials, and when a plea of insanity is likely to prove useful.[148]

Some institutions took identification photographs of patients soon after admission. Patients responded variably to this, from amusement to defensiveness, or feeling that it was degrading with the painful thought of figuring 'permanently in the records of this limbo of lost souls'.[149] Few patients smiled: while this was in keeping with the style of portrait photography at the time, many new patients may also have kept their mouths closed because of missing teeth.[150]

Initially, the patient was expected to stay in bed, as in a general hospital. Psychiatrist Charles Shaw of the Royal Mental Hospital, Montrose, Scotland taught that:

> Rest is the first essential. When any machine is out of order you cease using it until it is repaired. We cannot stop the activities of the organs of the body, but their task can be eased by throwing as little strain on them as possible, and this can be done most readily by putting the patient to bed. There he is comfortable and can get

> into the easiest position to relieve his discomfort. Also, he can be examined more readily, and observations made on his various symptoms and, if necessary, the amount of nourishment taken, urine passed, and hours of sleep can be recorded. Sleep itself is 'a closing for repairs,' and comes more readily when one is comfortably at rest.[151]

Ideally, following admission, patients would be nursed in the open air, day and night, under a deep glass-roofed verandah. Fresh air was considered a 'material aid to healthy metabolism' and 'a valuable corrective in cases of insomnia'.[152] The General Board of Control for Scotland was proud of the 'spacious verandahs' for treating 'acute forms of mental disorder' in all their institutions.[153] More often, in England, new patients were placed in a Nightingale-style ward, or – if particularly disturbed, noisy or destructive – confined to a single room.[154]

Across medicine generally, there was a tendency not to inform patients about their illness and treatment, in part because doctors sought to protect them from bad news and wanted to maintain hope. For patients certified as insane, the tendency not to tell was compounded by assumptions that mental disorders disturbed all aspects of thought and intellect.[155] Empathic insight that some patients were distressed by receiving little direct information on matters such as their health, having visitors and their rights under the Lunacy Act was far from universal. The Cobb Inquiry report advocated providing more information,[156] but the Board of Control argued that, although such information was important, displaying it on notice boards might 'distress sensitive patients'.[157] Those who opposed information on notice boards argued that explanations would be given at the appropriate time for each patient,[158] or that 'the more you put up notices of this kind the more you are going away from what you would expect in an ordinary hospital', thus reinforcing differences at a time when the prevailing aim was to treat mental and physical disorders in a similar way.[159]

Close relatives or friends could also benefit from information at the time of admission. Usual practice was to send a designated person information incorporating 'Visiting Regulations' and other rules and rights for the patient and themselves.[160] Some of the content was arguably inappropriate, such as expressing the intention to undertake a post-mortem in the event of the patient dying in the institution. At the time of admission, a relative was likely to be hoping for recovery rather than expecting death, and publicity about harsh treatment in the early 1920s could conjure up fears that their loved one would be a victim of such practices. John Lord suggested sending relatives written explanations about mental illness and treatment together with the standard information,[161] but this was not widely implemented. Informing them of practicalities was one thing; educating them about mental illness and giving them the tools to ask questions did not fit with the more common paternalistic 'doctor knows best' ethos.

For the relatives of patients admitted, there was almost no support from the institutions or other statutory services. However, friends and neighbours could be helpful, suggesting that the depth of mental illness stigma in the community was less than might be expected: Gerald Langston Day commented on 'the astonishing kindness of people' when his wife was admitted to a mental hospital in 1929. Most striking was the

> man living at the end of the row, a man who had several times been exposed in *John Bull* as a particularly mean crook. He was a surly-looking fellow and I had never spoken to him, yet he sent me word that I could have the unreserved use of his car![162]

Reflections

Certainties understood by the general public were the bricks and mortar of the institutions and the inflexibility of the Lunacy Act, associated with certification, the pauper lunatic designation and the fear of prolonged incarceration. Much public misunderstanding of related matters did not depend upon social class or level of education. Potentially influential people, such as parliamentarians, displayed understanding ranging from accurate to erroneous, sometimes expressed in a manner suggesting irrefutable truth. Errors and misunderstandings in the minds of government officials had the potential to result in inappropriate policies.

Many books and reports were written to inform the public. They included memoirs written by patients who were keen to tell their stories, good and bad. Novels were important. Their intense portrayals expressed experiences of individuals with whom readers could identify, and the images created could be hard to shift from the public mind. Some described acts of compassion despite an oppressive and hostile institutional atmosphere – facets which aligned closely with accounts published as factual.

Publications such as Montagu Lomax's book about standards of care, and reports about crime, insanity and wrongful detention, were recipes for public anxiety and suspicion, but also had the potential to raise awareness and influence change. Negative ideas were compounded by public mental hospitals often being located in walled, gated rural estates, remote from the population they served. They were mysterious places hidden from view, which had the potential to add to public conjecture. For some new patients, their first experiences upon admission were distressing and humiliating, much as Erving Goffman described in *Asylums*.[163] They could reinforce pre-existing fears, contributing to removing the sense of hope which the medical profession sought to instil.

Various lay-led organisations such as MACA, the NCMH and the NSLR sought improvements, including public education and legal changes, and options for early care and after-care. These organisations, along with some pioneering individual psychiatrists such as Henry Devine and John Lord, sought to understand and tackle the concerns of both patients and public. The charities had limited means, and it is difficult to gauge how many allies innovative doctors had in their profession. Drs Devine and Lord stood in stark contrast to others who would not enter into discussion with people they regarded as uneducated, on the grounds that their ignorance was impossible to overcome. Doctors' negativity and judgemental attitudes towards the public outside the institutions was likely to be mirrored inside.

In the community, people with mental disturbances faced a mixed bag of healthcare provision and attitudes and ideas prior to mental hospital admission. In the context of competing societal concerns, the plight of shell-shocked soldiers faded from public priority. Lack of access to outpatient clinics disadvantaged people who sought care early in the course of a mental disorder. Mental observation wards had the potential to provide prompt care close to a patient's home, but their location in workhouses added a layer of stigma, and in England and Wales their staff were not experts in the field.

The certification process, although aiming to be just, could be far from it, with potential inpatients having fewer rights than criminals regarding their detention. Separate admission blocks within the mental hospitals might aim to give new patients a greater hope of recovery, but they further isolated the main buildings and long-stay wards behind closed doors and away from new eyes which might provide insights and constructive criticism. Good intentions might be thwarted by ignorance, such as when tickets donated for patients to attend a matinée subjected them to public ridicule, with the potential to leave indelible and distressing impressions in the minds of patients and public, including children.

Notes

1 Anon., Northumberland County Asylum, Morpeth.
2 Newspapers, journals and periodicals: correspondence on mis-statements 1925–47, TNA MH 51/530.
3 Scott, *Sane in Asylum Walls*, 30.
4 e.g. Anon., High Court of Justice; Bulwer-Lytton, *A Blighted Life*; Reade, *Hard Cash*; Rickard, *Cathy Rossiter*.
5 Grant-Smith, *The Experiences of an Asylum Patient*, 57.
6 Elgood, The asylum as it should be, 295.
7 BoC, *Conference on Lunacy Administration*, 81.
8 Hwang, Women and depression.
9 Civis, Our 'mad' asylums, 212.
10 Lord, *Mental Hospitals and the Public*, 17.
11 Richards, Britain on the couch, 199.
12 Richards, Britain on the couch, 189.
13 Pierce, Psychiatry a hundred years ago, 233–4.
14 Long, Changing public representations, 17, 23.
15 Local inquiry, 4 Jul 1924, Shenley Village Hall, TNA MH 52/107.
16 MoH, *Report of the Committee on Administration* (Cobb Report), 77.
17 Local inquiry, 4 Jul 1924, Shenley Village Hall, TNA MH 52/107.
18 Letter, BoC to MoH, 12 Jul 1927, TNA MH 52/107.
19 Noble and Heale, Triangulation in research.
20 Smith and Pear, *Shell Shock and its Lessons*, xiv.
21 Smith and Pear, *Shell Shock and its Lessons*, 84, 125.
22 Smith and Pear, *Shell Shock and its Lessons*, 125.
23 Smith and Pear, *Shell Shock and its Lessons*, xiv.
24 Lomax, *The Experiences of an Asylum Doctor*; Weatherly, *A Plea for the Insane*.
25 Weatherly, *A Plea for the Insane*, 217.
26 Riggall, *Reminiscences of a Stay in a Mental Hospital*, 23.
27 Davidson, *Remembrances of a Religio-Maniac*; Riggall, *Reminiscences of a Stay in a Mental Hospital*; Grant-Smith, *The Experiences of an Asylum Patient*; Scott, *Sane in Asylum Walls*; Warmark, *Guilty but Insane*.
28 Beers, *A Mind that Found Itself*.
29 Sara Ellingham, managing director of Arthur H Stockwell publishers, email, Mar 2024.
30 Dickson, Experiments in life, 102, 112.
31 Rickard, *Cathy Rossiter*; Oxonian, Confined as a lunatic.
32 Rickard, *Cathy Rossiter*, 307.
33 Grant-Smith, *The Experiences of an Asylum Patient*, 50.
34 Wells, *Christina Alberta's Father*.
35 Bennet, *What Jung Really Said*, 93.
36 MacGuire and Hull (eds), *CG Jung Speaking*, 42.
37 BoC minutes, 9 Sept 1925, 134; 7 Oct 1925, 148, TNA MH 50/53.
38 Cole, Presidential address, 98.
39 National Society for Lunacy Reform, rough notes of AGM, 14 Jul 1925, WL SA/MIN/A/1/3.
40 Reade, *Hard Cash*.
41 A patient for five months, A living death.
42 Lunacy and Mental Disorder, *Hansard*, 24 Feb 1927.
43 Woolf, *Mrs Dalloway*.
44 Anon., Wrongful detention in an asylum; Anon., What makes a lunatic?
45 Butler, Representations of paternal child killing, 10.
46 Ward, A terrible responsibility, 369.
47 Anon., No Harley-Street law.
48 Anon., Publicity in cases of suicide; Anon., Imitative suicides.
49 Ward, Law, common sense, 348.
50 Ward, Law, common sense, 357–8.
51 Gordon, *Broadmoor*, 81.

52 Anon., Abstract of the Report of the Lord Chancellor's Committee, 108–9; Committee on Insanity and Crime, *Report*.
53 Royal Commission on Lunacy and Mental Disorder, *Report*, 16, para. 39.
54 Lunatics (Detention in workhouses), *Hansard*, 4 Aug 1925.
55 Isabel Wilson, The Board of Control and the mental health services 'seen from the centre' (unpublished manuscript), 10, WL MS.7913/19.
56 Mental Treatment Bill, *Hansard*, 17 Feb 1930.
57 Mental Treatment Bill, *Hansard*, 3 May 1923.
58 Reverend Professor Chris Cook, University of Durham, discussion, Apr 2024.
59 Read, Familial care of the insane, 187.
60 Lomax, *The Experiences of an Asylum Doctor*, 229.
61 Lord, *Mental Hospitals and the Public*, 17.
62 Lord, *Mental Hospitals and the Public*, 26.
63 Lord, *Mental Hospitals and the Public*, 18–19.
64 Long, *Destigmatising Mental Illness?*, 4.
65 Macmillan, Mental hygiene, 183.
66 Weatherly, *A Plea for the Insane*, 163.
67 Mental Treatment Bill, *Hansard*, 17 Feb 1930.
68 BoC, *Annual Report for 1928*, Part 1, 7.
69 Mould, Our asylums.
70 Soanes, Reforming asylums, 120.
71 Freud, *The Interpretation of Dreams*; Freud, *The Psychopathology of Everyday Life.*
72 Richards, Britain on the couch, 212.
73 Anon., Disorders of the mind.
74 Society for Psychical Research, https://www.spr.ac.uk.
75 Day, *Rivers of Damascus*, 60.
76 Society for Psychical Research, https://www.spr.ac.uk.
77 Richards, Britain on the couch, 189.
78 Richards, Britain on the couch, 201.
79 Richards, Britain on the couch, 183–4.
80 Christie, *The Murder of Roger Ackroyd*, 82.
81 Janowitz and Mayer, *The Cabinet of Dr Caligari*; Krakauer, *From Caligari to Hitler*, 3.
82 Lord, Lunacy law, 156.
83 Jones, *Asylums and After*, 111.
84 BoC, *Annual Report for 1919*, Part 1, 23.
85 BoC, *Annual Report for 1922*, 5.
86 Beers, *A Mind that Found Itself*; Scull, Creating a new psychiatry, 392.
87 Freebody, *Work and Occupation*, 202, 42; Scull, *Madhouse*.
88 Mary de Vere Hunt, The National Council for Mental Hygiene (unpublished manuscript), 2, WL MS.7913/4; Anon., National Council for Mental Hygiene, *BMJ* 1922.
89 Thomson, Mental hygiene as an international movement, 283–4.
90 Thomson, Mental hygiene in Britain, 135.
91 Anon., National Council for Mental Hygiene, *JMS* 1922, 279; Anon., Mental Hygiene; Anon., National Council for Mental Hygiene, *JMS* 1923, 404.
92 Robertson, The seventh Maudsley lecture, 491.
93 Anon., The causes of insanity.
94 Anon., Poverty and insanity.
95 National minimum wage, *Hansard*, 7 Mar 1923; Trades Union Congress and the Labour Party, *The Labour Movement and the Hospital Crisis*, 20.
96 Thane, *Divided Kingdom*, 75–6.
97 Lunacy Act 1890, s. 238.
98 *Mental After Care Association, Year 1928*, 3, WL SA/MAC/B.1/40.
99 BoC, *Annual Report for 1925*, 50.
100 Mental Treatment Bill, *Hansard*, 3 May 1923.
101 London County Council (Parks, etc.) Act 1915.
102 Royal Commission on Lunacy and Mental Disorder, *Report*, 15, para. 38; BoC, *Annual Report for 1925*, 51; Royal Commission on Lunacy and Mental Disorder, *Report*, 50, para. 104.
103 Soanes, Reforming asylums, 118, 126–7.
104 Soanes, Reforming asylums, 127.

105 *Mental After Care Association, Year 1925*, 4, WL SA/MAC/B.1/37.
106 Soanes, Rest and restitution, viii, 26.
107 Royal Commission on Lunacy and Mental Disorder, *Minutes*, Miss Vickers, q. 7,761; Lunacy and Mental Disorder, *Hansard*, 24 Feb 1927.
108 Based on archived records of Worcester County and City Lunatic Asylum, researched by Annie's great-great-niece, Julia Bynorth, 2023.
109 Med sup's reports, Colney Hatch, 19 Mar 1920, 14 May 1920, TLA H12/CH/A/08/001.
110 Annie K, Colney Hatch Sub-Com, 12 May 1922, 115, TLA LCC/MIN/01011.
111 Lunacy Act 1890, s. 20.
112 Royal Commission on Lunacy and Mental Disorder, *Minutes*, Dr J Dudgeon Giles, Harold Senior and George Usher, q. 3,029–467.
113 Isabel Wilson, The Board of Control and the mental health services 'seen from the centre' (unpublished manuscript), WL MS.7913/19.
114 Cowan, Mental observation wards, 422.
115 Lunatics (Detention in workhouses), *Hansard*, 4 Aug 1925; Mental Treatment Bill, *Hansard*, 17 Feb 1930.
116 Evidence to Cobb Inquiry, Miss Vickers, q. 2,153, TNA MH 58/220.
117 Allen Daley, The London County Council and developments in the mental health services (unpublished manuscript), WL MS.7913/20.
118 Cowan, Mental observation wards, 423.
119 Cowan, Mental observation wards, 421, 423.
120 JSC, The mental patient as he feels himself, 347.
121 Wells, *Christina Alberta's Father*, 224–5.
122 Wells, *Christina Alberta's Father*, 221.
123 Voluntary Mental Treatment Bill, *Hansard*, 22 Jul 1914.
124 Crichton-Browne, *The Doctor's Second Thoughts*, 49–50.
125 Royal Commission on Lunacy and Mental Disorder, *Minutes*, Frederick Willis, q. 734.
126 Medico-Psychological Association, Report of the Committee on the Status of British Psychiatry, 669.
127 Cooke and Bond, *History of the Asylum War Hospitals*, 32.
128 Royal Commission on Lunacy and Mental Disorder, *Minutes*, HWS Francis, MoH, q. 1,419.
129 Letter, solicitor representing mother of Constance S to med sup, TLA H12/CH/B/47/037.
130 Sclare, John Carswell, 266.
131 General BoC for Scotland, *Twelfth Annual Report*, xi.
132 Fairfield, Mental observation wards, 108; Cowan, Mental observation wards, 420; BoC, *Annual Report for 1926*, Part 2, 48.
133 General BoC for Scotland, *Twelfth Annual Report*, xi.
134 Robertson, Mental disorders.
135 Keane, Mental health policy in Scotland, 35.
136 BoC, *Conference on Lunacy Administration*, 81.
137 Letter, father of Leonie A to Colney Hatch, 22 Jan 1919, TLA H12/CH/B/47/018/01-3.
138 BoC, *Annual Report for 1924*, 12.
139 Soanes, Rest and restitution, 10–11.
140 Goffman, *Asylums*, 14, 46, 48.
141 Royal Commission on Lunacy and Mental Disorder, *Minutes*, Mrs M, q. 13,915–17.
142 Oxonian, Confined as a lunatic, 532.
143 Royal Commission on Lunacy and Mental Disorder, *Minutes*, Dr Bond, q. 845.
144 Morrison, Conversing with the psychiatrist, 19.
145 Royal Commission on Lunacy and Mental Disorder, *Minutes*, Mrs M, q. 13,928.
146 Younger, *Insanity in Everyday Practice*, 7.
147 Turda, Legacies of eugenics, 2,471–2.
148 Younger, *Insanity in Everyday Practice*, 7.
149 Warmark, *Guilty but Insane*, 119.
150 Nellie D, Case notes 1920, TLA H12/CH/B/14/004.
151 Charles Shaw, General considerations in mental nursing: An address to the staff of the Retreat, York, delivered 10 May 1924, 14, WL RET/5/11/13.
152 BoC, *Annual Report for 1924*, 23–4.
153 General BoC for Scotland, *Twelfth Annual Report*, xii.
154 Royal Commission on Lunacy and Mental Disorder, *Minutes*, Dr Bond, q. 845.

155 Mercier, *The Attendant's Companion*, 2.
156 BoC, Circular 616, Summary of Cobb Inquiry recommendations, 9 Feb 1923, TNA MH 51/240.
157 BoC, *Annual Report for 1925*, 152.
158 Mental Cases, *Hansard*, 16 Jun 1921.
159 Royal Commission on Lunacy and Mental Disorder, *Minutes*, Dr Bond, q. 450.
160 BoC, Circular 652, Notice to Patients (visitors and letters), 13 Mar 1925, MH 51/240; Royal Commission on Lunacy and Mental Disorder, *Report*, 165, para. XVII.
161 Lord, *Mental Hospitals and the Public*, 19.
162 Day, *Rivers of Damascus*, 24.
163 Goffman, *Asylums*, 14, 46, 48.

3

Certified under the Lunacy Act: patients' daily life in hospital, and after

Inveterate campaigner-psychiatrist Lionel Weatherly described the worst scenarios of 'our large asylums for the insane, wherein individualism is so much lost and where, to a very large extent, patients are herded in large numbers together'.[1] Arthur Trevor, a senior lawyer working at the Board of Control, expressed his shock at the suggestion that patients were 'herded' – a term which suggested that they were treated more like livestock than human beings. Nevertheless, in the same discussion, Mr Trevor himself remarked that patients 'trot' up to Board members during official inspections, a word usually reserved for quadrupeds.[2] Around the same time, the *Times* referred to patients 'branded' as lunatics, and an article by a former patient in a literary magazine described mental hospital ward staff as 'keepers'.[3] Taken together, these terms – herding, trotting, branding and keepers – suggest that standards of care in some institutions were animalistic. It is disturbing that senior people like Mr Trevor, who could influence institutional standards, used animal imagery in a way which suggested that he was comfortable with such language. The Ministry of Health acknowledged a range of standards in the mental hospitals, from inadequacy to providing models worth emulating.[4] Several historical studies have highlighted the diversity of patients' experiences within them, from therapeutic to detrimental.[5]

All patients in public mental hospitals in England and Wales were detained under the Lunacy Act 1890. Compulsory detention was standard practice in the 1920s, including in European countries such as France and Germany, where to do otherwise would have been considered unacceptable infringements of medical authority.[6] In England and Wales, however, the rigid legal system under which the mental hospitals functioned was at least as influential as medical authority regarding admissions. Admissions increased after WW1, probably associated with more beds becoming available when the asylums previously requisitioned for military purposes returned to civilian use, rather than reflecting an avalanche of mental illness. By the mid-1920s, the total population of England and Wales stood at about 39 million, so with about a hundred thousand public mental hospital beds, around one in four hundred people were certified pauper lunatics at any one time.[7]

This chapter aims to describe patients' experiences in the public mental hospitals across the long 1920s, drawing on their own words wherever possible. Some of the reasons for the happenings are discussed in this chapter, but those related specifically to patients' illnesses are discussed in the next chapter, and institutional leadership aspects in chapter five. In this chapter I explore patients' interactions with staff, and their freedoms and restrictions associated with the institutional culture, rules and regulations. I also consider patients' ward companions, who came from a diversity of social, cultural and religious backgrounds. With the emphasis on group living, a communal environment and communal activities, there were also issues of privacy, dignity and having personal possessions. Maintaining contact with the outside world was vital, and families and friends went above and beyond to do that and offer support. This chapter also explores patients' more sporadic experiences, including convalescence, discharge and after-care, and how death was dealt with in the social context of the institution.

Much of the narrative may appear straightforward, but the sources from which it is drawn may be biased, tending to focus on complaints and how to solve them, the detection of unsatisfactory practices and the need for improvement, rather than good practice. The bias of source materials means that observations on patients' lives in the institutions can only be qualitative and not quantitative. Among the discussions about problems and complaints, however, there are also letters of thanks from patients and relatives sent post-discharge. Annie Gi, for example, discharged in 1928 after a 17-year stay, wrote to the Colney Hatch committee and medical superintendent, telling them she was looking positively towards the future and sending thanks to them for 'Past Kindnesses'.[8]

Interacting with staff: hospital-like or prison-like?

In a lecture to nurses in 1924, Dr Charles Shaw explained that the word 'hospital' related to hospitality, guest house and shelter, so that if a patient was detained under the Lunacy Act, it 'makes it the more incumbent upon us to treat him with every consideration'.[9] Dr John Lord reiterated the need for sympathy, kindness and 'true friendliness' to patients.[10] Some patients were treated in this way, such as George Stephen Penny, admitted to Broadmoor State Criminal Asylum in 1923 after being found 'guilty but insane' regarding the murder of his daughter. He found that Broadmoor provided kindness, true asylum, and individual support to assist his recovery and rehabilitation.[11] Broadmoor, as a criminal asylum for the most dangerous patients, had a better staff-to-patient ratio than most public mental hospitals, to minimise risk from violence. It had around one staff member to every four patients, compared to the more typical one-to-nine in public mental hospitals. With more staff, it had the potential to create a better therapeutic environment. Broadmoor's approach indicated that therapeutic methods were understood, and that they could be provided if staff had adequate training and resources under the authority of a psychologically and therapeutically minded leadership. In her 2017 study on psychiatric practice in Scotland, Hazel Morrison argued that much was known about what to do to benefit patients, but to implement it required a culture shift.[12] Sometimes though, a kindly, almost parental approach, as Mr Penny described, could extend too far, towards infantilisation.[13] Like other mental hospital practices, it too could deprive patients of adult agency.

Outside the mental hospitals, punishment was culturally acceptable in the early twentieth century, viewed as a means to teach good behaviour, to deter others or as retribution. Hilaire Belloc's poems for children demonstrate the punitive ethos: Rebecca 'slammed doors for fun and perished miserably' and Matilda 'told lies, and was burned to death'.[14] There was corporal punishment in schools, and we hear of WW1 soldiers being executed for desertion and other offences.[15] Inside the mental hospitals, staff were prohibited from inflicting physical punishments on patients and could be dismissed or prosecuted for doing so. However, while retributive punishment was considered inappropriate, there was some support for the notion that reformative or deterrent measures 'may be appropriate for patients capable of understanding good and bad behaviour'.[16] If doctors prescribed harsh deterrents, they were reframed as treatment. This was construed under the psychological banner of 'behaviourism' then in vogue, where environmental influences were considered important to reinforce subsequent behaviours. The simplistic behaviourist approach did not convince everyone, wrote Joanna Bourke in her 2005 study on *Fear*, and, as Jeffrey Adler pointed out in 2015, introducing harsher laws and punishment in the USA in the inter-war years was associated with a rise, rather than a fall, in crime.[17] If staff understood procedures to be beneficial, they were likely to repeat them, including when patients perceived them as punitive. One such repeated and permitted measure was to relegate a non-compliant patient to a 'lower' or 'refractory' ward containing the most disturbed patients – a 'deplorable form of punishment' according to the National Society for Lunacy Reform.[18]

Suggestive of punishment, prison language was integral to the Lunacy Act 1890, and it was adopted in the mental hospitals, including words such as 'escape', 'recapture', 'detain' and 'release'.[19] This aligned mentally unwell people with wrongdoing and had the potential to influence how staff treated patients. Patients used words such as 'wardresses' and 'cells', indicating their perceptions of being in a prison rather than a hospital. Mental hospital staff often displayed bunches of 'jingling keys' on chains – a prison-like flaunting of signs of power and control which could reinforce patients' sense that they were prisoners, with the medical superintendent the 'Governor of the Gaol'.[20]

Regarding 'escape' and 'recapture', one patient recalled her friend's failed attempt to escape: 'She had not reached the first low fence when she was detected and brought back. All her little hard-won "privileges" were over for ever now. She was taken that night to the Infirmary, and afterwards to one of the "Back Wards." I never saw her again.'[21] The punitive response was also expressed in the novel *Cathy Rossiter*, after Cathy attempted to escape. The staff 'treated her like a child in disgrace, and clad her finally in a coarse chemise, which the elder wardress of the two told her she could not tear or fashion into a rope: therefore, as there was nothing about for her to do herself a mischief, she would be safe enough'.[22] Restrictions, often punitive, were implemented as alternatives to staff attempting to understand patients' distress and the reasons for their behaviour.

In the event of a patient's disturbed behaviour putting themselves or others at risk, staff were likely to resort to physical restraint, rather than to kindness or reasoning with them.[23] The term 'physical restraint' covered both 'manual' methods, meaning person-to-person contact, and 'mechanical' methods, using objects such as straitjackets. Mechanical methods were generally frowned upon, as they were deemed to have the potential for prolonged punitive misuse. By law, the use of mechanical restraint had to be recorded in a dedicated register. There was no similar system for monitoring the use of manual restraint. The 'nonrestraint movement' advocated avoiding physical restraint, especially by mechanical means, while recognising that manual restraint may be necessary in extremis. According to historian Jennifer Wallis, the nonrestraint movement, closely associated with the Quaker-run Retreat in York, argued that cultivating better relationships between staff and patients would help reduce the need for manual restraint. Despite controversy about using them, some psychiatrists preferred mechanical means, on the grounds that they were safer than manual methods which could result in broken bones or other serious injuries if the patient resisted.[24] Former asylum attendant Paul Elgood was also suspicious about manual methods, commenting that staff could deliberately inflict 'much pain, leading often to fatal results ... easily explained away by the two words: "Necessary restraint"'.[25]

One prison punishment term not adopted was 'solitary confinement'. Instead, the mental hospitals referred to 'seclusion', meaning putting a patient in a room alone and fastening the door so that they were unable to leave as they wished.[26] Seclusion was meant to be therapeutic, allowing a patient 'time out' when they were extremely disturbed. However, it was also used when insufficient staff numbers made it impossible to care for disturbed patients in any other way. Some seclusion rooms were cell-like, fear-inducing and oppressive, with poor ventilation, no artificial lighting and no heating. Some were so unsatisfactory that the Board of Control recommended that they should only be used as storerooms.[27] Like mechanical restraint, seclusion required documenting in an official register to avoid it being used punitively as solitary confinement for prolonged periods.

Linked to an institutional punitive ethos, staff might favour a harsh approach to a patient perceived as a troublemaker, especially if the patient criticised them. An inquiry was carried out into allegations of harsh treatment made by a discharged patient, Charles Cox, a former Metropolitan Police inspector. The *Times* reported on the inquiry, stating that Mr Cox was

> treated kindly at first and he had nothing to say against many of the attendants, except that they failed to report acts of cruelty and brutality by their comrades. When he saw how some of the weaker patients were treated several of the attendants seemed to turn against him. His letters were read by them; his food was tampered with; and the wrong medicine was given.[28]

Mr Cox was distressed when he witnessed cruelty towards other patients. By the time the inquiry took place, the patients who had suffered abuse had all died or were too mentally unwell to give evidence. The attendants against whom allegations were made 'absolutely and strenuously denied that anything of the sort had taken place', as did some patients.[29] Their response was probably influenced by a broader defensive, harsh and punitive institutional culture: staff avoided informing on their peers, and patients 'dare not complain for fear of the consequences to themselves. They know that they are entirely and absolutely in the power of their keepers'.[30] The inquiry concluded that the charges were due to Mr Cox's mental disturbance.[31] Ultimately, the more extreme a patient's allegations about punitive approaches, the less likely the authorities were to believe them. It was also convenient for an institution's leadership, or an inquiry committee, to ignore medical understanding that when patients suffered from persecutory or paranoid delusions, their fears usually concerned their own wellbeing, so that when a patient alleged ill-treatment of someone else, it was likely to be true.

Historian Vicky Long described a scenario from a coroner's inquest in 1929 into the death of a mental hospital patient, allegedly at the hands of staff. When the doctor assured the coroner that statements made by patients were unreliable, the jury decided not to hear the testimonies of patient-witnesses and returned a verdict of death by misadventure.[32] This vignette not only illustrates deference to the doctor by the coroner and the jury, but it also indicates the doctor's viewpoint that a patient's memory, interpretation and understanding of events were all inevitably distorted, despite this hypothesis being questioned in medical circles at the time.[33]

A patient's protest or complaint was likely to be regarded as evidence of insanity (probably as it contradicted the views of the 'sane' leadership), whereas gratitude (amounting to agreeing with those leaders) meant that a patient was either well enough for discharge or 'in the right place'.[34] Repeatedly sweeping patients' complaints under the carpet on the grounds that their reports were inevitably distorted was detrimental to their sense of personal integrity, and could provoke profound despair and a sense of helplessness and hopelessness. Coupled with the institutional assumptions that staff were excellent, generalisations about patients' words precluded impartial investigation of any allegations. Two instances of lost keys at Colney Hatch Mental Hospital provide an example concerning patients' dissimilar degrees of reliability: on one occasion a missing key was found concealed in a patient's clothing, whereas on another, a patient found a lost key and handed it in.[35] Rather than provoking consideration that patients differed, such examples were overlooked, reinforcing generalisations that patients were 'out of their minds and not responsible for what they do or say'.[36]

Freedoms and restrictions

Mental hospitals generally had a culture of obedience to unquestioned and inflexible rules and regulations, with responses to infringements automatic. One former patient wrote that patients' lives were 'under rigorous, frost-bound rule' which 'must eventually break the human spirit'.[37] Some psychiatrists recognised this and sought to abolish those rules they considered pointless. Henry Devine, medical superintendent of Portsmouth Mental Hospital, took this approach concerning rules prohibiting patients from having visitors until a month after admission. He agreed with his colleague Charles Mercier (a former president of the Medico-Psychological Association) that the only reason for this was to save staff trouble – 'a purpose which ought not to be served'.[38] Dr Devine likewise challenged a rule forbidding patients from smoking on Sundays until they had been to church:

> Such a rule smacks of the middle ages. The patient might not wish to go to church if he were at home, then why should he be penalised for not so doing when in hospital! The attendance at church may now be smaller than it used to be, but the patients are happier, and this is the chief thing.[39]

Alongside apparently purposeless blanket rules and regulations, others restricted the liberty of many patients in ways argued to be in the interests of their safety, but also aligning with staff convenience. The Board was rightly concerned about self-injury and monitored adverse incidents. However, data collected over the years were inconsistent, hindering useful comparisons at the time and historical analysis today. It is unclear, for example, how 33 deaths in England and Wales due to 'self-inflicted injuries' in 1919 compared statistically to 69 deaths attributed to suicide in 1927, 13 of which took place among twelve thousand patients granted time off the wards.[40] Medical superintendents were generally reticent to allow more freedom, fearing adverse verdicts in coroners' courts, and detrimental effects on their own careers and institutions.

Contrary to the intuition of the leadership of most institutions, that patients were safer behind locked doors than when given more freedom, there was evidence that locking patients in removed their sense of adult agency and could provoke fear and despair. There was, for example, the 'nightly terror' when ward doors were locked from the outside, with staff and patients 'like rats in a trap', should a fire break out.[41] Former patient Mrs M, who gave evidence to the Royal Commission on Lunacy and Mental Disorder (1924–6), referred to locked doors creating 'human tigresses': 'You cannot take adult animals and put them in any zoo and expect them to thrive. They will knock themselves against the bars. You cannot take human beings and shut them up like that.'[42] Mrs Rickard made similar observations in her novel *Cathy Rossiter*: when locked in a 'padded cell', Cathy felt that she 'was losing her courage, and the thought that she had drifted to the waste places where the wanderers roamed in their misery, became oppressive and awful … [I]f she could now find the means to end it all, she knew that she might use them.'[43] Historian Alice Brumby, in her study of WW1 mentally unwell veterans, likewise indicated that such constraints left patients feeling that 'the only option left was to resort to the last act of human self-control, the act of taking one's own life'.[44]

'Parole', another Lunacy Act and prison term, usually meaning release of a prisoner while under sentence on condition of good behaviour, was also common mental hospital terminology. 'More parole, more freedom, less curtailment of liberty, more open-door wards and more unblocking of windows on the ground floor,' urged Board of Control commissioner Dr Rotherham in 1922, despite prevailing fears of catastrophe.[45] Some medical superintendents agreed with him. The same year, at Littlemore Mental Hospital, Oxford, Dr Thomas Saxty Good took initiatives which paved the way for more liberal practices elsewhere.[46] He permitted high rates of parole, wards with unlocked doors, and unblocked sash windows on both floors. More liberal mental hospitals suffered no more disasters than those with the most restrictive regimes.[47]

Giving patients more freedom required a shift in opinion, particularly by a defensive mental hospital leadership, but it also needed acceptance by the public. The means of achieving this was less certain, although the five hundred-bed Old Manor mental hospital in Salisbury had to some extent done so, as about a fifth of its patients went into town daily, unaccompanied by staff and free to interact with local people.[48] While the shift towards giving patients additional freedom was piecemeal and hesitant, more advocates for doing so were speaking up, such as Robert Steen, medical superintendent of the City of London Mental Hospital,[49] and Dr Montagu Lomax, who commented: '[T]he more you show patients that they are worthy of trust, the more readily will they respond. Asylum authorities, of course, are far from believing this; the principle they act upon is just the opposite.'[50] In 1922, Joseph Shaw Bolton, medical superintendent of the West Riding Mental Hospital, Wakefield, endorsed 'the valuable therapeutic influence of freedom'. His hospital also paid patients for tasks undertaken while out and about, such as 'taking carts into the town'.[51] Colney Hatch began charabanc trips for patients to Southend-on-Sea in 1925.[52] On one occasion three patients escaped, but were returned via the local workhouse infirmary; on another, a patient jumped from the pier and had to be rescued.[53] Apart from these incidents, the outings were considered successful. In the year before his discharge from Colney Hatch in 1929, John H went to Southend, watched films at the Wood Green Empire cinema, and attended a Tottenham Hotspur football match at White Hart Lane.[54]

Ward companions

Mental hospitals followed established convention by being gender segregated – an acceptable pattern of social organisation at the time when many of the institutions were built. This practice also aligned with schools, colleges and some workplaces, as well as prisons and workhouses. The mental hospital architecture, however, was increasingly out of date, particularly regarding gender segregation in the context of societal change giving women more rights and freedom to make choices. Nevertheless, the culture of 'domestic paternalism' prevailed, emphasising the need to protect people seen as vulnerable.[55] Changing from a gender-segregated model was not a priority, in part associated with the increasing influence of eugenics ideology.[56]

Despite patients' legal designation as pauper lunatics, they came from many walks of life and many were in stable employment until illness struck. That included many women with a diversity of occupations, such as millinery, nursing, tailoring, and jobs as governesses, teachers, lavatory attendants, cigarette makers, and maids, often in addition to domestic roles in their own home. Occasionally a child as young as 10 might be found on an adult ward, at a time when children were also likely to be admitted to a general hospital adult ward if they needed treatment for a physical malady.[57]

Within the gender-segregated system, many hospitals sought to 'classify' their patients into different wards according to the degree to which they disrupted the daily lives of themselves and others, and by whether they were considered recoverable or chronic. In addition to symptoms often running a fluctuating course, the large, old-fashioned wards created challenges for achieving these divisions.[58] Dr Robert Turnbull of Severalls Mental Hospital, Colchester informed his colleagues that patients 'complain very bitterly of the enforced uncongenial companionship from which they have to suffer'.[59] No system of classification would meet everyone's approval, but the ideal, expressed by the Board of Control in 1924, was that the essential factor should be the 'adequate consideration of the real needs of each patient with corresponding effort to see that their fulfilment does not entail distress or discomfort to others'.[60] This was far from accomplished.

Having other patients to talk to was a means of survival for some: 'The days became less intolerable as intimacy with some of my companions increased,' wrote Oxonian in 1920.[61] Some patients offered a sympathetic ear to others: one day

> an old man gave me a quavering smile, and drew a photograph from his breast-pocket. 'I'm glad you've come,' he said; 'I wanted to show you this.' It was a handsome young soldier, his only child ... 'He is dead?' I questioned presently, and the old man nodded. 'He was so kind to his old father,' he said brokenly. 'I have prayed to be allowed to see his grave.'[62]

Little specific attention was paid to the needs of patients grieving their relatives killed in combat or to other civilian patients likely to have been traumatised by their wartime experiences. Such patients included refugees from Belgium who fled their homes when the German army invaded in 1914. At Colney Hatch, refugees and German prisoners of war (who were gradually being repatriated) were hospitalised alongside British ex-servicemen and civilians.[63] Colney Hatch visiting committee minutes do not reveal discussion about how members of these disparate groups related to each other, suggesting that their coexistence was uneventful.

In the early 1920s, British ex-servicemen suffering mental disturbances associated with their military service comprised about one-tenth of male mental hospital patients nationally.[64] Historian Peter Barham noted that at Whittingham Mental Hospital, Lancashire they were scattered across the wards, and with mental hospital emphasis on group conformity rather than individual need, he was sceptical that ex-servicemen were treated any better than the civilian pauper lunatics around them.[65] As Dr Smith and Mr Pear had predicted, the humanity and higher standards of care shown to them initially were 'merely temporary'.[66]

There was other social diversity, since some urban areas were ethnically, culturally, linguistically and religiously diverse. If several mental hospitals served such an area, as in London, one might take the lead in providing care for these minority groups. The London County Council (LCC) designated Colney Hatch to fulfil that role. Religion was regarded as important in patients' lives, but not always constructively. As historian Ute Oswald argued in her study of recreation in nineteenth-century asylums, it was considered to both prompt mental breakdown and to be therapeutic.[67] The Lunacy Act stipulated that each asylum must employ a Church of England chaplain.[68] It also permitted employing ministers of religion for patients of other faiths, although Ministry of Health records suggest that providing for groups other than Church of England and Roman Catholic believers was rarely considered.[69] Colney Hatch, however, had a Church of England chaplain, a Roman Catholic priest, and Jewish and Free Church ministers. The hospital also funded items for prayer and ritual for members of these faith groups and held religious services for them.[70] In addition, on Sundays some Catholic patients, accompanied by nurses, took the tram to church at Wood Green.[71]

In 1920, about 10 per cent of patients in Colney Hatch were Jewish, rising to about 25 per cent a decade later.[72] Many were recent immigrants, with their homes and families in the East End of London. The hospital had a kosher kitchen and an interpreter to translate for Yiddish-speaking patients.[73] Many patients from traditional families did not travel on the sabbath and festivals, so religious services and celebrations took place on site, including the Passover 'seder' and the 25-hour fast on the Day of Atonement, with meals provided before and after.[74] In some countries, such as the Netherlands, religious groups established their own mental hospitals.[75] In England this was near impossible under the Lunacy Act, given the legalistic processes of admission and discharge, and the Act's goal of stopping the proliferation of private 'licenced houses'.[76] In a study of healthcare of 'the Jewish poor' in the East End before WW1, no specifically Jewish mental healthcare institution was mentioned which could parallel the London Jewish (general) Hospital or the community's maternity homes.[77]

Others from abroad included crew and passengers arriving via the London Docks, some of whom had come to seek their fortune. Among them were students, language teachers, interpreters, governesses, cooks and musicians. John D's hospital notes refer to him as a 35-year-old 'African Negro' seaman in the merchant service who was admitted for 'prolonged stress' and discharged 'recovered' after a few months.[78] There were 'Mahomedan' and Buddhist patients. Ah Kee Y was a Buddhist children's nurse who received support from the Ayahs' and Amahs' Home (London City Mission) when discharged:[79] I found no evidence of discussion on the ethics of placing her with a Christian missionary organisation. Some patients were repatriated, with expenses defrayed by their relatives or by the Home Office. That might necessitate transatlantic travel by ship, including fares for escorts. When Paz A's family requested her return to Mexico, they funded her voyage, including the return passage for her escorts – one of Colney Hatch's interpreters (who was also a nurse) and his wife.[80]

There are few historical studies on the subject of life-changing repatriation of mental patients from the UK. However, one by Matthew Heaton discussed repatriation to Nigeria from various countries including the UK, mainly after the Second World War. It indicated the complexities of the decision making. Heaton noted that repatriation was framed as a medical intervention which aimed to help the patient, especially by returning them to a more familiar cultural milieu. Nevertheless, given that some may have been away from their country of origin for years, that may not have been realistic. Although Heaton argued that financial considerations were of secondary importance to achieving what was considered best for the patient, he also made the point that 'the UK government was more than willing to foot the bill in order to be rid of individuals considered to be a drain on public resources and a potential future public nuisance'.[81]

Although some evidence points to the authorities doing their best to accommodate the needs of religious and cultural minorities, attitudes towards patients from abroad could also be unwelcoming or intolerant. Hospital staff threw doubt, for example, on one Jewish woman's statement that she was born in Calcutta (perfectly plausible given the geography of the Jewish diaspora), implying that she was lying.[82] High usage of sedative medication at Colney Hatch was blamed on 'the Insane Alien population of London, which yields a large proportion of acute cases who are noisy, violent and destructive'.[83] This statement was probably referring to Jewish patients, who may have felt particularly disempowered by their admission outside their community, despite the hospital's efforts to provide for them. Theo Hyslop, a psychiatrist, also commented: '[A]liens have flocked to our shores, and it is a strange irony that once a lunatic is on the sea his only landing-place appears to be England, which has thus become the asylum of the world.'[84]

The ward environment: space and sound

The ideal that the entire mental hospital environment should be therapeutic could fall short at the first hurdle – that is, on the wards, where patients spent much of their time.[85] The 'patients should be the first consideration', said Charles Shaw, and wards should be bright and cheerful, well decorated, pleasing and soothing, and more homely than those in general hospitals which were characterised by impeccable neatness.[86] Overcrowding and inadequate space indoors could result in frayed tempers, so safe outdoor space was also important.[87] Such spaces, often referred to as 'airing courts', originated when it was considered necessary to 'air' patients to counter the 'miasmas' thought to spread infections in communal living environments.[88] Some resembled 'a prison yard with no view except the walls around and the sky above'.[89] Others were large gardens, but not all reached the ideal standard of being well tended and readily accessible to the patients to 'promote contentment and health'.[90]

Sounds passed through walls. In the days before ward telephones this could provide a way to summon help in an emergency, but other noises also drifted in. Oxonian recalled hearing patients being moved by staff, 'struggling and bawling, down the corridor', and 'an endless screaming wail: "God have mercy! Lord, have mercy! God have mercy upon me, a sinner!"' Such sounds could terrify patients.[91] Within the ward one could 'hear every sound', including distressed patients shouting, crying or being forcefully medicated.[92] Cathy Rossiter was described as reeling in an atmosphere 'full of uncouth noises', including foul language.[93] Language could be more obscene on women's wards than men's, observed newly qualified Dr Octavia Wilberforce in 1920 after a few weeks working in a mental hospital. She explained this by drawing on fashionable Freudian theory: 'they've been taught to repress it',[94] implying that when mentally unwell, women were unable to do so, and the words flooded out.

Noise at night, including from staff, could disrupt patients' sleep.[95] Some psychiatrists acknowledged that this was a problem, but others regarded it as a non-issue because patients did not complain about it. On the wards, patients were often expected to be in bed for 12 hours each night.[96] This fitted with institutional convenience of two 12-hour nursing shifts covering each 24 hour period, and aligned to the much debated medical teaching that just as a sick body needed physical rest, a sick mind needed sleep.[97] Some patients neither needed, nor expected, to sleep soundly for the 12 hours prescribed for them, which might have accounted for their lack of complaints. Expectations could affect whether an issue was regarded as a problem. Together with the psychological and social ramifications of protesting, number of complaints was not an accurate estimate of adequacy of care.

Privacy, dignity and personal possessions

Indignities, such as those concerning personal hygiene experienced by patients at the time of admission, continued. Some wards with beds far from toilets relied on commodes, sometimes only emptied when 'quite full, brimming over, and then it was always a patient who had to empty it', said Mrs M.[98] With an ethos of safety at all costs and toilets and bathrooms deemed to be 'places of danger for suicidal patients', they might be kept locked except at specific times, despite such practices distressing patients and going against Board of Control recommendations to keep them accessible. Further, to enable staff to observe patients, toilets might lack doors, despite the Board urging that they should at least be fitted with half-height 'dwarf' doors.[99] The number of toilets – sometimes only three for 60 patients – was insufficient, and the Royal Commission recommended a 'higher uniform standard' of provision.[100] The Commission's words did not motivate Colney Hatch to tackle the problem: the visiting committee considered building work too expensive and inconvenient and ignored the patients' distress.[101] Expenditure on patients 'had no political capital', remarked historians Niall McCrae and Peter Nolan in their study of mental nursing.[102]

The Royal Commission asked Mrs M numerous questions. Here is a précis of her answers regarding bathing:

> Directly dinner was over the charge nurse would call out: 'Ladies for the bath,' and we would all have to line up. The bathroom would be crowded with people either drying themselves or waiting to get in and have their turn in the bath. They allowed five towels for the whole of the 40. The first five would get a towel and be able to put it round them, and the rest would have to go on as they were. Some of the patients used to get an old nightdress and put it round them. They might stand stark naked in the queue, but some would undo their clothing and wait until the last moment, drop it off and then make a run for it. There were two baths, in a very tiny bathroom, a big crush. Each person had clean water. But you had to do what you were told, and if you made a fuss then you had a paraldehyde draught [dose of a liquid sedative]. You had to step into the bath, and the nurse soaped your head and rubbed your head, and then she poured the bath water over your head, and then you got out. The bath towels were the size of an ordinary bath towel, but not made from towelling but sheeting. If you were not one of the first five you had a very wet towel to dry yourself with; in fact, you could not get dry.[103]

A former hospital chaplain and a local councillor were among those who raised concerns about bathing practices. The chaplain described the 'positively indecent and harmful' situation of patients being 'made to strip themselves some distance away' from the baths.[104] The councillor, Mrs Mary Hatfield, on an unannounced official early morning inspection visit to her local mental hospital, observed indignity and unhygienic practices such as more than one patient using the same bathwater and the same bath towel. The authorities rejected her complaints as implausible, and accused her of deliberately stirring up trouble and trying to draw attention to herself.[105] Their motivation for rejecting criticism from patients and others appears to have been to protect their own reputation. Doing what was therapeutically beneficial for patients was a secondary concern.

There were no alternative, more private facilities for a woman who was menstruating. In the 1920s, discussion about menstruation and sanitary protection was becoming less taboo, and sanitary towels could be purchased, or were home-made from cloth or paper.[106] However, some mental hospitals did not provide sanitary towels when required, and a patient might be denied access to those she had brought in with her.[107] Mrs M attributed this to staff fearing that 'some patients would have strangled themselves with them'.[108] Dr John MacArthur, a psychiatrist who wrote the *Mental Hospital Manual* while an assistant medical officer at Colney Hatch, before promotion to medical superintendent elsewhere, referred to menstruation as 'the monthly illness', mentioning it only in the context of ward records about weight loss or gain, or pregnancy, as an aspect of biology. He did not mention sanitary protection.[109]

Patients were deprived of other items of daily life relating to bodily function and wellbeing. They might only be allowed their spectacles with the medical superintendent's agreement.[110] Toothbrushes were not always supplied; if a patient had one, they tended to keep it in their pocket.[111] Hairbrushes and combs were often shared, although, as Mrs M said, 'you would not dream of using one brush that was used by 40 other patients'.[112] Dentures could be misplaced or handed to the wrong patient. Only at the end of the 1920s did the Board of Control recommend using the novel 'aluminium baths, with a device to take a name card' to store dentures at night.[113] Given that when Mabel B at Colney Hatch lost her dentures and they cost the substantial sum of £5 to replace, this seemed wise, both for the patient and for the authorities.[114]

Closely aligned with personal hygiene was personal appearance. Women were not allowed hairpins[115] – a problem for those with long hair accustomed to wearing it in an up-do. Men were not entrusted with any sort of razor, and staff would shave patients intermittently. The Board of

Figure 3.1 Self-portrait of James Scott as an inpatient, from his memoir *Sane in Asylum Walls*, 1931 (facing p. 24). © orphan work; owner sought but not found. I am grateful to Hugh Fowler-Wright for his advice.

Control acknowledged that 'the appearance of some of the younger male patients will be much improved by being regularly shaved'.[116] James Scott, a journalist and a patient in Brentwood Mental Hospital in the 1920s, illustrated his hospital memoir with a self-portrait (Figure 3.1).

Patients' clothing usually belonged to the hospital, marking them out as pauper lunatics. The clothing was often outdated in style and did not fit properly, and the rough fabrics could be scratchy and uncomfortable, creating an ongoing sensory reminder of a patient's predicament.[117] In Mrs M's view, 'you could not wear it without looking a lunatic'.[118] Patients resented what they considered to be prison-like attire, regarding it as humiliating and destructive of self-respect. In some mental hospitals the clothing was shabby, even by the standards of the Poor Law Guardians. When the Leeds mental hospital authorities regarded the patients as 'suitably and neatly dressed' the Guardians thought that the '"dame" in pantomime was not more amusing in appearance than the female inmates of the asylum', and 'such dreadful clothing' was 'pathetic'.[119] Post-WW1, clothing could even be 'ragged'.[120] At Colney Hatch, three years after the Armistice, the visiting committee finally decided that their stock was beyond repair and needed replacing.[121]

In 1922, advocating for the psychological benefits of personal clothes, the Board of Control commented on the 'growing practice' of allowing patients to wear their own attire.[122] The claim that it was a growing practice is hard to substantiate, and the Board's perception may have been wishful thinking, or a ploy to encourage more institutions to introduce the practice. The mismatch between rhetoric and reality is also evident in the LCC's own-clothes policy introduced that same year.[123] It had an extremely slow rate of implementation, as with other changes which primarily aimed to benefit patients. In this case, the practicalities of keeping records of personal clothes when sent to the hospital's laundry would be time-consuming for nurses and a deterrent to complying with the policy.[124] Some hospitals also argued that clothes from home might carry 'infectious disease',[125] but it seems unlikely that hospital clothing would be any less of a potential source of infection (especially if soiled) and risks could be mitigated by adequate laundering. In 1925, even at exemplary public mental hospitals such as Littlemore, where 20 per cent of patients wore their own clothes, it was considered a privilege rather than a right.[126]

For patients who had a tendency to destroy their clothing, arguments were polarised about what they should wear. Some advised indestructible strong linen, of the sort used for straitjackets, securely fastened at the back to avoid the patient removing the garment, becoming cold and succumbing to some infectious malady.[127] Charles Shaw, on the other hand, advised that 'a patient who is given to tearing her clothing, and who picks to pieces a strong dress will cease operations if dressed in her Sunday best. Our patients are very human, just like ordinary people, only more so, and react when treated accordingly.'[128] Some medical superintendents let patients personalise their hospital clothes with trinkets which they were allowed to have in their possession,[129] but others regarded that as unsafe. Dr MacArthur envisaged a patient 'hoarding half a dozen buttons … He may swallow them, he may sharpen one on a stone with intent to injure himself, he may supply one to another patient for the same purpose, or he may use the edge to turn the screw fastening a window sash.'[130]

Personal possessions, including clothes, have meaning for individuals and help them express their identity. Based on his study of institutions in the 1950s, Erving Goffman explained that where patients were stripped of their possessions on admission, they might fill their pockets with 'bits of string and rolled up paper' – a habit 'usually seen as engaging in symptomatic behaviour befitting a very sick patient, not as someone who is attempting to stand apart from the place accorded him'.[131] Regarding acquiring personal items as pathological also promoted the demeaning practice of searching patients.[132]

Mrs M told the Royal Commission of the distress caused by enforcing a lack of belongings:

> They never allowed you to keep anything. If you had any parcels or any food it had to be put in the storeroom, and then it was often taken by other people. There were only two little shelves where patients could put their belongings, and the charge nurse used to go and clear those out and burn all the things; and the patients used to grumble about it very terribly.

Mrs M also experienced having all the letters received from her husband incinerated. When she suggested to the Royal Commission that individual lockers and keys could be provided, the chairman responded, 'I suppose if some patients had a key they might try to swallow it,' to which Mrs M replied, 'They might, but you would not give a locker to a patient like that.'[133] She proposed selective caution rather than, as occurred more commonly, blanket precaution.

In the absence of safe storage, not having personal possessions minimised – but did not eliminate – the risk of theft, and the thieves might not be fellow patients.[134] Following a father enquiring about why his son had not received the contents of a food parcel sent to him, Colney Hatch Nurse C told the visiting committee that he had given 'part of the contents to the patient, but fearing that the remainder would not keep', he took it upon himself to 'distribute various articles to other patients'. Nurse C's story, though, was incomplete: he had been off duty at the time, leaving the question as to why he had charge of the parcel in the first place. One wonders how much of the food went to patients, to staff, or to Nurse C himself. Reprimanded by the medical superintendent, he was warned of the consequences of 'a repetition of his conduct'.[135]

There were other reasons for possessions disappearing. When Mr Moffatt visited his mother shortly after her admission, he was disturbed to see her without her wedding ring.[136] If a patient was transferred from workhouse infirmary to mental hospital without their wedding (or any other) ring and the mental hospital did not request it from the Guardians 'within a reasonable time from the commencement of chargeability, the rings were sold, the proceeds contributing towards the cost of maintenance'.[137] Patients and relatives were neither consulted nor informed. When raised in Parliament, Minister of Health Neville Chamberlain denied knowledge of the Guardians taking patients' possessions as collateral.[138] Occasionally, there were also reports of patients being discharged from mental hospitals in England to find their shop or dwelling 'sold up, and their means of living so reduced as to bring them to the brink of destitution'.[139] This attitude towards covering costs contrasted with directives in Scotland, which supported keeping patients' funds intact if discharge was envisaged, 'so that the patient may resume his independence and so help towards the complete restoration to and retention of mental health'.[140]

Value was perceived in monetary rather than psychological terms, as with other aspects of hospital practice. When Sarah S died at the age of 78 in 1923, a small silver spoon in safe keeping was returned to her friend, but other belongings, including photographs of her as a young nurse, and the regimental Christmas card she received from the friend in 1917, were not considered of 'value' and were not offered to him. A century on, they remain archived, attached to her Colney Hatch file.[141]

Meals

In 1919, the *Times* called the Board of Control to account for the high wartime mortality in the asylums, suggesting that patients had been starved.[142] John Crammer's historical investigation of WW1 asylum deaths concurred with this claim, and he concluded that expenditure on food was minimised to save ratepayers' money.[143] When Board commissioner Dr Charles Hubert Bond addressed the Medico-Psychological Association in 1921, he referred to 'the bitter lessons of the war' and ongoing 'serious blemishes' concerning hospital diets, including their monotony and inferiority to what patients would have eaten at home.[144] Kathleen Jones pointed out that food was important not merely as a means of survival: familiar dishes provided reassurance, and 'a generation accustomed to fish and chips cannot be expected to eat steamed cod with anything but reluctance'.[145] Stephen Soanes also noted the social importance of food to patients, and that they particularly appreciated the good food and generous catering provided in Mental After Care Association convalescence homes following discharge from mental hospital.[146]

In the mental hospitals post-WW1, breakfast and 'tea' – at around 5pm with nothing later in the evening – often comprised only bread, margarine and a hot drink.[147] When, in 1925, a new meal plan at Winwick Mental Hospital added an extra item to both of these meals every day – at breakfast: jam on Monday, honey on Tuesday, dried fish on Wednesday, cold boiled bacon on Thursday, marmalade on Friday and so on – the National Asylum Workers' Union magazine encouraged others to follow their example.[148] This, however, did not overcome Charles Shaw's warning that people lose interest in food 'when you can diagnose the days of the week' by what you eat.[149] Winwick's improved breakfast and tea menus were still far from ideal in terms of variety and nutrition, notably the lack of fresh fruit and vegetables. The Union's enthusiasm and encouragement reinforces the impression of widespread dietary inadequacies.

If members of the Board of Control or the visiting committees saw patients eating a good meal on inspection days, they were reassured that food was generally adequate, despite patients complaining that it was 'vile' or insufficient: 'My wife brought in food. Else I should have been starved,' Mr Sale told the Committee on Administration of Public Mental Hospitals (Cobb Inquiry) in 1922.[150] Sometimes better food – a 'committee day soup'[151] – was rustled up on inspection day, unrepresentative of usual provision. On those occasions it is no wonder that inspectors reported patients enjoying their special meal. If the meals were leisurely, inspectors ignored patients' reports of them usually being rushed. As Mr Donaldson described to the Cobb Inquiry: 'Toothless old men had sometimes to wrestle with chunks of fat or gristle; they swallowed their food somehow or other, but had no time to masticate it properly.'[152] Mealtime etiquette might also be degrading, as the Board of Control observed on a women's ward in 1928: as there was no cutlery and patients had to use their fingers, '[w]e venture to think that an extended use of knives and forks might safely be made'.[153] This was yet another one-size-fits-all safety rule, reassuring for staff but demeaning for patients.

Mental hospitals in the USA introduced cafeteria-style meals in the 1920s, linked with the understanding that encouraging patients to make choices was part of rehabilitation. It also reduced waste, adding an economic dimension. However, some psychiatrists, drawing on established social principles, considered that eating meals 'family-style', rather than cafeteria-style, was beneficial. Others took the view that patients' mental disorders resulted from them having made poor choices in a broad sense, meaning that others should make their choices for them while in hospital.[154] Despite a lack of consensus, the subject of food choice did not appear on the Board of Control's agenda concerning 'dietaries'. In England, patients continued to eat their meals 'family-style', either in a central hall or on the wards. Where they ate was often determined by practicalities such as the time lag between hot food leaving the kitchen and arriving on patients' plates, rather than by ideals or philosophies.[155]

Work, occupational therapy and recreation

Dr Philippe Pinel, physician to the Bicêtre and then the Salpêtrière hospitals in Paris in the late eighteenth and early nineteenth centuries, is attributed with coining the term 'moral treatment' – a therapeutic method based on patients' psychological and emotional needs. The York Retreat took a similar approach, aiming to restore an insane person's reason based on humane practices and individualised approaches, including recreation, family living, fresh air, exercise and good diet.[156] These practices were introduced at a time of optimism about the curability of mental disorders, but doubts as to their efficacy arose. As the general population grew, more people suffering from incurable or chronic conditions were admitted to the public asylums, and as the institutions increased in size, moral treatment became more difficult to deliver.[157] Elements remained, such as encouraging occupation and religious practices, and providing entertainments, but the individualised components had largely been lost before WW1. Post-war, amid searches for treatments and cures across biological, psychological and social domains, some psychiatrists introduced similar sorts of individual treatment approaches. Henry Devine was one who marvelled at the outcomes of encouraging and supporting individual patients with activities tailored to their needs: 'The results are astonishing; and I believe we have but little conception as to how much we can rehabilitate our disturbed, restless and excited cases in this way.' Dr Devine berated himself and his colleagues who had 'unwittingly permitted our cases to sink into dementia because we have not taken sufficient individual trouble with them'.[158] A moral treatment approach might not cure chronic mental disorders, but it benefited patients nonetheless.

In some mental hospitals, patients' choices were valued. In her study of patients' narratives at the Glasgow Royal Mental Hospital during the 1920s, Hazel Morrison noted that 'a unique blend of psychoanalytic and biological psychiatry' was used to give patients a say in shaping their care and treatment.[159] For some, learning a new skill such as basketry or embroidery was beneficial, particularly if an 'occupations officer' had the patience, skill and time to encourage and coax. Scotland's first occupational therapist, Dorothea Robertson, working in the 1920s at Glasgow Royal where David Kennedy Henderson was medical superintendent, recalled one woman patient saying: 'The week I learned china painting has been the happiest I have spent in hospital.'[160] Dr Henderson, like Dr Devine, enthused about occupational activities developed to suit the needs of individual patients, which could distract them from morbid thoughts, help their 'self-confidence, self-esteem [and] self-pride become born anew', and help them realise that there were things they could achieve despite their mental problems.[161]

Experience of occupational rehabilitation methods in military hospitals and in some private and charitable mental institutions, alongside discussion about whether patients should engage in activities meaningful to themselves or routinely undertake ward-based domestic chores and work in the hospital utility departments, contributed to the early development of occupational therapy. Some middle-class patients objected to undertaking mundane, repetitive practical tasks, and patient James Scott, scathing about the suggested 'advantages' of doing utility work, refused to do any since it supported a regime which he loathed.[162] Historian Waltraud Ernst argued that, rather than patient choice, institutional profit, intolerance to idleness and work as the default setting prevailed.[163] The matter of choice chimed with a particular occasion at Colney Hatch when the asylum engineer suggested to the visiting committee that patients could help make coffins: the minutes give no indication that patients were asked for their views.[164] Some British psychiatrists, keen to learn more about occupational therapy, visited Dutch and German centres, including the Gütersloh Asylum, where Dr Hermann Simon had pioneered individualised 'active therapy' – patients had to work and take responsibility for the results of their activities.[165]

Over-emphasis on work, however, could be dangerous: Simon's reputation was later heavily tarnished by his support for Nazi ideology regarding people unable to contribute.[166]

At times, staff shortages were sufficiently severe that patients assisted staff in managing other patients.[167] When Mrs M told the Royal Commission that the night staff would wake her to help them, and thanked her by bringing her a cup of tea first thing in the morning, the chairman redirected the inquiry to a less controversial subject, rather than exploring the circumstances and nature of the help she was giving.[168] His response gives the impression that Mrs M's comment was too challenging to contemplate.

Patients willing to work could be given tasks which were distasteful to staff. Not only did patients empty commodes, but at Prestwich Mental Hospital, nine patients, supervised by two staff, comprised the 'closet-barrow gang'. Each night they emptied the earth closet sewage system which served the ward blocks.[169] Despite the visiting committee declaring its intention to replace the earth closets with water closets before WW1, in 1922 it continued to postpone modernisation due to expense.[170] All other mental hospitals in England originally fitted with earth closets had upgraded to water closets throughout, but they had been installed at Prestwich only in the accommodation provided for senior staff. The impression given is that the Prestwich committee considered that earth closets were adequate for patients and lower ranks of staff, and the work of the unpaid closet-barrow gang was acceptable.

Some patients were content with undertaking domestic chores and utility work and being trusted to do this. Others were irritated when not thanked for what they did or thought they should be paid.[171] Some authorities argued that board, lodging, clothing and daily necessities were sufficient payment, while others provided payment in kind, such as outings to the cinema.[172] The debate on payment for domestic tasks also played out in the wider community. Servants 'living in' who undertook menial tasks were paid a small salary in addition to their board and lodging. Housewives were unpaid, and young women who were expected to take on heavy caring and household duties in their parents' homes also often received no monetary reward. In an oral history study, Selina Todd mentioned some of these young women feeling very bitter about their restricted lifestyle as domestic drudges.[173] The mental hospitals' system of communal living in some ways aligned with family expectations, values and resentments.

The provision of equitable rewards for equitable work, especially when patients worked alongside paid staff, was missing from the Board of Control's agenda, although leaders of some mental hospitals sought to achieve this. Some drew inspiration from mental deficiency institutions where patients received cash payments for spending or saving,[174] or from Scottish mental hospitals where patients were encouraged to save their pay if discharge was likely.[175] At Broadmoor, as Mr Penny recounted, the reward system was 'ingeniously devised to mitigate the patient's sense of exploitation. Trades union rates were paid', with a fixed proportion deducted for maintenance and the rest banked for the patient.[176] The Cobb Inquiry recommended providing 'commensurate remuneration' to patients working for the institution.[177] 'Commensurate', however, was undefined and open to interpretation. That was clear when Colney Hatch won prizes for its mangelwurzels and other farm produce at an agricultural show. The distribution of the prize money was hardly equitable and was probably not commensurate: £3.12s.6d to the farm bailiff; £1 each to head cowman, first cowman and head pigmen; and 2/6d to each of the seven patients who worked at the farm. Those in charge received the highest dividends.[178]

Some mental hospitals gave cash rewards, while others used tokens. Although the 'token economy' system in mental hospitals is more associated with the 1950s and '60s, examples of token rewards date back to at least the early nineteenth century.[179] Tokens required a system for exchanging them into cash, or a shop in the hospital where patients could spend them. Hospital shops might start out with a stock of just tobacco, cigarettes and sweets,[180] but they provided patients with some opportunity for the ordinary, daily life activities of choosing and spending. Dr Mervyn Archdale, medical superintendent in Sunderland, provided paper tokens. The tokens were inspired by the teachings of the French psychologist Emile Coué. Coué's methods, popular at the time, included the auto-suggestion mantra 'Tous les jours, à tous points de vue, je vais de mieux en mieux en mieux'. The English translation, 'Every day, in every way, I am getting better and better and better', was printed on each token (Figure 3.2a).[181] The back of each token was stamped with a number and date of issue which could be recorded, thus identifying it with a particular individual and so reducing the risk of theft when patients lacked safe personal storage space (Figure 3.2b).

Despite some patients' reluctance to work, the Colney Hatch archives reveal few complaints about working, compared to other aspects of hospital life. Although an absence of complaints is not synonymous with an absence of problems, several factors may have influenced this apparent acceptance. Patients may have had better relationships with staff in work environments, partly because they were undertaking a shared activity with a common goal, or because staff-to-patient ratios were more satisfactory

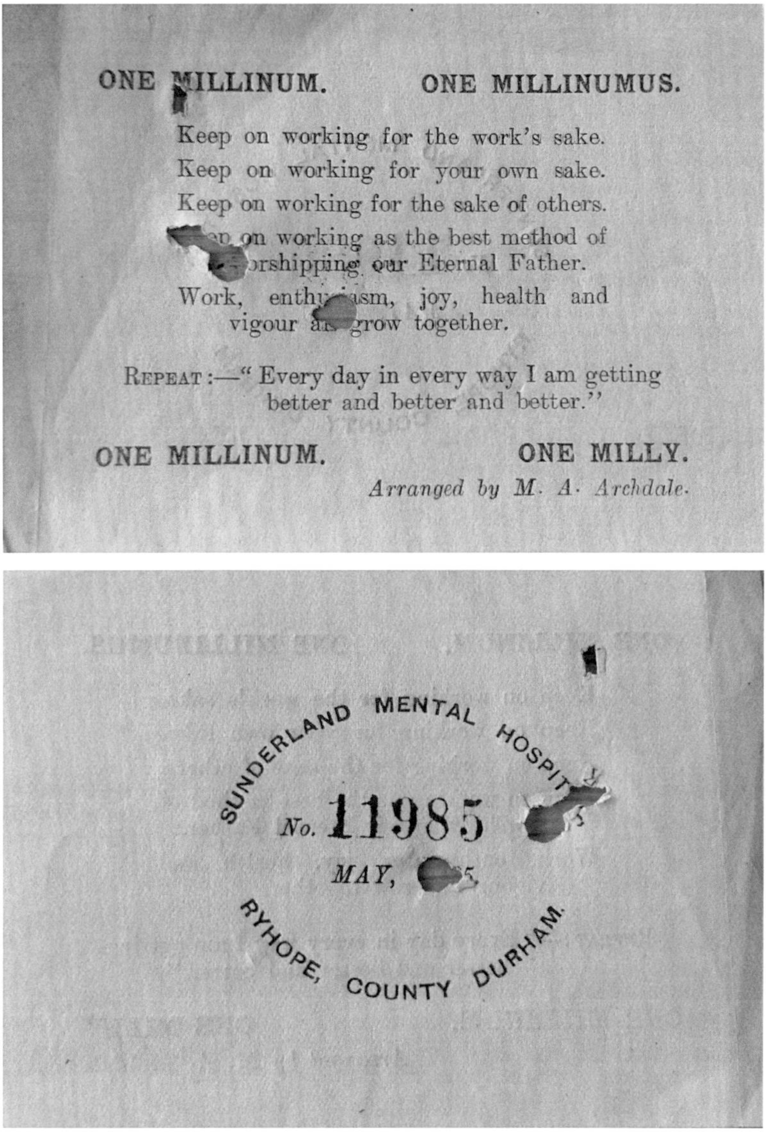
ONE MILLINUM. ONE MILLINUMUS.

Keep on working for the work's sake.
Keep on working for your own sake.
Keep on working for the sake of others.
...p on working as the best method of
...orshipping our Eternal Father.
Work, enth...asm, joy, health and
vigour a... grow together.

Repeat:—"Every day in every way I am getting
better and better and better."

ONE MILLINUM. ONE MILLY.

Arranged by M. A. Archdale.

Figure 3.2a and 3.2b Token reward from Sunderland Mental Hospital authorised by Dr Mervyn Archdale, 1925, with date of issue and number stamped on reverse. These tokens were damaged by being attached to other paperwork using treasury tags. Source: National Archives, ref. MH 51/353.

than on the wards. Also, workshops, laundry, kitchens and farms were subject to independent statutory inspection under employment legislation and were required to achieve the same standards of safety as workplaces outside the hospitals. Nevertheless, sometimes working patients lacked appropriate protective gear, and they had no recourse to trades unions (although some patients suggested that they should) to help them obtain it, or, if necessary, to seek compensation if they sustained injuries.[182] The institutional ethos of patient safety at all costs, and the assumption that patients were inevitably irresponsible, was inconsistent with expecting them to work to support the hospital economy.

In 1926 the Royal Commission recommended improving the organisation of occupational activities through workshops for handicrafts and rewards to motivate patients.[183] Some hospitals, but by no means all, began to make changes. In 1929 the Board of Control took the step of advising mental hospitals to shift the emphasis on occupation from patients whose input was of economic value to the institution to having trained staff encouraging 'apparently unemployable patients' with therapeutic occupation.[184] Again implementation was scanty, but the message indicated a shift in the Board's approach. However, the time lag between understanding, or relearning, the social and practical interventions regarded as beneficial for patients, and introducing or reintroducing them could be inordinately long.

Many leisure activities were gender-based, as they would have been in the community. For men, smoking was a respectable pastime. For women, before cigarettes were actively marketed to them (in the name of gender equality), their smoking was associated with being either very rich or 'indecent',[185] so institutions were unlikely to encourage it. At the City of London Mental Hospital, male patients tended to 'smoke like chimneys' and a weekly ration of tobacco was issued. Dr Steen, the medical superintendent, empathised with the women: he noted that it was 'a real hardship for a woman who has been accustomed to her daily smoke to be deprived of the same' and wanted to provide a smoking room for them, but anticipated that the visiting committee would not permit it.[186]

Women patients had fewer opportunities for outdoor recreation than men, and Mary Riggall was one who envied the men their cricket matches and long walks.[187] Some mental hospitals reportedly permitted men and women to mix on the cricket field on a summer evening, entertained by the hospital band, with 'dancing, mixed cricket matches and other games' taking place.[188] Such gender-mixed activities were unusual, and on occasions when men and women were together – at religious services, film shows, other entertainments or asylum balls – they were closely supervised.[189] Often, male staff, including doctors, got involved in male patients' recreational activities. The new women doctors, such

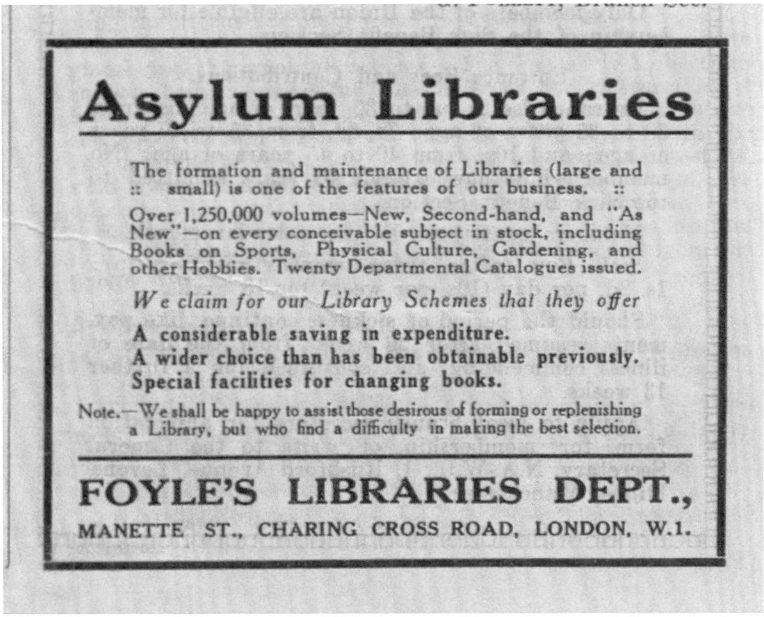

Figure 3.3 Foyle's Libraries Department advertisement for creating asylum libraries. Source: *NAWU Magazine* 1928, 17:3, 3. Reproduced with permission from UNISON.

as Dr Harriette Wilson at Wakefield, were beginning to organise separate activities for women patients, such as country dancing and drawing, sometimes assisted by volunteers from the community. Involving local people had the potential to reduce stigma and to help patients maintain community ties.[190]

Another line of activity was patients producing their own magazines, among them *Under the Dome*, the *Gartnavel Gazette* and the *New Moon* or *Crichton Royal Institution Literary Register*.[191] These fostered patient autonomy, individuality and independence. The content was upbeat and positive, and included stories, poems and reports on sports matches. Staff, who sometimes featured in the magazines, also read them, giving patients a measure of equality with them as human beings. Notably, the *Gartnavel Gazette* and the *New Moon* were produced in Scottish mental hospitals, and *Under the Dome* was the magazine of the Bethlem Royal Hospital in London, a charitable foundation. With charitable status, its rules and financial position contrasted with those of the public mental hospitals in England. Although some publicly funded institutions showed interest in this sort of project, they were hesitant to start.[192]

The Board of Control advocated that wards should have adequate supplies of magazines and books, and that electric lighting, rather than gas, would facilitate reading.[193] Some mental hospitals had libraries, with books purchased or borrowed, such as from Foyle's Libraries Department (Figure 3.3). Relatives, friends and local businesses also donated books, magazines and gramophone records, although the Royal Commission noted that mental hospitals were less likely than general hospitals to receive such gifts.[194] Patients also 'keenly anticipated' the arrival of daily newspapers in the wards, and some things were not so different from the outside world: 'the individual who collects two and sits on one until he has read the first is as unpopular as he is elsewhere'.[195]

Staff in some mental hospitals feared that activities considered harmless in the community might distress their emotionally vulnerable patients by exposing them to real or fictitious traumas. To protect them, newspapers were censored to avoid references to mental disorders, murders and suicides. Elsewhere, however, they 'discontinued that nonsense'. For a time, films were censored too. Dr Steen wrote:

> It is strange now to look back upon the suspicion with which we greeted the cinema. During the first year of its use we always had a rehearsal – the film was run through earlier in the day to ensure that nothing harmful should appear and all murders and suicides were carefully deleted.
>
> One evening we had 'The Old Curiosity Shop'. Here, towards the end, Quilp is seen struggling in the Thames before he is drowned; and this harrowing scene was cut out, and an unavoidable hiatus occurred. None are quicker than the patients to note anything suspicious, and the next day every 'Old Curiosity Shop' in the place (and there were not a few) was being read to find out what tricks the doctor had been playing; so that more harm was done than if the picture had been shown in the ordinary way.[196]

Relatives and friends: keeping in touch with the outside world

Lord Sandhurst, a barrister, magistrate and 'Lord Chancellor's Visitor' (a legal role concerning management of property belonging to someone mentally unwell), informed the Royal Commission: 'I am very much struck by the fidelity of the relations of the poor cases. They are constantly visiting. They visit once a week many of them, and the patients welcome the visits.'[197] Patients' relatives and friends were expected to obey the 'Visiting Regulations', a copy of which was sent to the closest relative or friend at the time of admission.[198] Not all followed the rules – one medical officer stopped Mrs W entering because the child with her had measles. Visitors who had 'given a great deal of trouble' might be summoned to attend before the visiting committee.[199] One was banned after bringing her husband a screwdriver, knife, fork and matches on different occasions; in spite of 'warnings as to the impropriety of her actions she seemed unable to realise the danger'.[200] The visiting committee minuted its discussion and conclusions about the visitor, but not the visitor's intentions, concerns or explanations for her actions.

Intermittently, Colney Hatch collected data about visitors, giving a glimpse of the extraordinary lengths to which some friends and family went to maintain contact. These records do not state how frequently Martha W's son travelled from Glasgow to visit her, but they indicate that he visited her 33 years after her admission.[201] Louisa S's siblings travelled from the west of England to see her, and Ernest Turner (whose relationship with Louisa was unclear) visited her weekly, offered to pay for her to be transferred to the 'private side' if that would benefit her, and later paid for her funeral.[202] Occasionally, rail companies offered reduced fares for visitors, and sometimes patients were moved between mental hospitals to facilitate visiting.[203]

Mary Riggall stated, 'one can form no idea what these visits mean to people who are thus cut off from the outside world'; for those without visitors, she noted, 'I have seen them cry with disappointment on visiting days as they heard the more fortunate ones called out to go down to the visiting-room.'[204] A dedicated visiting room excluded visitors from the wards, so they were unable to see the patients' living quarters, meet the nurses, see other aspects of ward life or encounter possibly less well patients or those who had no visitors. Hospitals often provided refreshments for patients and their visitors in the visiting room,[205] but those rooms also presented a window-dressed façade to the outside world regarding patients' lives.

As Mary Riggall observed, some patients had no visitors. Some lost contact before admission, or relatives may have become too frail, too poor or unable to travel, and others may have died. Relatives who lived in tied accommodation would have changed home address when they changed jobs, increasing the chances of losing contact. As had been done in the military hospitals, paid or voluntary 'social' workers befriended patients and helped them trace, and negotiate more contact with, their families, although sometimes this was a fruitless task.[206]

Some lost contact for other reasons, such as being moved from one mental hospital to another. In the early 1920s many patients were transferred back to the hospitals they had left early in the war when those institutions were requisitioned for military purposes.[207] Despite – or perhaps because of – the understanding that patients could be distressed by moving to a new institution, they could be given little warning about their impending transfer. Usually relocated as a group, these batch transfers suggest that they were organised for administrative convenience, to fit round hospital plans, such as emptying an entire ward so that it could be refurbished. Relatives might be informed of these impending transfers, and could give their opinion on whether the patient should be moved – ease of access for visiting being one of the criteria considered,[208] but patients themselves appear not to have been consulted. In the archives at Colney Hatch, the main documentation regarding such moves were medical statements that the patient was '[e]xamined and found fit to travel', the primary objective being to avoid transmitting infectious diseases between institutions.[209]

Mental hospital overcrowding also prompted the transfer of patients out of area. The Lunacy Act permitted a receiving asylum to charge a higher fee for these 'out-county' contract patients, compared to what it charged for patients from its own catchment area.[210] The prospect of making a profit could incentivise such deals, placing financial transactions above the needs of patients, and contrary to the Board of Control advocating the benefits of family and friends outside the institution maintaining contact with the patient.[211]

Administrative decisions led to other transfers. Annie A's daughter wrote to her in Colney Hatch in May 1928:

> How are you? Isn't this weather changeable? Mid-summer one day, freezing the next. Enclosed please find 1/6d not much but all I can afford at present. Have you received your goods from Highgate because I went up after them. Then they sent me a written notice to attend a committee meeting. I replied that I could not attend as they arranged it for 2.30 on a Tuesday afternoon …
>
> I shall not come out to Southgate this weekend as I really can't afford it. Have you heard from Lily yet? If you haven't its [*sic*] because she hasn't been very well. I think I am going away with her to Ramsgate for the holidays. The air is quite decent there. So it will do her good. I sold three hats today … Good, eh? I feel quite pleased.

Annie never received the letter. It arrived at Colney Hatch after she had been transferred to Storthes Hall Mental Hospital, Yorkshire, which served her official Poor Law 'parish of settlement'.[212] The parish of settlement was the parish of birth, or, for a married woman, the parish of her husband's birth, and Poor Law Guardians of that parish had responsibility for funding mental hospital care, rather than the Guardians where the person lived when they became ill. Annie, her husband and their daughters had moved from Yorkshire to London, so moving her back north gave her closest family little chance of visiting her.

Parish of settlement rules were particularly problematic for patients admitted to London mental hospitals, as costs in the metropolis were usually higher than elsewhere. The Guardians preferred the cheapest option, regardless of a patient's needs or their family's wishes. Annie M, for example, was a single 30-year-old domestic servant being treated in Colney Hatch, but her official parish of settlement was in Warwickshire. Annie's sister Mary lived in London and requested that Annie remain at Colney Hatch so she could visit her. The Warwickshire Guardians refused: they were only willing to pay the 22/2d a week charged by the Warwickshire institution, not the 28/7d for Colney Hatch.[213] If Mary was also a domestic servant, perhaps living in, her salary was likely to have been around 10/- a week: topping up 6/5d a week for Annie to remain at Colney Hatch was prohibitive.

Given Colney Hatch's role in providing for minority groups or those recently arrived from abroad or speaking little English, it would have been humane for such patients admitted from the London area to be permitted to stay there, near people they knew, to facilitate visiting and language and cultural exchange. However, practice was inconsistent. When Luba M arrived in England in 1917 she was placed in a transit camp in Eastleigh, Southampton, which was then designated as her parish of settlement. In the 1920s she was admitted to Colney Hatch, close to where she usually lived with her sister Leah, her only relative in England. Leah requested that Luba stay at Colney Hatch, but she was transferred to Knowle Mental Hospital near Southampton.[214] Luba was Jewish, and whereas Colney Hatch had provided for her religious practices, Knowle did not. There were other similar accounts.[215]

Other examples reveal a more empathic approach, such as the case of Annie G, born in Portsmouth. Her father was a tailor and the family moved to London for his work. The Portsmouth Guardians agreed that Annie could stay in Colney Hatch, as it would 'undoubtedly curtail the amount of expense and trouble of them having to come to Portsmouth on each occasion of their visit'.[216] Dr Henry Devine is not mentioned as being involved in this decision, but he was a strong advocate of care close to home and valued 'social contact of the ordinary kind' as beneficial for patients. It may be that his and the Guardians' benevolence was reciprocal, each influencing the culture and practice of the other in the Portsmouth area. Dr Devine's colleague Dr Helen Boyle, working in Hove, just along the south coast, held similar views: 'We should not be so hidebound about settlement. Sometimes their settlement is miles from their friends, and they do not want to go such a long way away.'[217]

By the end of the 1920s the Board of Control seems to have become more forthright and increasingly patient-centred in its recommendations. It asked mental hospitals to monitor who had visitors, and for those who did not, 'a letter should be sent on behalf of the patients to their relatives and friends pointing out the desirability of visiting and keeping in touch with them'. The Board asked to be informed about what action each hospital was taking to achieve this.[218]

When visits were not feasible, some maintained contact by letter. Incoming letters addressed to patients were likely to be opened by staff, on the premise that they might contain money or advice to facilitate escape, although patients could also receive both on visiting days.[219] Some people sent monetary gifts to the hospital authorities rather than directly to the patient: one man living in South Africa sent £400 to be put towards his brother's care.[220]

The Board of Control expected wards to supply patients with letter-writing materials, although the question of letters reaching their intended recipients was more complex. The Lunacy Act stipulated that patients could write in confidence to the authorities responsible for their detention and care, forbidding staff from reading them. The confidentiality rule did not extend to personal letters, so they were inspected, and if there was doubt about their propriety the medical superintendent had the final veto on whether to send them.[221] Frequently patients had no option but to hand all outgoing letters to ward staff. The Board received complaints from patients that staff were reading their letters, and stated its incredulity at such suggestions, attributing them to patients' imagination or delusions.[222] Nevertheless, to counteract the complaints, the Board recommended that each ward should install a locked, glass-fronted post box, to be emptied by an official rather than by the ward staff.[223] It was out of character for the Board to instruct hospitals to take action on the basis of false complaints, suggesting that it may indeed have been aware of infringements, despite voicing disbelief.

The new ward post boxes did not prevent senior hospital officials from examining personal letters, supposedly in the interests of the writer and potential recipient. The Board of Control advised that letters not posted would be discussed with the writer or 'laid before the Visiting Committee', but evidence of such discussions, or of the visiting committee minuting such happenings, has not come to light at Colney Hatch. Outgoing letters provide insights into patients' lived experience, with the caveat that fear of them being intercepted shaped their content.[224] Allan Beveridge studied unsent letters written by patients at the Royal Edinburgh Asylum before WW1, noting diverse experiences – from coercion to kindness. He also commented that writing letters could help patients come to terms with their plight and make sense of what was happening to them, to restore their self-esteem and regain control over events which had left them powerless.[225]

Convalescence and discharge

James Scott wrote that many patients had no more prospect of being discharged than 'a canary's being liberated from its prison because it sings merrily and continuously and thus proves that it is "happy and contented"!'[226] It was a provocative analogy for mental hospitals, where cages of canaries, alongside plants and flowers, were considered to enhance the ward environment.[227] Around 40 per cent of patients admitted were discharged, often 'recovered'; however, some were only 'relieved' or 'not improved', to use official terminology. The ideal mental hospital convalescence facility was envisaged in 1924 as a homely environment separate from the main building, preferably a 'villa' with between 12 and 30 single bedrooms, and from which patients could easily come and go.[228] Provision, though, was variable. By 1926, only about a quarter of mental hospitals had such facilities.[229]

Stephen Soanes argued that convalescence villas were a visible indication of psychiatrists' interest in curative treatment, recovery and discharge, and making their institutions more like general hospitals. He also noted that their practices of allowing patients into the community supported psychiatrists' views that treatment was feasible outside institutions.[230] Convalescence gave hope to recovering patients, and guided medical superintendents who might be overly cautious, ambivalent or fearful as to whether a patient was ready for discharge. Mary Riggall recalled a patient returning to the ward a week after going home, 'having hurled a knife at her family doctor'. The psychiatrist went to see the returned patient on the ward and commented: 'If people have to come back again as quickly as this, the doctors outside will say I don't know my job.'[231] No doubt he was concerned about his reputation, but this incident also suggests that he had a good relationship with his patients, and had sufficient humility, and perhaps courage, to acknowledge to them that he was not infallible.

A short period of 'trial leave', usually for up to four weeks, could be given to help pave the way to full discharge, plus a monetary grant for the period since social welfare payments were unavailable. As with other non-mandatory practices, their use varied. Trial leave could also be chaotic: patients might leave the hospital without their home front door key, or wearing someone else's dentures, or without any dentures, raising questions as to why they were not wearing them as part of their daily routine.[232]

The use of 'prolonged leave of absence on trial' was permitted under the Lunacy Act and encouraged by the Board of Control, in part as a response to mental hospital overcrowding, but it never became widely established.[233] It had longer-term relationship-building goals than standard convalescence, and was comparable to the long-established Scottish practice of 'boarding out' patients, and the centuries-old residential community support provided at Geel in Belgium.[234] In England some psychiatrists attributed lack of implementation to conservatism, inertia, ignorance and apathy on the part of the mental hospital leadership, and a public reluctant to accept a mentally unwell person into their household.[235]

Local authorities, such as the LCC, raised concerns with the Board of Control about prolonged leave. Since the patient was still certified, it was unclear who was responsible for paying for their clothes and medical treatment, and, if they died, whether their death would have to be reported to the coroner as for someone certified and in hospital.[236] Patients also had concerns, fearful that prolonged leave precluded any assurance of their 'freedom' and meant that they were 'liable to be sent back to the detention from which their friends wished to release them'.[237] Sometimes prolonged leave was arranged with a patient's own family. Occasionally these families managed to obtain a copy of the official form with which a general practitioner could terminate the Lunacy Act certification, thus achieving the outcome they desired. The LCC considered this practice particularly evident with 'the special type of patient received at Colney Hatch mental hospital, whose friends are commonly very wrongheaded, very persistent, and very definitely disposed to subterfuge'.[238] As with other criticisms of patients and their relatives, the source does not explain this further. At the time, the most likely 'special type' present in any number were Jewish people. Their actions may have been underpinned by various social factors, such as a sense of duty to care for their relative; the stigma of lunacy associated with marriage prospects; language and cultural difficulties impairing communication as an inpatient; or as a mainly immigrant community who had left their country of origin in the face of pogroms, associated with distrust of the authorities and fear of deportation.

In contrast to extended leave, some public mental hospital patients with ongoing symptoms were discharged under section 79 of the Lunacy Act. This required family or friends to sign an undertaking that they would look after the patient without drawing on public funds, and that they would prevent the patient injuring self or others. It was unrealistic in a domestic environment to guarantee, for an unspecified duration, that the patient would never cause harm, as such harm might arise from an entirely different cause. The obligations could be emotionally, practically and economically burdensome on the family. Nevertheless, patients did leave the hospitals via this route. One was Eleazor D, a former dock labourer, court martialled and imprisoned as a conscientious objector in WW1, who suffered from 'primary dementia'. He was discharged on his father's undertaking after several years as an inpatient. He appears to have remained out of hospital, and in 1939 was working as a street pedlar and living with his brother John, a dock labourer, and his sister Jessie, a waitress.[239]

The responsibilities imposed by section 79 may have deterred some relatives, but others complained that they had not been made aware of their right to request a patient's discharge. The Board of Control instructed visiting committees to display notices about this right and to include it in the information sent to a patient's nominated relative or friend at the time of admission.[240] The issue was raised in Parliament.[241] Minister of Health Sir Alfred Mond asserted that information should not be provided in advance, explaining that doctors were responsible, at the appropriate time during treatment, for telling a patient of the legal position and of the steps which relatives might take.[242] He did not endorse empowering relatives to raise matters as they felt appropriate.

There was inconsistency, however, between public and private mental hospitals concerning the right of relatives to discharge a patient. Relevant information was displayed in private mental hospitals, as a separate section (72) of the Lunacy Act applied to them, allowing the person paying the fees to withdraw the patient. Using social class and personal wealth to determine mental healthcare needs was medically illogical. Sometimes, a family of a patient in a public mental hospital might hear of section 72, find the money, transfer them to the private list, then use their right to discharge them a few days later.[243] Motivation for a family to discharge the patient was usually in the patient's interest, but not inevitably: Herbert Armstrong discharged his wife Katherine under section 72 in January 1921, and a month later she was dead. He was subsequently hanged for her murder.[244]

Some relatives went to great lengths to support the discharged person at home. Theo S, 'so as not to worry' his recently discharged wife Hertha, asked the hospital to send any correspondence about her to his work address.[245] Relieving her of worry and helping her settle outweighed his concerns about his colleagues seeing correspondence, usually identifiable by return-to-sender details stamped on the envelope. Sometimes, a family could not or would not accept a patient's return home,[246] and occasionally apprehension about doing so arose beyond the immediate family. An anonymous letter arrived at Colney Hatch during Annie K's trial leave, alleging that:

> she was drunk on Saturday … it is a disgrace to see a woman like her to go about the world not knowing what she was doing it is not as if her people will look after her … I am sure the woman is not fit to be allowed out by herself there is not a man, woman or child that can't tell a story about Mrs Annie K in Flower and Dean St.

When social workers visited Mr and Mrs K and other family members, they concluded that the letter reflected malicious gossip.[247]

After-care

The Mental After Care Association (MACA) was founded at Colney Hatch in 1879 and initially worked only with women patients. By the 1920s, the charity had broadened its remit and provided support to male and female patients and their families, sometimes to help prevent admission, but mainly around the time of discharge. It aimed to work with them as 'sympathetic, and personal friends, who are ready and anxious to stand by them'.[248] Miss Ethel Vickers took the helm at MACA, coordinating support for individuals, encouraging community services and helping shape national policy. MACA received over eight hundred applications for help in 1920, and in 1925 provided assistance to over fourteen hundred individuals.[249]

Certification on admission to hospital stripped patients of their status and rights of citizenship, and historian Hannah Blythe emphasised MACA's objectives in the context of helping restore them.[250] MACA provided support in many ways. It undertook post-discharge home visits, provided 'grants in kind or money towards maintenance' while the discharged person sought work, and helped them obtain 'necessaries such as clothing, glasses, dentures, etc and tools for their chosen occupation'.[251] It placed job-seeking advertisements in newspapers, informing potential employers that the person had 'been mentally ill, now quite strong and well'.[252] Many former patients found work this way, with MACA's individualised approach helping to allay the nervousness of employers about engaging someone who had been in a mental hospital. Some employers showed great compassion: the murder trial of former Broadmoor patient Mr Penny had been reported extensively in the press, and grocery manufacturer J Lyons and Co would have been well aware of it; nonetheless Lyons employed Mr Penny, providing a stepping stone towards his successful rehabilitation.[253]

Some patients went to a MACA 'cottage home' to convalesce following discharge. Often at the seaside or in the country, they were usually comfortable houses, grander than cottages, each with several convalescing guests. Some patients referred to the experience as a holiday – a testimony to the standards of care provided.[254] MACA homes took on immense challenges, such as when a patient was discharged following many years of hospitalisation, or when a family situation was problematic, such as a husband only wanting his convalescing wife home if she could support him.[255]

The Lunacy Act did not authorise local authority expenditure on after-care, even though successful reintegration into the community had the potential to reduce longer-term costs by avoiding readmission. The Royal Commission attempted to dispel the myth that former patients refused after-care because of stigma, and proposed to 'press local authorities' to fund it.[256] The Board of Control acknowledged the benefits of 'a talk with a sympathetic doctor' for patients discharged after a physical illness, and considered that similar opportunities would help those discharged from mental hospital. Inspired by practices at Maasoord Hospital, Rotterdam, which attributed its low readmission rate to its psychiatrists keeping in touch with discharged patients, the Board argued for similar practices to be established. However, as with other after-care, new legislation would be required to authorise expenditure on such innovations.[257]

MACA relied on charitable donations, and patients and their relatives were aware of its financial precarity.[258] MACA listed grateful patients among its donors in its annual reports.[259] It also cited patients' letters. One wrote:

> I can hardly express my thanks to you for what you have done for me: I was in a very bad way when I went down, but the three weeks' extension done me no end of good, I am going back to my little bit of work this morning, I think everything will be alright.
>
> I am enclosing 10s. note you so kindly gave me for rail fare, I can spare that this week as I have back Old Age Pension to draw this morning.
>
> I trust you will accept this with many thanks for all you have done for me.[260]

Death

Mr Lamborn's friend Alice W, a 36-year-old factory hand, died in Colney Hatch soon after being admitted. He wrote to the hospital:

> Sunday with two of my nieces we were talking together. Tonight Thursday She Lyes in the Dead-house, and I can not have Her Removed. I will call Saturday Afternoon & may I have the Final Look at Her and will also Attend the Funeral 10.30 Tuesday morning.[261]

Unable to 'have her removed' to provide the funeral himself, Alice would have a pauper's funeral at the expense of the Guardians. Some mental hospitals still used cemeteries on their own estates, often hidden away.[262] Burial within the mental hospital grounds, combined with the pauper lunatic label and place of death, added to relatives' and friends' grief. The Board of Control highlighted its awareness of the stigma attached to place of burial when it stipulated that ex-service patients must not be buried in an asylum cemetery, nor in any area of a church or municipal cemetery set aside for pauper lunatics.[263]

Occasionally the Board commented that practices around the time of death could be disrespectful to the deceased and their families.[264] They could also profoundly disturb patients. Mrs M recounted what she saw through a window of the admission ward:

> Every now and then you would hear a very terrifying whistle blown. When the nurse heard that whistle she had to go outside into the courtyard, walk down a little path and open a wooden door, and then some man, a male attendant, with male patients, would come through with a stretcher and the nurse would let them into the corridor; then the whistle would blow again, and that was the attendants going off with the corpse. The male patients would carry the stretcher on their shoulders. The corpse would be simply lightly covered over; sometimes there would be two on it, and you could see them wobbling; that was taking the bodies to the mortuary. This whistle made you all look.[265]

Local customs and religious ideas sometimes helped shape how death was managed in the mental hospitals,[266] suggesting that public views could influence institutional practice. However, nationally, death and mourning rituals were in transition associated with WW1. During the war many families lost close relatives who were buried where they fell rather than brought home. Without a local funeral, there was a shift from open expressions of grief to more suppressed private mourning. The soldiers' deaths also eclipsed deaths from disease, according to historian Pat Jalland, 'foreshadowing the silences surrounding domesticated deaths in the inter-war years'.[267] The country also had to contend with the Spanish influenza pandemic – yet more deaths for which public displays of grief were attenuated in an emotionally drained population, with mourning rituals impacted on by the war, by fears of infection, and by the difficulties of overworked undertakers, gravediggers and coffin makers, associated with the pandemic and in the context of many servicemen still not demobbed.

Post-mortems frequently took place in mental hospital mortuaries, with the aim of furthering scientific understanding of insanity and determining causes of death – including to demonstrate that death had not been caused by violence. Relatives had to consent to a post-mortem, but there was little agreement on how to obtain that consent. In 1920, the practice in LCC mental hospitals was to inform relatives at the time of admission that the patient would undergo a post-mortem, expecting them to reply in writing if they objected. No further consent was sought at the time of death. On admission, given that the mental hospital authorities sought to instil hope, this was incongruous. Relatives were more likely to be hoping for recovery than envisioning death, and they might overlook the instruction to inform the authorities if they objected to a post-mortem. Furthermore, after possibly several decades, an agreement made on admission might be said to be of dubious validity. Nevertheless, the LCC, backed by the Board of Control, claimed that their procedure was an 'advantage'.[268] It probably was advantageous to the authorities, but it ignored the needs of grieving relatives. The Wandsworth Guardians challenged the LCC and the Board about the consent procedure and explained that in general hospitals consent was sought after death. Given the ideals of making mental hospitals more like general hospitals, the LCC conceded grudgingly, despite the institutional inconvenience.[269]

Figure 3.4a and 3.4b Heska Breemer's pauper's grave at the Jewish Cemetery, East Ham. Photographs by author.

If a patient with no relatives or friends died in a mental hospital or other public institution, a decision needed to be made about disposal of the body. Medical schools were eager to receive unclaimed bodies to assist with teaching anatomy to medical students, preferably without them having been subject to a hospital post-mortem. Aligned with medical schools' needs, the Anatomy Act 1832 (passed to stop the crime of bodysnatching) provided a way for 'insane paupers' to 'repay their welfare debt to society'.[270] The Ministry of Health raised these matters with the Board of Control in 1920, and the Board wrote to inform the medical superintendents accordingly. The subject then fell from the agenda. Five years later the Board sent a follow-up letter, asking to be informed of current practices. Medical superintendents provided diverse responses: some reported complying with the Anatomy Act, but the number of bodies was very small; others commented that bodies had been refused by the medical schools on the grounds of old age; one wanted to discuss the matter with his committee; while another did not think it was a suitable topic to raise with them.[271] Colney Hatch appeared to adopt a clear process: if no friends or family were contactable after sending letters to the various addresses on file, the body was transferred to a medical school.[272]

In her 2012 paper on the 'dissection and interment of the insane poor', Elizabeth Hurren scrutinised this 'body trade' and estimated that, between 1832 and 1929, at least one-third of pauper lunatics who 'entered a public asylum and died on the premises were sold on for dissection'.[273] This contrasts with my analysis of a random sample comprising three hundred patients, all officially pauper lunatics, who died at Colney Hatch between 1919 and 1930. This revealed only five patients' bodies being sold on, nearer to one in 50. Given the institutional tendency to keep official documents, and since removal of a body under the Anatomy Act required a warrant and other documentation, records suggest that the practice was uncommon there. Of the five identified, all had been in institutions for over a decade – and one of them, Ann M, had been institutionalised for 34 years.[274] None had any known relatives at the time of admission, and attempts over the years to find them had failed. The precise reasons for the divergence in findings from Colney Hatch compared to Hurren's figures are unclear, but they may have been related to interpretation of the term 'pauper lunatic', and they point to the need for caution when making generalisations from case studies.

Colney Hatch's approach may also have been linked to the large number of Jewish patients within that institution. Aware that many Jewish people were opposed to post-mortems on religious grounds, it did not recommend that their bodies be transferred for dissection, reflecting respect for their religious beliefs. When Heska Breemer died in 1922 after a two-decade hospital stay and with no known friends or relatives, she was buried in a pauper's grave in the Jewish Cemetery at East Ham (Figure 3.4, a and b).[275]

Reflections

Some patients experienced the institutional culture as 'petty tyranny and soulless discipline',[276] or worse, but that was far from the whole picture of mental hospital life. Horror stories of asylums as uniformly and determinedly cruel and abusive[277] do not hold when an in-depth inquiry is made as close as one can get to patients' experiences. Both harsh and caring practices existed. Patients showed their gratitude for good care when they left hospital in published reminiscences and personal letters. After her discharge, Minnie M wrote to Colney Hatch: 'Thanking you and your staff for the splendid treatment I received at the hospital.'[278]

In some ways, the institutional culture reflected aspects of the wider community, such as the acceptability of punishment and not paying patients for utility work, as with family members in a household. The use of animalistic and prison language, including by those in authority, indicated cultural and emotional challenges which informed practice and policy and would need to be overcome to improve patients' experiences.

Making generalisations from the localised is fraught with risk. Although I have drawn on information from a variety of people, places and organisations in this chapter, much stems from the archives of Colney Hatch, where committee meetings tended to gloss over good practice, instead emphasising problems and what needed to be done to overcome them. Some of the gloom and doom in this chapter reflects the sources available for investigation, rather than the proportions of good and bad practice experienced by patients. However, in the early twentieth century, as public mental hospitals became larger, more unwieldy and relatively understaffed, many individualised, humane approaches to care used previously were overlooked, ignored or forgotten. Wartime austerity added to the neglect of civilian patients.[279] Post-war, despite good intentions stemming from treating shell-shocked soldiers, lessons did not transfer to civilian patients. Through much of the 1920s the Board of Control accepted custodial batch living as satisfactory rather than prioritising an individual patient focus. Staff could be insensitive to patients' predicaments, and lack respect, empathy and understanding towards them as human beings. There were inhumanities, which those with responsibility for the institutions and formal inquiries concurred were never acceptable. Nevertheless, typically they responded defensively when faced with allegations of such happenings, expressing disbelief that they could take place, except possibly as isolated occurrences on the rarest of occasions.

In the 1920s, mental hospital practices conformed to the stipulations of the Lunacy Act, but there was little effort on the part of the authorities to exceed the minimum requirements, even when there was evidence that change would benefit patients. Innovations like installing locked letterboxes on the wards to ensure that patients' letters remained confidential only brought practice up to the basic standards enshrined in the Act, and not beyond. Ideas from Scotland and further afield, and from different types of institutions, such as Broadmoor, received some attention, but overall, public mental hospitals in England lagged behind. When new practices were introduced, or when old practices were reinvigorated, patient-focussed change and innovation tended to be spearheaded by individuals, often psychiatrists, and charities such as MACA, which demonstrated liberal, flexible, patient-empowering, psycho-social and occupational approaches. Official decision making revolved around physical safety, economy, convenience for staff and providing custodial care rather than achieving the greatest possible benefit for patients. The welfare of the institution appeared to be more important than that of the patients.

The mental hospital leadership took decisions about patients which were internally inconsistent. For example, although obsessed with safety and minimising physical risk to patients regarding suicide and self-harm, they encouraged patients to work, sometimes undertaking hazardous utility tasks. They considered patients inevitably unreliable, but at the same time regarded them as sufficiently trustworthy to work to support the institution. Inconsistencies and idiosyncratic assumptions tended to go unchallenged. Deeply embedded institutional culture perpetuated practices, a subject which will be taken up again in chapter five.

Notes

1 Weatherly, The treatment of incipient and unconfirmed insanity, 497.
2 Evidence to Cobb Inquiry, Arthur Trevor, q. 27, 36, TNA MH 58/219.
3 Anon., Asylums and mental hospitals; A patient for five months, A living death.
4 Memo (illegible signature) to Aubrey Symonds, 1921, TNA MH 58/222; Anon., Oxford County and City; Mental Treatment Bill, *Hansard*, 3 May 1923.
5 Beveridge, Life in the asylum; Chaney, 'No "sane" person', 39; Wallis, *Investigating the Body*, 13–14.
6 Chaney, 'No "sane" person', 40.
7 UK Government, Population data tables.
8 Letter, Annie Gi, 2 Dec 1928, Reception orders etc, TLA H12/CH/B/47/038.
9 Charles Shaw, General considerations in mental nursing: An address to the staff of the Retreat, York, delivered 10 May 1924, 23, WL RET/5/11/13.
10 Lord, *Mental Hospitals and the Public*, 23.
11 Warmark, *Guilty but Insane*, 182, 185.
12 Morrison, Henderson and Meyer in correspondence.
13 Warmark, *Guilty but Insane*, 171.
14 Belloc, *Cautionary Tales for Children*.
15 Oram, *Military Executions*, 3–5.
16 Royal Commission on Lunacy and Mental Disorder, *Report*, 117, para. 214.
17 Bourke, *Fear*, 152–7; Adler, Less crime, more punishment.
18 Royal Commission on Lunacy and Mental Disorder, *Report*, 116–17, para. 214.
19 Lunacy Act 1890, ss. 85–9.
20 Evidence to Cobb Inquiry, Rev JJ Brownhill, q. 2,445, TNA MH 58/220.
21 Oxonian, Confined as a lunatic iii, 142.
22 Rickard, *Cathy Rossiter*, 318.
23 Elgood, The asylum as it should be, 294.
24 Wallis, *Investigating the Body*, 104–5.
25 Elgood, The asylum as it should be, 295.
26 Frederick Willis's definition of seclusion, 24 Jan 1923, TNA MH 58/224.
27 BoC, *Annual Report for 1926*, Part 2, 143, Long Grove Mental Hospital, LCC, 8 Oct 1926.
28 Anon., 'Death chamber'.
29 BoC, *Annual Report for 1922*, 99.
30 A patient for five months, A living death, 586.
31 BoC, *Annual Report for 1922*, 6.
32 Long, Changing public representations, 108.
33 An ex-patient, The asylum environment, 344; Editor, At the periphery, 8 Mar 1922, 188; Royal Commission on Lunacy and Mental Disorder, *Report*, 7, para. 15.
34 Evidence to Cobb Inquiry, Mr WH Skevington, q. 2,591, TNA MH 58/220.
35 Med sup's reports, Colney Hatch, 6 Aug 1919, TLA H12/CH/A/08/001; minutes for med sup, Colney Hatch, 24 Nov 1923, TLA H12/CH/A/02/005.
36 Mercier, *The Attendant's Companion*, 2.

37 Oxonian, Confined as a lunatic iii, 138.
38 Mercier, *Lunatic Asylums*, 240.
39 BoC, *Conference on Lunacy Administration*, 82.
40 BoC, *Annual Report for 1919*, Part 1, 36; *Annual Report for 1927*, Part 1, 32.
41 Evidence to Cobb Inquiry, Rev JJ Brownhill, q. 2,446–8, TNA MH 58/220.
42 Royal Commission on Lunacy and Mental Disorder, *Minutes*, Mrs M, q. 14,105.
43 Rickard, *Cathy Rossiter*, 319.
44 Brumby, 'A painful and disagreeable position', 49.
45 Evidence to Cobb Inquiry, Dr Rotherham, q. 305, TNA MH 58/219.
46 McCrae and Wright, Work, rest and play, 620.
47 Anon., Oxford County and City; Dr Bond, Précis of evidence, 1922, TNA MH 58/223.
48 Royal Commission on Lunacy and Mental Disorder, *Minutes*, Cecil Chubb, q. 6,522–3.
49 Anon., Reform in asylum administration.
50 Lomax, *The Experiences of an Asylum Doctor*, 68–9.
51 Evidence to Cobb Inquiry, Joseph Shaw Bolton, q. 2,890, TNA MH 58/220.
52 Colney Hatch Sub-Com, 19 Jun 1925, 29, TLA LCC/MIN/01014.
53 Colney Hatch Sub-Com, 8 Oct 1926, 113, TLA LCC/MIN/01015; 21 Oct 1927, 36, TLA LCC/MIN/01016.
54 John H, Colney Hatch case notes, TLA H12/CH/B/15/009.
55 Nicolaou, Countering the narrative, i.
56 Bond, The position of psychological medicine, 423.
57 Frederick H, Colney Hatch case notes, TLA H12/CH/B/26/006.
58 Royal Commission on Lunacy and Mental Disorder, *Report*, 116, para. 213; 115, para. 211.
59 BoC, *Conference on Lunacy Administration*, 78.
60 BoC, *Conference on Lunacy Administration*, 89; BoC, *Annual Report for 1924*, 11.
61 Oxonian, Confined as a lunatic iii, 139.
62 Oxonian, Confined as a lunatic iii, 142.
63 Colney Hatch Sub-Com, 1 Oct 1920, 129, TLA LCC/MIN/01009.
64 BoC, *Annual Report for 1923*, 12.
65 Barham, *Forgotten Lunatics*, 287.
66 Smith and Pear, *Shell Shock and its Lessons*, xv.
67 Oswald, Entertaining the insane, Abstract.
68 Lunacy Act 1890, s. 277.
69 Provisions in the MDA to safeguard religious persuasion of patients 1922–40, TNA MH 51/391.
70 Colney Hatch Sub-Com, 21 May 1926, 11, TLA LCC/MIN/0101521; Mar 1930, 4 Apr 1930, 313, TLA LCC/MIN/01017.
71 Med sup's reports, Colney Hatch, 16 May 1919, TLA H12/CH/A/08/001.
72 Colney Hatch Sub-Com, 8 Feb 1929, TLA LCC/MIN/01017.
73 Colney Hatch Sub-Com, 28 Sept 1923, 141, TLA LCC/MIN/01012; 2 Sept 1921, 166–7, TLA LCC/MIN/01010.
74 Colney Hatch Sub-Com, 1 Oct 1920, 132, TLA LCC/MIN/01009; Med sup's reports, Colney Hatch, 8 Jun 1923, TLA H12/CH/A/08/003.
75 Oosterhuis, Between institutional psychiatry and mental health care, 413–28.
76 Lunacy Act 1890, s. 207.
77 Black, Health and medical care of the Jewish poor.
78 John D, Case notes 1921–2, TLA H12/CH/B/15/004.
79 Ah Kee Y, Reception orders etc 1928, TLA H12/CH/B/47/037.
80 Paz A, Reception orders 1922, TLA H12/CH/B/47/027; Colney Hatch Sub-Com, 2 Sept 1921, 166–7, TLA LCC/MIN/01010; 18 Aug 1922, 181, TLA LCC/MIN/01011; 16 Jul 1926, 52–3, TLA LCC/MIN/01015.
81 Heaton, Contingencies of colonial psychiatry, 50.
82 Simcha C, Reception orders etc 1929, TLA H12/CH/B/47/039.
83 Report on expenditure for dispensary, Colney Hatch Sub-Com, 1 Oct 1920, 134, TLA LCC/MIN/01009.
84 Hyslop, *The Borderland*, 240.
85 Royal Commission on Lunacy and Mental Disorder, *Report*, 124, para. 226.
86 Charles Shaw, General considerations in mental nursing: An address to the staff of the Retreat, York, delivered 10 May 1924, 16, WL RET/5/11/13.

87 BoC, *Annual Report for 1926*, Part 2, 131, Cane Hill Mental Hospital, LCC, 17 Nov 1926; *Annual Report for 1929*, Part 2, 166, Severalls Mental Hospital, Colchester, 26 Jun 1929.
88 Cherry and Munting, 'Exercise is the thing', 47.
89 Charles Shaw, General considerations in mental nursing: An address to the staff of the Retreat, York, delivered 10 May 1924, 16, WL RET/5/11/13.
90 BoC, *Annual Report for 1926*, Part 2, 200, Menston Mental Hospital, Yorkshire, 25 Jun 1926.
91 Oxonian, Confined as a lunatic, 535–6.
92 Royal Commission on Lunacy and Mental Disorder, *Minutes*, Mrs M, q. 13,854–5.
93 Rickard, *Cathy Rossiter*, 259.
94 Wilberforce, *The Autobiography of a Pioneer Woman Doctor*, 126.
95 JSC, The mental patient as he feels himself, 347.
96 Royal Commission on Lunacy and Mental Disorder, *Minutes*, Maurice Craig, q. 20,952, 20,958; Mrs M, q. 14,105.
97 Mercier, *A Textbook of Insanity*, 14.
98 Royal Commission on Lunacy and Mental Disorder, *Minutes*, Mrs M, q. 13,880.
99 BoC, *Annual Report for 1926*, Part 1, 32; Part 2, 201, Menston Mental Hospital, Yorkshire, 25 Jun 1926.
100 Hunter and Macalpine, *Psychiatry for the Poor*, 147; BoC, *Annual Report for 1926*, Part 2, 89, Durham Mental Hospital, 22 Jun 1926; Royal Commission on Lunacy and Mental Disorder, *Report*, 168, para. XXV.
101 Colney Hatch Sub-Com, 25 Jan 1929, 21, TLA LCC/MIN/01017.
102 McCrae and Nolan, *The Story of Nursing*, 82.
103 Royal Commission on Lunacy and Mental Disorder, *Minutes*, Mrs M, q. 13,952–73.
104 Evidence to Cobb Inquiry, Rev JJ Brownhill, q. 2,422, TNA MH 58/220.
105 Anon., Willerby Asylum inquiry committee breaks up.
106 Bullough, Merchandising the sanitary napkin; Mandziuk, 'Ending women's greatest hygienic mistake'.
107 Royal Commission on Lunacy and Mental Disorder, *Minutes*, Miss H (former probationer nurse), q. 19,691–3.
108 Royal Commission on Lunacy and Mental Disorder, *Minutes*, Mrs M, q. 14,027–30.
109 MacArthur, *Mental Hospital Manual*, 60.
110 Letter, Colney Hatch to Holborn Guardians, 27 Jul 1921, Reception orders etc, TLA H12/CH/B/47/023.
111 BoC, *Annual Report for 1926*, Part 2, 129, Bexley Mental Hospital, Kent, 19 Mar 1926.
112 Royal Commission on Lunacy and Mental Disorder, *Minutes*, Mrs M, q. 13,979.
113 BoC, *Annual Report for 1929*, Part 2, 197, Bracebridge Mental Hospital, Lincolnshire, 19 Dec 1929.
114 Mable B, Med sup's reports, Colney Hatch, 11 Jun 1920, TLA H12/CH/A/08/001.
115 Royal Commission on Lunacy and Mental Disorder, *Minutes*, Mrs M, q. 13,974–95.
116 BoC, *Annual Report for 1926*, Part 2, 205, Storthes Hall Mental Hospital, Yorkshire, 16 Oct 1926.
117 Hamlett and Hoskins, Comfort in small things, 113.
118 Royal Commission on Lunacy and Mental Disorder, *Minutes*, Mrs M, q. 13,975.
119 Anon., Asylum patients.
120 Royal Commission on Lunacy and Mental Disorder, *Minutes*, Mr R Montogomery Birch Parker, q. 11,738.
121 Colney Hatch Sub-Com, 2 Sept 1921, 177, TLA LCC/MIN/01010.
122 BoC, *Annual Report for 1922*, 17.
123 BoC minutes, 31 May 1922, 145, TNA MH 50/50.
124 Hamlett and Hoskins, Comfort in small things, 113.
125 Steen, *The Modern Mental Hospital*, 20.
126 Anon., Oxford County and City.
127 MacArthur, *Mental Hospital Manual*, 79.
128 Charles Shaw, General considerations in mental nursing: An address to the staff of the Retreat, York, delivered 10 May 1924, 17, WL RET/5/11/13.
129 Hamlett and Hoskins, Comfort in small things, 113.
130 MacArthur, *Mental Hospital Manual*, 119.
131 Goffman, *Asylums*, 307.
132 MacArthur, *Mental Hospital Manual*, 59–60.

133 Royal Commission on Lunacy and Mental Disorder, *Minutes*, Hugh Pattison Macmillan and Mrs M, q. 14,010.
134 BoC, *Annual Report for 1921*, 44.
135 Nurse C, Colney Hatch Sub-Com, 25 Mar 1927, 231, TLA LCC/MIN/01015.
136 Ellen M, Reception orders etc 1928, TLA H12/CH/B/47/036.
137 Colney Hatch Sub-Com, 9 Aug 1929, 138; 4 Oct 1929, 178, TLA LCC/MIN/01017.
138 Asylum Inmates (Property), *Hansard*, 2 Apr 1925.
139 Anon., Pauper asylum patients (property).
140 General BoC for Scotland, *Sixteenth Annual Report*, x.
141 Sarah S, Reception orders etc 1922, TLA H12/CH/B/47/025.
142 Anon., Lunacy during the war.
143 Crammer, Extraordinary deaths.
144 Bond, The position of psychological medicine, 436.
145 Jones, *Mental Health and Social Policy*, 127.
146 Soanes, Rest and restitution, 316–17.
147 Committee on Dietaries, *Report*, 65–9.
148 Anon., Patients' dietary scales at Winwick Mental Hospital.
149 Charles Shaw, General considerations in mental nursing: An address to the staff of the Retreat, York, delivered 10 May 1924, 19, WL RET/5/11/13.
150 Evidence to Cobb Inquiry, Mr Sale, q. 664, TNA MH 58/219.
151 Claybury Asylum, meeting, 8 Nov 1917, notes of conference on staff food, between pages 231–2, TLA LCC/MIN/00948.
152 Evidence to Cobb Inquiry, Mr AM Donaldson, q. 619–21, TNA MH 58/219.
153 BoC, *Annual Report for 1929*, Part 2, 280, Storthes Hall Mental Hospital, Yorkshire, 14 Jun 1929.
154 Kearin, Dirty bread, forced feeding, 111.
155 Committee on Dietaries, *Report*, 36.
156 Oswald, 'Distraction from hurtful thoughts'.
157 Freebody, *Work and Occupation*, 75.
158 BoC, *Conference on Lunacy Administration*, 82.
159 Morrison, Conversing with the psychiatrist, 19.
160 Robertson, Occupational therapy, 77.
161 Henderson, Occupational therapy, 66; Henderson and Gillespie, *A Text-book of Psychiatry*, 475.
162 Scott, *Sane in Asylum Walls*, 48.
163 Ernst, Therapy and empowerment, 8.
164 Colney Hatch Sub-Com, 29 Oct 1920, 163–4, TLA LCC/MIN/01009.
165 Isabel Wilson, The Board of Control and the mental health services 'seen from the centre' (unpublished manuscript), 25, WL MS.7913/19; Freebody, *Work and Occupation*, 142; Hall, From work and occupation to occupational therapy.
166 Walter, Hermann Simon.
167 Anon., Macclesfield Asylum.
168 Royal Commission on Lunacy and Mental Disorder, *Minutes*, Mrs M, q. 13,943–5.
169 Lomax, *The Experiences of an Asylum Doctor*, 106–7.
170 BoC, *Annual Report for 1922*, 86, 93.
171 Freebody, *Work and Occupation*, 38.
172 Colney Hatch Sub-Com, 15 Apr 1921, 12, TLA LCC/MIN/01010.
173 Todd, Young women, 794.
174 Farmfield Institution, Monetary rewards to patients, 1928, TNA MH 51/424.
175 General BoC for Scotland, *Sixteenth Annual Report*, x.
176 Rewards to patients for industry and good conduct at Occupational Centres, 1920–60, TNA MH 51/424; Warmark, *Guilty but Insane*, 115, 153.
177 BoC, *Annual Report for 1921*, 95.
178 Showing of farm produce, Colney Hatch Sub-Com, 24 Jan 1930, 254, TLA LCC/MIN/01017.
179 Stilitz, A token economy.
180 BoC, *Annual Report for 1926*, Part 2, 132, Cane Hill Mental Hospital, LCC, 17 Nov 1926.
181 Letter, Mervyn Archdale to BoC, 14 Oct 1926, TNA MH 51/353.
182 Anon., 8-hour day for lunatics, citing *Manchester Evening News*, 27 Aug 1919; minutes for med sup, Colney Hatch, 10 Jun 1921, TLA H12/CH/A/02/005.
183 Royal Commission on Lunacy and Mental Disorder, *Report*, 120, para. 219.

184 BoC, *Annual Report for 1928*, 4.
185 Fielding, Smoking and women, 1,343.
186 Steen, *The Modern Mental Hospital*, 13.
187 Riggall, *Reminiscences of a Stay in a Mental Hospital*, 6–7; Cherry and Munting, 'Exercise is the thing', 50.
188 Cherry and Munting, 'Exercise is the thing', 50.
189 Cherry and Munting, 'Exercise is the thing', 46.
190 BoC, *Annual Report for 1929*, Part 2, 180, Chartham Mental Hospital, Kent, 19 Jul 1929; 272, Wakefield Mental Hospital, Yorkshire, 21 Feb 1929.
191 *Under the Dome*, Bethlem Royal Hospital, Museum of the Mind Archives; *Gartnavel Gazette*, Records of Gartnavel Royal Hospital, Glasgow, Scotland, WL HB13/2; *New Moon*, 1907–37, Records of Crichton Royal Hospital, WL DGH1/7/1/1/7; Morrison, Conversing with the psychiatrist.
192 Royal Commission on Lunacy and Mental Disorder, *Minutes*, Dr Dixon, med sup, Leicester, q. 3,877.
193 BoC, *Annual Report for 1926*, Part 2, 68, Cambridgeshire and Isle of Ely Mental Hospital, 14 Dec 1926; 129, Bexley Mental Hospital, LCC, 19 Mar 1926.
194 Royal Commission on Lunacy and Mental Disorder, *Report*, 99, para. 186.
195 Anon., What patients like.
196 Steen, *The Modern Mental Hospital*, 65–6.
197 Royal Commission on Lunacy and Mental Disorder, *Minutes*, Lord Sandhurst, q. 17,964.
198 BoC, Circular 652, 1925, TNA MH 51/240.
199 Med sup's reports, Colney Hatch, Edward W, 17 Jun 1925, 88, TLA H12/CH/A/08/004; 13 Jun 1919, TLA H12/CH/A/08/001.
200 Med sup's reports, Colney Hatch, 18 Oct 1929, 118, TLA H12/CH/A/08/006.
201 Martha W, Reception orders etc 1923, TLA H12/CH/B/47/029.
202 Letter, concerning Louisa S from Ernest Turner, Reception orders etc, 1923, TLA H12/CH/B/47/029.
203 Anon., Visits to patients in mental hospitals; Colney Hatch Sub-Com, 15 Apr 1921, 11, TLA LCC/MIN/01010.
204 Riggall, *Reminiscences of a Stay in a Mental Hospital*, 9.
205 Anon., The administration of public mental hospitals, 97.
206 BoC, *Annual Report for 1929*, Part 2, 173, Park Prewett Mental Hospital, Basingstoke, 29 Nov 1929.
207 Case notes 1921, TLA H12/CH/B/14/005.
208 Colney Hatch Sub-Com, 26 Sept 1924, 109–12, TLA LCC/MIN/01013.
209 Case notes 1926, TLA H12/CH/B/14/009.
210 Letter, Colney Hatch to Brentford Union, 3 Nov 1926, Reception orders etc, TLA H12/CH/B/47/034.
211 BoC, Circular 652, 1925, TNA MH 51/240.
212 Annie A, Reception orders etc, 1928, TLA H12/CH/B/47/037.
213 Annie M, Reception orders etc, 1926, TLA H12/CH/B/47/034.
214 Letter from Leah M about Luba M, Reception orders etc 1927, TLA H12/CH/B/47/035.
215 Letter from Mrs S about Ada C, minutes for med sup, Colney Hatch, 17 Dec 1920, TLA H12/CH/A/02/005.
216 Annie G, Reception orders etc 1926, TLA H12/CH/B/47/034.
217 Royal Commission on Lunacy and Mental Disorder, *Minutes*, Dr Helen Boyle, q. 18,729.
218 BoC, Circular 738, Visitors of friends and family, 1930, TNA MH 51/240.
219 Lomax, *The Experiences of an Asylum Doctor*, 69.
220 Colney Hatch Sub-Com, 9 Jul 1920, 45–6, TLA LCC/MIN/01009.
221 BoC, Circular 652, 1925, TNA MH 51/240.
222 Royal Commission on Lunacy and Mental Disorder, *Minutes*, Dr C Hubert Bond, q. 445.
223 BoC, *Annual Report for 1926*, Part 2, 141, Long Grove Mental Hospital, LCC, 8 Oct 1926.
224 Brumby 'A painful and disagreeable position', 49.
225 Beveridge, Life in the asylum, 463–5.
226 Scott, *Sane in Asylum Walls*, 49.
227 BoC, *Annual Report for 1926*, Part 2, 129, Bexley Mental Hospital, LCC, 19 Mar 1926.
228 BoC, *Annual Report for 1924*, 15.
229 Memo, Percy Barter, 6 Oct 1926, 7, TNA MH 58/216.

230 Soanes, Rest and restitution, 108, 110.
231 Riggall, *Reminiscences of a Stay in a Mental Hospital*, 12.
232 Reception orders etc 1920, TLA H12/CH/B/47/021; Elizabeth L, Reception orders etc 1922, TLA H12/CH/B/47/027; Ethel H, Reception orders etc 1923, TLA H12/CH/B/47/029.
233 Lunacy Act 1890, s. 55; Letter, LCC to BoC, 27 Oct 1925, TNA MH 51/331; Soanes, Rest and restitution, 69.
234 Allmond, Liberty and the individual, 29.
235 Read, Familial care of the insane, 194; Royal Commission on Lunacy and Mental Disorder, *Minutes*, Dr Guy Barham, q. 7,502.
236 Letter, LCC to BoC, 27 Oct 1925, TNA MH 51/331.
237 Mental Patients (Detention and Discharge), *Hansard*, 3 May 1928.
238 Chief officer, mental hospitals department LCC, to BoC, 28 Jan 1933, TNA MH 51/331.
239 Eleazor D, Case notes 1930–1, TLA H12/CH/B/15/010; England and Wales Register 1939, https://www.ancestry.com.
240 BoC minutes, 1 Dec 1920, 295, TNA MH 50/48; Lunacy Acts, *Hansard*, 15 Jun 1921.
241 Lunacy Acts, *Hansard*, 24 Nov 1920; Lunacy Act (Private Patients), *Hansard*, 19 Dec 1921; Lunacy Act, *Hansard*, 8 Oct 1924.
242 Mental Cases, *Hansard*, 16 Jun 1921.
243 Jane B, Reception orders etc 1927, TLA H12/CH/B/47/035.
244 Hilton, A mysterious diagnosis.
245 Letter, Theo S to Colney Hatch, Nov 1925, Reception orders etc, TLA H12/CH/B/47/033.
246 Letter, mother of Beatrice D to Colney Hatch, Jan 1929, Reception orders etc, TLA H12/CH/B/47/039.
247 Annie K, anonymous letter, 6 May, and after care workers' letter to med sup, 8 May 1924, Reception orders etc, TLA H12/CH/B/47/032.
248 MACA, *Report of the Council*, 1925, 6, WL SA/MAC/B.1/37.
249 MACA, *Report of the Council*, 1920, 5, WL SA/MAC/B.1/33; 1925, 4, WL SA/MAC/B.1/37.
250 Blythe, Mental recovery.
251 MACA, *Report of the Council*, 1925, 7, WL SA/MAC/B.1/37.
252 MACA, individual case files, Isabella F, advert, *Nursing Mirror*, 26 Nov 1921, WL SA/MAC/G.3/8.
253 Hilton, George Stephen Penny.
254 Soanes, Rest and restitution, 282.
255 Memo, MACA to Colney Hatch re: Beatrice B, 7 Mar 1929, Reception orders etc, TLA H12/CH/B/47/039.
256 Percy Barter, memo, TNA MH 58/216.
257 BoC, *Annual Report for 1928*, Part 1, 6.
258 Anon., The Mental After-Care Association, 344.
259 MACA, *Mental After Care Association, 1925*, 13, 14, 18.
260 MACA, *Report of the Council, for year ending December 1930*, 13, WL SA/MAC/B.1/42.
261 Alice W, Reception orders etc 1926, TLA H12/CH/B/47/034.
262 Philo, Troubled proximities, 91, 100.
263 BoC, Circular 518, Aug 1918, TNA MH 51/239.
264 BoC, *Annual Report for 1926*, Part 2, 141, Long Grove Mental Hospital, LCC, 8 Oct 1926.
265 Royal Commission on Lunacy and Mental Disorder, *Minutes*, Mrs M, q. 13,948.
266 Michael and Hirst, Recording the many faces of death, 43, 50.
267 Jalland, Bereavement and mourning; Jalland, *Death in War and Peace*, 34.
268 BoC minutes, 4 Feb 1920, 35, TNA MH 50/48.
269 Letters, Wandsworth Guardians to BoC, 24 Jan and 8 Jul 1927; LCC to BoC, 26 May 1927, TNA MH 51/532.
270 Hurren, 'Abnormalities and deformities', 65–6.
271 BoC to med sups, 16 Apr 1925, TNA MH 58/4.
272 Anne W, Reception orders etc 1919, TLA H12/CH/B/47/019.
273 Hurren, 'Abnormalities and deformities', 66–7.
274 Ann M, Reception orders etc 1929, TLA H12/CH/B/47/039.
275 Heska Breemer, Reception orders etc 1922, TLA H12/CH/B/47/028.
276 Our Medical Correspondent, Asylum horrors.
277 e.g. Scull, *Museums of Madness*.
278 Minnie M, Reception orders etc 1924, TLA H12/CH/B/47/032.
279 Hilton, *Civilian Lunatic Asylums*, 166, 201.

4
Challenges for the mental hospital doctors: medical knowledge and treating patients

In March 1919, a general practitioner in central London called in to his local police station. He reported that a woman in the street, scantily clad and lacking footwear, had thrown a cup of coffee at him. She was 39-year-old Marie R, from France, then a 'lodging-housekeeper' in London. The police fulfilled their duty of ensuring that she reached the mental observation ward of the workhouse infirmary.

These events occurred three months into Marie's first episode of mental disturbance. Marie described hearing the voices of her persecutors and being bitten by a serpent which came up through the kitchen floor. She was noted to be 'frightfully noisy and a persistent masturbator'. She had diarrhoea and had lost weight. Marie was diagnosed with 'non-systematised delusional insanity', attributed to the 'climacteric' (menopause) and prolonged stress. Certified under the Lunacy Act 1890, she was admitted to Colney Hatch Mental Hospital. She died there eight weeks later. Her post-mortem identified no single cause of death. Her death certificate recorded 'pulmonary congestion' (fluid in the lungs) and 'exhaustion of mania'. Marie's friend, Mr William Voss, a solicitor, arranged her funeral and wrote to the hospital thanking them for 'the care and attention that has been extended to this French woman, practically alone in England'. He also relayed the gratitude of the French Consulate.[1]

Despite Marie's death, it is cheering to note that her friends were satisfied with the care she received. Her case study illustrates the challenges faced by doctors when attempting to treat someone admitted to a mental hospital with disturbed behaviour. Mental hospitals had little access to laboratory investigations and technology, such as X-rays, to help distinguish mental illnesses, which lacked any detectable physical pathology in body or brain, from other mental disturbances caused by physical diseases.

Marie's story also highlights challenges for historians seeking to understand the patients' illnesses. Psychiatric concepts were, and are, shaped by socio-cultural contexts as well as scientific and clinical evidence. Terminology has changed, and the brevity of clinical notes, compounded by idiosyncratic archiving, contributes to making precise inferences about individual patients' illnesses often a matter of conjecture. Regarding Marie, her diagnosis – 'non-systematised delusional insanity' – is today an obsolete term. *A delusion is a* belief, not true to fact but which cannot be corrected by appeal to reason, and it is 'out of harmony with the individual's education and surroundings'.[2] That they were non-systematised meant that the delusions shifted and did not fit into a coherent scheme, either from the patient's perspective or in a way which people around the patient could detect. The pattern of non-systematised delusions might occur in 'delirium' caused by physical disorders. Delirious patients might be physically overactive, a symptom also characteristic of mania in 'manic depression' (today, bipolar disorder). The association between delirium and overactivity led psychiatrist Sir Maurice Craig to call delirium 'temporary mania',[3] but with entirely different causes and outcomes, the term was unhelpful.

John Lord, medical superintendent of Horton Mental Hospital, Epsom, regarded much terminology as 'confusing and meaningless', contributing to a situation where

> psychiatrists, not being able to understand each other, take their own lines, and hence the endless, confusing and seemingly contradictory psychological and clinical conceptions. The student, unable to make head or tail of this *melée* of contradictions, makes the best shift he can, and his psychology as a rule is peculiar and individual to himself.[4]

Ambiguous labels impaired communication of psychiatric knowledge in journals and textbooks, within and between institutions, and in discussion with colleagues at home and abroad.[5] Attempts were made, notably in Germany, to create more uniform scientific nomenclature.[6]

Marie's story resembles that of other certified patients whose mental symptoms due to physical illness were probably overlooked or ignored in the observation ward. One was 15-year-old Annie B, who died of pneumonia 21 days after the onset of her 'mania' and just five days after being transferred to a mental hospital.[7] Some were transferred to mental hospitals with terminal illness accompanied by disturbed behaviour, such as Kate Z, a 46-year-old mother of four children, admitted to Colney Hatch 'too ill to be answering questions'. Her husband Samuel was with her when she died six days later.[8] For these patients, their medical notes do not specify why decisions were made to transfer them from general to mental hospital. The general hospital doctors may have regarded the patients' mental symptoms as too disruptive for one of their wards, or they may not have identified the underlying physical pathology. A 1927 textbook of psychiatry offered an explanation, noting that a common excuse given by doctors working in both general and mental hospitals was that 'the patient is so disordered mentally as to be quite unco-operative, and on that account a complete examination is impossible. How seldom is that really the case!' It also criticised doctors who 'fail to get hold of the essential points of the case, either because of an undue sense of delicacy, or because their manner and method do not inspire confidence in the patient'.[9] A case vignette in Dr AJ Cronin's novel *The Citadel*, based on his experiences working as a GP in the 1920s, illustrates different diagnoses and outcomes when physical examinations took place. An experienced GP, Dr Bramwell, summarised his assessment of an acutely disturbed patient to his less experienced colleague Dr Andrew Manson:

> 'Acute homicidal mania. We'll have to get him into Pontynewdd straight away. That means two signatures on the certificate, mine and yours – the relatives wanted me to call you in. You know the procedure, don't you?'

After examining the patient, Dr Manson gave his view:

> 'In my opinion Hughes is only sick in mind because he's sick in body. I feel that he's suffering from thyroid deficiency – an absolutely straight case of myxoedema.' ... 'After all,' Andrew went on persuasively, ... 'Pontynewdd is such a sink of a place. Once Hughes gets in there he'll never get out. And if he does he'll carry the stigma of it all his life. Suppose we try pushing thyroid into him first?'[10]

Distinguishing a mental disorder from a primarily physical one causing the mental symptoms required astute bedside observation. In the story, and in keeping with clinical expectations, Hughes recovered when treated with thyroxine to correct his thyroid imbalance.

Serious physical disease in mental hospital patients was sometimes identified weeks or months after admission, raising the question of whether it had been present on arrival. That may have been the case for 50-year-old Swamanantha S, a barrister and teacher of languages in Colney Hatch, in whom tuberculosis (a bacterial infection) was detected eight months after admission, his death from it following a few months later.[11] Similarly, Sarah C, a young mother, was admitted with melancholia. Five months later, her notes state: 'Begs to be burned as she believes she is the most wicked woman in the world,' and, on the same day, physical examination suggested tuberculosis in her lungs. She died three months later.[12] Both Swamanantha and Sarah might have acquired tuberculosis after admission, but more likely they were admitted with it, basing this on the typical three-year duration from onset until death if untreated.[13] There were many others like Swamanantha and Sarah for whom pre-existing early stages of physical illness were probably overlooked. However, mental hospitals had no choice but to admit patients sent to them certified under the Lunacy Act. Arguably, if physically ill patients had remained in the general hospital, some may have benefited from the nursing and medical expertise there. Remaining there may also have benefited them socially and emotionally, staying local to family and friends rather than being moved further afield to the county mental hospital, avoiding the stigma of Lunacy Act certification, and of dying as a 'pauper lunatic'.

This chapter focusses on other conundrums regarding mental disturbances, both with and without physical malfunction of other bodily organs, in the context of the range of problems for which people might be admitted to mental hospitals. Doctors faced hurdles concerning diagnosis and treatment amid multiple biological and psychological theories, new research findings, and influences on medical ideology from a defensive institutional leadership. Biological aspects discussed in this chapter include the use (and misuse) of medication, dealing with infectious diseases, the newly identified condition of encephalitis lethargica, and 'focal sepsis', plus treating general paralysis of the insane (GPI – brain syphilis) by inoculation with malaria parasites. The chapter also explores ideology in the fields of heredity and eugenics, which, although not leading to direct biological interventions for patients in mental hospitals, is bound up with attitudes and expectations which influenced the care they received.

A confusion of theories

Early in WW1, doctors and psychologists sought to understand the causes of shell shock – the mental trauma and behavioural disturbances suffered by servicemen in the theatre of war. They initially considered physical causes, including forces of compression from exploding shells, or carbon monoxide released by them, or other toxins.[14] Finding no direct physical trigger shifted even the most biologically oriented psychiatrists towards multi-factorial causes.[15] Understanding the process of recovery was also a mystery, as it often occurred long after any recognised causes had ceased to operate. Recovery was ascribed to multifarious agencies, including suggestion, hypnotism, psychoanalysis, faith-healing and sudden emotion.[16] In her study of shell shock, historian Tracy Loughran argued that 'psychology, physiology and biology were all inseparably blended in many theories' about the condition.[17] Blended theories, however, gave little sense of direction as to how to disentangle them, whether for shell shock or other disorders.

A muddle of incongruent theories and observations connected co-occurring physical and mental symptoms. One of these co-occurrences, common in mental hospital patients, was 'insane ear', otherwise known as 'haematoma auris' or 'cauliflower ear': 'The affected ear swells up, loses its shape, and becomes a tense bluish tumour. If attended to and protected from further injury, this gradually subsides, leaving a hard, shrivelled, and misshapen appendage, often having but little resemblance to an ear at all.'[18] The subject was contentious. Some psychiatrists held that a faulty ear cartilage was a biological manifestation of mental disorder, making patients' ears particularly sensitive to even slight trauma. Psychiatrist Edward Hare, in his review of physical disorders found in patients in mental hospitals between 1850 and 1950, noted that insane ear usually occurred unilaterally on the left side – perhaps due to it being caused by a blow from a right-handed person? – and most commonly in men with disturbed behaviour. Occasionally, when staff were held responsible, new cases of insane ear stopped appearing.[19]

Hospital visiting committees typically rejected allegations from patients that staff pulled them around by their ears – a painful way of insisting that they move or obey commands.[20] When Mr S, a farm labourer at Colney Hatch, was supervising patients picking up potatoes, he decided that patient Mr B was not doing enough work, so he grabbed Mr B by the ear, forced him to the ground and called him a 'poor little imbecile'. Several patients reported the incident. The visiting committee considered the evidence, but, defensive of its staff and disbelieving of the patients, it concluded that Mr S had not used enough force to cause pain or injury.[21] Sometimes, staff explanations for injuries did not ring true, but neither did they alarm the hospital leadership. It was implausible, for example, that a patient described as 'accidentally' slipping off a settee would sustain a bruise on her head, or another 'putting [her] head on [a] radiator accidentally' would suffer second degree burns on her wrist.[22] For the committees it was easier, emotionally and practically, to concur that insane ear and other injuries were inherent to a patient's mental condition, rather than caused by staff assaulting them.

As well as insane ear, patients' broken bones attracted medical and public interest.[23] Surgeons backed theories that mental patients were intrinsically vulnerable to fractures: 'The bones of maniacs are frequently fragile. Fractures among the insane are not necessarily an indication of abuse,' advised surgeon John Chalmers da Costa in 1925.[24] Poor hospital diet might have contributed to bone fragility, as might bony abnormalities caused by syphilis or other diseases, but I found no reference to those underlying pathologies in post-mortem reports of patients at Colney Hatch who sustained fractures.

In the 1920s, mental hospitals were expected to notify the Board of Control in the event of death following a fracture. The Board would then decide if further inquiry was required into how it occurred, including whether a staff member had inflicted it. The Board was suspicious when Bertha M died at the age of 45 with fractures of her ribs and her collarbone following an 'accidental fall', since multiple breaks suggested an injury caused by greater force than a mere accident. However, the Board's minutes on the matter were cursory, accepting the medical superintendent's reassurance that staff were not to blame.[25] These sorts of superficial and defensive inquiries helped perpetuate biological theories linking mental illnesses and predisposition to physical injury, despite suspicions that alternative explanations existed.

Swiss-American psychiatrist Adolf Meyer at Johns Hopkins University in Baltimore, USA coined the term 'psychobiology' in the late nineteenth century, bringing together biological, psychological and environmental factors to account for mental symptoms – a 'whole person' approach to treating each patient.[26] Meyer's psychobiology also had the potential to bridge the geographical and intellectual gap between the USA, which tended to adopt psychoanalytic theories, and European countries, which favoured more biological models of mental illness.[27] Scottish psychiatrist David Kennedy Henderson was influential in bringing Meyer's ideas into clinical practice in Britain. Henderson had worked and studied with several internationally renowned psychiatrists including Meyer; Emil Kraepelin and Alois Alzheimer in Munich; and Frederick Mott in England, before being appointed medical superintendent at the Glasgow Royal Mental Hospital in 1921. In her study of correspondence between Meyer and Henderson, Hazel Morrison described Henderson's approach as a counterculture which 'challenged the established materialist views of Scottish psychiatry' with long-term effects.[28] Henderson's *Text-Book of Psychiatry for Students and Practitioners*, co-authored with Robert Gillespie, was first published in 1927 and revised to a 10th edition over the next 40 years.[29] It became the standard text for doctors undertaking postgraduate examinations in psychiatry, and was significant in propagating Meyer's ideas.[30]

Aligning with Meyer's and Henderson's teachings, Edward Mapother, medical superintendent of the new Maudsley Hospital in London, also favoured an eclectic approach,[31] and John Lord regarded failure to bring mind, body and sociological considerations together into psychiatry as impeding the progress of clinical work.[32] In 1925, Frederick Mott, despite having previously favoured biological theories of causation, suggested that the Medico-Psychological Association (MPA, later RMPA) should encourage a multi-faceted approach to research, incorporating biological, social and psychological causes of mental diseases with a view to preventing, alleviating and curing them.[33] In 1991, psychiatrist Michael Gelder reflected that Meyer's influence on the practice of psychiatry in Britain was so great that over a few decades it became

> quite difficult to discern. This is because his ideas have become so much part of the basic structure of British clinical psychiatry that it is easy to forget that there was a time when things were different. Whenever we take a case history, make a life chart, write a formulation, or work in a multidisciplinary team, we are likely to be using some of Meyer's ideas.[34]

In the mental hospitals of the 1920s, however, creating a multi-disciplinary approach was not so easy. The medical specialty of psychiatry and the disciplines of psychology (mainly focussing on measurement, development and behaviours in the contexts of education, industry and medicine) and psychoanalysis (theories and therapies relating to the unconscious mind) overlapped but were developing in different institutions, with each bound up in arguments about its own validity and utility. Of the three disciplines, psychiatrists led the mental hospitals (in accordance with the Lunacy Act) and could thus influence how the others might integrate into those institutions, but – as so often happened

– psychiatrists' opinions were polarised. Edward Mapother, for example, thought psychologists' techniques of measurement were useful and that collaboration would be beneficial, whereas William Menzies, medical superintendent at Stafford Mental Hospital and president of the MPA in 1920, considered that psychological theories were created primarily to satisfy mankind's intellectual needs.[35]

Regarding psychoanalysis, Sigmund Freud's theories received diverse responses from psychiatrists. At one extreme were the enthusiasts. They included Dr Ernest Jones, follower, friend and biographer of Freud, who founded the British Psychoanalytical Society in 1913 and the *International Journal of Psychoanalysis* in 1920. Psychiatrist William Stoddart also stood in awe of Freud, describing himself as 'one of Freud's disciples' but 'unworthy of assuming the role of an apostle'.[36] Despite his enthusiasm, he was doubtful about the place of psychoanalysis in the public mental hospital service: psychoanalysis was one-to-one and required trained staff and adequate time, both of which were expensive, and money was short.

Dr Stoddart regarded psychoanalysis as 'highly scientific work'. Other psychiatrists, such as John Macpherson, disagreed, describing it as being 'unassailable by direct argument or dialectic attack', with the result that the 'Freudian hypothesis is embarrassing to psychiatry'.[37] Dr Shaw Bolton called psychoanalysis an 'insidious poison', being instilled into people's minds and doing untold harm.[38] The ever-outspoken psychiatrist Charles Mercier, writing during WW1, also gave his opinion:

> psycho-analysis is past its perihelion, and is rapidly retreating into the dark and silent depths from which it emerged, but as it has in certain cases an unquestionable value, and as, moreover, the historian of medicine of the future will have difficulty in finding any account of it, it is well that it should be systematically described before it goes to join pounded toads and sour milk in the limbo of discarded remedies.[39]

By 'unquestionable value', he meant value to the practitioners: 'It is a god-send to them to be provided with a decent excuse for allowing their thoughts to dwell upon sexual matters and for freely talking and writing about them.'[40]

Other conundrums in the 1920s included whether mental disorders were a series of separate conditions or a continuum from mild to severe, from neurosis to psychosis, or from feeling 'run down', through 'nervous exhaustion', and into 'grave forms of mental breakdown'.[41] Meyer favoured a continuum, associated with failures of adjustment or 'reaction types' – the product of an individual's psychobiological make-up and the environmental challenges they faced.[42] A continuum model aligned with some physical disorders, such as tuberculosis, and supported the notion that early treatment could reverse the disorders and facilitate recovery. The continuum theory underpinned practice at the Maudsley Hospital. Recalling his psychiatric training there between the World Wars, Dr Eliot Slater wrote:

> Neuroses and psychoses shaded into one another; the distinction between them was arbitrary, misleading and almost meaningless. Diagnosis was of little service. To distinguish a patient as suffering from a schizophrenic or an affective state was often a labour lost, since both conditions could so easily co-exist in the same individual, and neither was more than a mode of 'reaction'.[43]

Questions also arose as to whether psychiatrists took a sufficiently scientific mindset in their daily work. With one doctor to about four or five hundred patients, ward rounds were often superficial. Former mental hospital attendant Paul Elgood described doctors who

> glance perfunctorily at the inmates who force themselves under their notice. Others of an unobtrusive, sulky disposition they never look at from one year's end to another, except in a case of [physical] illness. The medical officer always seemed to me to regard his patients as under restraint instead of under treatment ... They have neither the time nor, I fear, the inclination to tackle the greater job.[44]

Dr Menzies questioned the scientific content of those rounds: 'Are we to be content for ever to go round the wards daily, chatting pleasantly to the patients, without any thought as to what their blood pressure is, or what type of micro-organism they are harbouring, or why they are constipated or why noisy?' He blamed the unscientific approach, at least in part, on the non-clinical demands made on medical superintendents: '[M]ore kudos is to be gained from selling a sow than from sensitising a serum, from taking 2d off the maintenance rate than from discovering how dysentery is propagated.'[45]

Emphasising the overlap between daily clinical work and research may sound strange to a twenty-first-century medical reader, but, as Michael Gelder pointed out regarding Meyer's ideas, it is easy to forget that what is now considered routine in clinical practice was once new, and it needed investigation. In the 1920s, unexplored territory included determining relationships between different mental states and newly available biological parameters, such as blood sugar levels or markers of inflammation.[46]

An anonymous paper in the *Lancet* criticised the lack of research in psychiatry in England.[47] The Medical Research Council (MRC) established a mental disorders committee to encourage and fund more research. It was rare, however, for mental hospital doctors to apply to the MRC, despite the Board of Control urging them to do so.[48] Factors contributing to that may have been a lack of intellectual curiosity, a lack of research skills, the impossibility of undertaking research in addition to clinical duties of looking after large numbers of patients, or because the MRC had a reputation for being a difficult organisation to negotiate with.[49] However, some universities, such as Cardiff and Liverpool, collaborated on research with local mental hospitals, a model which the MRC, MPA and Board of Control wanted to be more widespread, as in Germany and the USA.[50]

Spanning the clinical and research interface were post-mortem examinations. In theory, they could both enhance understanding of the pathology of diseases and ensure accuracy of death certificates. In 1920, 4,600 post-mortems were carried out in English and Welsh mental hospitals, equating to 58 per cent of the number of deaths.[51] Some mental hospitals employed specialist pathologists, but more often, as at Colney Hatch, the post-mortems were performed by the doctors who had treated the patients. The value of post-mortems in mental hospital patients had long been debated: Johann Christian August Heinroth, professor of medicine at Leipzig in the early nineteenth century, recommended that doctors should focus more 'on analysing the living individual instead of the dead torso'.[52] Nevertheless, post-mortems continued in England – a legacy of the Victorian asylums which became a prescribed and expected part of 1920s mental hospital routine.[53]

Colney Hatch post-mortem records give the impression that the doctors had little curiosity or interest in the findings. This fits with Nicol Ferrier's historical analysis of post-mortems in Victorian asylums which found that causes of death ascertained from them seemed accurate but were very similar, with no unusual findings. The doctors appeared content to pigeonhole cases into accepted, and acceptable, causes of death.[54] This was also in line with Steve Sturdy's observation that a principal concern of pathology was to 'effectively … write out any idiosyncrasy from the clinical narrative' with the identification of 'typical rather than singular cases'.[55] It was unlikely to push forward frontiers of knowledge.

Lack of interest on the part of the doctors undertaking the large number of post-mortems may also have contributed to causes of death stated on death certificates differing from clinical presentations or post-mortem findings. When Marie B died in 1921 her death certificate recorded GPI as the immediate cause, then dysentery; the large cavity in her lung containing pus, identified at post-mortem and suggesting tuberculosis, was not mentioned.[56] The doctor completing the death certificate had to list first the 'disease which initiated the train of events leading to death'.[57] Marie B had been admitted with GPI, a fatal condition, so whether it or the more acute infections 'initiated the train of events' is open to debate. Inconsistencies between post-mortem findings and death certificates were problematic since data from the latter were incorporated into official statistics, undermining their potential to inform trends in disease occurrence, and thereby also the introduction of preventative measures.

In practice, the Board of Control, keen to introduce new therapeutic interventions, sometimes spurned scientific evidence. It urged that balance was needed between the 'statistics' which 'may be disappointing; but, psychologically it is worth much to inspire the patient and his relatives with the feeling that everything possible is being done to ensure his recovery'.[58] Maintaining hope was an essential ingredient of treatment, as the Board said, but other doctors voiced concern about its unscientific approach.

Investigations and medications

Given the recognised overlap between mental and physical disorders, geographical isolation from the general hospitals did not facilitate thorough clinical assessments, although a few medical investigations were undertaken in some mental hospitals to assist diagnosis. They included laboratory tests, such as the relatively new Wassermann antibody test for the treponema pallidum bacterium which caused syphilis. The test was not foolproof, but it was helpful in suspected GPI, and, importantly, it could be used on samples of both blood and cerebrospinal fluid – the fluid surrounding the brain and spinal cord. Cerebrospinal fluid for testing was obtained by lumbar puncture – inserting a needle between two vertebrae low in the back. Both the lumbar puncture technique and drawing off fluid for diagnostic purposes were late nineteenth-century innovations.[59]

The Board of Control wanted every mental hospital to have X-ray equipment, but part of their motivation for advocating this was defensive: by X-raying every patient on admission they could ensure there were no fractures for which they would later have to account.[60] X-rays were also of value, the Board advised, for detecting swallowed items and 'for the diagnosis of pulmonary tuberculosis, joint conditions, dental and other septic foci'.[61] Mental hospitals wanted their own X-ray equipment, rather than having the inconvenience of taking patients to the local general hospital. Some sought to purchase second-hand equipment, but even that could be prohibitively expensive.[62]

As well as providing clinical investigative technology, the general hospitals could easily arrange consultations with different specialists for patients with complex problems. Getting those experts in physical diseases to attend the mental hospitals was less easy to organise.

A limited range of sedative medications were available in the mental hospitals, used alongside practical methods in crisis situations, mainly if a patient's level of distress or behaviours were deemed to be putting themselves or others at risk. No medications yet existed aligned with modern 'psychopharmacology', which might change the ultimate course of a severe, chronic mental disorder.[63] There were sedatives, such as bromides and chloral hydrate, dating from the nineteenth century, and barbiturates from the early twentieth.[64] Clinical notes at Colney Hatch reveal little information about when, why and how much medication was prescribed or dispensed. Prescription charts revealing drug names, doses and frequency of use do not appear among the archives. This may mean that medication was given very infrequently, or that information has been lost. Rosetta S's story is not unusual, but her clinical notes tell us more than most about her medications and the management of her disturbed behaviours. Rosetta was a 63-year-old widow and mother of seven adult children, admitted to Colney Hatch in 1920 with a two-week history of disturbed behaviour. She was forgetful 'and cannot give a relevant account of her recent doings'. Her shouting, screaming, disorientation, delusions and restlessness disturbed the other patients, and she was considered at risk of falling. Some of the time she was kept in a 'pad' – a padded room – and was prescribed sedatives – hyoscine, sulphonal, paraldehyde and brandy – none of which was considered to have given her any benefit. She developed a fever, and diarrhoea which was treated with chalk and opium, a commonly used remedy at the time, but died two months later.[65]

Not all doctors, patients or their relatives supported the use of sedatives. Some preferred mechanical restraint, such as straitjackets, or seclusion in a 'pad'. When writing about his wife's mental illness,

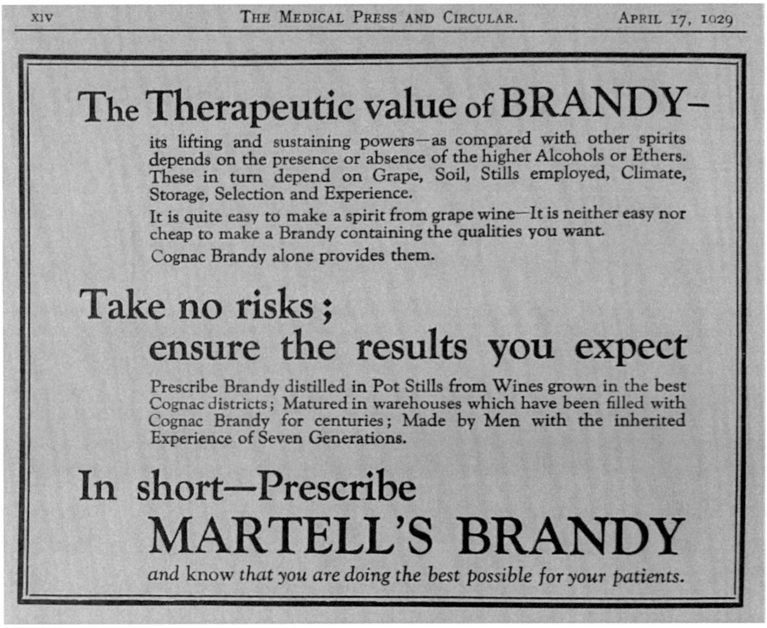

Figure 4.1 The therapeutic value of brandy. Source: *Medical Press and Circular*, 17 April 1929, xiv. © orphan work; owner sought but not found.

Gerald Langston Day cited Dr Thomas Dutton, a generalist rather than psychiatrist who regarded drugs as 'far more injurious and dangerous' than other means:

> Chloral, morphia, heroin, sulphonal, paraldehyde and bromide are now commonly used. Can we really say that such things are better means of restraint? These drugs ruin the physical stability of the patient and destroy every sense of value that he has. All shame disappears and the habitually doped patient sinks to depths of conduct impossible to describe.[66]

Colney Hatch psychiatrist John MacArthur was also sceptical about sedatives. Instead, he recommended that the first line of treatment for a restless patient should be 'warmth [and] good and plentiful feeding' which may help them rest. If that did not work, he recommended the 'continuous warm bath'. Only if that failed should a sedative be tried.[67] For insomnia, he also suggested practical interventions: moving the patient's bed to a darker part of the ward, prohibiting smoking after tea, giving a hot drink before bed, and in some debilitated patients 'a small amount

Table 4.1 Croton oil purchased by mental hospitals, 1919–21.

Mental hospital name or location	Total number of patients	Croton oil (g) purchased 1919–21
Prestwich	2,700	850
another in Lancashire	2,100	Nil
Colney Hatch	2,600	85
in Wales	1,700	28
in southwest England	1,100	14

Sources: Ministry of Health, *Report of Committee on Administration of Public Mental Hospitals*, 112–17, annotated copy, TNA MH 58/221; Board of Control, *Annual Report for 1922*, 106, 108.

of stout', despite that practice having become unfashionable.[68] Other alcoholic drinks (as for Rosetta S, above) were prescribed medicinally (Figure 4.1).

Regarding a patient refusing to take medication, Dr MacArthur had further advice: it should not be concealed in food or drink as this might make patients suspect that they were being poisoned or treated with illegal drugs; instead the doctor 'should personally see him, and if reasoning has no effect, the patient should be tube fed with it. This may sound drastic, but is better practice than any attempt to administer it by subterfuge.'[69] Dr MacArthur's advice suggests that he had some inkling that medication was being given covertly. That aligned with accounts in Dr Montagu Lomax's 1921 exposé, *The Experiences of an Asylum Doctor*, particularly relating to croton oil – a strong laxative easily concealed in food.[70] It might have been prescribed for constipation, but Dr Lomax claimed that the nurses did not give it for that reason: allegedly, croton oil was given punitively or to control a restless patient, who, once exhausted by the diarrhoea, would be less troublesome.[71] According to Dr Lionel Weatherly, croton oil was dispensed without being documented.[72] Given concern that use of croton oil did not match documented prescribing, the Ministry of Health collected data on quantities purchased in five hospitals between 1919 and 1921 (Table 4.1), to estimate usage.

Table 4.1 indicates the huge variation in quantities purchased. Different hospital diets, and patients' various mental and physical illnesses, were unlikely to have accounted for the variation. It is possible that one mental hospital placed a bulk order to share with neighbouring institutions, but no evidence for that has come to light. Prestwich Hospital, where Dr Lomax worked, was a clear outlier, purchasing 10 times more than Colney Hatch for a similar size patient population. Despite this disparity, and doctors and patients alleging punitive use of croton oil, the

Committee on Administration of Public Mental Hospitals (Cobb Inquiry) concluded that such allegations were false.[73] Alongside the croton oil investigations, the Ministry investigated the use of sedatives, publishing its results as part of the Cobb Inquiry report in 1922. The number of doses of sedatives administered to patients varied over a hundredfold between similar mental hospitals, and women were prescribed more than men. However, the report did not comment on these observations.[74]

In 1928, prompted by the Royal Commission on Lunacy and Mental Disorder, the Board of Control again enquired about quantities of sedatives and 'strong purgatives including croton oil'. If the mental hospitals could not give precise information, the Board requested estimates.[75] That risked introducing bias related to how much each hospital thought it should be using. Curiously, the Board's report did not mention croton oil, despite having specifically requested information on it, leaving the quantities used open to speculation. As regards the use of sedatives, the Board concluded that in 'no case are the quantities used excessive' – a bold statement given the methodology. It also noted that the 'order and tranquillity of mental hospitals bear little relation to the extent to which sedatives are used'.[76] This suggested that alternative approaches were also effective, raising questions about staffing levels and staff skills to provide those alternatives. The whole matter was ripe for research.

Dementia praecox and manic depression: psychotic disorders on the international stage

Lily F, an interpreter and shorthand typist in her early 20s, worked in Milan, Italy. She was admitted to an asylum there in 1919. Returning to London in 1920, she was certified and admitted to Colney Hatch. She said that her voice was not her own, God had sent her as the Messiah to reform the world, she had been tortured in Italy and her mouth had been stretched out of shape and boiling water poured down her throat. Physical examination was reported as showing no abnormalities. Her disorder was attributed to adolescence.[77] Lily probably suffered from dementia praecox, by then becoming known as schizophrenia. This condition was likely to run a chronic course, adding to the number of long-stay patients in the institutions.

Professor Emil Kraepelin in Munich took a lead on the world stage for research into dementia praecox and manic depression. Unlike the diagnostic tendency in the UK to label mental disorders according to their main symptom at a single point in time, and inspired by his forebear psychiatrist Karl Kahlbaum, who linked a patient's symptoms to their past history, Kraepelin explored combinations of symptoms over time.[78] He found dementia praecox and manic depression to be distinct entities, and not part of a continuum from normal mental wellbeing. His concepts entered the English language in 1902 with the publication of an abridged version of his *Lehrbuch der Psychiatrie.*[79]

Kraepelin's observations found a mixed reception in the UK, almost as diverse as Freud's.[80] Scottish professor George Robertson, one of the UK's foremost psychiatrists, challenged Kraepelin's research findings, and cited Charles Mercier's view that Kraepelin's account of dementia praecox was 'a rubbish-heap of symptoms with about as much definition of outline as a suet dumpling'. Robertson was also sceptical because he thought that neither chronic mental disability (dementia) nor onset in youth (praecox) were integral to the diagnosis, and that many patients fell outside the classification – a problem which Kraepelin himself acknowledged. Robertson, however, valued Kraepelin's clinical and research methods, which promoted accurate observation of patients.[81] Edward Mapother was also sceptical of Kraepelin's findings, more than his method, and contended that Kraepelin's views were widely accepted in Germany because of his personal networks with colleagues.[82]

Emil Kraepelin and Sigmund Freud were both born in 1856 and both were contentious figures. Nevertheless, among psychiatrists in Britain, Kraepelin's approach seems to have been appreciated more than Freud's. Kraepelin was elected an honorary member of the MPA, its highest honour, in 1909, just seven years after his work was translated into English; Freud had to wait until 1936 to receive the same, 23 years after his work began to enter the language.[83]

Infectious diseases, new and old

One of the mysteries challenging the medical profession by the 1920s was encephalitis lethargica. It was described as a new disorder in 1917 by Constantine von Economo, a neurologist and psychiatrist in Vienna. Increasing numbers of patients presented with symptoms following each receding wave of epidemic or pandemic influenza, but some patients had no clear history of that infection, and the nature of the encephalitis symptoms varied with each wave.[84] The sequence suggested that the influenza virus caused both disorders, although people suffering encephalitis were not infectious to others. The disorder gradually disappeared over the 1930s, but was immortalised in Dr Oliver Sacks' book *Awakenings* in 1973, and the subsequent film with the same title.[85] Psychiatrists in the 1920s described encephalitis lethargica's overlapping psychiatric and neurological symptoms as a 'picture of chaos', with a 'fickle course' that might end in recovery, death, or long-term neurological and behavioural symptoms.[86] Symptoms included restlessness, lethargy, and 'mental or moral deterioration with impulsive, mischievous or vicious behaviour … a contrast with the previous character'.[87] Patients responded poorly to all treatment, including exercise, occupational therapy and tonics. So-called improvements were probably part of the illness's fluctuating course rather than the effects of therapy.[88]

Encephalitis lethargica was difficult research territory. The nature of viruses, invisible under a traditional light microscope, was still speculative. The Board of Control, keen to work collaboratively to understand the cause and pathology and to develop treatments, took steps to bring patients to a few specialist centres, such as West Park Mental Hospital near Epsom and Littlemore Mental Hospital in Oxford, as well as other mental hospitals which had links to universities.[89] They made little progress; as Leslie Hoffman and Joel Vilensky wrote in 2017: 'Encephalitis lethargica was … the biggest medical mystery of the 20th century, and remains that to this day.'[90]

Patients in mental hospitals suffered high rates of infectious diseases. The mental hospital death rate attributed to the Spanish influenza pandemic of 1918–19 was around twice that of the general population.[91] Although epidemiological data were not age-matched between institution and community, given the large numbers involved the figures were likely to be statistically significant. As with many mental hospital problems, there was probably more than one reason for this. Patients' physical vulnerability associated with poor diet and overcrowding, failures to detect infections early on and to segregate those affected, and the practice of transferring mentally disturbed patients from general to mental hospitals when severely physically ill probably all contributed.[92] The high death rate from influenza was worrying, but that from tuberculosis, when eventually identified, was terrifying: in 1918 it was about 5,300 per 100,000 in the mental hospital population, compared to 170 per 100,000 in the general population – a 30-fold difference.[93]

To understand the occurrence and management of infectious diseases in the mental hospitals, particularly tuberculosis, one needs to step back to around the turn of the century. In 1899, Dr Francis Crookshank blamed the asylums for the high rates of tuberculosis, due to overcrowding, poor ventilation, lack of outdoor activity, unhygienic wards and poor diet.[94] An MPA committee was appointed to investigate. It concurred with Dr Crookshank and recommended urgent intervention.[95] Little was done. During WW1, the steep rise in mental hospital deaths did not point to staff directly failing in their duty of care resulting in suicide or injury, and since causes of death were the same as those pre-war, the Board of Control took little notice.[96] The Board finally became alarmed in September 1918. It sought the advice of the Chief Medical Officer, Sir Arthur Newsholme, and began to investigate.[97] Its 1919 report reiterated the earlier ideas, adding that the problems were compounded by wartime contingencies, including lack of fuel and heating, inadequate diet and the bitterly cold winter of 1916–17.[98] This emphasised causes outside the Board's direct control, enabling it to pass the buck rather than taking responsibility for vulnerable people under its care. In his historical analysis of the deaths, John Crammer argued that, in its zeal for the war effort, the Board 'abandoned the patients whose care they were supposed to safeguard' and that it was responsible for the excess mortality.[99] Crammer also laid some of the blame for the disaster of mental hospital infections on the fact that specialist healthcare institutions were governed by lay committees who lacked relevant understanding, 'ignorant of what work went on, or ought to have gone on', and who did not know when to seek specialist advice.[100]

The death rate from tuberculosis fell rapidly post-war, both in the community and in the mental hospitals. Why this happened is an unsolved mystery for which material changes do not fully account.[101] However, the fall may have contributed to a false sense of security in the mental hospitals regarding infectious diseases. Some visiting committees ignored the Board's report on tuberculosis, yet the Board affirmed its faith in them, stating: 'Asylum Authorities are alive to these difficulties, and … as far as possible, they will endeavour to improve existing conditions.'[102] The Buckinghamshire Mental Hospital, for example, continued to treat patients with tuberculosis 'amongst the ordinary sick', and the Board 'hoped', in 1919, that it would consider treating them separately and outdoors.[103] Given that mental hospitals had neglected the subject since Dr Crookshank's report, the Board's hope was perhaps wishful thinking.

In 1921, in addition to the established practice of the Board of Control receiving data on mortality in the mental hospitals, it began to obtain copies of the statutory notifications of infectious diseases at the time of diagnosis which the local authority Medical Officer of Health was obligated to collect. This had the potential to increase understanding of infections in the institutional setting and to lead to changes in practice.[104] However, the returns for some mental hospitals indicated that death rates from tuberculosis were higher than notifications of diagnosis, reinforcing the suspicion that some doctors failed to identify early stages of the disease, or did not inform the Medical Officer of Health, as was their duty. If the disease was not detected, patients suffering from it could not be separated from others, nor could they be given sanatorium-type treatment in the fresh air.[105] It seems likely that Lily F – mentioned earlier, admitted with dementia praecox in 1920 – suffered this fate, dying from tuberculosis in 1921.[106]

Many mental hospitals had designated isolation wards intended for patients with tuberculosis and other infections, but not all were used for the purpose, despite encouragement from the Board.[107] Mental hospitals which had more tuberculosis also had more instances of other infections, such as typhoid and dysentery,[108] suggesting a broader neglect of hygiene in some institutions than in others. While those diseases caused deaths in the public mental hospitals, they were almost non-existent in private and charitable institutions and in the community outside.[109] The rates of typhoid and dysentery fluctuated but did not decline during the 1920s, despite the Board reiterating advice on the safe handling of food and laundry, and on ward hygiene, such as using vacuum cleaners rather than brooms to avoid spreading germs.[110] The Board appeared surprised that typhoid was more common in women patients than men, and seemed to overlook the possibility that this may have been associated with women working in the hospital laundry, dealing with soiled and infected linen in less than ideal hygienic conditions. Tragically – and as the Board acknowledged – infectious diseases, and deaths from them, were potentially preventable.[111]

The assumption continued that mentally ill people were inherently more predisposed to injuries and physical illnesses than the general population. Given the limitations of research and statistical methodologies, distinguishing causes from chance associations was undoubtedly complicated, but also, much was known. The Board of Control intermittently offered sound advice, but blaming problems on patients or other factors outside its control was a convenient and inexpensive short-term management strategy, and that was what counted.

General paralysis of the insane (GPI): treating an infection with an infection

When 31-year-old Marjorie Eleanor A was admitted to Colney Hatch with early symptoms of GPI, she required transfer to the specialist unit at Horton Mental Hospital to receive the new treatment for the disorder:

inoculation with the parasites causing malaria. Permission to transfer her was sought from her father as her husband was abroad. Her father wrote to the doctor at Colney Hatch:

> Mrs A, my Daughter, has for some time been leading a sordid life and her child has been taken to a Fever Hospital suffering from Diptheria [*sic*]. The child I am willing to help as far as I am able if the Authorities will write and state what best to be done, but Mrs A I think is for her husband to deal with.[112]

Stemming from a sexually transmitted infection, much shame was associated with GPI. Despite this, confidentiality was not on the agenda regarding its treatment. Instead, the Board of Control was more concerned about gaining consent from relatives to protect the doctor and the hospital 'from the unpleasantness of an action at law', should the patient die during treatment.[113] Confidentiality and disclosure of clinical information is an ongoing subject of medical legal and ethical discussion,[114] but it is dubious whether disclosure to relatives to protect the practitioner in this way was, or is, ethical. Assumptions that mentally unwell people lacked judgement gave patients little opportunity to contribute to decisions about their own care, especially when combined with a paternalistic style of practice common across the medical profession, not just in psychiatry. Historian Agnes Arnold-Forster noted that, well into the twentieth century, surgeons considered a degree of paternalism necessary to manage the emotions and health of patients, especially those suffering from the most feared diseases.[115]

GPI was more common in men than women. In 1919, it accounted for 17 per cent of male mental hospital deaths, and 3 per cent of female. For men, it was second only to tuberculosis, which accounted for 24 per cent of deaths.[116] Clinical notes suggest that women with GPI tended to present at an earlier stage of the disease than men. Men were frequently admitted in extremis and close to death, giving the impression that their wife or lover had provided dedicated care for as long as possible. When George S, a commercial traveller, developed GPI and, typical of the disorder, became 'extravagant and foolish' and was found wandering in a confused state, he was taken to the police station, then to the workhouse and then certified. His wife accompanied him to Colney Hatch. She was aware that he had been 'going about with loose women'. She also knew he had been attending clinics at a local hospital, but did not know that it was for treatment of syphilis.[117]

In its late stages, syphilis could spread to various organs of the body, not just the brain. Highly toxic medications derived from mercury and arsenic could be used to treat it in most organs, but they did not cross into the brain so were ineffective for GPI.[118] Something different was needed. Over the centuries, some physicians had observed that fevers could alleviate symptoms of mental illness. In the 1880s, Dr Julius Wagner-Jauregg, working at the Vienna Asylum, observed this and it aroused his interest.[119] In 1917, he inoculated blood from a soldier with malaria, recently returned from Macedonia, into a patient with GPI.[120] He based the intervention on the theory that malaria produced high fevers which could kill the treponema pallidum, but, unlike other fevers, those caused by malaria could be controlled with quinine, allowing the treatment to be terminated should the patient react adversely to it. Nevertheless, it was still a desperate remedy for a desperate disease.

A combination of its mid-war timing, the need to translate reports from the German, incredulity at Wagner-Jauregg's findings, and other priorities post-war meant that malaria inoculation took time to reach clinicians in other countries.[121] It was first recorded as being used in the UK in 1922,[122] but only when a Wassermann test on cerebrospinal fluid confirmed the diagnosis.

As recognised for encephalitis lethargica, new medical challenges required collaborative approaches. The use of malaria-carrying mosquitoes to provide treatment necessitated cooperation between psychiatrists and tropical medicine experts. In 1922, Professors Stephens and Warrington Yorke at the Liverpool School of Tropical Medicine and Drs Ronald Clark and Alastair Grant at Whittingham Mental Hospital, Lancashire joined forces.[123] They inoculated three patients with malaria-infected blood from another patient. Two did well, and one failed to develop a fever.[124] This outcome inspired further activity. By the end of 1923, 19 institutions across England and Wales were providing the treatment, and a year later a total of 32 were doing so.[125]

There were two methods for inoculating malarial parasites to treat a person with GPI: blood from a person infected with malaria (whether or not they also had syphilis) could be injected into the recipient using a syringe, or an infected mosquito could be allowed to bite the recipient directly.[126] Families disliked the idea of blood from a patient with syphilis being injected into their relative, preferring the direct bite method. Fortunately, some evidence indicated that a direct bite was more effective.[127] To achieve that, an infective mosquito was transferred into a glass jar and the mouth of the jar covered with mosquito netting. The netting was placed against the patient's thigh, allowing the mosquito to bite through. The bites were painted with iodine to allay irritation and bandaged to prevent the patient from scratching them.[128]

Malaria treatment required close monitoring, so doctors needed to take a more medical approach than that which was customary on a mental hospital ward. Physical examinations and blood and urine tests underpinned decisions as to whether it was safe to continue treatment, or to terminate the fevers with quinine. With physical and mental debility due to GPI plus the malaria, some succumbed, and the rest were exhausted and profoundly anaemic by the end of treatment. Great efforts were made to improve their general health, including through good diet, fresh air and 'a moderate allowance of stout'.[129]

Not all institutions in the UK achieved the high cure rate reported from Vienna, but optimistic reports of malaria treatment appeared in newspapers, including the *Evening Standard* and the *Times*.[130] Patients began to request the treatment,[131] despite being aware of the risks of malaria due to their knowledge of wartime fatalities from it among soldiers stationed around the Mediterranean. Reports of locally transmitted infections from soldiers repatriated to England resulted in malaria being classed as a notifiable disease – also a requirement for the new treatment.[132] When an indigenous species of mosquito which could transmit malaria was found near mental hospitals which had not taken the precaution of nursing the patients 'in a mosquito proof ward during the period of their infectivity', the Ministry of Health demanded safer procedures.[133] Precautions also included arranging for mosquitoes to be bred in a 'mosquito-proofed' treatment block at Horton Mental Hospital, and from there dispatched to other hospitals.[134]

How best to evaluate the outcome of malaria treatment was a conundrum. A comparison group was needed, but treatment was being given, as far as possible, to everyone who was thought likely to benefit. Comparisons could not be made with past cohorts of untreated patients because earlier methods of diagnosis were less accurate than the new benchmark of diagnosis confirmed by a Wassermann test on cerebrospinal fluid. Ingeniously, Dr Edward Meagher decided to use data from 1922–4, just after malaria inoculation was introduced but before it became widespread, and to look at the long-term outcome (Table 4.2).[135]

Although not done by Meagher, a chi-square test on his data confirms his interpretation of the outcomes of treatment. Understanding the pathology of GPI and devising treatment for it inspired optimism that a physical basis would be found for other mental illnesses, which would then also become curable. This had implications for the direction of future

Table 4.2 Malaria treatment 1922–4 and its outcome in 1927.

	Died n, %	**In hospital in 1927 n, %**	**Discharged n, %**	**Total**
Treated with malaria 1922–4	191, 43.6	139, 31.7	108, 24.7	438
Untreated 1923–4	1016, 86.6	117, 10.0	40, 3.4	1173

Chi-square = 330.4892. p<0.0001

Data from: Meagher, *General Paralysis and its Treatment*, 37, 47. With thanks to Jacob Hilton for advice on statistics.

research and for clinical practice, including the need to treat at least some mentally unwell patients in general hospitals. Observations that treatment given in the early stages of GPI resulted in better outcomes[136] also backed up arguments supporting legal change, so that patients would be allowed to seek early help for mental disorders, rather than waiting for deterioration to justify Lunacy Act certification as a first step.

Other infections: focal sepsis and dentistry in the mental hospitals

Early in the 1920s, James Scott, a middle-aged journalist who 'engaged in literary and artistic work', became 'terribly run down'. A GP who visited him at home examined his teeth, told him that his troubles may have emanated from that source, and advised their extraction. He only had 13 teeth left at that time, and they were all removed. Mr Scott's mental state did not improve, so he was admitted to Brentwood Mental Hospital.[137] Removing his teeth was in line with the theory of 'focal sepsis', which postulated that a hidden and asymptomatic infection localised in one part of the body could affect other parts. London physician William Hunter, a stalwart of the theory, published his ideas in 1900, based on his own observations of individual patients, particularly after treating dental sepsis.[138]

With pointers that infections caused mental symptoms, psychiatrists seeking biological causes for mental disorders, and microbiology being a relatively new and in vogue discipline, psychiatry was not to be excluded from the fashion. One psychiatrist who believed that focal sepsis caused severe long-term mental disorders was Henry Cotton at Trenton State Hospital, New Jersey, USA. He treated his patients by surgically removing their teeth and their bodily organs which he considered harboured asymptomatic infections.[139] Thomas Chivers Graves, medical superintendent of the Birmingham Mental Hospitals at Rubery Hill and Hollymoor, was as close as Cotton got to a disciple in the UK. When Cotton visited Graves' hospitals in 1923, they concurred on much.[140] Graves had taken an unusual route into psychiatry: he trained first as a veterinarian, then in medicine, and then worked as a surgeon.[141] His surgical career probably drew him towards Cotton's methods. Graves, like Cotton, began by extracting the teeth of his mental hospital patients, and despite finding no benefit, he persisted on the strength of his belief in the theory, similar to the Board of Control advocating unproven practices in a desire to maintain a patient's hope.[142] Later, Graves encouraged patients to undergo removal of sinuses and tonsils, and introduced other anti-infection initiatives including vaccinations, colonic lavage and treatment with ultra-violet light.[143]

Concern about Cotton's methods in the early 1920s led to three US researchers, Drs Nicholas Kopeloff, George Kirby and Clarence Cheney, carrying out a case-controlled study.[144] The study demonstrated that Cotton's surgical procedures gave no benefit. Cotton, like Henderson, was a protégé of Adolph Meyer, and Meyer commissioned a third protégée, Dr Phyllis Greenacre, to investigate Cotton's methods. She presented her final results to Meyer late in 1925.[145] She was alarmed by the degree of harm Cotton was causing, but Meyer continued to encourage Cotton in his practice. The reasons for Meyer's stance, contrary to his more critical approaches in other areas of psychiatry, are unclear.[146] Cotton continued, and attended the RMPA's annual meeting in 1927.[147] William Hunter lectured at that meeting, reiterating his advice that '[t]he removal of the sepsis in all cases of mental disorder and insanity' was an urgent and initial treatment.[148] Henderson criticised Hunter's faulty methodology, stating that it was likely to 'make British psychiatry the laughing stock of the world'. Praising the recent studies by Kopeloff, Kirby and Cheney as 'infinitely better controlled than the work of Cotton', Henderson advised: 'Do not be led away by this toxic theory; investigate carefully the facts in every individual case, and do not jump to hasty conclusions.'[149]

In 1928, Graves lectured at Cotton's hospital. Unlike Cotton, Graves had moved to less aggressive surgical procedures. He no longer sought hidden foci of infection. Instead, he tried to treat chronic infections which followed obvious acute episodes, such as sinusitis after upper respiratory infection. He said that he had 'realized that most of the cases of more lasting improvement were those in which the patient had asked me to remove septic and aching teeth',[150] supporting the relationship between physically symptomatic infections and feeling mentally unwell, rather than hidden and otherwise asymptomatic assumed foci of infection. Graves shifted his practices in response to new evidence, in contrast to Hunter and Cotton who ignored feedback from multiple sources.

Sophisticated statistical approaches were emerging from the discipline of mathematics, but they were slow to be accepted in medical research.[151] Cotton was among those who ignored them. He also argued against other theories, claiming his own to be superior. He argued, for example, that 'Freudism has proven to be a tremendous handicap to psychiatry. For those who have built up this elaborate and fantastic scheme are not willing to consider any other factors, no matter what results have been shown.'[152] He opposed ideas of hereditary causes as fatalistic and stifling of investigation, and that they 'simply served as a cloak to hide our ignorance of other factors. For if we believed that the psychoses depended upon heredity, there [would be] no chance for us to prevent their occurrence.'[153] There was an element of truth in Cotton's words about other theories, but he failed to recognise that, like some of his colleagues who were also aggressively promoting their own ideas, he was blind to faults in his own theory. One is left with the impression that, despite the emergence of contradictory scientific evidence, arrogance and pig-headedness continued to underpin Cotton's attitudes and practices: as historian of psychiatry Andrew Scull noted, he 'had never been one to hide his light under a bushel'.[154]

Only after Henry Cotton's sudden death in 1933 were his disastrous methods abandoned. In other fields of medicine, focal sepsis theories continued to influence practice. In Ear, Nose and Throat surgery, for example, focal sepsis theory was the basis of what became known as 'routine' tonsillectomy for children.[155] In the UK, many thousands of children were subject to this procedure, and some died from it. Cotton is narrated as a historical pariah, but the historiography of tonsillectomy inspired by focal sepsis largely lets its advocates off the hook.[156] This suggests broader issues underpinning historical understanding of different medical specialties, such as suspicion towards psychiatrists primarily treating conditions affecting the brain and mind, contrasting with trust in surgeons and physicians treating physical disorders.

Frederick Broderick, a dentist in Cambridgeshire, opposed the wholesale removal of teeth in the search for so-called focal sepsis among mental patients. Instead, he regarded dental sepsis as 'the last straw in causing the breakdown and not the essential factor'.[157] Contemporaneous with the heyday of focal sepsis were discussions about dental hygiene and the need to improve dental services as part of preventative medicine for the whole population. In the mental hospitals, doctors caried out a basic oral examination when a patient was admitted, with a view to them receiving dental treatment while an inpatient. Reviewing admission notes for a hundred consecutive patients admitted to Colney Hatch between

1919 and 1921 (56 women, 44 men, aged 14–73 years, of whom eight were over 60 years) almost half had significant dental disease or decay.[158] One such patient was Vincenza G, an Italian-speaking domestic servant admitted with depression. She also had 'severe pyorrhoea' which was treated. She recovered mentally, was discharged, and she returned to her previous employment.[159] Treating both disorders may have facilitated her recovery, but coexisting conditions did not imply causation. The need to unravel correlation, causation and coincidental relationships between different conditions was recognised in the 1920s and remains challenging a century on.[160]

The Board of Control encouraged dental care in mental hospitals, including each patient having their own named toothbrush, and staff encouraging them to use it.[161] In 1923 the Board criticised hospitals which did not employ a dentist at least part time.[162] Appointing a dentist was part of making mental hospitals more like their general counterparts, providing active treatment and drawing on a range of specialties. Focal sepsis theory of physically asymptomatic infectious causes of mental disorders was wrong, but it nevertheless contributed to improving the standards of physical healthcare, and the mental wellbeing, of patients in mental hospitals in England.

Heredity, eugenics and sterilisation

It would be neglectful, in the context of 1920s biological theories about mental disorders, to overlook heredity and eugenics. The term 'eugenics' means influencing human reproduction through education, legal and biological means, justified by up-to-date scientific knowledge, to 'improve the biological quality of a population'.[163] Eugenics developed from the work of Sir Francis Galton (1822–1911) at UCL. His research, which assumed the primacy of genetics for many disorders, was tainted with Victorian race, sex and class prejudices, and statistical methods which failed to distinguish between cause and association.

Another nineteenth-century advocate for the importance of heredity was Bénédict Augustin Morel. His 'degeneration' theory proposed that insanity in a family arose at an earlier age and more severely in successive generations, so that in the third or fourth generation it is represented by severe mental deficiency, and the family line comes to an end. This mirrored Charles Darwin's theory on survival of the fittest, and aligned with the comment attributed to Victorian psychiatrist Sir Thomas Clouston, that it was 'Nature's method of killing off a bad stock'.[164] In the early twentieth century the opposite view was fashionable: the hereditarily diseased and insane would multiply until they swamped the rest of society.[165] These two standpoints could not both be correct, but in the context of the global traumas of WW1, the Spanish influenza pandemic and new thinking about the world's future, the envisioned population-swamping scenario frightened many. The Eugenics Society (founded as the Eugenics Education Society in 1907) aimed to promote public awareness of the existence of positive and negative hereditary qualities, and to encourage social responsibility regarding their transmission. In the 1920s, it also aimed to develop a research portfolio.[166]

Mental hospital patients in the UK in the 1920s were not directly subject to eugenics-related biological procedures such as sterilisation. However, debate about eugenics reflected, and had the potential to influence, public and professional conceptions of mental disorders, the people suffering from them, and the economics and policies around their care.[167] Eugenic ideas also linked to the organisation of mental institutions, including segregation by gender with little opportunity to meet the opposite sex.[168] In 1925, the MPA referred to 'the segregation from the public of those who, by reason of mental disorder or defect, impair the social machine by their inefficiency as citizens ... [T]he more thoroughly this is done the better for the home and for the nation.'[169] This pro-custodial message was out of keeping with the asylums' original recuperative purpose as envisaged by the County Asylums Act of 1845. It was also out of keeping with learning from shell shock and new moves towards establishing outpatient clinics, after-care and greater freedom for patients in the hospital environment. It was, however, in keeping with public concerns and social challenges, such as the state of the economy, restrictions on public expenditure and rising unemployment.[170]

Non-medical people latched on to the fear of those with mental difficulties overwhelming society and were vociferous in their call for eugenic measures. Lord Buckmaster was one who expressed his ideas in Parliament, with potential to influence a wide audience, but in a manner which did not promote debate:

> A matter that has struck every thinking man in recent years is the appalling fact that the reproduction of our population is taking place in inverse ratio to the value of the people who are reproduced, and, beyond all others, the people who are weak-minded reproduce their species at a rate that can only fill one with alarm ... the time has come when the whole question of this perpetuation of the utterly unfit, mentally weak and unsound should be the subject of full

investigation ... seeing whether it is not possible by some wise and humane means to extirpate from our race the curse under which, if we do not conquer it, we shall ourselves be ultimately destroyed.[171]

Given his preamble about 'every thinking man', it is unsurprising that no one opposed him. Politicians across the political spectrum, physicians, religious leaders and others interpreted eugenic theories variably to help formulate what they deemed to be their duties and responsibilities regarding future generations.[172]

Similar to focal sepsis, eugenic theories did not match evidence. The term 'hereditary tendency' was used speculatively in psychiatry to link disparate disorders.[173] In mental hospital practice a hereditary cause did not necessarily indicate a gloomy prognosis or preclude active treatment.[174] In 1921, David Bower, a psychiatrist in private practice, considered that 'hereditary insanity' might be more treatable than other forms, as 'it did not take much to send them over the border, neither did it require much of the right treatment to bring them back to normal'.[175] Sir Humphry Rolleston, president of the Royal College of Physicians, emphasised that despite 'the indubitable influence of *hereditas damnosa*', it is 'advisable to avoid exaggeration of such a fatalistic attitude by critical consideration of the limitations of this conception'.[176]

The message of improving the race through eugenics cut across geographies, cultures and religions, becoming an integral aspect of global modernity.[177] However, different countries had different views. Coming to terms with the huge loss of life in WW1, French officials feared population decline, while in Britain concerns were more about 'the over-prolific poor'.[178] In Germany in 1920, psychiatrist Alfred Hoche and lawyer Karl Binding proposed 'the destruction of life unworthy of life' for people considered a burden on the state.[179] Though debated, their call fell on fertile soil and germinated in the context of social, political and economic post-war turmoil.[180] Meanwhile, Ernst Rüdin researched psychiatric genetics in Kraepelin's department in Munich, where biological approaches to psychiatric illness were paramount.[181] Rüdin addressed the First International Congress on Mental Hygiene in Washington DC in 1930. John Lord attended the lecture and noted that Rüdin's views met with much opposition: the audience disputed his facts and urged caution because 'his scheme was not trustworthy and might lead to entirely fallacious conclusions'.[182]

Dr Redcliffe Salaman, a Cambridge University researcher in experimental genetics, was apologetic that he and his colleagues had held themselves aloof from the Eugenics Society at a time when they recognised that the Society was attempting to apply theories which lacked scientific genetic evidence.[183] The Eugenics Society proposed a Sterilisation Bill and, in 1927, sought guidance from the Board of Control to draw it up. It must have been a curious situation with discussions involving Major Leonard Darwin of the Eugenics Society and Ruth Darwin, a senior member of the Board of Control[184] – one a son, the other a granddaughter of Charles Darwin. Their personal Darwinian legacy may have created a conflict of interest regarding their objectives, a matter which is absent from the Board's archives.

Archibald Church, an MP and member of the Eugenics Society, introduced the Sterilisation Bill to Parliament in 1931. The bill was 'based on the willingness of those suffering mental defects to undergo an operation which will prevent them from bringing children into the world'; it would allow 'an experiment on a small scale' from which conclusions could be drawn with a view to introducing 'compulsory sterilisation of the unfit'. Hyacinth Morgan, a medically trained MP, opposed the bill. It was based on 'mostly moonshine … said to be in advance of public opinion, but it is really in advance of common sense and ordinary sanity'. It would

> lure the progressive world headlong into an abyss of degenerate civilisation. Some when inebriated see beetles; the eugenist, intoxicated, sees defectives … once the principle of maiming or mutilation is admitted, not for the benefit or health of the individual but for the good of others or the State acting for others, there is no brake to sliding down the slippery slope leading to the swamp of State penalisation, where we may get rid of all those obnoxious to the State.[185]

The bill went no further in Parliament, but led to a Departmental Committee on Sterilisation, of which both the panel and witnesses were largely medical. It reported in 1934, in favour of sterilisation.[186] By that time, Nazi Germany had introduced compulsory sterilisation for people with a variety of presumed hereditary mental and physical conditions. In Britain the sterilisation debate continued, but the committee's conclusions went no further towards legislation.

Reflections

Adolf Meyer announced optimistically in 1921 that 'modern psychiatry has found itself'.[187] Psychiatric practice in England was built on, challenged and intertwined with knowledge from earlier times, and incorporated new ideas, including from overseas. Conferences, journals and periods of study abroad contributed to psychiatrists' theories and practices. Better clinical research methodologies and analytical statistics were developing, albeit slowly. It was far from easy to judge the clinical relevance of research findings, but the self-congratulatory arrogance of some psychiatrists concerning their research, rather than a willingness to reconsider, was a dangerous trait. In England and Wales, clinical challenges in mental hospitals led to various lines of research, some undertaken collaboratively between hospitals and universities, with the potential for cross-fertilisation of research ideas.

From continental Europe came Freud's psychoanalysis, Wagner-Jauregg's malaria inoculation, Rüdin's eugenic explanations, and Kraepelin's longitudinal research approach and his insights into dementia praecox and manic depression. From the USA came Meyer's psychobiology, eclectic treatment approaches and theories of mental disorders as a continuum, as well as Cotton's discredited practices based on focal sepsis theory. In summing up how the USA and German-speaking countries informed UK psychiatry, historian Mathew Thomson commented that both contributed positive and negative theories and practices.[188]

New clinical ideas were slow to permeate mental hospitals in England. Hazel Morrison attributed this to an atmosphere of 'authority, influence, self-interest and deference',[189] but other more positive factors also contributed. There was a healthy professional scepticism in the UK regarding claims that certain practices benefited patients or cured mental diseases. Respected psychiatrists such as David Kennedy Henderson, Frederick Mott, John Lord and Edward Mapother critically evaluated new knowledge, which helped protect patients from harm arising from misleading research findings and unproven interventions proposed by dogmatic enthusiasts. In contrast to the caution urged by these and other like-minded psychiatrists, it is disconcerting that sometimes the Board of Control advocated ignoring statistics and adopting unproven methods.

Access to clinical investigations, alongside aims to treat patients in an 'atmosphere of cure',[190] raised issues of when and where patients should be offered help. More knowledge about the overlap between mental and physical disorders indicated the importance of accurate diagnosis to guide treatment, and the need to take advice from practitioners in other medical specialties. It also emphasised the importance of early diagnosis and treatment to achieve the best outcome for patients. For the population generally, that was advocated and offered for disorders deemed physical;

under the Lunacy Act, except for people able to pay privately, it was still unavailable for those with mental symptoms.

The desire to find preventative methods, helpful treatments and especially cures for severe chronic mental disorders remained inspiring and distant dreams. Though repeatedly thwarted, psychiatrists and their research collaborators did not abandon their hopes. Kraepelin summed up the combination of challenges facing psychiatrists:

> While we must be zealous in our immediate task of relieving symptoms, we must not lose sight of our main object – the struggle against the causes of insanity ... We must be prepared to face the fact that every step of the way will have to be trodden, and with untiring care and thoroughness.[191]

Whatever might be discovered, Dr Henry Devine offered sound advice to his colleagues: to 'look on our patients as persons and not as diseases – as human beings with difficulties to overcome'.[192]

Notes

1 Marie R, Reception orders etc 1919, TLA H12/CH/B/47/020; Autopsy book, female, 1918–19, 273, TLA H12/CH/B/22/015.
2 Henderson and Gillespie, *A Text-book of Psychiatry*, 89.
3 Craig, *Psychological Medicine*, 99.
4 Lord, The clinical study of mental disorders, 10.
5 Pereira, Psychiatry in Portugal; Evidence to Cobb Inquiry, Miss Bowhay, q. 822, TNA MH 58/219.
6 Berrios, British psychopathology since the early 20th century, 233.
7 Annie B, Reception orders etc 1922, TLA H12/CH/B/47/028.
8 Kate Z, Case notes 1928, TLA H12/CH/B/16/009.
9 Henderson and Gillespie, *A Text-book of Psychiatry*, 66–7.
10 Cronin, *The Citadel*, 67–9.
11 Swamanantha S, Case notes 1918–19, TLA H12/CH/B/17/003.
12 Sarah C, Case notes 1920–1, TLA H12/CH/B/16/004.
13 Tiemersma et al., Natural history of tuberculosis.
14 Jones, 'An atmosphere of cure', 414.
15 Loughran, Shell shock, 112.
16 Pierce, Psychiatry a hundred years ago, 233–4.
17 Loughran, Shell shock, 112.
18 MacArthur, *Mental Hospital Manual*, 165–6.
19 Hare, Old familiar faces, 86.
20 Anon., 'Death chamber'.
21 Colney Hatch Sub-Com, Mr Skipper, 5 Aug 1921, 145–8, TLA LCC/MIN/01010.
22 Injuries sustained by patients, medical journal, female 1924–5, TLA H12/CH/B/20/014.
23 Wallis, *Investigating the Body*, 101–40.
24 da Costa, *Modern Surgery*, 477.
25 BoC minutes, Bertha M, 2 Jul 1930, 119, TNA MH 50/58.
26 Lamb, Social skills.
27 Shorter, The history of nosology.
28 Morrison, Henderson and Meyer in correspondence, 72.

29 Henderson and Gillespie, *A Text-book of Psychiatry* (10th edn).
30 Morrison, Henderson and Meyer in correspondence, 73.
31 BoC, *Annual Report for 1927*, Part 2, 43.
32 Lord, The clinical study of mental disorders, 46.
33 Mott, The investigation of some of the causes of insanity, 647.
34 Gelder, Adolph Meyer and his influence, 419.
35 Miller, Twentieth century British clinical psychology and psychiatry, 158; Menzies, The mechanism of involutionary melancholia.
36 Stoddart, A brief résumé, 1.
37 Stoddart, A brief résumé, 8; Macpherson, The ninth Maudsley lecture, 389.
38 Bolton, The myth of the unconscious mind, 38.
39 Mercier, Psycho-analysis, 897.
40 Mercier, Psycho-analysis, 900.
41 Lord, *Mental Hospitals and the Public*, 20.
42 Scull, Creating a new psychiatry, 390.
43 Jones and Rahman, Framing mental illness, 114, citing Slater, Mapother memorial, 7.
44 Elgood, The asylum as it should be, 292, 293.
45 Menzies, The mechanism of involutionary melancholia, 413.
46 McCowan and Quastel, Blood-sugar studies; Anderson, The sedimentation velocity of erythrocytes.
47 Anon., The reproach of psychiatry.
48 Letter, Dr Bond to Dr Beaton, 15 Mar 1923, TNA FD 1/1396; BoC, *Annual Report for* 1925, 11.
49 Meeting and correspondence, Dr Beaton and Dr Thomson, 6–7 Apr 1922, TNA FD 1/1396.
50 MPA Sub-com on post-graduate teaching and the diploma in psychiatry. Draft letter to universities which do not have a DPM, 23 Feb 1922, Minute Book 1915–23, Royal College of Psychiatrists archives, Box B006.
51 BoC, *Annual Report for 1920*, 12.
52 Steinberg, The sin in the aetiological concept of Johann Christian August Heinroth, 442.
53 Ferrier, Mortality in Victorian asylums, 243.
54 Ferrier, Mortality in Victorian asylums, 240.
55 Sturdy, Scientific method for medical practitioners, 776.
56 Marie B, Post-mortem reg female 1919–22, TLA H12/CH/B/22/016.
57 Instructions for completing death certificate c.1920, TLA H12/CH/B/16/009.
58 BoC, *Annual Report for 1928*, Part 1, 3.
59 Sakula, A hundred years of lumbar puncture, 174.
60 BoC, *Annual Report for 1923*, 29, Horton Mental Hospital, LCC, 9 Nov 1923.
61 BoC, *Annual Report for 1924*, 20.
62 Minutes for med sup, Colney Hatch, 21 Mar and 11 Apr 1919, TLA H12/CH/A/02/005.
63 Braslow and Marder, History of psychopharmacology.
64 Lehmann, Before they called it psychopharmacology.
65 Rosetta S, Case notes 1920–1, TLA H12/CH/B/16/004.
66 Day, *Rivers of Damascus*, 198.
67 MacArthur, *Mental Hospital Manual*, 80.
68 MacArthur, *Mental Hospital Manual*, 83.
69 MacArthur, *Mental Hospital Manual*, 38.
70 Lomax, *The Experiences of an Asylum Doctor*, 103.
71 Lomax, *The Experiences of an Asylum Doctor*, 99–100.
72 Evidence to Cobb Inquiry, Dr David Thomson, q. 3,340, TNA MH 58/220; Lionel Weatherly, q. 1,677–9, TNA MH 58/219.
73 MoH, *Report of the Committee on Administration* (Cobb Report), 76, 77.
74 MoH, *Report of the Committee on Administration* (Cobb Report), 113.
75 BoC, Circular 715, Nov 1928, TNA MH 51/240.
76 BoC, *Annual Report for 1930*, Part 1, 48.
77 Lily F, Case notes 1920–1, TLA H12/CH/B/16/004.
78 Anon., Medico-Psychological Association, *JMS* 1906, 820; Mapother, Emil Kraepelin, 512; Kahlbaum, The clinico-diagnostic perspective.
79 Diefendorf, *Clinical Psychiatry*, v.
80 Shorter, *A History of Psychiatry*, 108–9.

81 Robertson, Is dementia præcox a definite clinical entity?, 529–30; Kraepelin, Ends and means, 117.
82 Mapother, Emil Kraepelin, 512–13.
83 Bewley, Online archive, 34, Honorary members and fellows.
84 Auden, Encephalitis lethargica, 648; Marshall, The mental aspects of epidemic encephalitis, 592.
85 Foley, *Encephalitis Lethargica*, 1–2; Sacks, *Awakenings*.
86 Mackenzie, Epidemic encephalitis, 567; Marshall, The mental aspects of epidemic encephalitis, 589.
87 BoC, Circular 634, Encephalitis Lethargica, 7 Apr 1924, TNA MH 51/240.
88 Gillespie, Treatment of post-encephalitis, 412, 415.
89 BoC, Circular 634, Encephalitis Lethargica, 7 Apr 1924, TNA MH 51/240; BoC, *Annual Report for 1925*, 99; Letters, BoC and med sup, Dr Vincent, South Yorks Mental Hospital, May 1926, TNA MH 51/617.
90 Hoffman and Vilensky, Encephalitis lethargica, 2251.
91 BoC, *Annual Report for 1919*, Part 1, 29.
92 County and City of Worcester Lunatic Asylum, *Sixty-Sixth Annual Report*, 11, 27.
93 BoC, *Annual Report for 1919*, Part 1, 29; Drolet, World War I and tuberculosis, 691.
94 Crookshank, The frequency, causation, prevention, and treatment of phthisis, 667.
95 Menzies, Some points connected with tuberculosis in asylums.
96 Hilton, *Civilian Lunatic Asylums*, 215.
97 BoC minutes, 18 Sept 1918, 240–1, TNA MH 50/46.
98 BoC, Circular 532, Increased annual death rate in asylums, 15 Jan 1919, MH 51/239.
99 BoC, *Annual Report for 1917*, Part 1, 23; Crammer, Extraordinary deaths, 441.
100 Crammer, Extraordinary deaths, 440.
101 Murray, Tuberculosis and World War I, 411–14.
102 Crammer, Extraordinary deaths, 437–8; BoC, *Annual Report for 1919*, Part 1, 35.
103 BoC, *Annual Report for 1923*, Bucks Mental Hospital, 29 Oct 1923, 120–1.
104 BoC, *Annual Report for 1922*, 22.
105 BoC, *Annual Report for 1930*, Part 1, 35.
106 Lily F, Case notes 1920–1, TLA H12/CH/B/16/004.
107 BoC, Circular 627, Isolation hospital queries, 2 Jan 1924, TNA MH 51/240; BoC, *Annual Report for 1930*, 35.
108 BoC, *Annual Report for 1924*, 45.
109 BoC, *Annual Report for 1921*, 39.
110 BoC, *Annual Report for 1928*, Part 1, 30; BoC, *Annual Report for 1925*, 27; Shaw, Infection in mental hospitals, 24.
111 BoC, *Annual Report for 1925*, 29.
112 Marjorie A, Reception orders etc 1927, TLA H12/CH/B/47/035.
113 Letter, BoC to Dr Ronald Clark, Whittingham, regarding consent from relatives about giving malaria inoculation, 25 Jun 1923, TNA MH 51/697.
114 Beauchamp, Informed consent, 515.
115 Arnold-Forster, *Cold, Hard Steel*, 40.
116 BoC, *Annual Report for 1919*, Part 2, 39.
117 George S, Case notes 1920–1, TLA H12/CH/B/17/004.
118 Marshall and Ffrench, *Syphilis and Venereal Diseases*, 251.
119 Whitrow, Wagner-Jauregg and fever therapy, 294–5.
120 Shorter, *A History of Psychiatry*, 193.
121 Monrad-Krohn, Regarding the treatment of general paralysis, 46.
122 Scripture, The treatment of general paralysis by malaria.
123 Grant, The treatment of general paralysis by malaria.
124 BoC, *Annual Report for 1922*, 81.
125 BoC, *Annual Report for 1923*, 71; *Annual Report for 1924*, 102.
126 BoC, *Annual Report for 1923*, 85.
127 Anon., The first international malaria congress.
128 Nicol, The care and management of induced malaria, 210–11.
129 Nicol, The care and management of induced malaria, 213–16.
130 Anon., Medico-Psychological Association, *JMS* 1923; Anon., To cure insanity. *Evening Standard*, 5 Mar 1923, TNA MH 51/697; Our Medical Correspondent, Disease as cure.

131 Letter, Dr Ronald Clark, Whittingham, to Dr Bond, BoC, 21 Jul 1923, TNA MH 51/697.
132 Brabin, Malaria's contribution to World War One, 10, 14; Anon., The Board of Control (England and Wales) and the malarial treatment of general paralysis, 338; BoC, Circular 631, Feb 1924, TNA MH 51/697; Public Health (pneumonia, malaria, dysentery, etc.) Regulations, 1919, TNA MH 51/697.
133 Letter, Col James to Dr Bond, 14 Nov 1923, TNA MH 51/697.
134 Nicol, Care and management, 209.
135 Meagher, *General Paralysis and its Treatment*, 37, 47.
136 Grant and Silverston, Malaria therapy, 88.
137 Scott, *Sane in Asylum Walls*, 13–14; MACA, Case agenda book, 4 Nov 1925, WL SA/MAC/G.2/6.
138 Hunter, Oral sepsis.
139 Cotton, The relation of chronic sepsis, 434.
140 Scull, *Madhouse*, 226–8.
141 Anon., Obituary notices, TC Graves.
142 Scull, *Madhouse*, 117; BoC, *Annual Report for 1928*, Part 1, 3.
143 Jones et al., The Maudsley Hospital, 373.
144 Kopeloff and Cheney, Studies in focal infection; Kopeloff and Kirby, Focal infection and mental disease.
145 Scull, *Madhouse*, 184.
146 Scull, *Madhouse*, 272.
147 Anon., Royal Medico-Psychological Association, the annual dinner, 729.
148 Hunter, Chronic sepsis, 561.
149 Anon., Royal Medico-Psychological Association, 721–2.
150 Graves, The relation of unresolved infective processes, 32.
151 Magnello, The introduction of mathematical statistics.
152 Cotton, The relation of chronic sepsis, 439.
153 Cotton, The relation of chronic sepsis, 438.
154 Scull, *Madhouse*, 61.
155 Hilton, Our values and our historical understanding.
156 Dwyer-Hemmings, 'A wicked operation'.
157 Broderick, Dental sepsis, 1,391.
158 Case notes 1919–21, TLA H12/CH/B/14/005 and H12/CH/B/15/003.
159 Vincenza G, Case notes 1930–1, TLA H12/CH/B/14/012.
160 Coombs, Mental disorder in cardiac disease, 253; Zaniletti et al., How to distinguish correlation from causation.
161 BoC, *Annual Report for 1923*, 254, Menston Mental Hospital, Yorkshire 19 Jan 1923.
162 BoC, *Annual Report for 1923*, 133, Denbigh Mental Hospital, North Wales, 26 Jun 1923.
163 Roelcke, Eugenic concerns, 19.
164 Robertson, The seventh Maudsley lecture, 474.
165 Lewis, Fertility and mental illness.
166 Eugenics Education Society to MRC request for funding, 24 Oct 1923, TNA FD 1/1396.
167 Fennell, *Treatment without Consent*, 83.
168 Bond, The position of psychological medicine, 423.
169 Anon., The ninth and tenth annual reports, 560.
170 Thomson, *The Problem of Mental Deficiency*, 60.
171 Mental Treatment Bill, *Hansard*, 3 May 1923.
172 Turda, Legacies of eugenics, 2470.
173 Younger, *Insanity in Everyday Practice*, 6.
174 Hilton, *Civilian Lunatic Asylums*, 91.
175 Bower, Medico-Psychological Association, 111.
176 Rolleston, Discussion on prophylaxis, 781.
177 Turda, Legacies of eugenics, 2,472.
178 Olszynko-Gryn and Rusterholz, Reproductive politics, 119.
179 Binding and Hoche, *Allowing the Destruction of Life Unworthy of Life*.
180 Mueller and Beddies, 'The destruction of life unworthy of living'.
181 Roelcke, Eugenic concerns, 20.
182 Lord, American psychiatry and its practical bearings, 459–60.
183 Salaman, Mental health.

184 BoC, FW memo, 8 Feb 1927, Sterilisation: Draft Bill proposed by Eugenics Society, 1927–30, TNA MH 51/547.
185 Sterilization, *Hansard,* 21 Jul 1931.
186 Departmental Committee on Sterilisation, *Report.*
187 Jones et al., The Maudsley Hospital, 371–2.
188 Thomson, Mental hygiene in Britain, 150.
189 Morrison, Henderson and Meyer in correspondence, 83.
190 Jones, 'An atmosphere of cure', 412–21.
191 Kraepelin, Ends and means, 143.
192 BoC, *Conference on Lunacy Administration*, 82.

5
Regulatory culture: structure and staff

In the immediate post-war climate of optimism, there was public and official energy to acknowledge deficits in healthcare and social welfare, and to seek improvements. Aiming to centralise and coordinate all health and welfare administration, the Liberal-Conservative coalition Government, led by David Lloyd George, established the Ministry of Health. A coordinated approach was a wise move politically and socially. It aligned with the ideals of the upcoming Labour Party, which recognised the importance of health to individual and national wellbeing, and with the view that the war had stemmed from a European mental malaise.[1] The new Ministry's remit was broad, and mental healthcare would need to fight for its position on the ladder of priorities.

Throughout the 1920s, mental hospitals across England and Wales had to conform to the Lunacy Act 1890. In addition to shaping patients' admission and discharge procedures, the Act set out the rules for the workings of the institutions. Many rules demanded detailed administrative record keeping so that the Board of Control could ensure compliance with the law, in line with its statutory duty of regulatory oversight of the institutions. At all levels, 'worship of red tape' and 'unnecessary clerical work' contributed to distracting staff from caring for patients.[2]

Organising and managing the public mental hospitals was a vast and complex enterprise. For comparison in terms of size, those institutions had around a hundred thousand beds, similar to the total bed complement across all medical specialties in the National Health Service in England in 2024, although clearly with different patterns of usage.[3] The Lunacy Act and the Board of Control delegated authority to the county and borough councils, which appointed the visiting committees to administer each mental hospital in conjunction with the institution's senior staff or 'officers'. Others from outside the control hierarchy asked questions, made demands, and required responses from it. They included patients and their relatives, medical and nursing individuals and professional organisations, trades unions, the press, parliamentarians, campaigners and reformers. Observations from outside could be a tool for parties inside to rethink their activities and sense of direction. However, within the system, fear of criticism, defensiveness, secrecy and the desire of the leadership at all levels to maintain their institutional and personal reputations did not facilitate optimum provision for patients.

The style of mental hospital administration resembled that often found in 'total institutions' in the 1950s, defined by Erving Goffman as places of 'residence and work where a large number of like-situated individuals, cut off from the wider society for an appreciable period of time, together lead an enclosed, formally administered round of life'.[4] Early in 1921, the *Medical Press and Circular*, a doctors' rag which flourished on controversy and challenged the reliability of unscientific medical authority, published a report stating that 'callousness and indifference' permeated the whole system of asylum administration. The culture involved all staff, who 'inhale this atmosphere all their lives, and this cannot help being reflected in their official attitude to their charges'.[5] The institutional leadership modelled a culture and behaviours which arguably influenced the way staff interacted with the patients. Therefore, to understand patients' experiences during their mental hospital stay, it is necessary to understand the workings of the whole system at all levels.

This chapter primarily concerns how the institutional hierarchy, and powerful others outside it, affected patients' daily lives. It includes leadership and decision making, and the roles, responsibilities and activities of hospital personnel mainly above the ranks of the frontline staff whose day-to-day contact with patients was probed in chapter three. The chapter begins by exploring some new challenges for the mental hospitals which arose at the end of the war, and which set an inauspicious start for them into the long 1920s. It then discusses the management and leadership, starting at the top with the Ministry of Health and Board of Control, then the local authorities, Boards of Guardians and visiting committees. It moves on to the doctors and nurses and how they dealt with the challenges they faced, from both within and beyond their own professional groups. I will also discuss one long-running matter which illustrates the complexity of making changes – that of crossing the gender line of the usually gender-segregated institutions, including employing women nurses to care for disturbed mentally unwell male patients, and women doctors to work across both 'sides' of the institution.

Archival and published sources concerning administrative processes reveal disparate and pressing agendas and require cautious interpretation. For both lay and professional readerships, the press provided information, but often with partisan motives. The magazine of the National Asylum Workers' Union (NAWU) provided a forum where staff could express their views about their workplace experiences anonymously, in a way which was impossible within the hospital where they feared recriminations for doing so. However, anonymity raises issues, touched on in chapter one – including about provenance, accountability and reliability – creating challenges applicable at the time and for historians today. The NAWU also had an editorial say in its magazine, and was more likely to publish submissions which aided its objectives. Alongside their criticisms, many contributors also made constructive suggestions about improvements.[6] Whether their comments stimulated action was another matter: WG from Warwick wrote that they would 'have as much effect as a mosquito kicking an elephant'.[7]

In the aftermath of the war

When the war ended, the population was exhausted and restless for change. For the nursing staff, as Niall McCrae and Peter Nolan described in *The Story of Nursing in British Mental Hospitals*, this early post-war time was a 'return to strife'. Nurses' wartime hundred-hour working week continued, and 'conditions of service had never been worse'. Staff were desperate, including for reduced hours, more palatable food, better bathroom facilities, and not to be expected to sew their own uniforms in their spare time. More of them joined the NAWU.[8] There were several strikes, such as when some 'small changes' were made to leave and pay: what was 'small' to the authorities was a last straw to a fragile workforce.[9]

The Government had no clear demobilisation strategy when hostilities ceased. It advised that those with jobs to go to should be demobbed first. On those grounds, the Board of Control sought early demobilisation for hospital staff.[10] However, many men with jobs to return to were also among the last to be called up. The Government's plan met with soldiers' protests, so it changed the strategy to allow the longest serving to be released first.[11] The Ministry of Labour, though, had other ideas. It sought early release of 'those persons whose services are most urgently required', and it invited visiting committees to submit a list of names, up to a maximum of 25 per cent of the total number still serving.[12] At Colney Hatch Mental Hospital, it took almost two years for the full cohort of servicemen to return to hospital employment.[13] The situation was particularly difficult regarding medical staff, given that most doctors were male, and that many were still needed in the war hospitals.

There were many staff changes in the mental hospitals, on both male and female sides, with people returning to or beginning work after four years of extraordinary experiences. Employers were obligated to re-engage their war-disabled former staff, which meant adapting to their needs – a departure from the usual practice of only employing staff who could conform to the institution's norms.[14] At Colney Hatch, former nurse Allison Bertie Gatward had been 'severely wounded', but returned to work in June 1919 on afternoon shifts only, to help ease him in. He later became head male nurse, leading the male side of the hospital.[15] Another former nurse, George Alfred Snowden, survived nine months in the Machine Gun Corps in France, and was re-employed as a telephone operator, only later returning to the more strenuous and emotionally taxing job of nursing.[16] Chief tailor Charles Henry Beamon had also served in France. His injuries meant that he was no longer able to cut cloth, but he was allowed to retain his status and leadership in the tailoring workshop, taking charge of the stock, keeping the accounts and supervising work. However, his salary was reduced to help pay for a new cutter to carry out the tasks he could not do.[17] Re-employment was offered, but without salary protection it was hardly in line with David Lloyd George's objective of making the country fit for heroes.

The urgency with which demobilised soldiers sought work could be exploited by visiting committees. An argument broke out at Exeter City Mental Hospital after the medical superintendent informed Mr Glanville, a carpenter with 28 years' service, that his wages would not be increased as 'he did not consider him worth Trade Union rates'. Mr Glanville replied that, as a carpenter, he could not judge a doctor's work, and a doctor lacked competence to judge his.[18] He was dismissed for insolence and, in his support, a strike followed.[19] Forty-one of a total 73 staff walked out from this small, two hundred-bed public mental hospital. It took just three days to fill the male vacancies, mainly with demobilised soldiers, and the female vacancies, mainly with married former staff living locally. The Ministry of Labour and the NAWU tried to mediate, but the visiting committee was adamant that it would not negotiate, on the grounds that it was a 'question of discipline'.[20] When the strike was finally called off after several months, the hospital refused to reinstate any of the strikers. Not only had they lost their jobs, but by being dismissed they had also forfeited their non-transferable pension contributions.[21] Rules took priority over showing compassion or trying to understand the needs of staff and patients as individual human beings.

The Ministry of Health and the Board of Control

The Ministry of Health brought fragmented preventative and ameliorative health services, social welfare and housing into a single government department, and oversight of the Board of Control shifted from the Home Office to the Ministry. Leaving a government department orientated to law and order, and joining one focussing on health and welfare, suggests a shift in government attitudes towards mentally unwell people, mental hospitals, psychiatry as a branch of medicine, and mental nursing as part of the nursing profession.[22] Bringing the Board under the Ministry also had the potential to better integrate mental and general hospitals, facilitate preventative public mental health measures and help alleviate mental hospital stigma.[23]

Despite the move, changes in the Board's practices were minimal. A contributory factor may have been its longstanding inflexible, defensive style of leadership. This rigidity may have been enhanced by its wartime experience of working with the military to create, staff and organise the war hospitals located in the requisitioned asylums.[24] The Lunacy Act 1890, then in its fourth decade, was correspondingly rigid; as Kathleen Jones summarised in *Asylums and After*: 'Nothing was left to chance, and very little to future development'.[25] Despite the unrelenting statutory obligations imposed by the Act, the Board had an 'astonishing degree of freedom' and autonomy in determining how it went about its tasks. Symbolic of its independence, for many years it had its own offices, away from those of other government departments, and it had an unconventional telegraphic address: 'Avicenna, Sowest, London'. Avicenna (or Ibn Sina) was an eleventh-century Muslim philosopher and physician.

According to Bridget Towers' historical analysis of the inquiry into the public mental hospitals in 1922, senior civil servants in the Ministry, notably Sir Arthur Robinson and Sir Aubrey Symonds, sought to maintain the impression that it was enlightened and reformist, and they were anxious to avoid adverse publicity about poor standards of healthcare. The Ministry therefore needed a clear understanding of the Board of Control's role, and intended to keep a close eye on its activities.[26] That included the Ministry forbidding the Board from sending circulars to medical superintendents and local authorities without it first vetting the contents.[27]

Dr Haydn Brown was not a psychiatrist but had visited a number of mental hospitals. He regularly wrote to the press and was not one to mince his words.[28] He commented in the *Medical Press and Circular* that the Lunacy Act made 'officials hardened and narrowed down to the strict performance of a sufficient duty and nothing more'.[29] The Board's obligation to ensure compliance with the Act meant that its main weekly meetings were preoccupied with legalities, administrative procedures and data collection – the vital statistics it was required to gather.[30] Promoting humane and therapeutic care appeared secondary, and not stepping beyond its remit could let harmful practices pass unaccounted for. One of the Board's duties was to monitor deaths of certified patients. However, if a patient sustained an injury, such as on a mental observation ward shortly before certification, but died after certification, the Board delved no further.[31] The responsibility for happenings on the observation wards was officially outside the Board's remit, and the minutes provide no indication that it requested the authorities responsible for those wards to investigate such incidents. The number of 'escapes' was likewise recorded regularly, but without evidence of discussion about why they were happening, how to prevent them, what happened to the patient when 'recaptured' or their longer-term outcome.[32] The Board prioritised compliance with the letter of the law. Dr Isabel Wilson, appointed to the Board in the early 1930s, wrote: '[T]here was a great burden of onerous, responsible and heartbreaking work which, however, went only a little way towards serving the purpose for which it was intended, and which we who were caught up in this elaborate machinery considered to be largely a waste of time.'[33]

In her study of mental institutions in England and Scotland, Gillian Allmond referred to a prominent safety-first approach across the administrative hierarchy in England, particularly regarding the risk of patients harming themselves. In contrast, the equivalent authorities in Scotland, bound by the Lunacy Act (Scotland) 1857, emphasised the importance of patients' liberty and individuality.[34] This may have been influenced by stipulations about inspecting the institutions. In England, the Lunacy Act 1890 demanded that each inspection must be carried out by a minimum of two Board members, at least one of whom must be a medical practitioner and another a lawyer. By contrast, lawyers did not undertake mental hospital inspections in Scotland, which may have contributed to the less legalistic, and arguably more successful, approach there.[35]

The Lunacy Act also listed various aspects of patients' daily lives which it required the Board to scrutinise. These included diet, attendance at religious services, and any 'system of coercion' taking place.[36] The Board sought to verify compliance by examining mandatory registers and other documents, without any serious attempt to gain perspectives from patients or ward staff. Inspection descriptions and recommendations were made public in the Board's annual reports in years when manpower and finances permitted the inclusion of such a lengthy appendix. The Board both praised high standards and named and shamed institutions and medical superintendents where it considered that practices fell short.

The Board's papers give the impression that enforcing the letter of the law took precedence over the wellbeing of patients and that it sought to protect its authority and reputation at all costs.[37] Its defensiveness inhibited impartial investigation of problems in which it might be implicated. The Board's self-protectiveness was also expressed by an entire file dedicated to 'misstatements' made in the press which might reflect negatively on its leadership. An internal memorandum in this file referred to any Board investigation of negative press comments being 'with a view to clearing up the obvious misstatements',[38] rather than trying to identify any truths behind them which might help put the alleged wrongs to right.

Distrust of the Board of Control surfaced repeatedly, from the public, the Chief Medical Officer, the Ministry, the medical profession, and others with various roles relating to the mental hospitals.[39] Dr Risien Russell, a neurologist and supporter of the National Society for Lunacy Reform, considered the Board's oversight 'an elusory safeguard'.[40] Dr Ethel Bentham MP described the Board as 'mysterious and awful', and Mr John Jones MP summed up as follows:

> Once sentenced to death so far as the ordinary mental institution is concerned, there is no hope of reprieve. One is under the control of the Board of Control – an unapproachable body. You can write letters, you can send appeals, but you get the old stereotyped reply every time.[41]

Lack of trust and respect for the Board did not inspire the confidence of people outside, or lower in the organisational hierarchy, in ways which might enable constructive dialogue. A 1930 Board memorandum following a meeting with Dr Edward Mapother of the Maudsley Hospital recorded that he wanted 'to build Maudsleys everywhere and to keep them as far as possible outside the jurisdiction of the Board of Control and, indeed, of all Government departments'.[42]

Local authorities, visiting committees and the dilemmas of managing an institution

Local authorities provided the tier of mental hospital organisation below the Board of Control. That might have been a single county or borough council with just one mental hospital, or a large urban amalgamation of boroughs, such as the London County Council (LCC), with multiple hospitals. These local authorities had direct responsibility for financing the institutions' buildings and estates, while the Poor Law Boards of Guardians paid the maintenance fees for each patient. Falling under the Poor Law designated each patient a 'pauper lunatic', although that term, widely disliked, was becoming obsolete. Instead, the less stigmatising term 'rate-aided patient' was being adopted in advance of formal legal change, in the hope that care would eventually be funded directly from local general taxation – 'the rates' – independent of the Guardians.

In 1922, Professor George Robertson noted that the 'financial burden of caring for the insane is not borne by the ratepayers without complaint'.[43] In the opinion of former asylum attendant Paul Elgood, mental hospitals were, 'so to speak, run by the ratepayers, and, as generally happens in all such cases, efficiency had to play second fiddle to economy'.[44] Around the same time, in *The Experiences of an Asylum Doctor*, Dr Montagu Lomax referred to the welfare of patients being 'pitted against the cost to the ratepayers' and psychiatrist Lionel Weatherly declared: 'Damn such economy.'[45] Extricating mental hospitals from the Poor Law might remove the 'pauper lunatic' label, but whether it could shift the associated cultural mindset of pauper un-deservingness, which was likely to influence standards of care, was less clear.[46]

Visiting committees, appointed from among elected local councillors, both managed the hospital and represented the ratepayers' interests.[47] The committees therefore faced a conflict of interests: on the one hand, keeping costs down in the interests of the local ratepayers, and on the other, providing adequately for patients. Prioritising low short-term expenditure kept them in favour with the electorate, but that encouraged cheaper custodial practices rather than therapeutic interventions, even though the latter had the potential to improve long-term outcomes for patients, and ultimately to reduce costs.

A visiting committee was responsible for managing each institution and providing for all aspects of patients' lives. The committee had to consider directives from above, which at Colney Hatch included instructions from both the Board of Control and the LCC. Within the hospital, the visiting committee took its lead from the medical superintendent, the institution's senior doctor, but he (as yet no woman had that role in a public mental hospital) was the visiting committee's employee. He had to reconcile his advice to meet the committee's goals, sometimes kow-towing to their demands, else he risked losing his job. The committee also worked with, and took guidance from, other salaried senior hospital staff including the matron, chaplain, farm bailiff, chief engineer, and those who led the various utility departments and workshops. Dr Charles Mercier's 1894 book on managing lunatic asylums was still the standard work on the subject,[48] suggesting that many well-entrenched practices were still accepted, and that there was little recent innovation or creativity to make provision more compatible with twentieth-century social expectations.

A visiting committee was obliged to inspect its institution at least every two months. That included seeing all the patients and providing them with 'full opportunity of complaint'.[49] In a large institution that was an unrealistic – if not impossible – task in terms of establishing a process that would be meaningful for patients, yet the law had to be obeyed. Consequently, attempts to comply included gathering patients together, often in the presence of staff, and asking them as a group if they wanted to say anything.[50] It was a near futile way of encouraging honest feedback, especially if the feedback was negative and patients felt intimidated by staff. Some staff regarded the inspection process as unhelpful, such as Dr Octavia Wilberforce, who was delegated to escort committee members round the hospital where she worked. She commented that they 'only come to pry and pick holes if they can'.[51] The Poor Law Guardians were also obligated to inspect the mental hospitals in which they paid for patients. Their inspection reports at Colney Hatch were formulaic and bland, and rarely criticised the institution – giving the impression that they had little real understanding of the needs of patients or interest in their welfare, other than from a safe custody point of view.[52]

In the early 1920s, only around one-third of visiting committees had any women members, despite there being more women patients than men. Contributing to debate on the role of women on these committees, women's organisations favoured the proposal that they should be involved, but the County Councils Association (representing councils and ratepayers) and the Mental Hospitals Association (representing visiting committees and mental hospital administration), comprised almost entirely of men, opposed it.[53] Co-opting members onto the committees, or mandating a minimum number of women, would require Lunacy Act amendment. Attempts to do this got as far as the first reading of a bill in Parliament in 1922, but this was dropped in favour of a more wide-reaching mental treatment bill which would include a clause on that point.[54] Ultimately, the amendment had to wait until the Mental Treatment Act 1930.

Colney Hatch had at least one woman on its visiting committee throughout the 1920s: Miss Ida Samuel.[55] Mid-way through one meeting the minutes record that Miss Samuel vacated the chair, and Mr Johnson took over. The reasons for this were not explicit but the swap immediately preceded an agenda item about allegations of indecent exposure by William C, a farm labourer, to a female patient. Considering that Miss Samuel was also a magistrate, it seems unlikely that she was unable to undertake the task or opted to vacate the chair, suggesting that the chair-swap may have been prompted by male members wishing to protect her sensibilities, or regarding her as unable to lead the discussion, or feeling uncomfortable about allowing a woman to do so. Afterwards, Miss Samuel resumed the chair.[56] Although formally of equal status with the men on the committee, in practice it seems that the men had the upper hand.

Managing the physical environment

Managing the physical aspects of a huge institution, comprising buildings, their contents and much land around them, was an unending task. The committee had to ensure that farm, laundry and kitchen machinery functioned safely and efficiently, including equipment such as coffee and pepper grinders, and the 'refrigerating plant and cold storage chamber'.[57] Items for leisure and recreation also needed maintenance, including sports equipment, and pianos which intermittently required retuning, repairs or, eventually, replacement. Colney Hatch's 40-odd pianos, plus other musical instruments, indicate the significant musical recreational resources in the hospital for both patients and staff.[58]

There was also the task of modernising 70-year-old buildings, making them fit for purpose for the twentieth century. One such project at Colney Hatch was to replace indoor gas lighting with electric lighting. The Board of Control extolled the virtues of the latter: it was safer and healthier, provided better illumination, and was free from indoor atmospheric pollution, benefitting both patients and staff.[59] It was also beneficial to the nurses' workload, as they would no longer have to undertake the daily task of lighting and extinguishing the many gaslights on each ward.[60] Cables reached some wards and the male-side operating theatre in 1927, but further progress was slow.[61] Doctors Richard Hunter and Ida Macalpine, who later worked at Colney Hatch and wrote its history – *Psychiatry for the Poor* (1974) – noted that the Board tried to 'ginger up the hospital management' about the changeover in 1929, but with an estimated cost of £22,500, its completion was not sanctioned until 1930 – to be paid for with a capital expenditure grant and not from the local rates.[62] Delays in completing electrical wiring hampered the installation of other technology, such as X-ray equipment, and vacuum cleaners – use of which was preferable to sweeping and dusting, especially in wards with a high risk of infection.[63]

Switching from gas to electricity would also reduce the risk of fire. Fire was a great fear – possibly more so at Colney Hatch than elsewhere, ever since its disastrous fire of 1903 which killed 51 patients. Colney Hatch, like other mental hospitals, had its own fire brigade. In the early 1920s it managed some serious fires, such as one attributed to high winds blowing hot soot from a neighbouring chimney through a louvre in the laundry's drying-room and onto the clothes hanging below.[64] The nearest professional fire brigade two miles away could also be called, but even if it was, there was no certainty that the hospital's water hydrant couplings would fit their pumps.[65] When the chief fire main broke just as the system was being demonstrated to the Board of Control, the hospital's fire safety credibility was in doubt.[66] That incident prompted the Board to send a circular to all mental hospitals, requesting information about their fire arrangements.[67] In its style of praising innovations worth emulating, the Board noted, in 1926, that the mental hospital at Wakefield had a telephone fire alarm system serving the entire institution.[68]

Despite reducing the risk of fire by installing electricity, mental hospitals had to contend with new fire risks. Cellulose nitrate X-ray films were 'well nigh explosive' and could produce large quantities of toxic carbon monoxide and nitrogen oxide gases if they caught fire. A heavy death-toll resulted from one such incident in the USA in 1929, prompting the Board to circulate guidance on the matter.[69] Cinema films had similar hazards, necessitating a fire safety certificate based on an inspection by the professional fire brigade chief in order to secure a licence to show films.[70]

Clean water supplies were essential. The well at Colney Hatch supplied around 30 million gallons a year. The pumps needed to be maintained, and the water had to be tested regularly for chemical and bacterial pollutants.[71] In the event of a failure of the well supply resulting in a shortage of water, Colney Hatch established a back-up plan of mains water via the Barnet Water Company.[72] However, laying mains water pipes under the estate was another major undertaking. A further modernisation was prompted by the death of one of the hospital cart horses – the committee considered whether to purchase a motor vehicle for taking coal and other commodities round the estate.[73]

A tranche of new rules accompanied modernisations, such as when the hospital extended its network of telephones. The name of every staff member who dialled out on official business was noted, along with the name and number of everyone called. Staff were only permitted to use the phones for private calls in an emergency, and then they were expected to pay for the privilege. The internal telephone system also had the positive effect of reducing the nurses' workload, as they no longer had to carry messages from their wards to other parts of the institution.[74]

Electricity, water, motor vehicles, telephones and cinema facilities were all technological advances, some fitting closely with government objectives, such as public health and standards of social housing. They comprised an arm of hospital reform requiring envisioning the future. The visiting committees were rightly proud of these achievements. They benefited patients, lightened staff workloads and were visible signs that they had improved the institution. Modernising facilities, however, did not require the degree of empathy or depth of self-reflection which would have been necessary had the committees attempted to change institutional cultures, routines and practices to modernise relational, psychological and social aspects of individual patient care.

Staff and patients: law and order

In the 1920s, workplace psychology was an embryonic discipline, spurred on by the aftermath of both shell shock and the gruelling work regimes of civilians during the war. It was also stimulated by increasing social discord, with the burgeoning trade union movement and the 1917 Russian Revolution prompting fears of a working-class uprising. It was hoped that an understanding of psychological factors at play in the workplace would help quell social unrest.[75] The mental hospitals showed little awareness of this.

Although visiting committees were responsible for staffing and providing for patients, neither patients nor rank-and-file staff were routinely represented at committee meetings.[76] Montagu Lomax quoted one mental hospital staff member as saying that employees were '"a cog in the wheels of an infernal machine. I hardly think that phrase expresses my point, as they are not so important as a cog".'[77] Regarding patients, when the Colney Hatch committee discussed the cost of 'making and serving tea in a household manner' on women's wards they decided to extend the project to all wards where the medical superintendent said that the patients would appreciate it.[78] The minutes implied that there were some wards where patients would not appreciate it, but there was no suggestion that the medical superintendent had sought their views.

In the event of a complaint, the committee might summon informants, witnesses, victims and alleged perpetrators before them. Neither visiting committees nor senior hospital staff were trained in managing complaints, although some may have gained experience from other work. Despite reports that nurses were harsh, or even cruel, to patients,[79] visiting committees remained incredulous that their nurses would ever deliberately behave that way. That assumption, reinforced by stereotypical beliefs about mentally ill people being inevitably untrustworthy, meant that if a staff member's perspective differed from that of a patient, the staff member's words typically took precedence.[80] If a more senior staff member witnessed an incident, such as a colleague of lower rank being harsh to a patient, visiting committees tended to believe the senior person.

The committee did not appear to try to understand the situations which gave rise to traumatic incidents involving patients and staff. It also rarely accepted a staff member's apology or remorse, or expression that they genuinely wanted to learn from their mistakes. When a probationer nurse (a nurse in training) at Prestwich Mental Hospital was prosecuted at the Manchester County Police Court for pulling a patient's hair, she said in her evidence: 'I had no intention of grabbing her by the hair ... I had no intention of ill-treating the patient in any way.' The magistrate criticised the hospital leadership, rather than the nurse. He said that both patients and staff needed care and attention, and 'with great respect ... if this girl is convicted her whole career is blasted. She is only 23, and as she has told you, whatever she did she did as she thought in accordance with her duty. There was no intention to ill-treat the patient.' The case was dismissed.[81] The magistrate showed more empathy and understanding towards the staff member than had the visiting committee. Rightly intolerant of abuse of patients, the committee had tried to demonstrate its institution's high standards by being rule bound, punitive and blaming individuals. It appeared blind, however, to more systemic potential contributory factors, such as the challenges faced by the nurses working long hours on under-staffed wards, or the fact that the committee itself was an unsympathetic role model.

Visiting committees' seemingly bizarre rules, some of long standing and others newly created, alongside harsh penalties for infringements, highlighted the punitive institutional culture. One such rule, at Stafford Mental Hospital, read as follows:

> All female members of the staff … must leave or enter the asylum by the Corporation Street [main] entrance. The Visiting Committee would very much regret if any member of the staff should, owing to insufficient consideration, commit an act of indiscipline by contravening this rule, and so render herself liable to the penalty prescribed for such acts by the regulations, viz., instant dismissal with the consequent loss of pension and other emoluments.[82]

Reasons for the rule were unclear, particularly as only female staff members were subject to it, as was the heavy penalty for contravening it. At another hospital, nurses returning at night later than their passes allowed were fined or refused entry, even if their lateness was unavoidable. The local press commented: 'The person responsible for these new rules seems to be endeavouring to introduce Prussianism' into the hospital.[83] In some instances, inflexible and apparently meaningless rules were associated with staff being deceptive in order to defy them.[84]

Nurses' employment was precarious, especially while probationers. It took little for a committee to dismiss them. They were passive recipients of decisions by the leadership, who only observed actions rather than seeking to understand them. At Colney Hatch, when probationer nurse Matilda C had been off sick with minor ailments too frequently, she was 'dispensed with on the ground of ill-health which made [her] unsuitable for the service'.[85] When fully trained nurse Sarah Q was attacked in the hospital grounds, she was reluctant to give the names of those bullying her, probably fearful of revenge if she did, and she too was considered unsuitable and given a month's notice.[86] The rules were also disrespectful of staff individuality, privacy and personal space. At Colney Hatch, the visiting committee reprimanded probationer nurse Sydney M for his untidy bedroom, informing him that 'any further laxity on his part in the performance of his duties will result in the termination of his services'.[87] If keeping his room tidy was one of his duties, it implied that staff, just like patients, had no real privacy or personal space on hospital premises.

Some staff objected to managerial intrusion into their personal lives. When Nurse H was called before the committee for various misdemeanours, such as playing her gramophone at 9.30pm, she replied that she could do whatever she wanted as she paid rent, and she criticised their intrusiveness. She was 'severely admonished by the Chairman' and informed that her conduct would be closely scrutinised over the following three months.[88] She was fortunate to keep her job, in contrast to Mr Glanville at Exeter, who was dismissed for insolence. Arguably unnecessary details of staff illnesses also appeared in the minutes, such as about John G, a long-serving farm labourer, who had carcinoma of the rectum and needed hospital admission.[89] The committee did not perceive themselves as intrusive or punitive, or that they modelled harsh and disrespectful methods which staff might replicate when working with patients.[90]

The medical hierarchy in the public mental hospitals

Dr Archie Cochrane, the mid-twentieth-century pioneer of evidence-based medicine, was said to have referred to some of his senior medical colleagues as having a 'God complex' – an overwhelming belief that they were infallible in their problem solving.[91] A former mental hospital chaplain regarded his medical superintendent as 'an absolute autocrat. More so than the "Czar of all the Russians".'[92] In his *Mental Hospital Manual*, Dr John MacArthur advocated a culture of obedience to seniors, and advised his colleagues on the need for 'loyalty' to the medical superintendent, who

> is primarily responsible for the administration and welfare of the institution, and is entitled to the fullest support and confidence of his medical colleagues. No deviation from the normal routine, even of the most trivial variety, should ever be sanctioned, much less initiated, without his full knowledge and consent, nor should any information affecting the building or any inmates thereof ever be concealed from him.[93]

It was a one-way flow of respect, often lacking reciprocal openness or space for discussing disagreements. Dr David Parfitt, a newly qualified doctor working in a mental hospital in 1929, was perturbed by the 'strong feeling' instilled into his cohort that their 'own opinions were more likely than not to be unwelcome'.[94] For doctors, as other staff, alleged so-called disloyalty to senior personnel could result in 'enforced resignation'.[95]

The Board of Control was aware of the limitations of lay committees regarding appointing medical staff, and offered to advise them on advertising for medical superintendents and selecting candidates.[96] Some committees valued this, but others did not, preferring their accustomed method of promoting the next in line in seniority – nepotism rather than open competition.[97] Automatic promotion from within was problematic, as it was unlikely to introduce fresh ideas. However, shifting to open competition, particularly if unexpected, could result in disgruntled medical colleagues. In her novel *Private Worlds*, Phyllis Bottome colourfully summed up the views of Dr Alec MacGregor, a defeated internal candidate who had applied for a medical superintendent post. He called the visiting committee 'a set of bloody swabs with the minds of rabbits!', and was immensely scathing of the newly appointed medical superintendent, Dr Charles Drummond: '[He] was born in a Scottish castle, and has a head full of highland maggots ... He is an Edinburgh man and has been at Broadmoor ... Imagine our hospital ... run by a reactionary, who treats the patients like criminals!'[98] Irritations similar to this played out in the real world, as when Dr Perceval, medical superintendent of the troubled mental hospital at Prestwich, retired in 1923 after over 20 years in post. When he left, the institution was in a sufficient state of disarray and poor morale that many staff did not contribute to his retirement gifts.[99] The Lancashire Mental Hospitals Board, which oversaw Prestwich and the county's other mental hospitals, appointed an outsider, Dr Frederick Rogers, to replace him, instead of Dr David Orr who was next in line. The 'medical men of the Manchester District' protested. Lack of local medical support for Dr Rogers would not help him succeed in his new role. How much that lack of support contributed to Dr Rogers resigning after just a few months is uncertain. Despite the committee's good intentions to introduce new blood to make changes, challenging a forthright local medical culture and changing the system to appoint an external candidate probably had unforeseen ramifications. When Dr Rogers left, Dr Orr finally took over. However, his tenure was also fraught with difficulties, perhaps as the visiting committee had feared. Two years later, after extended sick leave, Dr Orr also resigned.[100]

The medical superintendent was responsible for daily oversight of both the clinical and the business sides of the hospital – a vast responsibility. He was obliged to live on site, close to the hospital. The house could be so close that, as Bill Boyd, son of a medical superintendent appointed in 1927, recalled, as a young child he was told not to listen when someone was shouting obscenities on the hospital terrace.[101] Medical superintendents typically remained in post for many years, creating a bottleneck for career progression. Most who aspired to that position would never achieve it. That was one of the factors, identified pre-war, which deterred doctors from entering, and remaining in, mental hospital work. Other factors included the intrusive rules, poor living accommodation (all doctors were required to live on site), plus 'stigma by association' – the attaching of negative characteristics of a disadvantaged group to those who support them.[102]

In the 1920s, typically between four and six doctors worked as assistants to the medical superintendent in a mental hospital with around fifteen hundred to two thousand patients. It was near impossible for so few to carry out their medical responsibilities adequately. The Board of Control devised a strategy to improve recruitment and retention of doctors based on experiences in other medical specialties, on proposals from formal inquiries and on the pre-war recommendations of the Medico-Psychological Association (MPA, later RMPA), the psychiatrists' professional body.[103] The Board's proposed remedies included paid study leave to allow doctors to attend lectures for the Diploma in Psychological Medicine, then the sole university-taught postgraduate qualification in psychiatry; a salary rise on passing the exam; and removing the rule that doctors had to seek the medical superintendent's permission to marry.[104] The Board sought to improve links between mental hospitals, general hospitals and universities to help achieve educational and research objectives. It also aimed to establish a laboratory in each mental hospital to spur on doctors' 'spirit of inquiry'.[105] The MPA was keen to suggest ways to achieve these goals, but appeared to continue with its placid pre-WW1 public profile, or, as Trevor Turner, psychiatrist and historian, commented, '[s]taying sane while critics raved around them' was its central outward-looking achievement.[106]

Some historians have concluded that the Board's and the MPA's desire to improve medical staffing was driven primarily by wanting to improve the professional respectability and status of psychiatry and psychiatrists relative to other branches of medicine.[107] On the basis of the evidence uncovered during the course of researching this book, status seems a minor driver for change relative to concerns about the adequacy of mental hospitals' medical staffing and the practicalities of providing care.

The doctors' day in the mental hospitals usually began with a meeting in the medical superintendent's office, to discuss patients, any other concerns and what actions to take. Ward rounds then took place, with a senior nurse accompanying each doctor.[108] Among their other tasks, doctors might be asked to assess ailing resident staff.[109] They also had night duties and gave lectures to the nurses. Other staff appreciated them joining in with out-of-hours events.[110] Public health tasks cropped up from time to time, such as asking a doctor to inspect a delivery of cans of meat to ensure they were fit for consumption.[111] They also carried out surgical procedures and attended women during childbirth.[112] It was apt that the Cobb Committee on Administration of Public Mental Hospitals should recommend in 1922 that mental hospital doctors should have some general hospital experience as house surgeons and house physicians (optional at that time) before entering psychiatric practice.[113]

In some hospitals doctors took on pharmacists' roles. The Board of Control deplored this: 'Medical Officers have not been specially trained in the dispensing of drugs … their time would be much more valuably spent in giving individual treatment to patients in the wards than in this somewhat irksome duty.' It could also be dangerous. At Powick Mental Hospital, Worcestershire in 1921, nine patients became ill, of whom three died, after the medical officer misread the labels on concentrated solution stock bottles. He had mistaken the toxic 'Glyc Belladon' for the laxative 'Ext: Casca c Glyc'.[114] The *Times* reported the inquest, naming the doctor, Alexander O'Flaherty, and giving the verdict of death by misadventure.[115] I have found no evidence of Dr O'Flaherty being prosecuted, but according to the General Medical Council's register he ceased practising medicine, giving the impression that he was devastated by his errors.[116]

Nursing

Shortly after the war, Dr Bedford Pierce, medical superintendent of the Retreat, York, berated his medical colleagues for neglecting the wellbeing of nursing staff, both male and female, when nursing problems were well known:

> Long before the war the pay and the conditions of service of the mental nurse left much to be desired … The work, as we know well, is often very arduous, and brings little reward beyond the satisfaction of doing difficult work well, the pay has been miserably poor, and there have been few signs of appreciation from patients, their friends or from managing committees … conditions of service ought to be good and the remuneration liberal. Yet we, who knew all this, did not, I fear, press upon our committees in season and out of season the urgent necessity for their giving attention to these aspects of the question.[117]

Montagu Lomax doubted whether nurse staffing levels were sufficient to manage patients humanely.[118] He found little trust between senior staff and their subordinates on the wards, or between ward staff and patients. As with the doctors, nursing culture was rule-based, and hierarchical obedience to seniors was paramount. Ordinary nurses were subservient to the matron and her ward sisters on the women's side, and on the men's side, to the head male nurse and his charge nurses. There was also 'an atmosphere of servility where the doctors are concerned'.[119] A nurse accompanying a doctor on a ward round should stand 'in the same relation to him as a non-commissioned officer in the army does to his superior', advised Dr MacArthur.[120] Orders were orders: all medical instructions had to be followed faithfully, which risked ignoring any other needs of the patients and creating 'a cut-and-dried unintelligent course of procedure'.[121] Articles in the nursing periodicals of the time suggest that mental nurses were more concerned about working conditions than patient care, and that they accepted – uncritically – concepts of mental disorders and treatment as medical matters. Many nurses 'retained the outlook of a lay occupation' and dragged their heels on the 'ascent to the sunny uplands of professionalism'.[122]

Nursing, however, was undergoing a process of change. The Nurses Registration Act 1919 established the General Nursing Council (GNC). Just as the General Medical Council (since 1858) was the statutory body for regulating, registering and setting standards for the medical profession, the GNC did likewise for nursing, establishing it as an independent profession. However, incorporating mental nursing into the GNC scheme was complicated. GNC leaders lacked practical experience of mental nursing; general nurses tended to be elitist and disparaging of mental nurses; and the male nurses in the mental hospitals were an oddity in the overall female-dominated profession.[123] Miss Musson (later Dame Ellen Musson), former matron of Birmingham General Hospital, was appointed chairman of the GNC in 1927. According to Michael Arton in his history of the professionalisation of mental nursing, she 'had no wish to register the mental nurses for whom, in general, she voiced the greatest contempt'.[124] She sat on the GNC's Mental Nurses Committee, which ensured that her voice was heard on all related matters.[125] While psychiatrists were regarded condescendingly by some of their medical colleagues, arguably, the tensions between general and mental nurses were even more profound.

The MPA instigated training for mental nurses in the 1880s, comprising a programme of nurse-led ward experience, and lectures mainly given by psychiatrists. This led to the MPA's examination for the Certificate of Proficiency in Nursing the Insane – the only formal qualification for mental nurses until the 1920s.[126] The MPA also produced a textbook, originally called the *Handbook for Instruction of Attendants on the Insane*, which it regularly revised, renamed and reissued.[127] The *Handbook* was very bio-medical, but it also emphasised the personal qualities necessary for a good mental nurse, including kindness, sympathy, tact and patience, and being cheerful, forbearing and gentle.[128] Despite its limitations, Niall McCrae and Peter Nolan described the *Handbook* as a 'major contribution' to the development of mental nursing.[129]

In the early 1920s, the ward-based practical training varied in quality. Some nurses were scathing about it. One male nurse commented that it was

> vested in the arts of window-cleaning, floor and wall scrubbing … fire drills and first-aid lectures … the fine art of shifting coal and wood, and farming and gardening. We are expected to become acquainted with our patients' ailments, but how can an attendant do so when he is being shifted about from one ward to another? ... I have found nothing interesting or edifying about the duties as taught at this hospital.[130]

In 1925, Minister of Health Neville Chamberlain signed off a syllabus and plan for practical skills training agreed with the GNC, for 'Mental Nurses and those Nursing Mental Defectives'. The first year of the three-year programme was the same for all nurses, on the 'theory and practice of nursing', including skills such as bed making, preventing and managing bed sores, hospital etiquette, and care of the dead.[131] Specialist training followed over the next two years. Although for mental nursing the syllabus still conformed to the MPA's *Handbook*, the GNC ceased to recognise the MPA's certificate as a qualification entitling admission to the new State Register.[132] The GNC contested the right of doctors to organise nurse training. It wanted nurses to be independent from doctors as a matter of principle. Despite acknowledging earlier contributions of the MPA, Miss Musson was unwavering: 'When a State body comes in the Voluntary Associations should give up':

> One realises in those great mental hospitals one must have sort of a General to manage, but we cannot see any reason why the members of one profession should hold such absolute power over the training and liberties of another profession. It is quite time the mental nurses took firm charge of their own affairs.[133]

Michael Arton referred to GNC-RMPA meetings as 'high-level bickering', with neither side showing any desire to settle the dispute.[134]

Another new nursing body entered the fray: the Mental Hospital Matrons' Association – known as the 'Tabbies' (although the precise reason for this name is elusive). A fearsome body of nursing women, the Tabbies sought to ensure 'maintenance of a progressive attitude towards the nursing of mental illness'.[135] They were adamant about nursing independence, particularly away from doctors, and they condemned trades union membership 'in any branch of Nursing': nurses were expected to be selflessly dedicated, putting the needs of others before their own.[136]

Frequently probationer nurses were expected to attend lectures and training demonstrations outside duty hours[137] – an indication of both the rigidity of their duty rotas and the expectation of their dedication to their work. It was also expected that they would pay their examination fees up front (although a pay rise if they passed would reimburse them).[138] To enter for the GNC examination the cost was £5.5s (equating to several weeks' wages) and for the MPA's it was £1.15s.[139] Fewer nurses than the GNC had hoped entered for their examination, at least in part due to the cost.[140]

One outcome of Dr Lomax's book, *The Experiences of an Asylum Doctor*, was that the Board of Control appointed a committee to investigate nursing in the public mental hospitals. The NAWU viewed this cynically, as a ploy by the Board to show that it was doing *something* to avoid the need to have to face a Royal Commission which might otherwise be appointed.[141] The Committee on Nursing comprised 10 people, of whom only one, Miss Mary Mitchell Thorburn, matron of Horton Mental Hospital (where John Lord was medical superintendent), had any mental nursing experience.[142] It took evidence from some nurses, but evidence from patients as recipients of care is elusive, confirming the impression that their views did not count, at least in the eyes of the Board. The NAWU criticised the committee's lack of nursing expertise, and that in its report the 'wages suggested are scandalous; the hours' scheme is idiotic, and the few recommendations that are of value are redundant' as they had already been made by the Joint Conciliation Committee comprising the Mental Hospitals Association and the NAWU.[143]

One of the recommendations of the Committee on Nursing was for a mental hospital matron to be trained in both general and mental nursing.[144] Since the first year of training was universal across all nursing specialties, the GNC specified two additional years of training for a qualified mental nurse to become a fully trained general nurse. However, this was far from easy to achieve. General nursing training schools were not keen to accept women mental nurses on such a programme, and almost all excluded men.[145] By 1923, only Hackney Union Infirmary and the National Hospital for the Paralysed and Epileptic, both in London, enrolled men for general training, although a handful of others followed gradually.[146]

Despite doubly trained nurses being a potential benefit to patients, some mental hospitals were reluctant to second their nurses to general hospitals for additional training. In part, their hesitancy was due to concerns that those nurses might choose not to return to the mental hospitals or that, as employers, they would be unable to offer types and grades of employment commensurate with their additional qualifications. There were also barriers of unequal remuneration for equivalent grades of nurse in different institutions, and non-transferable pension schemes.[147]

While some mental nurses obtained a general nursing qualification, the potential benefits of general nurses knowing how to treat mentally unwell patients received little attention. Patients in general hospitals might become mentally disturbed, but the most likely response was to dispatch them as rapidly as possible to a mental hospital on the assumption that their mental state was the primary problem. It was therefore a great achievement when Littlemore Mental Hospital and the Radcliffe Infirmary in Oxford paved the way by establishing reciprocity of mental nurse and general nurse training, each having placements in the other's hospital.[148]

Rotas, recruitment and retention

According to the upcoming Labour Movement, across both mental and general hospitals, nurses did arduous and risky work, for long hours, lived in unhealthy hospital accommodation and were 'grossly under-paid'. It attributed this to the origins of nursing within religious orders, and to women providing nursing care for little or no monetary reward, to help support charity-funded hospitals. When nursing developed into a skilled profession, salaries and conditions of service did not keep pace.[149]

The International Labour Organization was founded in 1919 on the premise that internationally agreed rules for social justice in the workplace would help promote peace. From the start, it stressed the need for a 48-hour working week (eight hours a day, six days a week) in industrial settings, bolstering the NAWU's demands that asylum staff hours should average no more than that.[150] The NAWU regarded an eight-hour day as 'quite long enough for anybody to be in contact with the insane … [N]o system can be regarded as satisfactory which contemplates the continuance of 10, 12 or 14 hour spells of duty as a normal arrangement.'[151]

Shortening the working week was controversial generally. In industry, it had not yet been determined that shorter hours could be associated with higher hourly productivity. Instead, it was assumed that industry would suffer because fewer hours would mean lower productivity.[152] Likewise, the potential for better therapeutic 'productivity' was not automatically assumed to align with shorter nursing hours. It would also disrupt the well-established 12-hour nursing shift pattern, which fitted neatly with the regime of sending patients to bed at around 7pm for 12 hours each night. The Board of Control regarded long hours as beneficial for staff and patients, who 'suffer by the constant changes of the personnel of the staff looking after them. Neither, in our opinion, do the long hours off duty, when they are almost bound to be spending money, tend to the contentment of the female staff, especially when they are far away from their own homes.'[153] Despite the male-dominated Board of Control making this comment, it was not entirely misogynistic: the all-female Tabbies also deplored the move to shorten hours of work, as it was 'killing the spirit of fellowship between the nurse and the patient'.[154]

The theory that mentally unwell people benefited from 12 hours' sleep each night may have determined the practice of 12-hour shifts, or vice versa. However, with long shifts associated with economy of staffing, particularly with almost skeletal ward staffing at night, the practice became embedded in institutional routines, unquestioned and hard to shift. The Board's Committee on Nursing did not promote the theory that patients needed so much sleep. Indeed, it encouraged more evening activities for patients. Neither, however, did it reconcile conflicting views on the optimum length of shifts. Maintaining nurses' weekly salaries, with three shifts in 24 hours and fewer total hours worked per week, would be more expensive and 'wasteful and extravagant in staff'.[155] When three shifts with shorter hours were introduced without recruiting more staff, as reported from Stafford Mental Hospital, there were fewer nurses on the ward at any one time, with more untherapeutic custodial methods and potential additional risk to patients.[156]

Some doctors referred to a 'nurse famine' across hospitals generally, attributing this to more employment doors opening for women which gave them a greater choice of paid work.[157] Mental hospitals advertised widely and repeatedly for nurses, in daily, weekly, national, local and nursing newspapers and magazines.[158] Disappointing responses to adverts led some hospitals to appoint all applicants even if they were unsuitable, risking practices becoming even more custodial, mechanistic, untherapeutic and neglectful of patients' wellbeing, and raising fears about ward safety.[159]

Once on a ward, an idealistic new nurse might be disappointed:

> We are not allowed to participate in or develop the social life of the institution, to play games, or even to converse with the patients, and very little opportunity for recreation is provided for the staff. The whole duty lies in rigid routine – not a very promising outlook … as a profession.[160]

It is not known how representative this sort of experience was, and it is not reported whether or how this particular nurse coped with his disappointment. However, we know that resignations in the first year of training were 'very frequent', particularly among women. According to an analysis conducted in 1925, of the entire female mental nurse complement, only 20 per cent remained in the service for over five years.[161] Resignation rates at later career stages were lower. The staff who stayed probably acclimatised to the way of life, saw it as acceptable and perpetuated it.[162]

The day-to-day working life of mental nurses received little serious scrutiny as to its possible contribution to staff turnover, but the authorities discussed various remedies to improve staff retention. The Mental Hospitals Association gave its view that even higher wages would not 'bring to the service the type of nurse required'; it blamed the 'unpleasant' work, stating that 'girls were so appalled at the conditions which obtained' that only 'a class of girl inferior to the class taking up general nursing was recruited'. The Association did not mention improving the work environment. Instead, it proposed a punitive deterrent: non-return of pension contributions for resignation during the first five years of employment.[163] The Committee on Nursing also abrogated responsibility for the difficulties of nursing retention: the Tabbies and the Board of Control agreed that nursing was 'a vocation which, for its proper fulfilment, will always demand a large element of devotion and self-sacrifice in the service of humanity, and cannot be judged by general occupational standards'.[164] The Committee threw the onus back on the individual nurse to adapt, rather than offering them a voice within the institutions.

An editorial in the *British Medical Journal* commented that 'the true nursing spirit flourishes with difficulty in an atmosphere of chronicity', but whether nurses were asked about their preferences for working with people who were chronically or acutely unwell is not stated.[165] Many years later, when nurses caring for long-stay psychogeriatric patients were asked, it was apparent that their choices about work preferences did not match the doctors' assumptions. For example, whether the patients were pleasant or gloomy affected nurses' work satisfaction more than whether the care they provided was heavy or messy.[166] There was little chance of making the work more intrinsically rewarding, or understanding the sense of pride and satisfaction which staff took in it and sought to achieve from it, without asking them.[167] The Board of Control also did not grasp the potential psychological rewards associated with work. In the late 1920s, it was surprised to find that those hospitals which insisted that all new nursing entrants study for a recognised qualification, giving them intellectual and emotional satisfaction alongside a pay rise on achieving it, found recruitment easier.[168]

To help with recruitment and retention, the Board of Control proposed to build nurses' homes in hospital grounds, although this idea was not new. Charles Mercier, for example, had drawn attention to the need for separate accommodation with adequate leisure facilities in 1894.[169] Nurses' bedrooms had traditionally been allocated adjacent to the wards, so that in the event of an emergency they could be called to help even when off duty. However, if staff accommodation was provided elsewhere on site, those rooms could be repurposed to accommodate more patients. The building of dedicated nurses' homes was therefore regarded as acceptable capital expenditure. The homes would have single bedrooms and places for relaxation when off duty.[170] Facilities for nurses 'who may wish to smoke when off duty' would also be provided, to avoid fire risks associated with them smoking in their bedrooms.[171] The Board also advised, for women nurses, that

> [t]he semi-collegiate and corporate life which is possible in a nurses' home should form a prominent part of a probationer's training. The opportunities it provides for promoting *esprit de corps* and the acquiring of nursing etiquette, for mutual discussion, the making of friends, and social enjoyment, are of the highest value in the formation of character.[172]

The Sex Disqualification (Removal) Act 1919 'in principle, abolished disqualification by sex or marriage for entry to or continued employment in the professions or the exercise of any public function'.[173] In practice, the 'marriage bar' remained in many public sector areas, including in many mental hospitals. Women were generally required to resign on marriage, although some avoided doing so by not informing the authorities that they were indeed married. Visiting committee minutes from 1923 highlighted this in a note that police telephoned Colney Hatch enquiring about

Nurse H, 'as they had found a man seriously injured who was evidently her husband'. The visiting committee terminated Nurse H's contract forthwith.[174] When Nurse G gave birth in the hospital, '[p]aternity was fully admitted by a man who states that he is about to marry the woman at once', although the committee later heard that 'she had been married for some time'. She too was dismissed.[175] Legal changes giving women greater opportunities and equal rights to men did not equate with cultural change to implement them. One medical superintendent in 1929 described being 'compelled to engage a married woman', on a temporary contract, to fill a post because there was absolutely no alternative.[176] If women wished to continue their nursing careers and to seek more senior posts, they had to forgo marriage, remain single and continue to live in the institution.

In contrast, men choosing to work in mental nursing were allowed to marry and live with their families, either in a tied cottage or off the estate 'so that the family may have an opportunity of developing its life untrammelled by the routine and regulations of the hospital'.[177] Although not living in the institution, male nurses also networked with their colleagues, often regarding NAWU matters. Men were more active in the NAWU than women. This was partly because, once settled in the service, a greater number of men considered their mental hospital work a career for life, making it worth their while to invest time in negotiating for improved wages and terms and conditions of employment. The gender difference in NAWU leadership is shown in a photograph from the NAWU annual conference in 1929. Of a total of around a hundred executive committee and delegates, there were only three women: Miss Phillips from Portsmouth; Miss Wiese, a member of the union executive; and Miss Brown from the GNC (Figure 5.1).

The hospitals generally tolerated NAWU activities, although it was alleged that some tried to intimidate staff who wanted to join, such as warning them that they would be 'sent down the drive'.[178] While union activity was one arm of male collegiality, other collaborative efforts verged on criminality. The local Customs and Excise Officer wrote to Colney Hatch alleging that two male nurses had been trading in tobacco and cigarettes. Called before the visiting committee, the nurses stated that they had collected money from staff to purchase tobacco and cigarettes at wholesale prices. They then distributed the goods, they said, without making a profit. The visiting committee ordered the practice to cease.[179]

Mental nurses did not have a national pay scale.[180] In rural mental hospitals, male nurses' salaries were set to be comparable with those of farm labourers in the locality.[181] Farm labourers disliked the comparison, as in their view nurses 'have nothing to do but stand about, keep an eye on the patients, and play cricket and football'.[182] This comment indicated the visibility of outdoor leisure pursuits in the mental hospitals, and suggested that, when convenient for outsiders, stereotypes of mad and dangerous patients could be wiped away.

Figure 5.1 NAWU Annual Conference 1929. Note that only three women were present and one man had a child on his knee. Source: *NAWU Magazine* 1929, 18:8, 5. Reproduced with permission from UNISON.

Women nurses in the mental hospitals were paid 20 per cent less than men in equivalent jobs, and the Committee on Nursing made no recommendations to disturb that differential.[183] Equal pay for men and women featured in campaigns to achieve equal citizenship for women, but some opposed it, such as the conservative press, including the *Daily Mail* which, according to historian Pat Thane, 'insistently promoted stereotypes of "embittered" "hysterical" feminists'.[184] The assumption that women employees had no dependants also overlooked realities.[185] One married woman, Nurse EM, needed work to support her two children because her husband had deserted her. Colney Hatch compromised and employed her on a temporary contract. However, this gave her no job security, and she sought a safer, permanent contract. Nurse HM was in a similar position, needing secure employment after her husband in West Africa 'met with considerable misfortune' and was 'unable to support her'.[186] It may have been a coincidence that these two unusual requests for permanent contracts were raised at the same meeting of the visiting committee. Alternatively, it hints at women staff supporting each other to raise personal matters with the authorities. The minutes do not relay the outcomes of their requests, but, contrary to the expectations and advice of the Board of Control, for these women, just as for the male nurses, collegiality could exist without them residing in a nurses' home.

Crossing the gender line: women nurses on male wards

Gender segregation was almost total in the mental hospitals, for both staff and patients. Hospital doors were locked, and male staff could not open doors on the female side and vice versa. Very few staff, except doctors and the hospital chaplain, had keys for both sides.[187] There were three main issues regarding gender and mental nursing: women nurses working with physically unwell men; matron having charge of nurses on both sides; and women nurses nursing mentally unwell but physically fit male patients. With the recognition that there was benefit in having doubly trained nurses taking charge of wards where patients also required physical nursing, women nursing physically unwell men was the least contentious of the three issues, particularly given that male mental nurses had difficulty accessing general nurse training. The second issue – that matron (a woman) should be in charge of male nurses, rather than them being led by their own chief male nurse, was more contentious.[188] Arguments for male nurses having their own chief at a level equivalent to matron included the fact that men's roles extended into the farm, recreation ground, band and fire brigade – matters in which matron was assumed to have little practical experience, even though she was likely to be better trained in nursing.[189]

The third and most contentious issue was women nursing mentally unwell men who were physically fit. That was done as a temporary expedient during WW1, and was deemed to be beneficial, suiting both patients and staff. Post-war, and without clear evidence, the popular press expounded on the 'widespread evils' which would result should the practice continue.[190] The NAWU opposed the practice, adamant that it was degrading and put women at risk – a message which could also increase stigma towards mentally ill people and fear of mental hospitals, and deter potential recruits. The NAWU also advocated that unemployed ex-servicemen should have priority for work on the men's wards, even if they were not suitable for the job.[191] It described employing women in place of men as a cost-cutting manoeuvre, although in Scotland, where the practice of women nursing mentally unwell men had long been accepted, two women nurses were employed in place of one male when necessary, making it more expensive.[192] Other arguments related to injuries. Regarding injuries to patients, some doctors observed that when women nurses cared for male patients, injuries which had previously been accounted for as 'accidents', such as slipping or falling, had ceased, implying that in the past they had probably been caused by rough handling.[193] In Scotland, psychiatrist George Robertson reported that relatives of male patients preferred women nursing them, as 'to them it is a guarantee that no violence will be employed'.[194] Robertson also explained that the practice had been found safe for the nurses: '[A]lthough a man is deranged in mind, it does not necessarily mean that he loses all his faculties and all his intelligence.'[195] However, psychiatrists' views varied, and the 1923 edition of the MPA *Handbook* contradicted Robertson, cautioning that 'in the insane there is frequently no self-restraint, the lower animal nature is no longer in subjection, the thoughts cannot be controlled, so that the conversation and the whole behaviour is shameless and indecent'.[196]

Risk of injury in mental hospitals was an important matter, and staff and patients could be both perpetrators and victims. From time to time patients did assault staff, including doctors, resulting in physical injury or 'considerable nervous prostration'.[197] However, staff also assaulted patients, independent of excessive force when undertaking restraint procedures. Attendant Mr H attempted 'immoral sexual relations' with patient Margaret S: when intoxicated, he had found his way into a scullery to which women patients had access. He was dismissed, and the Director of Public Prosecutions consulted.[198] Homosexual acts involving staff and patients were also alleged, including a drunk male doctor who 'attempted to behave indecently' to a male patient. The doctor was dismissed, but continued to practise medicine as a public health specialist in a different locality.[199]

By 1924, only about a quarter of public mental hospitals across England and Wales had adopted the system of women nursing mentally unwell men. When the Board surveyed medical superintendents, many of those averse to it had not tried it, whereas many in favour had. Where the practice ran into problems, it was attributed to the way it had been implemented, not the principles behind it.[200] In 1926 the usually conservative Board – perhaps surprisingly on such a controversial matter – recommended that the practice be extended, but the response was half-hearted.[201] The controversy continued, drawing in, among others, Neville Chamberlain, who was broadly in support. The National Conference of Labour Women raised the subject, commenting that allowing women to nurse mentally unwell men was detrimental to the patients and that it subjected nurses to 'perversion of the emotions or actual violence'.[202] Such views had the effect of perpetuating unfounded generalisations about mentally ill men.

Absent from discussions within the hospital hierarchy were the women nurses who wanted to work on men's wards, and expressed their choice in the pages of NAWU's magazine:

> the moral tone in a male mental ward will compare favourably with that of a 'military hospital' ... I have always been treated with respect by the patients, and heard much less bad language than one hears in most workshops where both sexes are employed. Moreover, I believe that the mere presence of a woman acts as a restraining influence upon most male patients.[203]

Clinical, employment, financial, moral, emotional and safety aspects of arguments were diverse and entangled. The vociferousness of the debate, little evidence of discussion other than among the select membership of the Committee on Nursing, and the inability of both public and professionals to distinguish evidence from hearsay probably contributed to risk-averse institutions maintaining the status quo.

Crossing the gender line: women doctors

Dr Octavia Wilberforce trained in medicine at the London School of Medicine for Women, qualifying in 1920. Her first paid work was as a locum, for one month, at Graylingwell Mental Hospital, Sussex. When she told medical superintendent Dr Harold Kidd that she had 'no special experience with lunatics', he reassured her: 'Oh they are mostly exactly like ordinary patients, though you may be told by one that she is Queen Victoria.' On the morning she arrived, she was handed a bunch of keys:

> I felt I was thrown to the lions. I walked down a corridor feeling rather numb. Oh well this is a challenge I said to myself as with beating heart I unlocked the ward door. The sister came to meet me and I found my self confidence returning as I faced the first patient.[204]

Dr Wilberforce described her experience on a men's ward in a letter to a friend:

> There is an ex-service man who uses the most awful language and is very violent. I was warned about him. He began as soon as I entered the ward. I stopped that man, and he talked to me quite more or less civilly. The attendants can't stop him, he goes on with them all day. Another spits in your face by way of playing up. I didn't know till after which he was. And I bent right over him and asked about the book he was reading. I noticed attendants rather restive but all went happily.[205]

Her experiences echoed the respect which women nurses reported they received from male mental patients. When Dr Wilberforce left the hospital, she considered that she had learned much and had benefited from the experience. She also thought she had broken through some of the negative expectations and stereotypes of women doctors and done 'quite good spade work here for any future woman who might like to come'.[206]

Women doctors were still few and far between, and – as with women nurses – practice varied regarding employing them, especially when it came to working with male patients. In 1920 the MPA had 23 women members – about four per cent of the total. Some of them had undertaken military medical service during the war: they were forthright, courageous and determined, but still struggled to gain recognition in their civilian professional roles.[207] One of the best known of that cohort was Dr Helen Boyle of the Lady Chichester Hospital for the Treatment of Early Mental Disorders, in Hove. To undertake her pioneering approach, she opted to work outside the public mental hospital system, keeping the Board of Control at arm's length as much as she could.[208] Dr Jean (or Jane) Shortt became medical superintendent at The Lawn, Lincoln, a private mental hospital with about 70 patients, although the Board of Control was dubious about the wisdom of the hospital committee 'appointing a Lady Superintendent so long as there are so many male patients': at that time there were 15.[209] As with women mental nurses, their ability to cope with male patients was under scrutiny. Dr Shortt stayed in post for two years, probably resigning because of her impending marriage.[210] The Lawn's committee was happy to appoint another woman, Dr Mary Barkas, who had worked at the Maudsley Hospital, and who in 1924 was the first woman to be awarded the MPA's prestigious Gaskell Medal and Prize.[211]

The Medical Women's Federation (founded in 1917) sought appointments for women doctors on an equal footing with medical men, including interchangeable duties, equal pay and equal opportunities for promotion.[212] The Federation preferred the term 'women', in contrast to the Board of Control which often referred to 'lady' doctors – maybe a title of respect but it also implied that they were not real members of the workforce. During its hospital inspection visits, the Board noted the presence of these doctors on the staff, usually neutrally.[213] Outside the mental hospital system there was encouragement for more women doctors to be employed. The National Council of Women of Great Britain wanted women doctors primarily for women patients. The Council wrote to Sir Frederick Willis, chairman of the Board of Control, proposing at least one woman doctor on the staff of every public mental hospital with that objective in mind.[214] Supporting this view, Dr Francis Fremantle, a medically trained MP, explained to a parliamentary committee, unfortunately using an uncomplimentary analogy: '[I]t takes a thief to catch a thief, so it takes a woman to find out things appertaining to women, and a woman doctor to find out things appertaining to women patients.'[215] Envisioning women doctors working primarily with women patients avoided the controversy of women being part of a team which worked across an entire mental hospital.

By 1929, no public mental hospital had a woman medical superintendent, although Dr Isabella Gillespie was deputy at Upton, Cheshire.[216] In 1930 the RMPA had at least 60 women members – 12 per cent of the total – but still only one in 12 medical staff in the public mental hospitals were women, whereas the ratio of female to male patients was about four to three.[217] The culture was slow to shift. Some hospitals, such as Colney Hatch, despite having women on its committee, cited the organisation and domestic staffing of the doctors' residence as a reason for not appointing women.[218] There seemed little intention of following the trend which the Medical Women's Federation stated was emerging in several European countries, North America and South Africa.[219]

Reflections

At the beginning of the decade, the hospital authorities needed to deal with a backlog of measures dating back to before the war, and other measures encompassing post-war needs and expectations. Women were speaking out more vociferously and representing women's interests, both for the professions and on behalf of patients. Influential new organisations included the Ministry of Health and the GNC. Trades unions such as the NAWU – a largely male voice – were stronger and sought to improve terms and conditions of employment. Some in authority regarded these shifts as a threat to the established hierarchical system. Others, such as Dr Bedford Pierce, considered that this 'new era of democratic control' was likely to be beneficial.[220]

For most of the 1920s, the Board of Control prioritised the letter of the law, the NAWU represented the interests of staff, professional organisations represented themselves, and visiting committees focussed on maintaining discipline in the mental hospitals and managing them according to budget. The perception that the medical profession had a 'God complex' extended to others at the top of their individual hierarchies, such as the Tabbies. Each group was self-protective and defensive of its own position. There was a lack of negotiation and compromise within and across professional and organisational boundaries and each faction held tight to its own agenda, often creating a stalemate rather than collaboration.

Projects undertaken to improve the material environment for patients and staff were important, such as new buildings and installing electric lighting. However, these developments were a public display of what was being done for patients, likely to reassure the ratepayers that patients were being well treated. An image of material adequacy was unlikely to encourage local authorities to offer more, or medical superintendents to work with visiting committees to demand additional resources to improve therapeutic approaches for individual patients, with the possibility of longer-term benefits to their wellbeing. In the context of public understanding and expectations regarding mental disorders, plus broader social priorities, national constraints on public expenditure and financial conflicts of interest of the visiting committees, the façade that all was well was likely to satisfy most.

Obtaining adequate resources was only one mental hospital challenge. Arguably, at least as important, were the deeply embedded values and culture which influenced the daily lives of those within. Unless scandals arose, the culture was almost invisible to those outside the system, and to those within who regarded themselves as unwaveringly beneficent. This study cannot quantify how many institutions operated within a culture that was harsh or punitive or otherwise detrimental, but there are many pointers to suggest that care and kindness towards the workforce and the patients was too often lacking. For most of the decade, in the eyes of the leadership, if something worked satisfactorily it was unwise to change it. If problems arose, the buck was passed to others, often lower in the hierarchy, rather than acknowledging that the problem may have stemmed from the decisions of those at the top. Self-assured by means of status, the leadership controlled the institutions in ways which appeared correct to them. The leadership pattern tended towards being military, rigid and top-down, dominated by obedience to seniors' orders. Lower ranks of staff had little or no opportunity to raise concerns with the leadership. If they did not like their work they could leave, and contesting the rules or opposing seniors could lead to a speedy dismissal. Arguably, leadership style contributed to how staff understood how to care for patients in their charge. If staff and visiting committees stayed in post long enough, they tended to acclimatise to the culture and perpetuate it. The regime fitted with Goffman's later descriptions of 'total institutions'.

Some individual leaders advocated a more empathic and patient-centred approach, but a more compassionate culture would require all ranks to acknowledge that they were not omnipotent over those lower on the scale, and that they did not hold all the answers. In 1928 Mr Bartlett, president of the NAWU, addressed its annual conference, commenting that the time was ripe for a shift from the Union's preoccupation with wages and work conditions, and towards 'our duty to see that the patients are properly cared for'.[221] The NAWU took on a new name – Mental Hospital and Institutional Workers' Union – and its magazine became less confrontational, less of a call to arms and more a vehicle for disseminating information. The change of NAWU stance was concurrent with other transformations, including the Local Government Act 1929 and the Labour Party coming into power, albeit as a minority government. There was also much consideration of the *Report of the Royal Commission on Lunacy and Mental Disorder*, associated with important changes in lunacy law, and a shift in the attitude of the Board of Control towards advocating that low expenditure was not necessarily the best marker of institutional efficiency.[222]

Notes

1 Trades Union Congress and the Labour Party, *The Labour Movement and the Hospital Crisis*, 19; Thomson, Mental hygiene as an international movement, 283.
2 Lomax, *The Experiences of an Asylum Doctor*, 41.
3 NHS England, Bed availability and occupancy data: average daily number of available and occupied beds, Jul–Sept 2023.
4 Goffman, *Asylums*, xiii.
5 Anon., Asylum and lunacy law reform.
6 Anon., My impressions at Exminster.
7 WG, Re: Impressions of a probationer.
8 McCrae and Nolan, *The Story of Nursing*, 65.
9 BoC, *Annual Report for 1922*, 16–17.
10 BoC, Circular 527, 23 Dec 1918, TNA MH 51/239.
11 Thane, *Divided Kingdom*, 69–70.
12 BoC, Circular 527, 23 Dec 1918, TNA MH 51/239.
13 Colney Hatch Sub-Com, 10 Jun 1921, 82, TLA LCC/MIN/01010.
14 BoC, Circular 516, Suggested employment of disabled officers and men in institutions with which the Board of Control are concerned, 10 Aug 1918, TNA MH 51/239.
15 Private Allison Bertie Gatward, Med sup's reports, Colney Hatch, 11 Jul 1919, TLA H12/CH/A/08/001; Imperial War Museum, Lives of the First World War.
16 George Alfred Snowden. Colney Hatch Sub-Com, 8 Jul 1921, 103–4, TLA LCC/MIN/01010; WW1 service medal and awards roll, 1914–20, and Nursing Register, 1925, http://www.ancestry.com.
17 Private Charles Henry Beamon, minutes for med sup, Colney Hatch, 19 Mar 1920, TLA H12/CH/A/02/005; LCC Record of War service, http://www.ancestry.com.
18 Anon., The strike at Exeter Asylum.
19 Anon., The Exeter strike.
20 BoC, *Annual Report for 1919*, Part 1, 18.
21 Anon., Exeter Asylum strike terminated.
22 McCrae and Nolan, *The Story of Nursing*, 66.
23 BoC, *Annual Report for 1920*, Part 1, 1.
24 Cooke and Bond, *History of the Asylum War Hospitals.*
25 Jones, *Asylums and After*, 107.
26 Towers, The management and politics of a public exposé, 50–1.
27 BoC minutes, 30 Jul 1919, 191, TNA MH 50/47.
28 General Medical Council, *BMJ.*
29 Brown, Asylums, 148.
30 Lunacy Commission and BoC, Minutes and Seals 1919–30, TNA MH 50/47–58.
31 BoC minutes, 10 Aug 1921, 233, TNA MH 50/49.
32 e.g. BoC minutes, 7 Jan 1920, TNA MH 50/48.
33 Isabel Wilson, The Board of Control and the mental health services 'seen from the centre' (unpublished manuscript), 13, WL MS.7913/19.
34 Allmond, Liberty and the individual, 38.
35 Allmond, Liberty and the individual, 33.
36 Lunacy Act 1890, s. 187.
37 Letter, F Willis to WA Robinson, MoH, 2 Nov 1921, TNA MH 58/221.
38 Memo (illegible signature) to F Willis, 18 Dec 1925, TNA MH 51/530.
39 Memo, LGB: BoC and Dr Mapother meeting, 4 Feb 1930, TNA MH 51/714.

40 NSLR deputation (John Withers MP, R Sorensen MP, JWJ Cremlyn, FJ White, R Montgomery Parker, Dr Risien Russell), 16 Dec 1929, to Arthur Robinson, Mr Brock and Mr Barter, TNA MH 51/714.
41 Mental Treatment Bill, *Hansard*, 17 Feb 1930.
42 Memo, LGB: BoC and Dr Mapother meeting, 4 Feb 1930, TNA MH 51/714.
43 Robertson, The hospitalisation of the Scottish asylum system, 323.
44 Elgood, The asylum as it should be, 292.
45 Lomax, *The Experiences of an Asylum Doctor*, 56; Weatherly, *A Plea for the Insane*, 83.
46 Royal Commission on Lunacy and Mental Disorder, *Report*, 143, para. 252.
47 Lunacy Act 1890, s. 239.
48 Mercier, *Lunatic Asylums*; MacArthur, *Mental Hospital Manual*, 1.
49 Lunacy Act 1890, ss. 169, 188.
50 Hilton, 'I have to-day seen all the 671 patients', 395.
51 Wilberforce, *The Autobiography of a Pioneer Woman Doctor*, 131.
52 Reports Boards of Guardians visiting patients chargeable to them, 1887–1929, TLA H12/CH/A/06/001.
53 Anon., National Conference of Labour Women; Deputation: County Councils Association and Mental Hospitals Association to MoH and BoC, 28 Jan 1930, TNA MH 51/714.
54 Asylums Visiting Committees (Women), *Hansard*, 22 Dec 1919; Lunacy (Visiting Committees), *Hansard*, 21 Jun 1922; Lunacy (Visiting Committees) Bill, *Hansard*, 24 Jul 1922; Lunatic Asylums (Women Visitors), *Hansard*, 2 Aug 1922; Lunacy (Visiting Committees) Bill, *Hansard*, 4 Aug 1922.
55 Colney Hatch Sub-Com, 11 Jun 1920, TLA LCC/MIN/01009; 30 Nov 1928, 293, TLA LCC/MIN/01016.
56 Colney Hatch Sub-Com, 27 Jul 1928, 205–8, TLA LCC/MIN/01016.
57 Minutes for med sup, Colney Hatch, 8 Aug 1919, TLA H12/CH/A/02/005.
58 Colney Hatch Sub-Com, 9 Aug 1929, 149, 135, TLA LCC/MIN/01017.
59 BoC, *Annual Report for 1926*, Part 2, 91, Brentwood Mental Hospital, 29 Jul 1926.
60 McCrae and Nolan, *The Story of Nursing*, 48.
61 Colney Hatch Sub-Com, 25 Feb 1927, 221, TLA LCC/MIN/01015.
62 Hunter and Macalpine, *Psychiatry for the Poor*, 149.
63 BoC, *Annual Report for 1926*, Part 2, 137, Colney Hatch Mental Hospital, LCC, 17 Jul 1926.
64 Colney Hatch Sub-Com, 17 Mar 1922, 81, TLA LCC/MIN/01011.
65 Colney Hatch Sub-Com, 5 Aug 1921, 139, TLA LCC/MIN/01010; BoC, Circular 621, requesting information about fire procedures, 1923, TNA MH 51/240.
66 Colney Hatch Sub-Com, 22 Dec 1922, 254, TLA LCC/MIN/01011.
67 BoC, Circular 621, requesting information about fire procedures, 1923, TNA MH 51/240.
68 BoC, *Annual Report for 1926*, Part 2, 195, West Riding Mental Hospital, Wakefield, 24 Jun 1926.
69 BoC, Circular 737, Storage arrangements for X-ray films, Apr 1930 (based on British X-Ray and Radium Protection Committee, Recommendations with reference to the handling and storing of celluloid x-ray films, Oct 1929), TNA MH 51/240.
70 Colney Hatch Sub-Com, 1 Nov 1929, 210, TLA LCC/MIN/01017; 3 Oct 1930, 100, TLA LCC/MIN/01018.
71 Colney Hatch Sub-Com, 13 May 1921, 50, TLA LCC/MIN/01010; BoC, *Annual Report for 1926*, 26.
72 Colney Hatch Sub-Com, 18 Jun 1926, 31, TLA LCC/MIN/01015.
73 Med sup's reports, Colney Hatch, 21 May 1926, 277, TLA H12/CH/A/08/004.
74 Colney Hatch Sub-Com, 10 Jun 1921, 64, TLA LCC/MIN/01010; McCrae and Nolan, *The Story of Nursing*, 48.
75 Wallace, Making a healthy change.
76 Anon., Mental hospitals' administration.
77 Lomax, Searchlight on asylums.
78 Colney Hatch Sub-Com, 7 Jul 1922, 159, TLA LCC/MIN/01011.
79 Anon., Struggle with a mental patient.
80 A patient for five months, A living death; Evidence to Cobb Inquiry, Edward Mason, q. 2,113, TNA MH 58/220.
81 Anon., Struggle with a mental patient.
82 Anon., County Mental Hospital: Users of front drive.
83 Anon., Prussian practices at Powick.

84 Colney Hatch Sub-Com, 13 May 1921, 39–40, TLA LCC/MIN/01010.
85 Matilda C, Colney Hatch Sub-Com, 7 Sept 1928, 236, TLA LCC/MIN/01016.
86 Nurse Q, Med sup's reports, Colney Hatch, 15 Feb 1924, 245–6; 14 Mar 1924, 270, TLA H12/CH/A/08/003.
87 Sydney M, Colney Hatch Sub-Com, 5 Aug 1921, 139, TLA LCC/MIN/01010.
88 Nurse Hinchley, Colney Hatch Sub-Com, 9 Jul 1920, 59–60, TLA LCC/MIN/01009.
89 John G, Med sup's reports, Colney Hatch, 13 Jun 1919, TLA H12/CH/A/08/001.
90 BoC, *Report of the Departmental Committee*, 33.
91 Robbins, Profiles in medical courage, 65–73.
92 Evidence to Cobb Inquiry, Rev JJ Brownhill, q. 2,438, TNA MH 58/220.
93 MacArthur, *Mental Hospital Manual*, 17–18.
94 Parfitt, A mental hospital in 1929, 467.
95 BoC minutes, 3 Nov 1920, 269, Enforced resignation of Dr SEM, on the allegation of disloyalty to Dr R, TNA MH 50/48.
96 Memo, PB to Brock, 1 Aug 1922, Action by the MoH, BoC circular, TNA MH 58/224.
97 BoC minutes, 5 Feb 1930, 29, TNA MH 50/58; 17 Mar 1926, 53, TNA MH 50/54.
98 Bottome, *Private Worlds*, 13.
99 Anon., Retirement of Prestwich superintendent.
100 BoC minutes, 3 Oct 1923, 142; 1 Aug 1923, 124; 17 Oct 1923, 145, TNA MH 50/51; 28 Aug 1925, 127, TNA MH 50/53.
101 Bill Boyd, oral history interview by author, 2021.
102 Olshansky, Stigma.
103 BoC, *Annual Report for 1919*, Part 1, 19; MoH, *Report of the Committee on Administration* (Cobb Report), 77–8; Medico-Psychological Association, Report of the Committee on the Status of British Psychiatry.
104 BoC, *Annual Report for 1919*, Part 1, 19–20; BoC, Circular 583, 8 Mar 1921, TNA MH 51/240.
105 BoC, *Annual Report for 1925*, 10.
106 Turner, 'Not worth powder and shot', 15.
107 Long, *Destigmatising Mental Illness?*, 13; Takabayashi, Surviving the Lunacy Act.
108 MacArthur, *Mental Hospital Manual*, 10.
109 MacArthur, *Mental Hospital Manual*, 23.
110 MacArthur, *Mental Hospital Manual*, 22, 19.
111 Minutes for med sup, Colney Hatch, 2 Sept 1921, TLA H12/CH/A/02/005.
112 Med sup's reports, Colney Hatch, 21 Feb 1919, 21 Mar 1919, 12 Sept 1919, TLA H12/CH/A/08/001.
113 MoH, *Report of the Committee on Administration* (Cobb Report), 77.
114 BoC, *Annual Report for 1921*, 32–3.
115 Anon., The wrong bottle.
116 General Medical Council, *Medical Register 1926*.
117 Pierce, Some present-day problems, 198–9.
118 Lomax, *The Experiences of an Asylum Doctor*, 73.
119 Trades Union Congress and the Labour Party, *The Labour Movement and the Hospital Crisis*, 5–6.
120 MacArthur, *Mental Hospital Manual*, 18.
121 Trades Union Congress and the Labour Party, *The Labour Movement and the Hospital Crisis*, 5–6.
122 McCrae and Nolan, *The Story of Nursing*, 71.
123 Anon., General Nursing Council.
124 Arton, The professionalisation of mental nursing, 196, 209.
125 Mental Nurses Committee, 29 Jan 1929, 2, TNA DT 6/100.
126 McCrae and Nolan, *The Story of Nursing*, 49.
127 Medico-Psychological Association, *Handbook for the Instruction of Attendants*; Medico-Psychological Association, *Handbook for Mental Nurses*.
128 Medico-Psychological Association, *Handbook for Attendants on the Insane*, 363.
129 McCrae and Nolan, *The Story of Nursing*, 49.
130 Anon., My impressions at Exminster.
131 Mental Nurses and those Nursing Mental Defectives, with schedule of subjects given in practical instruction. Signed (approved) Neville Chamberlain, Minister of Health, 23 Jan 1925, TNA DT 38/170.
132 Mental Hospital Matrons' Association, 12 Apr 1929, TNA DT 16/322; BoC, *Report of the Departmental Committee*, 10; Anon., Medico-psychological examinations still to be carried on.

133 Mental Hospital Matrons' Association, 12 Apr 1929, TNA DT 16/322.
134 Arton, The professionalisation of mental nursing, 194.
135 Anon., Mental Hospital Matrons' Association; BoC, *Report of the Departmental Committee*, 21.
136 Mental Hospital Matrons' Association, 12 Apr 1929, TNA DT 16/322.
137 Anon., Lectures and demonstrations.
138 Colney Hatch Sub-Com, 11 Jun 1920, TLA LCC/MIN/01009.
139 BoC, *Report of the Departmental Committee*, 10, 29.
140 Mental Hospital Matrons' Association, 12 Apr 1929, TNA DT 16/322.
141 Anon., Another attempt to dodge the Royal Commission?
142 Anon., The nursing service in county and borough mental hospitals.
143 Anon., Departmental Committee on Mental Nursing: NEC's resolution.
144 BoC, *Report of the Departmental Committee*, 21.
145 Anon., Double training for mental nurses.
146 Anon., New training school for male nurses; Anon., Hospitals for training male nurses.
147 Anon., Seconding of mental nurses to general hospitals; BoC, *Report of the Departmental Committee*, 10.
148 Anon., Oxford County and City.
149 Trades Union Congress and the Labour Party, *The Labour Movement and the Hospital Crisis*, 5.
150 Anon., National Programme.
151 Anon., 48-hour week.
152 Scott and Spadavecchia, Did the 48-hour week damage Britain's industrial competitiveness?
153 BoC, *Annual Report for 1921*, 5.
154 Anon., Hours of work.
155 BoC, *Report of the Departmental Committee*, 34.
156 Anon., Stafford Branch.
157 Anon., Nurse famine in the country.
158 Colney Hatch Sub-Com, 12 May 1922, 112, TLA LCC/MIN/01011; 31 Jul 1924, 51, TLA LCC/MIN/01013; Med sup's reports, Colney Hatch, 3 Aug 1923, 89, TLA H12/CH/A/08/003.
159 BoC, *Annual Report for 1930*, 15; Med sup's reports, Colney Hatch, 23 Jan 1920, TLA H12/CH/A/08/001.
160 Anon., Impressions of a probationer.
161 Summary of evidence of Mental Hospitals Association and other bodies, c.1925, 2, TNA HLG 52/475.
162 Lomax, *The Experiences of an Asylum Doctor*, 68.
163 Summary of evidence of Mental Hospitals Association and other bodies, c.1925, 2, TNA HLG 52/475.
164 BoC, *Report of the Departmental Committee*, 33.
165 Anon., Nursing of mental patients, 964.
166 Arie, Discussion.
167 Colney Hatch Sub-Com, 17 Mar 1922, 83, TLA LCC/MIN/01010.
168 BoC, *Annual Report for 1928*, Part 1, 4.
169 Mercier, *Lunatic Asylums*, 56.
170 BoC, *Annual Report for 1926*, Part 2, 61, Beds, Herts and Hunts (Three Counties) Mental Hospital, 27 Jul 1926; 91, Brentwood Mental Hospital, Essex, 29 Jul 1926.
171 Minutes for med sup, Colney Hatch, 20 Dec 1918, TLA H12/CH/A/02/005; Colney Hatch Sub-Com, 25 Jul 1930, 58, TLA LCC/MIN/01018.
172 BoC, *Report of the Departmental Committee*, 15.
173 Thane, *Divided Kingdom*, 81.
174 Colney Hatch Sub-Com, 13 Apr 1923, 15, TLA LCC/MIN/01012.
175 Colney Hatch Sub-Com, 15 Apr 1921, 72–3, TLA LCC/MIN/01010.
176 Colney Hatch Sub-Com, 29 Nov 1929, 228–9, TLA LCC/MIN/01017.
177 BoC, *Report of the Departmental Committee*, 42.
178 Anon., Trade union membership.
179 Colney Hatch Sub-Com, 3 Dec 1926, 148–9, TLA LCC/MIN/01015.
180 Anon., Joint Conciliation Committee for the Mental Hospital Service.
181 BoC, *Annual Report for 1919*, Part 1, 17–18.
182 Anon., Cushy jobs.
183 BoC, *Annual Report for 1919*, Part 1, 17–18; BoC, *Report of the Departmental Committee*, 33.
184 Thane, *Divided Kingdom*, 98–9.

185 Thane, *Divided Kingdom*, 83.
186 Med sup's reports, Colney Hatch, 6 Nov 1925, 152, TLA H12/CH/A/08/004.
187 MacArthur, *Mental Hospital Manual*, 7.
188 BoC minutes, 6 Oct 1926, 143, TNA MH 50/54; 4 May 1927, 66, TNA MH 50/55.
189 BoC, *Report of the Departmental Committee*, 22.
190 Anon., John Bull, Female nurses.
191 Anon., Female nursing in asylum male wards must go!; Anon., More applicants – but unsuitable.
192 Anon., Female nursing in male wards of asylums; Anon., Montrose Asylum Board.
193 National Society for Lunacy Reform, *Annual Report 1925*, 4.
194 Robertson, The employment of female nurses, 362.
195 Royal Commission on Lunacy and Mental Disorder, *Minutes*, George Robertson, q. 16,047.
196 Medico-Psychological Association, *Handbook for Attendants on the Insane*, 252; Medico-Psychological Association, *Handbook for Mental Nurses*, 423.
197 BoC, *Annual Report for 1923*, Part 2, 168, Rainhill Mental Hospital, Lancashire, 27 Nov 1923, Dr Ernest Reeve returned to work; General Medical Council, *Medical Register 1925*; minutes for med sup, Colney Hatch, 27 Oct 1922, TLA H12/CH/A/02/005; Colney Hatch Sub-Com, 24 Oct 1924, 128, TLA LCC/MIN/01013; Med sup's reports, Colney Hatch, 11 Apr 1924, 192, TLA H12/CH/A/08/003.
198 BoC minutes, 21 Nov 1928, 183, TNA MH 50/56.
199 Med sup's reports, Colney Hatch, 5 Sept 1919, TLA H12/CH/A/08/001; Dr J B-B, med sup's reports, Colney Hatch, 31 Jul 1924, 254, TLA H12/CH/A/08/003; General Medical Council, *Medical Register 1932*.
200 BoC, *Report of the Departmental Committee*, 41.
201 BoC, Circular 677, The nursing service in mental hospitals, 4, Jan 1926, TNA MH 51/240.
202 Anon., Female nursing in male wards; Anon., National Conference of Labour Women.
203 Anon., Female nurses in male asylum wards.
204 Octavia Wilberforce, The Eighth Child, Part 2, Backsettown Farmstead, Henfield, Sussex, 264, 266, LSE Fawcett Library Archives, 7/0cw/A2.
205 Wilberforce, *The Autobiography of a Pioneer Woman Doctor*, 132.
206 Wilberforce, *The Autobiography of a Pioneer Woman Doctor*, 131.
207 Medico-Psychological Association, Members of the Association.
208 Westwood, A quiet revolution in Brighton, 447, 449.
209 BoC minutes, 6 May 1925, 73, TNA MH 50/53; BoC, *Annual Report for 1925*, 378; *Annual Report for 1926*, Part 2, 257.
210 Jean (or Jane) Elder Shortt; England and Wales, Civil Registration Marriage Index, 1916–2005, 1928, http://www.ancestry.com.
211 BoC, *Annual Report for 1927*, Part 1, 25; Bewley, Online archive 36, Prizes and prize winners.
212 Medical Women's Federation, memo, medical women in mental hospitals c.1929, WL SA/MWF/D.11.
213 e.g. BoC, *Annual Report for 1923*, 211, Northumberland Mental Hospital, 20 Jul 1923.
214 Letter, National Council of Women of Great Britain to F Willis, BoC, 27 Oct 1926, TNA MH 58/215.
215 House of Commons, *Standing Committee A*, 293.
216 BoC, *Annual Report for 1929*, Part 2, 146, Upton Mental Hospital, Cheshire, 23 Apr 1929.
217 Royal Medico-Psychological Association, Year Book; Medical Women's Federation, memo, medical women in mental hospitals c.1929, WL SA/MWF/D.11.
218 Med sup's reports, Colney Hatch, 17 Jun 1927, 77, TLA H12/CH/A/08/005.
219 Medical Women's Federation, memo, medical women in mental hospitals c.1929, WL SA/MWF/D.11.
220 Pierce, Some present-day problems, 201.
221 Anon., Report of proceedings.
222 BoC, *Annual Report for 1929*, Part 1, 7.

6
Reform

When the Prince of Wales visited the Bethlem Royal Hospital in 1921 and shook hands with all the patients, there was 'a pronounced improvement in the mental condition' of every one of them.[1] Over many centuries it was believed that the royal touch could cure scrofula, a manifestation of tuberculosis,[2] and now it was improving mental hospital patients! This was no miracle of course, but the royal handshake helped restore self-respect, hope and a sense of being valued as a human being. That personal approach was too often lacking in mental hospitals. To achieve it would require shifts in the lunacy law, attitudes to patients, funding and institutional culture, to allow a style of treatment which was more flexible and individualised. An anonymous correspondent in the magazine of the National Asylum Workers' Union (NAWU) commented that if the Prince of Wales' new 'mental treatment' was so effective, he should 'go to the House of Commons and shake hands with our Coalition legislators' to set them on the right track too.[3]

Bringing about social welfare change is a complex, 'wicked' problem. The Multiple Streams Framework is used in social science research to help explain the process. It comprises three basic streams. 'Problems' need to be identified and clarified and 'policy' solutions proposed. These need to enter a 'political' stream, influenced by public mood, various interest groups and elected officials. All three must come together to open a 'window' to take matters forward. Reform was, and is, a multi-faceted process spanning far wider than professional groupings.[4] Its complexity is far removed from the dualist explanations that Andrew Hubbard, in his historical analysis of risk and confinement in England and Wales, and other commentators, have offered – of 'resurgent medicalism' being associated with the medical profession embarking 'on a determined campaign to make certification primarily a medical concern and overturn the legalism of the 1890 Act'.[5] Debate between legal and medical leaders was only part of the story. Tensions between the legal and medical professions intertwined with calls for reform from people from multiple spheres, including patients, politicians, parliamentarians, trades unionists and magistrates.

After WW1 there were campaigns in countries within and beyond Europe to raise standards of care for mentally unwell people and to modernise the restrictive legislation that had dominated practice. These moves were accompanied by international exchanges of ideas. The geographical spread of these activities adds weight to the hypothesis that shell shock was only one of many stimuli for reform, rather than its main driver.[6] In the USA, for example, improvements were spurred on more by the mental hygiene movement, which was established pre-war. Shell shock was less of an issue there because the country only declared war against Germany in 1917, with the first American military offensive taking place in May 1918, just months before the Armistice.[7]

Many of the reasons why reform of the mental hospitals and lunacy law were needed are described and explained in earlier chapters of this book. Forthright advocates sought to create more liberal and humane institutional practices and to provide treatment without compulsion whenever possible. This chapter explores chronologically the principles, processes and outcomes of the campaigns, debates and inquiries which sought to achieve those goals, what hampered them and what enabled them, what made the Government act, and what was achieved.

Reforming the Lunacy Act

Continuing from the pre-war attempts to reform the Lunacy Act 1890 discussed in chapter one, early in 1918, while the war still raged, Dr Lionel Weatherly, then in his 60s and thus not eligible for military service, published his book, *A Plea for the Insane*. It was written for both a public and professional readership. He argued that the 'obnoxious' and 'pernicious' Lunacy Act should be abolished.[8] While the war continued, but now at a point where the country was able to look forward to a period of reconstruction, the Medico-Psychological Association (MPA, later RMPA) established its English Lunacy Legislation Sub-Committee.[9] This 13-person group included psychiatrists working at lieutenant-colonel rank in military roles, Dr Helen Boyle from the Lady Chichester Hospital, Dr Bedford Pierce from the Retreat, York, and Dr Robert Steen from the City of London Mental Hospital.[10] Notably, these psychiatrists worked at the periphery of the Board of Control's gaze and away from the constraints of the unwieldy, local authority-funded county and borough mental hospitals. They had practical experience of doing things differently, and were known to provide more flexible and humane care than that often found in the public mental hospitals, which were constrained by resources, the Lunacy Act and long-standing institutional culture. At its meeting two weeks after the Armistice, the MPA praised the work of the Sub-Committee and stated its support for a Mental Treatment Bill in 1919 which would 'compel' local authorities to provide facilities for treating 'incipient mental disease', aiming to prevent the conditions from worsening and therefore avoiding the need for admission under the Lunacy Act.[11]

In *A Plea for the Insane*, Lionel Weatherly also spelt out why the standard of care in asylums required improvement, and how to achieve it: 'we must get at the public and they must agitate' to influence the officials. Those officials he said, spanned the breadth of asylum administration, including 'a crocodile and a python' in central government.[12] Dr Weatherly's book, neither particularly well written nor easy to read, faded from public view, but the man behind it did not. Weatherly reflected that he may have been 'too fearlessly out-spoken',[13] and that

> while fighting for reforms, I have had the uncongenial task of 'kicking against the pricks' [Acts of the Apostles 26:14] [but] as long as my poor old brain is able to work, I shall still keep on 'kicking,' in the fervent hope that, though some harm may come to me, some progress may yet be made toward those more altruistic reforms which I and others have advocated.[14]

Weatherly kicked with an almost religious zeal to reform the asylums and asylum law. He later wrote to the Board of Control: 'I feel sure you will not mind if I bombard you [with questions] at any time.' Evidently, judging from the Board's internal memos, it did mind.[15]

Societal changes abounded post-war. The school leaving age rose from 12 to 14 years, campaigning for women's rights was ongoing, and there were more and stronger trades unions representing workers. The new Ministry of Health took a lead across many aspects of healthcare and social welfare. Nursing reform was also proceeding, associated with ideas of professionalism, education, employment and leadership, especially for women. For mental deficiency (rather than mental illness), changes envisaged by the Mental Deficiency Act 1913 but delayed by the war were at last underway. Assumptions and social attitudes enshrined in the Lunacy Act 1890 were increasingly outdated, such as the pauper lunatic designation and providing different access to care depending upon wealth rather than illness and need. Discussion about the Act centred on principles of liberty, choice, detention and stigma.

The subject of the provision of institutional care for mentally ill people frequently entered debate in both Houses of Parliament. Repeated themes were suspicion or distrust of the institutional regime, and financial costs.[16] Standards of care within the mental hospitals were raised less often. In 1920, several damning reports about asylum standards appeared in the national press.[17] When Dr Sara White wrote 'The living dead' in a women's magazine, the Board of Control sought advice from the Director of Public Prosecutions as to whether it should take legal proceedings against her.[18] Another report came from Ernest Parley, a conscientious objector who worked in an asylum during the war. He noted a lack of anything which could be construed as 'mental treatment', referring instead to a gloomy, unnatural silence among the patients, their wandering aimlessly in the airing courts, and the 'deadly monotony' of asylum life, 'sans freedom, possessions, friends, incentive, and therefore, in so many cases, the desire to live'.[19] The *Medical Press and Circular* was typically forthright in criticising the state of care, and emphasised the urgent need for asylum and lunacy law reform.[20] Advocating for reform, it said, was its duty.[21] Lionel Weatherly 'rejoiced' at its stance, which endorsed reports published elsewhere and increased awareness of the issues so that 'the Government will see the necessity of some very wholesome reforms'.[22]

Mr Parley, like Drs Weatherly, White and Lomax, did not stop at his initial disclosures. He became active with the newly founded National Council (later Society) for Lunacy Reform (NCLR/NSLR). The NCLR had broad objectives, including dealing with systemic organisational difficulties; enhancing recovery through community measures; safeguarding 'the liberty of the subject' – meaning protecting the public from wrongful detention; and reducing 'the burden of our ever increasing and mainly unproductive asylum expenditure' – a nod towards eugenics.[23] Members of the NCLR included well-connected and veteran campaigners, suffragists, and others from across the political spectrum. The organisation joined forces with others with shared goals, such as the Ex-Services Welfare Society. It sought to publicise its campaign through the press and at public meetings. It also encouraged 'drawing room' meetings, where 'people of influence' would invite their friends to their homes to hear suitable speakers, to stimulate interest and help with fundraising.[24]

Medically trained doctor Christopher Addison was appointed as the first Minister of Health in 1919. His intentions to improve access to mental healthcare were but a small part of an overwhelmingly large welfare reform agenda. He introduced the Ministry of Health (Miscellaneous Provisions) Bill in 1920. One of its clauses sought to enable the general population to access publicly funded psychiatric outpatient clinics and admission for treatment on a voluntary basis. Dr Nathan Raw MP (later president of the MPA) voiced his approval that 'the Minister of Health is treating mental disease and insanity in precisely the same way as he would treat any other affliction'. However, the multi-faceted bill faced opposition in the Commons on the grounds of its structure and content, which ranged from mental hospitals to public housing. William Ormsby-Gore MP called it 'an omnibus, ill-drafted, hotch-potch of a Bill'. It was also controversial in terms of the financial cost that would be required to implement it, although Thomas Myers MP was derisive of those members who appeared to take the attitude of 'save the rates and the taxes, even if the people perish'.[25]

A different set of objections arose in the Lords, including the bill's timing. On 14 December 1920 Lord Sheffield said:

> it is not fair for the Government to bring in an important Bill and ram it through the House of Commons by an all-night sitting with no opportunity for discussion, and then ask us at the very close of the session to deal with these important proposals ... the Bill should be thrown out ... it is unreasonable to ask us to meet between Christmas Day and the New Year.[26]

The collapse of the Ministry of Health (Miscellaneous Provisions) Bill provided the *Medical Press and Circular* with an opportunity to censure the Government: 'For a Government Department ... to be so widely trounced, and afterwards snubbed, can only mean some loss of prestige to the Administration generally ... Is all well with the Ministry of Health?' Addison was 'a man in a hurry' with good ideas, but perhaps too radical.[27] Soon after, during the financial crisis which followed, the Treasury slashed public expenditure and, with many of his plans thwarted, Addison demitted office.[28] Both the Board of Control and the MPA were keen to try again to change lunacy legislation, but preferably with a bill specific to the issue.[29]

Dr Montagu Lomax and his book

Dr Montagu Lomax's exposé, *The Experiences of an Asylum Doctor*, appeared in the summer of 1921. Lomax was a retired general practitioner who had worked in two asylums between 1917 and 1919, to cover for the usual doctors who were then serving in the military. Some of his experiences, as described in earlier chapters of this book, shocked him. They included witnessing a lack of meaningful activity for patients, patients being punished, purged and drugged, severe understaffing prohibiting good care, and a want of tact, kindness, sympathy and patience on the part of staff.[30] He was more forthright about standards of care than Dr Weatherly, but they agreed that there was a systemic failure, where rules were put above the needs of patients, and that to achieve change the public must be aware of the facts.[31] Public mood, as the Multiple Streams Framework later explained, was crucial to mobilise change.

The Board of Control was defensive and in disbelief of Dr Lomax's allegations, although the Ministry of Health readily acknowledged, at least initially and in private, that some institutions were inadequate. Dr Lomax did not mention the name of the institution on which his book was based, but it was obvious to the Ministry, which wrote:

> It is unfortunate that nearly all [of Lomax's] experience was gained at one of the least satisfactory asylums ... buildings are antiquated, and the Medical Superintendent is not conspicuously efficient. It may safely be said that Dr Lomax saw the English asylum system at its worst, the normal defects of Prestwich being aggravated by [wartime] shortage of staff and strict rationing of food ... the book is important because the main criticisms apply in a greater or lesser degree to all public asylums ... Broadly speaking it is true that our asylums are barracks rather than hospitals and the insane are treated more like prisoners than patients.[32]

Prestwich, just north of Manchester, was one of the five Lancashire asylums. Shortly before publication of *The Experiences of an Asylum Doctor*, it had been investigated concerning an allegation made by Benjamin Tillett MP that ex-service patients were being neglected.[33] Dr Cunyngham Brown of the Ministry of Pensions, which had responsibility for their care, accompanied Dr Marriott Cooke and Mr Arthur Trevor of the Board of Control to interview the patients.[34] In two days, they interviewed 279 ex-servicemen. Only 11 had any complaints, most of which the Board concluded had 'no substantial foundation' but resulted from delusions or hallucinations such as a belief that their food had been drugged.[35] The conclusions fitted with standard defensive rhetoric: the patients' statements were tainted by their mental condition.[36] Dr Weatherly was scathing about Dr Cooke's and Mr Trevor's claim to have interviewed so many people in so little time, suggesting that their interviews were superficial at best.[37] Dr Cunyngham Brown's views, that standards were indeed unsatisfactory, were overruled by the so-called experts of the Board.[38]

Much to the chagrin of the Board of Control,[39] *The Experiences of an Asylum Doctor* attracted press attention. The *Times* paraphrased Dr Lomax's words, commenting that 'many of the pictures painted of petty tyranny and soulless discipline are calculated to fill the reader with horror'.[40] 'Civis' in the *English Review* praised Dr Lomax's 'timely public service', 'revelations which demand at once public attention and inquiry, for truly if this is Bedlam in our midst, it is a ghastly and pitiable tale'.[41] The *Medical Press and Circular* expressed admiration for the book's 'judicial and impartial' approach, called for an inquiry and praised the way in which 'the newspaper press has figuratively tumbled over upon itself in devoting columns to the discussion of the maladministration of the asylums'.[42] Dr Weatherly, among others, was delighted by the 'almost universal opinion in lay and medical newspapers that an investigation of a searching and independent nature was absolutely necessary'.[43] Dr Lomax worked closely with the NCLR leadership. They responded to letters about ill-treatment and wrongful confinement in institutions across England; where possible, they visited patients and interviewed them in hospital, to gain better 'inside knowledge'.[44] The NCLR arranged lecture tours for Dr Lomax, and his publisher provided copies of *The Experiences of an Asylum Doctor* at wholesale prices which the charity could sell at the standard retail rate.[45] It also lobbied members of Parliament and gave Dr Lomax influential contacts in political, literary and medical circles. It managed press interest and published supporting literature. The NCLR attracted the attention of prominent figures, such as members of the aristocracy, authors GK Chesterton and HG Wells, and psychiatrists such as Helen Boyle and Lionel Weatherly. The Labour Party Public Health Advisory Committee asked the NCLR for input into its programme of lunacy reform and the Board of Control invited it to send a representative to its conference in 1922.[46]

Scottish psychiatrist Professor George Robertson referred to *The Experiences of an Asylum Doctor* as 'essentially a correct statement of the back-ward condition of Lunacy Administration generally in this country, more especially in England'. He also commented that Dr Bond, a senior member of the Board of Control, was 'a very strong adverse critic of Dr Lomax's book, being apparently of the opinion that there is little or nothing in it which is either good or true'.[47] This suggested that Dr Bond's further involvement in analysing the situation was likely to be prejudiced. Nevertheless, Dr Bond, accompanied by his Board of Control colleague Dr Rotherham, made an unannounced visit to Prestwich in September 1921. Given the furore, it may have been unannounced, but it could not have been unforeseen. Drs Bond and Rotherham found problems but regarded them as minor. They thought, for example, that patients' clothing 'might be improved', but to call the clothing 'humiliating' as Dr Lomax had was 'a travesty of the truth'. Neither did the earth closet system from which the 'closet-barrow gang' removed excreta each night seem to disturb them. They did not report, though, on whether the nine patients in the gang did the work and the two staff supervised it, or whether the staff took part in the physical labour. Discussion with Prestwich's medical superintendent, Dr Frank Perceval, who was in post when Dr Lomax worked there, appeared to convince Drs Bond and Rotherham that Dr Lomax was wrong in almost every way.[48]

The Board's confidence in Dr Perceval was far removed from that of the Ministry of Health.[49] Similarly, the Ministry acknowledged the poor state of provision at Prestwich, but the Board did not, suggesting that low standards were acceptable. The Board employed classic techniques of undermining the complainant's credibility, noting, for example, that since Dr Lomax had no formal psychiatric training, he lacked the knowledge and authority to comment. The Board described Dr Lomax as 'confused in his ideas', and that publishing his allegations was 'ungentlemanly' and 'unprofessional', as he ought to have discussed his concerns with Dr Perceval.[50] Dr Lomax recognised the ethical dilemma of delaying raising the issues, which allowed inadequate practice to continue, but in a regime where employees who spoke up were usually dismissed and their concerns ignored, dismissal would have hampered his ability to gather ammunition for his book.[51]

The style of the official response to Montagu Lomax and his exposé was replicated when other authorities received complaints. One such occasion was when Councillor Mary Hatfield, the only woman member of Hull City Council, undertook an official, unannounced early morning inspection visit to the local mental hospital. As mentioned in chapter three, she witnessed women patients being bathed in the same bathwater and sharing bath towels, and was shocked by what she considered callous, unhygienic and undignified standards of care.[52] When she reported her findings to the Council, the Lord Mayor alleged that her sole objective was publicity for herself. The Council accused her of lying, but, to protect itself, asked the Board of Control to investigate.[53] The Board vindicated the hospital, challenged Mrs Hatfield's integrity and motivation, and referred to what she had observed as an 'exceptional occurrence', implying that it was unlikely to recur.[54] Mrs Hatfield wrote of the Council's response to her: 'Had I been a low grade animal and the committee and chairman a gang of German brutes, the treatment meted out to me could not have been more of a virulent type.'[55] The Council's defensive response to criticism would not lead to improvements, and the publicity around the episode was likely to deter others from reporting unacceptably low standards.

Reflecting on his book in 1922, Montagu Lomax wrote:

> I was quite unprepared for the immense amount of public interest it immediately excited ... The fact that a book written by an obscure and hitherto unknown medical man, and having no pretensions to do more than skim the surface of the matter dealt with, should have such a striking and immediate effect proved at least two things: that the subject was recognised to be of pressing importance and appealed to public interest, and that I had quite unexpectedly struck the 'psychological moment' for its discussion.[56]

Setting up the Cobb Inquiry: the Committee on Administration of Public Mental Hospitals

Shortly after publication of *The Experiences of an Asylum Doctor*, Dr Bouverie McDonald MP asked Minister of Health Sir Alfred Mond whether he intended to inquire into Dr Lomax's allegations 'in order to relieve the anxiety of many of the public who had relatives confined in these institutions'.[57] One medical superintendent, Dr Percy Hughes, wrote to the Board of Control, expressing the need to protect the staff from Lomax's 'lying statements'.[58] Both Dr McDonald's and Dr Hughes' statements indicated their disbelief about poor standards, and emphasised prioritising the institutions' public image.

In August 1921 the Ministry suggested the setting up of a Royal Commission, because an inquiry would need to be sufficiently authoritative to deal with financial and legal aspects of the asylum system as well as the specific allegations.[59] Sir Frederick Willis, chairman of the Board of Control, wrote to Sir Arthur Robinson, a senior Ministry of Health civil servant, stating that the Ministry should not establish an inquiry into any of the recent exposés: 'The Board of Control is the proper body to deal with these ... Any other course would undermine our authority.' Mental hospital organisation and administration, Willis wrote, had evolved as a 'result of long experience and there is nothing radically wrong with them. But many improvements are possible most of which however would cost money.' Diverting attention away from the sensitive issues of standards of care and the need for additional expenditure, Willis shifted to recommending legal changes. What needed to be done was to 'facilitate the treatment of early cases without certification', a task which would not be too expensive, and with which the Board was well equipped to deal as '[they] alone possess the requisite knowledge and are in close touch with the agencies which should be used'.[60] The Board was defensive, appeared deaf to the possibility that inadequate care existed on its watch, and was self-opinionated about its own ability to take the next steps.

In November 1921 the Ministry retracted its earlier proposal for a Royal Commission, on the grounds that there was insufficient evidence for such a major investigation and that it would take too long to organise.[61] It also rejected the Board of Control's proposal that it should undertake the inquiry itself. It followed a third line, deciding that the best option was an independent inquiry under its authority.[62] Nevertheless, the Ministry consulted the Board on the composition of the inquiry committee: the Board still wanted one of its members on the panel because anything less would undermine its influence.[63]

The Ministry appointed Sir Cyril Cobb to chair the Committee on Administration of Public Mental Hospitals. Cyril Cobb was knowledgeable, having previously chaired the LCC Asylum and Mental Deficiency Committee.[64] The other committee members were Dr Bedford Pierce of the Retreat, and Dr Percy Smith who had worked at the Bethlem Royal Hospital and then mainly in private practice. Mr Percy Barter, a civil servant at the Ministry, who will be referred to again later, was appointed as secretary to the committee.[65]

Some dismissed the inquiry as farcical before it even began.[66] Lionel Weatherly was among those disturbed by the committee's composition of two psychiatrists plus a former LCC asylum committee chairman, which meant that it lacked independence and would, in a sense, be judging itself.[67] That Dr Pierce had already described Lomax's book as 'a grossly unfair attack' suggested that he was likely to be prejudiced in his committee role.[68] The inquiry panel satisfied Board of Control convention that only those deemed trained and experienced in providing services had a right or ability to judge, rather than others approaching the subject with an independent mindset. A report in the *Times* criticised the Ministry of Health for 'doing everything in its power to confuse the issue and "side-track" the reform', merely paying lip-service to public concern, and that when the committee finally offered its report, it would be treated as 'a final and authoritative finding on the point on which the public is interested', with the result that more awkward questions would be shelved.[69]

1922: the year of the Cobb Inquiry

The Board did not want the inquiry, preferring to do things its own way. It took the unusual step of planning a conference on 'Lunacy Administration' for January 1922, just before the Cobb Inquiry was due to begin. Arthur Robinson did not feel he could oppose it.[70]

The conference included much reassuring rhetoric, such as Alfred Mond declaring that asylums 'really are hospitals for persons suffering from mental diseases', to which the *Times* responded: 'That apology has been used before on many similar occasions. It will not bear a moment's scrutiny.'[71] Nevertheless, the conference was not devoid of criticism, including opprobrium from mental hospital medical superintendents. Dr Robert Turnbull of Severalls Mental Hospital, Essex expressed concern that wards of 60 or more patients were too large: smaller wards would be better for patients, albeit more expensive to run.[72] The conference took place contemporaneously with the Government's drive for public economy and retrenchment, so implementing Dr Turnbull's ideals and other proposals was unrealistic in the short term. In particular, higher running costs would require local authority – and hence ratepayers' – approval, which was unlikely to be forthcoming when authorities were challenged by 'the blight of poverty and the necessity of reducing expenditure to absolute essentials'.[73] Dr Henry Devine of Portsmouth Mental Hospital complained about the financial constraints, the existence of too many rules and a lack of focus on patients as human beings requiring help, noting that 'those cases who walk day by day round the ward gardens are our own failures – and the nurses' failures'.[74] Those patients were 'asylum-made lunatics' – an acknowledgement of institutional failure, aligning with the later terms 'institutionalisation' and 'institutional neurosis'.[75]

The MPA was delighted with the conference, declaring it to be 'one of the most important departures in the history of lunacy administration'.[76] Uniquely at the time, it provided a forum for discussion between interested parties inside and outside the institutions. However, despite giving opportunities for participation, the Board maintained a tight grip. The main outcomes were two resolutions, reported as being unanimous. First, that the option to obtain early treatment for mental problems on a voluntary basis without certification should be available to the whole population, not just those able to pay for it. Second, that the Board was the appropriate authority to oversee current and new provision. The first of these was important but hardly new, and the second would have been difficult for delegates to oppose. The conference also spurred the Board to appoint separate multi-disciplinary committees to investigate nursing, diet and record keeping.[77]

The Cobb Inquiry was not permitted to take witness statements on oath, nor was legal representation allowed. For these reasons, the NAWU instructed its members not to give evidence, and Dr Lomax, having discussed the matter with Lionel Weatherly and others, decided likewise. Shortly before the inquiry began, Dr Lomax wrote in a letter to the *Times* that it would be 'one-sided and likely to prove unsatisfactory and abortive', and proposed a Royal Commission, comprising two women, a senior doctor, a barrister, MPs and social workers, presided over by a judge.[78] Replying in the *Times*, Alfred Mond justified the appropriateness of the Cobb Committee as it could begin its work quickly, rather than entailing the longer process of establishing a Royal Commission.[79] Members of Parliament were concerned at the proliferation of reports 'by responsible persons' appearing in newspapers 'almost daily' which supported Dr Lomax's allegations, but Mond also ignored MPs' requests for a Royal Commission.[80]

In the run-up to the formal hearing, the Cobb Committee visited Prestwich. Given the passage of time since the end of the war, the attention drawn to Prestwich by the Ministry of Pensions and the six months that had elapsed since Dr Lomax's book appeared, one might have expected improvements to have taken place. The committee did not find things to be as bad as Dr Lomax had described, but neither was it as forthright as the Board of Control about the hospital's adequacy.[81] Indeed, it was shocked by some of its observations, such as unacceptable strategies for managing restless and distressed patients. It also found that 'Dr Perceval's personal attitude towards the study of modern methods was unsympathetic'.[82]

The Cobb Inquiry took evidence formally between February and April 1922, mainly in public. A typed transcript of the minutes is preserved at the National Archives.[83] It includes some handwritten alterations, but who made them, and on what authority, is unclear. Shorthand note-takers may have misheard or misunderstood statements which legitimately required later correction, but the minutes may also have been adjusted to make them less incriminating. Dr Perceval was one witness who gave evidence in private. The reason for that privilege, usually reserved for maintaining the anonymity of patients and frontline staff fearing stigma or recriminations, was not made explicit, but in the light of some of his words being redacted, there may have been concern about him making libellous statements. The minutes as they stand now record his description of his wartime staff as 'the flotsam and jetsam ~~and scum of the earth~~'.[84] Although staffing should have improved three years post-war, there was little evidence of that for either doctors or nurses.[85] Unlike elsewhere, Prestwich had no general hospital trained nurses as Dr Perceval 'could not get the money for it'.[86] Lectures for staff had not resumed, perhaps because of Dr Perceval's negativity that an 'elaborate course of training would not be suitable' as the staff were mainly former domestics and factory workers.[87] Neither were doctors at Prestwich allowed study leave, because they were 'too busy and could not be spared'.[88] Dr Perceval gave the impression of being resigned to poor standards, blasé, evasive, uncreative in attempting to solve problems, and having little interest in the wellbeing of those over whose lives he presided.[89]

Some other evidence given to the Inquiry was disrespectful of patients, including Mr Trevor's comment about patients who 'trot' up to him during hospital inspections[90] – a word usually reserved for animals. Other evidence included sweeping statements with dubious grounding in fact, such as from Dr David Ogilvy, Long Grove Mental Hospital's medical superintendent: 'Bad language as far as I know, not only in mental hospitals, but in my general knowledge of the world, is a thing that has diminished just exactly the same as the use of alcohol has diminished.'[91] Other evidence caused consternation among the committee members, such as when Mr Mears, a non-medical mental hospital staff member, proposed that for a long-stay patient who had become bedridden: 'I should let them sleep. I think that is a humane thing to say: to put them to sleep'; moreover, for anyone else, if they could work on the land they should be discharged. Dr Pierce replied: 'It would save the ratepayers' money.' Mr Mears answered: 'Indeed it would.'[92]

The committee was uncivil to some witnesses to a degree which could discourage them from giving their testimony. When Dr Sara White was called, Cyril Cobb greeted her: 'Now Dr White, there is some particular point on administration which has arisen … If you will kindly keep yourself to the point.'[93] He could be more courteous, as he was when welcoming Dr Weatherly: 'Good afternoon, Dr Weatherly, we are obliged to you for being willing to give us some results of your experience.'[94] Sir Cyril's words suggested assumptions about the value of some people's evidence before they offered it.

Diversity of opinion regarding problems and solutions, even just among the doctors, may have hindered the committee from drawing conclusions. Whereas, for example, Dr Ogilvy regarded seclusion as a 'very useful form of treatment', Dr Weatherly was averse to it.[95] Regarding the size of institutions, Dr Ogilvy thought a thousand beds was reasonable, but Dr Laurence Fuller of the Three Counties Mental Hospital proposed ten thousand, even more than the Milledgeville State Hospital, USA, where numbers were rising close to it.[96]

The Cobb Inquiry achieved what the Ministry and Board of Control had sought: while noting that some things could be improved, the report reassured the public that 'the present provision for the care and treatment of the insane is humane and efficient' and compares 'favourably with that in any other country'.[97] The latter statement was meaningless since there was no international comparative data, and it gives rise to the question whether other of their conclusions were also speculative. The recommendations, however, concurred with the underlying thesis of Dr Lomax's work, even if they failed to address the dysfunction at Prestwich. Some of Cobb's recommendations would not require heavy financial commitment, among them advertising medical superintendent vacancies rather than automatically promoting from inside the institution; appointing 'visiting' medical, surgical and dental specialists to the mental hospitals; employing staff specifically to improve patients' occupational activities; and 'payment of commensurate remuneration to patients doing useful work',[98] all discussed in earlier chapters of this book. All required shifts in culture and outlook towards patients' welfare and threw the onus for change on the individual hospitals.

In her analysis of the Cobb Inquiry, Bridget Towers commented on the pros and cons of admitting to having problems in an institution. Admitting to them risked personal discredit of the leadership and creating public alarm. However, it might also generate sufficient concern to promote creative solutions and buttress the case for improvement, with the potential for longer-term benefits. Finding that all was well encouraged maintenance of the status quo, and reassured the leadership, the public and their elected representatives of the need to do nothing.[99]

The Board of Control visited Prestwich again, late in 1922. Its report disappointed the Ministry, which commented that it was 'to all intents and purposes just as bad now as when the Cobb Committee began their investigations'.[100] In the context of the committee ignoring specifics, paying lip service to patients' needs and being unable to mandate change, it was unlikely to stimulate action in places which demonstrated little interest in taking it. The Ministry and the Board went no further to reflect on their own approaches, or that the Cobb Inquiry may have ignored crucial factors or underestimated the severity of the problems, or that recommendations alone were unlikely to create meaningful and speedy change.

Not everyone took the Cobb Report at face value. The press was alive to the possibility of further revelations, and responded with interest to the publication of the pseudonymous, autobiographical book by Rachel Grant-Smith, *The Experiences of an Asylum Patient*, with an introduction and notes by Montagu Lomax.[101] The periodical *Truth* dubbed the Cobb Report a 'whitewash', and supported Dr Lomax's and the NCLR's calls for a Royal Commission.[102] In Parliament, MPs continued to ask questions, such as about the pauper taint, the lack of women on visiting committees, and low standards of care provided for both ex-service and civilian patients detained in the institutions.[103]

The MPA was heartened by the Cobb Report – unsurprising since most public mental hospital medical superintendents were also members of that body. When Professor Robertson gave his presidential address to the MPA in 1922 on making mental hospitals more humane and more like general hospitals, he referred to successful developments in Scotland.[104] For the mental hospital leadership south of the border it was a prompt to reconsider their approach, but the MPA did not seem to latch on. Rather, the MPA was emphatic about 'the cult which has taken Dr Lomax for its high priest', whose 'devotees continue unabatedly to inveigh that creation of their imagination, "the system"'. Dr Lomax, the MPA stated, demonstrated 'mental agility at misinterpretation and innuendo' and appeared 'undeterred and unrepentant as to his method of propaganda'.[105]

Although labelled a traitor to the medical profession because his writing 'offended against every canon of professional etiquette', Dr Lomax did not give up. He rationalised that the leadership had to disprove his allegations in their own interests.[106] For him, though, the issues raised were ones of 'common humanity', stating: 'I am a man before I am a doctor.'[107] Even his brief obituary in the *Lancet* in 1933 reiterated little more than the 'sensational' nature of his book, and that his allegations were refuted.[108] Reminders of Montagu Lomax were lost from other places: images of him are missing from family photo albums, suggesting that he may have been an embarrassment to his family too.[109] Almost forgotten, his contributions to raising awareness of problems, and his remarkable personal steadfast approach to remedying them, have re-emerged at the hands of historians, but a century on, similar patterns of official defensiveness and disregard of criticism continue.[110]

1923 and the Mental Treatment Bill

1923 began in celebratory fashion when the LCC's Maudsley Hospital opened its doors to civilian patients after eight years as a military mental hospital. Its opening for public use was the culmination of an extraordinarily long project. Frederick Mott, a scientist, physician and psychiatrist in London, visited Professor Emil Kraepelin and his institute in Munich in 1907, and sought to create similar facilities in London. Before the war, Mott negotiated initial funding for the project from the wealthy psychiatrist Henry Maudsley, with a view to further capital and longer-term funding being continued by the LCC.[111] The new institution (subsequently named in honour of the donor) would function like a university-linked teaching hospital, aiming to treat patients suffering from mental disorders of recent onset, and only accepting voluntary admissions when both doctor and patient agreed to it, without certification under the Lunacy Act. Implementation of this plan required new legislation. This was secured as a private Act of Parliament, the London County Council (Parks, etc.) Act 1915, making the Maudsley Hospital the first publicly funded mental hospital in the country to allow admission without certification.[112]

The hospital's opening was regarded as highly significant for the practice of psychiatry in England and for the future design of mental healthcare provision for the majority of the population who could not afford private fees. Nevertheless, it was a relatively minor event in the LCC calendar. A flimsy, postcard-size 'Order of Proceedings' for the opening ceremony is preserved, bound into a volume of LCC pamphlets. It is sandwiched between another Order of Proceedings of the same size and flimsiness, for the opening of the Eltham By-pass Road, and another, much larger, with colour pictures on glossy paper for the opening of the LCC's new headquarters, County Hall. Most of the large Orders of Proceedings were produced when royalty had agreed to perform the opening ceremonies, the small ones when a lesser official, such as a government minister, was to undertake the duty. The Ministry of Health had wanted royalty to open the Maudsley Hospital, but archival sources hint that civil servants mishandled the invitation.[113] In the absence of royalty, the honour of opening the hospital fell to the new Minister of Health, Sir Arthur Griffith-Boscawen, who had succeeded Sir Alfred Mond when David Lloyd George's Government fell the previous October.

In line with pre- and post-WW1 recommendations and the principles behind the new Maudsley Hospital, a Mental Treatment Bill was introduced into Parliament in 1923. Just as in earlier bills, it aimed to permit outpatient and inpatient psychiatric treatment for 'incipient mental disease', for the whole population, without certification and regardless of ability to pay.[114] Various safeguards regarding personal liberty would be created: the institution into which the patient would be received would have to be approved and monitored by the Board of Control;[115] two doctors would need to make the recommendation; and the patient would have to request admission. Duration of admission would be limited to one year. The patient would have the right to discharge himself with 48 hours' notice, although some thought 72 hours was more realistic, to ensure that families were notified and that patients could be returned into their care, given that most households had neither telephone for contact nor car for travel.[116] Dedicated wards for these voluntary patients could be in general or mental hospitals, and outpatient clinics could be provided along the lines of those at Oxford's Radcliffe Infirmary.[117] The bill also proposed that visiting committees would arrange after-care for patients, paid for through public funds, to assist with readjustment to community life, with the aim of preventing readmission. Other clauses in the bill included allowing visiting committees to co-opt people who were not elected local councillors, which would help ensure that each had at least two women members.[118]

The debate on voluntary admission ranged from eagerness, such as from the Bishop of Worcester, who urged that if a new law might do some good 'for God's sake, go on and try ... you are doing something to bring mercy and hope of recovery to what is the most pitiable section of our great community', to hostility, such as from Lord Buckmaster, who emphasised the importance of detention to protect the community, and with eugenic overtones.[119] The bill proceeded through the Lords, but the timing was unfortunate: arriving in the Commons immediately before the summer recess, the matter was adjourned.[120] Its passage from one House to the other resonated with the awkward timing of the Ministry of Health (Miscellaneous Provisions) Bill in 1920. The postponements suggested that neither bill was considered to warrant urgent consideration. The Board of Control described the new bill as 'abandoned'. However, yet another turn was on the horizon.[121]

Questions of wrongful detention: the cases of *Everett* and *Harnett*

The public feared the possibility of wrongful mental hospital detention when mentally well. Sometimes cases were reported in the press, which attracted much public attention. In the early 1920s, two such cases reached the House of Lords for judgement by the Law Lords.

The first of these was the alleged wrongful certification of Harry Everett by Dr Kaiku Anklesaria and magistrate Mr Griffiths, resulting in Mr Everett's admission to Colney Hatch Mental Hospital. Dr Anklesaria, medical superintendent of St John's Road Infirmary, Islington, took a special interest in patients on the mental observation ward and generally made the medical recommendation under the Lunacy Act if they required mental hospital admission.[122] Harry Everett was on the observation ward for several days before Dr Anklesaria concluded that mental hospital admission was appropriate. Mr Griffiths' assessment included discussion with staff members, the Poor Law relieving officer who brought Mr Everett to the ward, and Mr Everett's mother, who emphasised that she feared her son's violent behaviours.[123] Dr Anklesaria and Mr Griffiths appeared to have made their decisions with care.

On transfer to Colney Hatch, Mr Everett was deemed to be suffering from 'primary dementia'. When his mental state began to improve, he was 'employed in the Clerk's office, and was practically on parole'. He escaped and, evading recapture within the legally stipulated 14 days, his certification lapsed. Mr Everett then took legal action, claiming wrongful certification by Dr Anklesaria and Mr Griffiths.[124] The case was tried before the Lord Chief Justice and a jury, and subsequently passed to the Court of Appeal and the House of Lords. The Law Lords found no evidence to support Mr Everett's claim, and the case was dismissed. The outcome, reported in the *Times*, confirmed that Mr Everett had not been wrongly detained, reassuring the public that the workings of the mental hospital system, including the Lunacy Act, were satisfactory.[125] The reassurance had the same flavour as the Cobb Report, but publicity around the case added to concerns about wrongful detention – a subject embedded in public consciousness, alleged in memoirs and appearing in popular novels. An unanswered broader question was whether a doctor who made such a decision in good faith in the course of his public duty should be legally protected from charges of negligence.[126]

The second case was the long-running, and ultimately influential, drama and legal proceedings concerning William Harnett's alleged wrongful detention. It overlapped in content with the *Everett* case, and in timing with the planned post-adjournment reintroduction of the Mental Treatment Bill 1923 into Parliament. The bill was not reintroduced, because the House generally refrained from discussing issues which were under consideration in a court of law.

To understand the *Harnett* case, it is necessary to track its development, beginning in 1912, when 51-year-old William Harnett, a farmer, was admitted to a private mental hospital at Malling Place, Kent, run by Dr George Adam. As per the Lunacy Act for private patients, William's brother, Arthur Harnett, petitioned for his admission and agreed to follow up on his wellbeing. With the brothers having the same surname, I will refer to each by their first names for clarity, not out of disrespect. William's admission papers referred to his firmly held beliefs that he should rescue prisoners at Borstal prison and draw everybody to Christ. He was also 'deeply steeped in sexual topics, now trying to get some publications, in ethical questions of sex', and regarded the servants as insane because they could not spell parallelogram. He was labelled as suffering from 'religious mania'.

Soon after admission, William wrote to the Board of Control complaining that he had been wrongfully detained. The following month, he escaped when out on leave with Arthur. William returned to his own home, collected his cheque book, booked into a hotel in London, and went to the Board's office. There, he spoke to Dr Bond who telephoned Dr Adam, who sent 'a motor and 2 Attendants' to return him to Malling Place.[127]

William's disturbed mental state persisted. He had delusions about his wife and refused to see her, and persecutory delusions about a conspiracy against him, about which he declared that Scotland Yard was aware, and that the police had arrested one of the conspirators. From Malling Place he moved through several other private institutions. Still detained in 1921, he contacted a solicitor, on the grounds that both Dr Bond and Dr Adam, back in 1912, had detained him illegally. Shortly after that he escaped again and was not recaptured.[128]

In 1922, a High Court writ informed Drs Bond and Adam of an impending court case against them.[129] The hearing, early in 1924, took place before a judge, Charles Lush, and a jury.[130] Mr Justice Lush awarded William £25,000 damages against Drs Bond and Adam.[131] The *Times* reported: 'The Harnett case will have awakened the general public to the possibility of wrongs which most of us have hitherto supposed to be confined to the realm of fiction,' suggesting the need for urgent reform to 'ensure that no sane person shall ever again be subjected to the dreadful ordeal' which William Harnett had undergone.[132] A photograph of a smiling, convincingly 'normal'-looking William Harnett appeared in the

THE ILLUSTRATED LONDON NEWS, March 8, 1924.—393

PERSONALITIES OF THE WEEK: PEOPLE IN THE PUBLIC EYE.

Photographs by Elliott and Fry, L.N.A., Photopress, Sport and General, C.N., and Barratt.

A FAMOUS ANTHROPOLOGIST RETIRING: DR. ARTHUR SMITH WOODWARD.

THE HOME SECRETARY INTRODUCED TO THE HOUSE OF COMMONS BY HIS M.P. SONS: (L. TO R.) MR. ARTHUR HENDERSON JUN., M.P., MR. ARTHUR HENDERSON, M.P. (THE NEW MEMBER FOR BURNLEY), AND MR. W. W. HENDERSON, M.P.

A FAMOUS EGYPTOLOGIST AND ASSYRIOLOGIST RETIRING: SIR ERNEST A. WALLIS BUDGE.

THE BELGIAN PREMIER, WHO HAS RESIGNED: M. THEUNIS.

HEROINE OF A ROYAL ELOPEMENT: THE LATE PRINCESS LOUISE OF BELGIUM.

TESTATOR OF A MYSTERIOUS £4,250,000: THE LATE MR. J. T. MILLS.

AWARDED £25,000 FOR 9 YEARS IN ASYLUMS: MR. W. S. HARNETT.

THE NEW KEEPER OF EGYPTIAN AND ASSYRIAN ANTIQUITIES AT THE BRITISH MUSEUM: DR. H. R. HALL IN HIS OFFICE.

THE NEW UNIONIST CHIEF AGENT: MR. H. E. BLAIN, TUBES MANAGER, OF "SAFETY FIRST" FAME.

DISTINGUISHED AS RAILWAY ENGINEER IN INDIA: THE LATE SIR STEPHEN FINNEY.

THE NEW KEEPER OF GEOLOGY AT THE BRITISH MUSEUM: DR. F. A. BATHER.

RETIRING AFTER 37 YEARS IN THE WAR OFFICE FINANCIAL DEPARTMENT: SIR CHARLES HARRIS.

Dr. Smith Woodward, the retiring Keeper of Geology at the British Museum, is famous for his work on the Piltdown Skull.——Dr. F. A. Bather has been Deputy-Keeper since 1902.——Mr. Arthur Henderson, who took his seat in the Commons on March 3, is probably the first M.P. introduced by his sons.——Sir Ernest A. Wallis Budge has been Keeper of Egyptian and Assyrian Antiquities at the British Museum since 1893. His successor, Dr. H. R. Hall, has excavated for the Egypt Exploration Fund, and directed the Museum excavations at Ur of the Chaldees, Tell-el-Obeid, and elsewhere.——M. Theunis, Premier of Belgium, resigned on the rejection of his Cabinet's motion to ratify the Franco-Belgian Economic Convention.——Princess Louise of Belgium, daughter of Leopold II., was married at 16, in 1875, to the late Prince Philip of Saxe-Coburg-Gotha, and was divorced in 1906 after eloping with Count Geza Mattachich.——Mr. J. T. Mills, whose fortune provides £1,640,000 in Estate Duty, was Lord of the Manor of Leighton Buzzard, and a director of several companies. He left two Murillos to the National Gallery ——Mr. W. S. Harnett was confined in asylums from December 1912 to 1921, when he escaped.——Mr. H. E. Blain has shown exceptional organising power as Manager of the London Underground Railways and General Omnibus Company.——Sir Stephen Finney was for eight years Manager of the North Western Railway in India, and later served on the India Railway Board. In 1872-3 he played Rugby football for England.——Sir Charles Harris has been Joint Secretary of the War Office since 1920, and a member of the Army Council. As Assistant Financial Secretary he introduced a new system of Army accounts.

Figure 6.1 Personalities of the week: Mr William Harnett, 'Awarded £25,000 for 9 years in asylums', *Illustrated London News*, 8 Mar 1924, 393. © Illustrated London News Ltd/Mary Evans Picture Library.

Illustrated London News with the caption 'Awarded £25,000 for 9 years in asylums', without further explanation: it would likely have roused readers' interest – and their fear (Figure 6.1).[133]

Charles Lush's entry in the *Oxford Dictionary of National Biography* noted: 'Sometimes he allowed his feelings to master his judgement, as in Harnett *v.* Bond.'[134] His decision spurred on campaigners for lunacy reform. The NSLR lost no time. It held a public meeting to demand a Royal Commission and 'urgent reform'. Scrawled across the top of a flyer advertising their meeting (Figure 6.2), someone wrote: 'Nemesis!! First chapter of the Book of Revelation your end', probably referring to the opening verse, about recent revelations and 'things which must shortly come to pass' – that is, a Royal Commission.[135]

The MPA took a back seat, drawing its information from the *Times* reports, but the medical profession more broadly voiced its alarm.[136] Clearly, in Mr Justice Lush's opinion, doctors acting in good faith in the course of their duty were not protected from charges of negligence: might any of them also have to pay such damages for improper certification? Perhaps they should refuse to certify anyone?![137] It was a dilemma: if a doctor failed to certify a case which ended in suicide, homicide or other tragedy, he may also be 'held responsible and subjected to public censure'.[138] Given the innumerable attempts to define insanity from both medical and legal standpoints, but with none wholly satisfactory, plus a lack of training on mental disorders in medical schools, and the fact that generalists rather than specialists usually undertook the clinical assessment to determine whether certification was warranted, infringing the rules or causing harm was many doctors' nightmare.

Within days of the judgement, Moss Turner-Samuels MP described the Lunacy Act as a 'scandalous menace to personal liberty',[139] rather than the usual rhetoric that it enshrined a safe system, and Leonard Costello MP asked the Prime Minister to appoint a Royal Commission.[140] In the same debate, Mr Turner-Samuels read from letters he had received about cruelty in asylums, aligning them with Stalinist labour camps in Siberia. Other MPs were supportive on the issue of personal liberty, but during the debate shouted 'Rubbish!' at the mention of cruelties.[141]

The defendants appealed against the judgement, and the Court of Appeal ordered a new trial by the House of Lords.[142] In the interim, the Royal Commission was appointed. By the time the Law Lords overturned the original decision, having concluded that William had not been wrongfully detained and the £25,000 need not be paid, the Royal Commission was underway.[143]

Nemesis!! First Chapter of the Book of Revelation

NATIONAL SOCIETY
FOR
LUNACY REFORM

A
PUBLIC MEETING

Your end

to support the Society's Memorial for a Royal Commission on Lunacy Law Administration and to demand urgent reform will be held in

CENTRAL HALL
(Small Hall),
WESTMINSTER, S.W.

On Wednesday, February 27th, 1924,
at 8 p.m.

Speakers:

THE LORD BISHOP OF EXETER.
Rt. Hon. LEIF JONES, M.P.
JOHN MARLEY, M.P.
Sir ROBERT NEWMAN, M.P.
Dr. BERNARD HOLLANDER, M.D.
Dr. MONTAGU LOMAX, M.R.C.S.
Miss MARGARET MACMILLAN, C.B.E.

Mrs. PETHICK LAWRENCE in the Chair.

ADMISSION FREE.

A few Reserved Seats at One Shilling.
All who are interested in this very important question should attend without fail, and bring their friends.

N.S.L.R. 32-33, Avenue Chambers, Southampton Row, W.C.

The Paternoster Press, 26-27, Ivy Lane, E.C. 4.

Figure 6.2 Flyer for NSLR public meeting: 'Nemesis!! First chapter of the Book of Revelation your end', Feb 1924. Photographed as filed, with treasury tag in place. Source: National Archives, ref. MH 86/46.

It was an unhappy state of affairs for the Harnetts. In 1925, despite the Lords' decision, William decided to continue his fight. Despairing of William's plans, Arthur threw himself from a moving train. The coroner's verdict was 'suicide during temporary mental derangement'.[144] Financially, William was ruined.[145] In 1927, his body was washed ashore on the River Thames at Poplar. The coroner's verdict was 'found drowned'. The coroner was also reported to have said that 'for the last four years or so Mr Harnett had acted perfectly normally'.[146] That comment raises questions of lay perceptions of normality and whether William's pursuit of justice after the Lords' ruling was realistic, or whether his actions were based on grandiose or persecutory delusions caused by a severe psychotic illness.

Following the publication of Lomax's book, the Minister of Health argued that a Royal Commission would take too long to organise.[147] Concerning *Harnett v. Bond*, it took a matter of weeks. Rather than standards of patients' care, the sane public's fear of being wrongly certified as insane and a crisis in the medical profession, with doctors fearful of being sued for wrongful certification, triggered the Commission. In contrast to the reassurances given by the Cobb Inquiry and *Everett v. Griffiths*, Mr Justice Lush's decision fuelled public and professional fears. As the Multiple Streams Framework sets out, problems were recognised, the policy solution (in this case a Royal Commission) was formulated, and political action to implement it was enabled by the concerns of various interest groups and a fearful public mood.[148]

The Royal Commission on Lunacy and Mental Disorder, 1924–1926

The *Harnett* case shaped the Royal Commission. Its terms of reference concerned 'the existing law and administrative machinery in connection with the certification, detention, and care of persons who are or are alleged to be of unsound mind' in England and Wales, and the consideration of treatment without certification.[149] Even this contained loaded terminology, the word 'alleged' implying that the person had done wrong, rather than being ill. The Commission defined 'care' as 'all the factors involved in the environment and treatment of patients', including legal and administrative factors.[150] The standards of care within the institutions were only part of the Commission's brief.

Regarding independence of judgement, the Commission's membership was as far removed professionally and administratively from the mental hospitals as the Cobb Committee's had been entwined with them. Hugh Pattison Macmillan (later Baron Macmillan), a Scottish-born advocate, judge and parliamentarian, chaired the Commission. Alongside him sat Earl Russell, who had a longstanding interest in lunacy law reform. Other members included MPs, lawyers, civil servants and senior doctors. The two doctors were Sir Humphry Rolleston, president of the Royal College of Physicians, and Sir David Drummond, recently president of the British Medical Association. There were two women: Mrs Anna Mathew, an LCC councillor, and Miss Madeline Symons, a trades unionist and Labour activist. Mr Percy Barter, who served as secretary to the Cobb Inquiry, took on the same role for the Commission.[151] In summary, the make-up of the Commission was much as Lomax had suggested before the Cobb Inquiry.[152]

The Royal Commission was a vast undertaking. It received oral evidence from 111 witnesses over 42 days between October 1924 and December 1925.[153] Sixteen of the witnesses were women, five of whom were former patients. Eight male former patients also gave evidence. Other witnesses included trades unionists, civil servants, local government officers, campaigners, magistrates, nurses, doctors and ministers of religion.[154] Some tireless campaigners, such as Miss Ethel Vickers of the Mental After Care Association and Dr Helen Boyle of the Lady Chichester Hospital, fought their corner, giving evidence to both the Cobb Inquiry and the Royal Commission. Unlike the Cobb Inquiry, the Commission had the power to call witnesses, take evidence on oath and allow witnesses legal representation.[155] Montagu Lomax, the NSLR and the NAWU had confidence to give evidence. Evidence was generally taken in public with the press present, although for most former patients and some nurses it was taken in private when considered prudent to maintain anonymity.[156] As with the Cobb Inquiry, the intention behind this was to alleviate fears of publicity contributing to stigma for patients or recriminations for staff.

Inpatients who applied to give evidence did so when the Commission visited their hospitals.[157] In addition, over five hundred current and former patients sent written evidence. The Commission denied making automatic assumptions that patients' complaints were due to their mental condition, but nevertheless it commented, without further elaboration, that a 'considerable proportion' of their letters 'bore unmistakable signs of mental instability'[158] and therefore 'failed to carry conviction to our minds'.[159] Similar to the Cobb Committee, the Commission thought that patients' evidence did not make 'any constructive contribution of material value to the main purpose of our Inquiry, though it proved useful in informing us at first hand of incidental defects in the system'.[160]

The Commission's remit was specific to mental illness in England and Wales, so it did not delve into mental deficiency, or law and practice in Scotland, or the interface between crime and insanity.[161] Nevertheless, it explored these subjects, when necessary, to help inform its analysis. It also avoided some subjects which were already under investigation, notably mental nursing and patients' diet.[162] For those matters, it studied the published reports, combining that information with testimony which arose during its inquiry. The one million words of minutes indicate the depth to which the Commission probed the subject of their investigation. The minutes also give the impression that the Commission was repeatedly dismayed by legal, administrative, medical and social aspects of the mental hospitals, and at times bewildered by the testimony it received. The chairman requested clarification, for example, when baffled that the term 'pauper' was used to define a patient's status 'when he is an excellent member of society ... I can well conceive that the expense of treatment may be beyond the means of the wage-earner, but at the time when he becomes afflicted he is not a pauper in any sense of the term; he is a self-respecting and self-sustaining citizen.'[163] It was also dismayed by other aspects, such as having different rules for admitting and discharging pauper and private patients, with criteria 'out of harmony with modern views upon treatment of sick persons'.[164]

The Commission's report and changing the law

The Commission's report was published in July 1926 in turbulent times, soon after the General Strike. It was unlikely to bring about an immediate government response, given their other preoccupations, although the Commission's independence, authority and extensive analysis meant that at least some of its recommendations would have to be considered at ministerial level.

Like the Cobb Inquiry, the Commission attempted to weigh the evidence regarding allegations of abusive practices in the mental hospitals, and the reports of both reveal tropes of reassurance and defensiveness. Both concluded that, overall, patients were well cared for and the 'wholesale allegations of neglect and ill-treatment which are sometimes made' were unjustified,[165] although '[i]solated instances of brutality or perhaps more often of rough handling or neglect occasionally occur'.[166] It acknowledged a range of reasons, such as 'temperamentally unfit' staff, provocative 'refractory' patients or 'wet and dirty' patients, and stated that sometimes heavy handedness was justifiable, such as 'to control the maniacal fury of a violent case'.[167] All these factors were located at the level of individual frontline staff and patients, with those more senior being deemed to lack influence on the matter, other than by having the authority to remove the staff member. The Commission's remedies were practical, and far from original: provide staff with better training, work conditions and accommodation, with more staff and more supervision on the wards, and continue with the 'detection and the elimination of unsatisfactory nurses'.[168]

The report advocated humane practices, some controversial at the time, such as having women nurses care for male mental patients, and it warned about frugality – for example that 'a cheap and dull dietary may well prove a false economy by reducing the number of recoveries'.[169] It also demonstrated the wicked nature of providing mental healthcare, bound up with multiple and hard to shift issues including outdated laws, unclear medical theories, and often negative societal values and priorities.[170] It described some reforms as long overdue, and endorsed many proposals made in earlier bills which had not become law, such as public funding for after-care.[171] Little, however, in the way of new ideas emerged from the Commission. The NSLR was wary, fearful that the new set of proposals might meet the fate of others, reiterated over many years but to no avail.[172]

The report did not shy away from other contentious issues, such as the Board of Control. The LCC, Mental Hospitals Association and County Councils Association regarded the Board as 'unduly interfering', secretive and difficult to challenge.[173] The Commission noted no 'want of zeal' on the part of Board members'[174] – a statement which hinted that they were overzealous towards the tasks allocated to them, notably monitoring practices and enforcing rules over and above paying attention to patients' wellbeing. Seemingly cautious about criticising a central government authority, the Commission advised restructuring the Board. That meant more staff, including a senior woman member 'who might be non-technical', which appeared to mean one with neither medical nor legal qualification.[175] With their role undefined, this seems somewhat tokenistic, and out of step with women entering the medical and legal professions. A larger team might make tasks easier to complete, but whether it would or could change the culture, making the Board more approachable or more individual patient-centred, was less certain. Like the MPA, the Board of Control seemed complacent and unable to read between the lines. Its chairman, Frederick Willis, was characteristically relieved that allegations of wrongful detention and of widespread cruelty were 'for the most part, made by irresponsible and reckless persons' and had 'no foundation'.[176] His words point to him having little intention of finding out more about those which were not 'the most part'.

In the post-*Harnett* context, the Commission acknowledged underlying public concern about balancing the liberty of the sane individual with the detention of mentally unwell people in order to 'protect' society from those who 'will not or cannot conform to the accepted code of social conduct'.[177] The existing Act, it said, emphasised compulsory detention and 'bristles with precautions against improper detention', but '[n]o safeguards that can be devised can be absolute'.[178] However, given the recent furore about doctors being sued for damages for wrongful detention, it recommended that the Lunacy Act should be amended so that a doctor would not be liable to civil or criminal proceedings unless he had acted 'in bad faith or without reasonable care'.[179] Not all agreed with the Commission's stance of protecting the doctor. Josiah Wedgwood MP was one who regarded the threat of prosecution as a beneficial public safety matter. Without it, he wrote, there was 'not the slightest risk to the doctor', meaning that more people might be detained in mental hospitals with the 'terror confronting and dominating that man – that he may never get out'.[180]

The Commission was obliged to weigh up evidence concerning legal formalities for obtaining treatment. Existing legislation was out of keeping with recommended best clinical practice, which aimed to treat mental problems in the same way as physical problems, particularly allowing early treatment with access to outpatient clinics and inpatient care without certification.[181] Mental problems, the Commission said, were a public health matter, and – just as for some infectious diseases – there could be elements of compulsion for treatment, and services in both general and specialist hospitals.[182] Compulsory detention should be a 'last resort, not the pre-requisite of treatment', and certification should have 'one object only, the protection, treatment and, if possible, cure of the patient'.[183] Based on the success of the voluntary admission scheme at the Maudsley Hospital and, by then, also at the City of London Mental Hospital, and the flexibility of admission practices in Scotland, the Commission recommended establishing admission on a voluntary basis for psychiatric assessment and treatment across England and Wales.[184]

Nevertheless, on the principle of habeas corpus, it decided to continue to involve a magistrate for certification for compulsory detention, despite evidence that the duty was sometimes performed in a perfunctory way. Magistrates were *meant* to provide an independent voice to safeguard the liberty of the subject. Standards ranged from undertaking a thorough assessment and making an informed judgement (as Mr Griffiths did concerning Mr Everett), to giving a cursory glance at the patient, or automatically rubberstamping the doctor's recommendations.[185] One example given was that of a patient 'put into a taxicab and taken to the door of the justice's home ... [T]he justice ran down the garden, poked his head into the cab and then signed the certificate.'[186] Safeguards were important, but 'do not let us overload the Bill with so many safeguards that we cannot get the cure that we all want', warned Derrick Gunston MP.[187]

The Commission's words were recommendations and were not binding. Seeking a more liberal approach, it recommended new legislation to replace the complex and anachronistic Lunacy Act, because a superimposed amending Act would increase complications. In mid-1926 Percy Barter, the Ministry of Health civil servant who had acted as secretary to both the Cobb Committee and the Royal Commission, advised that despite a full replacement being an ideal, the Ministry would be confronted 'by the limitations of parliamentary time. It can be argued in favour of an amending Bill that it will probably take less time to prepare and less time to pass and will expose a shorter front for criticism in the House.' 'Parliamentary convenience' would also be a crucial factor. Given the experiences with the Ministry of Health (Miscellaneous Provisions) Bill 1920 and the Mental Treatment Bill 1923, suggesting simplicity and brevity to avoid Parliament feeling overwhelmed by matters about which it had demonstrated variable understanding and concern, was a reasonable consideration. Although the Lunacy Act was not being abolished just yet, Mr Barter was optimistic that a 'consolidating measure' would follow within a few years, which would have the benefit of incorporating learning from the legal changes then being introduced.[188]

Mr Barter wanted a short bill to be put to Parliament soon, but he gave no clue as to timing. When, in November 1926, William Davison MP urged Minister of Health Neville Chamberlain to introduce the new legislation, Mr Chamberlain replied that the Commission's recommendations were under consideration.[189] In May 1928, Mr Chamberlain reassured MPs that the Ministry was dealing with the issue, but that it was unable to give a date for the bill.[190] In December 1928, Lord Sandhurst raised his concern in the House of Lords regarding the lack of progress.[191] With frustrations about the delays piling up, a reference to *Christina Alberta's Father* appeared in the *Manchester Guardian* in 1929:

> Five years have elapsed since the scandalous condition of our lunacy laws led to a public outcry and to the appointment of a Royal Commission. Those who have forgotten its recommendations may at least remember *Christina Alberta's Father*. But we cannot expect

> Mr HG Wells to expose each of our social scandals every year. We must fall back upon the National Society for Lunacy Reform, whose annual report once more reminds us that an evil does not mend because a Royal Commission explains its nature.[192]

In 1929, just as in 1920 at the time of the Ministry of Health (Miscellaneous Provisions) Bill, the Ministry had numerous good intentions. It was again attempting to navigate multiple threads of legislation through Parliament which could impact on mental and physical wellbeing. That included a Housing Bill, to ensure that slum dwellers were rehoused in more favourable surroundings at affordable rents. There was also a Local Government Bill, which would transfer health and welfare responsibilities from the Poor Law Guardians to the county and borough councils.[193] This would also officially abolish the 'pauper lunatic' term, so people admitted to mental hospitals would instead be known as 'rate-aided patients' – terminology which put those admitted to mental and general hospitals on the same footing.

The impression from archive sources is that the Ministry dragged its heels over mental hospital matters, and the Board of Control and RMPA did little to cajole them. There may have been sound reasons for delaying the Mental Treatment Bill, but the impression given is more of difficulty in getting mental disorders to the top of the priority list in the real world of competing agendas. In 1929, the NSLR noted the delays but was optimistic that something would happen under the new Labour Government of Ramsay MacDonald.[194]

By 1930, the Ministry and Board of Control were feeling perturbed at the lack of support they were receiving from those they perceived as allies, including the RMPA. The Board's new chairman, Laurence Brock, wrote to Dr Thomas Saxty Good, president-elect of the RMPA (rather than to the incumbent, Dr Nathan Raw, who may have had conflicting interests since he also held a paid central government position):

> As usual, the friends of the Bill are doing nothing. This generally happens, because there is an idea that if the Government introduce a Bill they can and will see it through. But this is not at all the case with Bills of this type which are not Party measures. No Government will give more than a certain amount of time to a Bill of this kind and sufficient obstruction by its critics, combined with the apparent apathy of its friends, may very easily result in the Bill being dropped.[195]

Laurence Brock criticised the RMPA's inactivity, in keeping with Trevor Turner's historical analysis pointing to its institutional docility before WW1.[196] If the RMPA was in support of the bill, it needed to bring its views to the notice of the House of Commons. Mr Brock also asked Dr Bond to 'ginger up' his friends in the organisation: 'All the cranks and opponents are circularising Parliament and if bodies like the RMPA do not take any steps to counteract this pernicious propaganda, an impression may easily be created [among parliamentarians] that nobody wants the Bill.'[197] The political wheels of change were unlikely to move without external pressure, but the RMPA seemed to lack initiative regarding mobilising its membership or expressing its views.

The Minister of Health echoed the Royal Commission's report: 'Certification should be a last resort and not a necessary prerequisite for treatment.'[198] The possibility of voluntary status raised new conceptual and ethical issues: what was meant by 'volition'? Was it more than just an automatic agreement? Lord Dawson, a medically qualified peer, attempted to clarify the concept of volition in the House of Lords. He explained that decisions about providing treatment for patients who lacked volition did not just apply to mental illness: 'If one of your Lordships were delirious and in a fever you would be without volition within the meaning of this Act ... Nobody hesitates in those circumstances to restrain personal liberty.' In that situation, a magistrate would not be required to authorise treatment, so a similar non-legal approach was appropriate for treating a primarily mental disorder which impaired a person's ability to make decisions about treatment.[199] Nevertheless, the whole subject was fraught with intellectual, ethical and legal challenges. Defining and determining 'real volition' was contentious: could someone who has a disturbed mind have 'real volition in the full sense', and how might that be assessed? What would happen if a voluntary patient wanted to leave, but had neither resources nor support because his friends who had promised to fetch him had not arrived as they said they would? Although 'escaping' would not be covered by the law, would 'retaking' the patient fall under a duty of care? What if a voluntary patient wanted to sign legal documents or vote in an election, and how might the situation be managed if the voluntary patient ceased to have volition?[200]

The debate on volition overlapped into an important deviation from the Commission's recommendations: the Ministry of Health introduced an additional 'temporary' legal category for patients. Temporary status would be appropriate for someone suffering from a mental disorder who was considered likely to benefit from a short period in hospital, but at the time of assessment was 'incapable of expressing himself as willing or unwilling to receive such treatment'.[201] Admission as a temporary patient would require an application made by a relative or friend, supported by two medical recommendations, but without a magistrate's order. The person would not be certified since the rationale for the option was to treat to facilitate recovery, just as for admission to a general hospital for a physical disorder. It was also in line with the legal situation in Scotland, which allowed treatment for up to six months in a mental observation ward without certification.[202]

New legislation would not offer an instant solution. Other challenges had to be overcome to facilitate implementation, such as providing suitably staffed outpatient clinics and admission wards in general and mental hospitals. Without the commitment of local authorities and visiting committees there was a risk that the new Act would fail, with proposals becoming no more than a 'mere detail of nomenclature'.[203] Whether the Ministry of Health could influence local authorities to implement the Commission's recommendations, which had the potential to achieve better longer-term outcomes, was unclear. Likewise, there was uncertainty as to whether it could convince the Treasury that central government funding would be worthwhile, especially to stimulate activity in 'backward authorities' such as Prestwich. The Ministry was consistently fatalistic, expecting that financial considerations would probably limit the 'extent to which effect can be given' to proposals.[204]

In contrast, the Board of Control, although not holding the purse strings, persisted with new financial tactics as the Commission had indirectly permitted it to do. Prioritising low costs was now a matter for criticism: expenditure was 'not a safe criterion of efficiency', 'it is never economical to under-staff a hospital', and 'it is far more economical to promote as many discharges as possible, preferably on recovery, than to lower the maintenance rate' which risked 'penalty in the shape of expenditure on additional beds'. In a similar way, well-staffed outpatient clinics could reduce bed use, and would be a 'remunerative expenditure'.[205] Similar messages circulated about improving standards in mental deficiency institutions, although that had not been part of the Commission's terms of reference: better provision there might also improve skills and behaviours, and facilitate discharge back into the community.[206]

However, the new philosophy had no time to embed. The Wall Street Crash of October 1929 was followed by the Great Depression – a prolonged and worldwide economic downturn. Minister of Health Arthur Greenwood rejected the need for additional funding, offering sticks rather than carrots. He justified his approach on the grounds that the new legislation was 'not so much a new duty as the application of an old duty in a different way ... [It is] part of the public health work of the local authorities ... [I]f they do not carry out their duties they may, under the Local Government Act, suffer a diminution in their State assistance.'[207]

The psychiatrists, despite being at the pinnacle of the individual mental hospitals, were only one component of policy decision making. They could advocate but were not always heard. On the other hand, sometimes they were not sufficiently forthright, and the (R)MPA could be complacent. Psychiatrists had to juggle their advocacy with walking tightropes between clinical safety and risk; between advocating for (probably more expensive) innovation and considering the perspectives of their visiting committees; and between maintaining their reputation locally in order to remain in post, or jeopardising the wellbeing of themselves and their family. Obligations to family, especially in isolated communities, have continued to be a factor in psychiatrists' decisions as to whether to rock the boat.[208]

Reflections

In the 1920s, greater middle- and upper-class prosperity stood in stark contrast to the poverty, unemployment and slum housing of many working-class people. Better mental healthcare and associated fit-for-purpose legislation were among the many social and welfare concerns for which improvements were sought in the initial period of post-war optimism. By the end of the 1920s many proposals had only partially materialised. Ongoing social difficulties were associated with a broad public disillusionment.[209]

This chapter brings together mental health themes featured earlier in the book, including public understanding, medical priorities regarding early treatment, and organisational hierarchies, cultures, processes and policies, all of which ultimately affected patients' lives. No single individual, profession or other group could achieve the necessary widespread changes. Many contributed, much was known about what to do, and there were pockets of change. The importance of the Royal Commission lay in the authority of its report, derived from its independence, rigour and ability to combine and evaluate many voices, rather than it creating ideas from scratch.

Following the conclusion of the Royal Commission, government action was largely focussed on bringing about the Mental Treatment Act 1930. The process was long and drawn-out, with the result pleasing to some but less so to others such as the NSLR.[210] The 1930 Act tinkered with the Lunacy Act 1890, rather than completely recasting it as the Commission had recommended. Based on ideas which had arisen over decades, the substance of the Act was little different from the succession of earlier bills which had failed to become law. The inveterate campaigner Dr Lionel Weatherly reminded the Board of Control after the Act was passed: 'As you doubtless know, I have been urging many things mentioned … from the year 1884.'[211]

At this stage in the narrative, the heading of 'Reflections' also needs to be looking forward. The Board was pleased with the new Act, which marked 'an epoch in the treatment of mental disorders in this country'.[212] It was indeed a new epoch, with the potential to improve access to treatment, but the Board also had concerns, as the Act was mainly an 'enabling measure' rather than a mandate for change.[213] Clauses regarding providing additional services were permissive rather than mandatory, and under those circumstances, they would not automatically reach the top of local authority and mental hospital agendas, particularly in the context of economic retrenchment. Aware of the likelihood of slow progress in implementing the Act,[214] within a fortnight of Royal Assent the Board arranged a conference for local authorities, visiting committees, medical superintendents and others to discuss opportunities. The conference resembled their previous one in January 1922. With 250 delegates, and high volumes of sales of the published proceedings afterwards, the Board summarised the outcome as indicating a general interest in the subject, and congratulated itself.[215]

One aspect of reform which attracted reasonably speedy action was that of local authorities establishing outpatient clinics.[216] Clinics would be relatively inexpensive, at least when starting on a small scale, and had the potential to reduce mental hospital overcrowding and demand for beds, thus avoiding additional building costs. In the first year under the new Act, voluntary patients accounted for around 40 per cent of new admissions in some mental hospitals, but elsewhere there were none.[217] The Board considered the higher rates as examples of what could be achieved, and continued its tactic of naming and shaming the worst performers in its annual reports. Admission in the 'temporary' patient category was 'disappointingly small', non-volitional patients being certified as before.[218] The Board was tentative about the reasons for this, but mentioned the possibility that GPs were unwilling to use the new option for admitting those patients. The Board jumped to the conclusion that GPs 'shirk their medical responsibility'.[219] Given that GPs often worked alone and encounters with non-volitional patients would have been relatively rare, compounded by the difficulties of defining and assessing volition and fears of making errors, it was likely that they would stick to doing what they knew best. The Board may genuinely have been trying to be constructive, but without addressing the GPs' concerns and educational needs, passing the buck appeared to be a continuing part of its modus vivendi.

The new Mental Treatment Act of 1930 had limitations, yet by enshrining the right of all adults to seek outpatient and inpatient mental healthcare, it took a radical conceptual step which primed further consideration of voluntary treatment, volition and autonomy. Such debate contributed to shaping legislation in the longer term,[220] but Percy Barter's reassurance that a consolidating act would be passed after a few years did not materialise. Instead, it took almost 30 years, when the Mental Health Act 1959 repealed both the Lunacy Act and the Mental Treatment Act.

Notes

1 Anon., Lunacy treatment (new style).
2 Grzybowski and Allen, History and importance of scrofula.
3 Anon., Lunacy treatment (new style).
4 Kingdon, *Agendas, Alternatives and Public Policy*.
5 Hubbard, Risk and confinement, 124.
6 Hilton, *Civilian Lunatic Asylums*, 59–60.
7 Scull, Creating a new psychiatry, 390; Imperial War Museum, Voices of the First World War.
8 Weatherly, *A Plea for the Insane*, 47, 63.
9 New Ministries Bill, *Hansard*, 8 Aug 1917; Medico-Psychological Association, Report of English Lunacy Legislation Sub-Committee, 36.
10 Westwood, A quiet revolution in Brighton; Medico-Psychological Association, Report of English Lunacy Legislation Sub-Committee, 36.
11 Medico-Psychological Association, Report of English Lunacy Legislation Sub-Committee, 44; Anon., Medico-Psychological Association, *JMS* 1919, 49.
12 Weatherly, *A Plea for the Insane*, 74.
13 Weatherly, *A Plea for the Insane*, 15.
14 Weatherly, 'A plea for the insane' (*Medical Press*), 32.
15 BoC, correspondence and memoranda, 5–7 Oct 1930, TNA MH 51/249.
16 Bond, The position of psychological medicine, 406; Pauper Lunatics, *Hansard*, 1 Mar 1920; Pauper Lunatics (Maintenance), *Hansard*, 8 Mar 1920; Lunatic Patients, *Hansard*, 11 Mar 1920; Pauper Lunatics (Maintenance) *Hansard*, 15 Mar 1920; County Lunatic Asylums, *Hansard*, 21 Apr 1920; Pauper Lunatics (Maintenance), *Hansard*, 29 Jun 1920; Pauper Lunatics, *Hansard*, 3 Nov 1920.
17 Oxonian, Confined as a lunatic; Oxonian, Confined as a lunatic ii; Oxonian, Confined as a lunatic iii; Mould, Our asylums; Bishop, Our asylums; Gwynn, Our asylums.
18 BoC minutes, 15 and 22 Dec 1920, 'The Living Dead' (*Englishwoman*, Dec 1920) by Dr SE White, TNA MH 50/48; 'Sarah' in General Medical Council, *Medical Register 1926*; 'Sara' in *Medical Directory* 1925.
19 Parley, *Life in a Madhouse*, 9–10.
20 Anon., The asylum and lunacy law reform, 44.
21 Anon., The question of asylum and lunacy law reform.
22 Weatherly, Asylum and lunacy law reform.

23 NCLR minute book, 19 May 1920, WL SA/MIN/A/1/1.
24 NCLR minute book, 30 Sept 1920, 25 Oct 1920, 7 Apr 1921, list of names, WL SA/MIN/A/1/1.
25 Ministry of Health (Miscellaneous Provisions) Bill, *Hansard*, 9 Nov 1920.
26 Ministry of Health (Miscellaneous Provisions) Bill, *Hansard*, 14 Dec 1920.
27 Anon., The collapse of the Miscellaneous Health Bill.
28 Thane, *Divided Kingdom*, 76.
29 BoC, *Annual Report for 1920*, 2; Wolseley-Lewis, Ministry of Health (Miscellaneous Provisions) Bill.
30 Lomax, *The Experiences of an Asylum Doctor*, 38.
31 Lomax, *The Experiences of an Asylum Doctor*, 13.
32 Memo, Laurence Brock to Aubrey Symonds, MoH, Aug 1921, TNA MH 58/221.
33 BoC, *Annual Report for 1920*, 15.
34 BoC minutes, 13 Oct 1920, 246, TNA MH 50/48.
35 BoC, *Annual Report for 1920*, 17.
36 Anon., The asylum inquiry.
37 Weatherly, Lunacy reform, 262.
38 Towers, The management and politics of a public exposé, 47.
39 BoC, *Annual Report for 1921*, 6.
40 Our Medical Correspondent, Asylum horrors.
41 Civis, Our 'mad' asylums, 214.
42 Anon., The question of asylum administration.
43 Weatherly, Lunacy reform, 261.
44 NCLR minute book, 1923–33, 16 Dec 1927, WL SA/MIN/A/1/3.
45 NCLR minute book, 1921–2, 26 Apr 1922, WL SA/MIN/A/1/2.
46 NCLR minute book, 1921–2, 20 Dec 1921, WL SA/MIN/A/1/2.
47 Notes, Chalmers Watson, 18 Oct 1921, TNA MH 58/79.
48 BoC, *Annual Report for 1922*, 89–90; Dr Bond and Dr Rotherham, Report of visit to Prestwich Asylum, 27–9 Sept 1921, TNA MH 58/221.
49 Memo, Laurence Brock to Aubrey Symonds, MoH, Aug 1921, TNA MH 58/221.
50 Memo for Minister of Health on Mr Montagu Lomax's book, 21 Sept 1921, TNA MH 58/222.
51 Lomax, *The Experiences of an Asylum Doctor*, 17.
52 Anon., Willerby Asylum inquiry: Lady councillor's sensational charges.
53 Anon., Seventeen lunatics to a bath.
54 Anon., Cloud of suspicion lifted.
55 Anon., Willerby Asylum inquiry committee breaks up, 18.
56 Lomax, *A Reply to the 'Report of the Committee on the Administration of Mental Hospitals'*, 1.
57 Anon., Parliamentary news, 571.
58 Letter, Dr Percy Hughes, Worcestershire Mental Hospital, to Dr Bond, 28 Oct 1921, TNA MH 58/221.
59 Memo, Laurence Brock to Aubrey Symonds, MoH, Aug 1921, TNA MH 58/221.
60 Letter, F Willis to WA Robinson, MoH, 2 Nov 1921, TNA MH 58/221.
61 Memo, Laurence Brock to Aubrey Symonds, c. Aug 1921; Memo, WA Robinson to MoH, 9 Nov 1921, TNA MH 58/221.
62 Chief Medical Officer, minute sheet, 11 Oct 1921, TNA MH 58/222.
63 Memo, F Willis to WA Robinson, 18 Nov 1921, TNA MH 58/221.
64 Anon., Sir Cyril Cobb.
65 MoH, *Report of the Committee on Administration* (Cobb Report), 4.
66 Anon., The Board of Control and asylum administration.
67 Towers, The management and politics of a public exposé; Weatherly, Asylum administration, 113.
68 Lomax, Lunacy reform, citing *The Friend*, 2 Sept 1921.
69 Anon., Asylums and mental hospitals.
70 Memo, WA Robinson to Minister of Health, 9 Nov 1921, TNA MH 58/221.
71 Anon., Asylums and mental hospitals.
72 BoC, *Conference on Lunacy Administration*, 78–80.
73 BoC, *Annual Report for 1922*, 5.
74 BoC, *Conference on Lunacy Administration*, 82.
75 Henry Maudsley, cited in Lomax, *The Experiences of an Asylum Doctor*, 39; Argyle, *Psychology and Social Problems*, 85; Barton, *Institutional Neurosis*.

76 Anon., The ninth and tenth annual reports, 559.
77 BoC, *Annual Report for 1922*, 1–2.
78 Lomax, Lunacy reform; Evidence to Cobb Inquiry, Lionel Weatherly, q. 1,565, TNA MH 58/219.
79 Mond, Lunacy reform.
80 Lunatic Asylums (Administration), *Hansard*, 15 Feb 1922.
81 Letter, BoC to Dr Perceval, 17 Jan 1922, TNA MH 58/221.
82 Cobb Committee visit to Prestwich, 26–7 Jan 1922, TNA MH 58/221.
83 Committee on Administration of Public Mental Hospitals (Chair: Sir Cyril Cobb), 1922, TNA MH 58/219 and 58/220.
84 Evidence to Cobb Inquiry, Frank Perceval, q. 410, TNA MH 58/219.
85 Evidence to Cobb Inquiry, Frank Perceval, q. 497–8, TNA MH 58/219.
86 Cobb Committee visit to Prestwich, 26–7 Jan 1922, TNA MH 58/221.
87 Evidence to Cobb Inquiry, Frank Perceval, q. 485, TNA MH 58/219.
88 Cobb Committee visit to Prestwich, 26–7 Jan 1922, TNA MH 58/221.
89 Evidence to Cobb Inquiry, Frank Perceval, q. 486–9, TNA MH 58/219.
90 Evidence to Cobb Inquiry, Arthur Trevor, q. 27, TNA MH 58/219.
91 Evidence to Cobb Inquiry, David Ogilvy, q. 1,970, TNA MH 58/220.
92 Evidence to Cobb Inquiry, Mr Mears, q. 972, 979, 980, TNA MH 58/219.
93 Evidence to Cobb Inquiry, Sara White, q. 1,504, TNA MH 58/219.
94 Evidence to Cobb Inquiry, Lionel Weatherly, q. 1,565, TNA MH 58/219.
95 Evidence to Cobb Inquiry, David Ogilvy, q. 1,876, TNA MH 58/220; Lionel Weatherly, q. 1,681, TNA MH 58/219.
96 Evidence to Cobb Inquiry, David Ogilvy, q. 1,705; Laurence Fuller, q. 2,207, TNA MH 58/220; Shorter, *A History of Psychiatry*, 190.
97 MoH, *Report of the Committee on Administration* (Cobb Report), 80.
98 BoC, *Annual Report for 1922*, 94–6.
99 Towers, The management and politics of a public exposé, 55.
100 Memo, Percy Barter to Laurence Brock, 18 Dec 1922, TNA MH 58/224.
101 Anon., Another book of asylum 'revelations'.
102 Scrutator, Asylum whitewash.
103 Lunacy (Visiting Committees), *Hansard*, 21 Jun 1922; Lunatic Asylums (Women Visitors), *Hansard*, 2 Aug 1922; Mental Cases (Detention), *Hansard*, 4 Aug 1922; Mental Cases, *Hansard*, 4 Dec 1922; Mental Cases, *Hansard*, 12 Jul 1923.
104 Robertson, The hospitalisation of the Scottish asylum system.
105 Anon., The administration of public mental hospitals, 91–2.
106 Lomax, The asylum report and asylum reform, 850.
107 Lomax, The asylum inquiry.
108 Anon., Obituary: Montagu Lomax.
109 Correspondence with Dr Clare Groves, currently researching the life of Montagu Lomax.
110 Harding, 'Not worth powder and shot'; Hilton, *Improving Psychiatric Care*; Towers, The management and politics of a public exposé.
111 Jones et al., The Maudsley Hospital, 358, 362.
112 London County Council (Parks, etc.) Bill, *Hansard*, 24 Jun 1915.
113 Memo, Hospitalisation of asylums, MoH, 1922–3, TNA MH 58/79.
114 Mental Treatment Bill, *Hansard*, 3 May 1923; Lunacy Act Amendment (London) Bill, *Hansard*, 5 Apr 1905; Voluntary Mental Treatment Bill, *Hansard*, 22 Jul 1914.
115 BoC, *Annual Report for 1922*, 1.
116 Mental Treatment Bill, *Hansard*, 3 May 1923; Mental Treatment Bill, *Hansard*, 30 May 1923.
117 EM, T Saxty Good.
118 Mental Treatment Bill, *Hansard*, 3 May 1923; Mental Treatment Bill, *Hansard*, 30 May 1923.
119 Mental Treatment Bill, *Hansard*, 3 May 1923.
120 Mental Treatment Bill, *Hansard*, 12 Jun 1923; Date of Adjournment, *Hansard*, 24 Jul 1923.
121 BoC, *Annual Report for 1923*, 3.
122 RCF, KA Anklesaria.
123 Anon., House of Lords.
124 Med sup's reports, Colney Hatch, 11 Apr 1919, 5 Sept 1919, TLA H12/CH/A/08/001.
125 Anon., House of Lords.
126 *Everett v. Griffiths and another* [1920] 3 KB 163 (Court of Appeal); [1921] 1 AC 631 (House of Lords).

127 BoC to MoH, 1 Jun 1922, TNA MH 86/45.
128 Mr Whatley to BoC, 31 May 1921; BoC to MoH, 1 Jun 1922, TNA MH 86/45.
129 Writ, 31 May 1922, delivered 7 Jul 1922, TNA MH 86/46.
130 Anon., High Court of Justice King's Bench Division. Alleged wrongful detention.
131 Anon., Wrongful detention in an asylum.
132 Anon., What makes a lunatic?
133 Anon., Personalities of the week.
134 Mathew, Lush, Sir (Charles) Montague.
135 Flyer for NSLR public meeting, 27 Feb 1924, TNA MH 86/45; Book of Revelation 1:1 (King James Version).
136 Anon., Medico-legal notes: Harnett v. Bond and Adam, 264.
137 Editor, At the periphery: The Harnett case.
138 Royal Commission on Lunacy and Mental Disorder, *Report*, 40–1, para. 90.
139 Lunacy Laws, *Hansard*, 3 Mar 1924.
140 Harnett v. Bond and Adam, *Hansard*, 3 Mar 1924.
141 Lunacy Laws, *Hansard*, 3 Mar 1924.
142 Anon., Court of Appeal; Lunacy Laws, *Hansard*, 10 Mar 1924; Anon., Medico-legal 1924, 692.
143 Anon., Medico-legal 1925, 989.
144 Railway tragedy, *Beckenham Journal, Penge and Sydenham Advertiser*, Oct 1925 (cutting), TNA MH 86/46.
145 Mr WS Harnett, *Hansard*, 28 Jul 1925.
146 Anon., Mr Harnett's death.
147 Mond, Lunacy reform.
148 Kingdon, *Agendas, Alternatives and Public Policy*.
149 Royal Commission on Lunacy and Mental Disorder, *Report*, iii.
150 Royal Commission on Lunacy and Mental Disorder, *Report*, 94–5, para. 182.
151 Royal Commission on Lunacy and Mental Disorder, *Report*, iii.
152 Lomax, Lunacy reform.
153 Royal Commission on Lunacy and Mental Disorder, *Report*, 4, para. 10.
154 Royal Commission on Lunacy and Mental Disorder, *Report*, 178–82.
155 Tribunals of Inquiry (Evidence) Act, 1921.
156 Royal Commission on Lunacy and Mental Disorder, *Report*, 7, para. 15.
157 Royal Commission on Lunacy and Mental Disorder, *Report*, 4, para. 9.
158 Royal Commission on Lunacy and Mental Disorder, *Report*, 7–8, para. 17.
159 Royal Commission on Lunacy and Mental Disorder, *Report*, 113, para. 209.
160 Royal Commission on Lunacy and Mental Disorder, *Report*, 7, para. 15.
161 Royal Commission on Lunacy and Mental Disorder, *Report*, 2, para. 3.
162 BoC, *Report of the Departmental Committee*; Committee on Dietaries, *Report*.
163 Royal Commission on Lunacy and Mental Disorder, *Minutes*, chairman, q. 269–70.
164 Royal Commission on Lunacy and Mental Disorder, *Report*, 31, para. 73.
165 Royal Commission on Lunacy and Mental Disorder, *Report*, 95, para. 182.
166 Royal Commission on Lunacy and Mental Disorder, *Report*, 113, para. 209.
167 Royal Commission on Lunacy and Mental Disorder, *Report*, 95, para. 182; 113, para. 209.
168 Royal Commission on Lunacy and Mental Disorder, *Report*, 114, para. 210.
169 Royal Commission on Lunacy and Mental Disorder, *Report*, 110, para. 204; 124, para. 224.
170 Turner et al., The history of mental health services.
171 Royal Commission on Lunacy and Mental Disorder, *Report*, 23, para. 53.
172 Royal Commission on Lunacy and Mental Disorder, *Report*, 49, para. 103; NSLR, rough notes of AGM, 14 Jul 1925, WL SA/MIN/A/1/3.
173 Royal Commission on Lunacy and Mental Disorder, *Report*, 150, para. 262; Letter, LCC to MoH, 26 Jul 1927, TNA MH 58/215; Deputation, County Councils Association and Mental Hospitals Association, to Arthur Robinson, Miss Lawrence, Mr Brock and Mr Barter, 28 Jan 1930, TNA MH 51/714.
174 Royal Commission on Lunacy and Mental Disorder, *Report*, 150, para. 263.
175 Royal Commission on Lunacy and Mental Disorder, *Report*, 154, para. 266.
176 Memo, F Willis to Minister of Health, 11 Nov 1926, TNA MH 51/640.
177 Royal Commission on Lunacy and Mental Disorder, *Report*, 16, para. 39.
178 Royal Commission on Lunacy and Mental Disorder, *Report*, 19, para. 46.

179 Lunacy Act 1890, s. 330; Royal Commission on Lunacy and Mental Disorder, *Report*, 41, para. 90.
180 Josiah Wedgwood, 'New lunacy terror', reprinted from *John Bull*, 24 May 1930, WL SA/EUG/D/142.
181 Royal Commission on Lunacy and Mental Disorder, *Report*, 20, para. 47.
182 Royal Commission on Lunacy and Mental Disorder, *Report*, 22, para. 50.
183 Royal Commission on Lunacy and Mental Disorder, *Report*, 19, para. 45; 17, para. 43.
184 Royal Commission on Lunacy and Mental Disorder, *Report*, 51, para. 106.
185 Royal Commission on Lunacy and Mental Disorder, *Report*, 36–7, paras 82–4.
186 Mental Treatment Bill, *Hansard*, 10 Dec 1929.
187 Mental Treatment Bill, *Hansard*, 17 Feb 1930.
188 Memo, F Willis to Minister of Health, 11 Nov 1926, TNA MH 51/640; Memo, Percy Barter, 24 Aug 1926, TNA MH 58/216.
189 Lunacy, *Hansard*, 15 Nov 1926.
190 Lunacy Law, *Hansard*, 17 May 1928.
191 Voluntary Boarders at Public Asylums, *Hansard*, 4 Dec 1928.
192 *Manchester Guardian*, 13 Jun 1929, reprinted and circulated by NSLR, WL SA/EUG/D.142.
193 Anon., Local government reform.
194 Anon., Insanity and its treatment.
195 Letter, Laurence Brock to Dr Good, 10 Feb 1930, TNA MH 51/714.
196 Turner, 'Not worth powder and shot', 15.
197 Letter, Laurence Brock to Hubert Bond, 10 Feb 1930, TNA MH 51/714.
198 Mental Treatment Bill, *Hansard*, 17 Feb 1930.
199 Mental Treatment Bill, *Hansard*, 28 Nov 1929.
200 Royal Commission on Lunacy and Mental Disorder, *Report*, 51–2, para. 106; see file: Voluntary patients: intention to leave: notice to be given 1931–59, TNA MH 51/246.
201 Mental Treatment Act 1930, s. 5.
202 General BoC for Scotland, *Twelfth Annual Report*, xi; Mental Treatment Act 1930, s. 5.
203 BoC, *Annual Report for 1929*, Part 1, 2.
204 Royal Commission on Lunacy and Mental Disorder, *Report*, 144, para. 253; 173, para. XXXV; Percy Barter, Note on financial implications, 6 Oct 1926, TNA MH 58/216.
205 BoC, *Annual Report for 1928*, Part 1, 5; *Annual Report for 1929*, Part 1, 7.
206 Anon., 300,000 mental defectives.
207 Mental Treatment Bill, *Hansard*, 17 Feb 1930.
208 Author's personal experience on a small Caribbean island in the 1990s.
209 Jalland, *Death in War and Peace*, 30.
210 NSLR, Deputation to Minister of Health, 16 Dec 1929; Special meeting, 30 Dec 1929; AGM, 27 May 1930, WL SA/MIN/A/1/3.
211 Dr Weatherly to BoC, 5 Oct 1930, TNA MH 51/249.
212 BoC, *Annual Report for 1930*, Part 1, 1.
213 BoC, *Annual Report for 1930*, Part 1, 3.
214 BoC, *Annual Report for 1930*, Part 1, 1.
215 BoC, *Annual Report for 1930*, Part 1, 3.
216 BoC, *Annual Report for 1931*, Part 1, 1–2.
217 BoC, *Annual Report for 1931*, Part 1, 1.
218 BoC, *Annual Report for 1931*, Part 1, 3; *Annual Report for 1932*, Part 1, 2.
219 BoC, *Annual Report for 1932*, Part 1, 2.
220 Royal Commission on Lunacy and Mental Disorder, *Report*, 51–2, para. 106; see file: Voluntary patients: intention to leave: notice to be given 1931–59, TNA MH 51/246.

7
Epilogue: reflections then and now

In the long 1920s, framed by the Armistice in 1918 and the Great Depression at the end of the decade, many societal goals of post-WW1 reconstruction remained unfulfilled. Although there were steps towards gender equality and improvement in some aspects of housing and social welfare, much remained unsatisfactory. The population experienced high unemployment, social unrest and the effects of financial constraints across the public sector. The poorest in society benefited least from 'progress',[1] and among them were the hundred thousand people in the mental hospitals. This contrasted with rapid developments in other domains, such as technological innovation including radio broadcasts, television and automatic traffic lights, and medical discoveries such as insulin and the first glimpses of penicillin.

In the context of healthcare, happenings of long ago are often overlooked, unless they are groundbreaking scientific or clinical technology discoveries, or notable policy and practice innovations such as the opening of the Maudsley Hospital in 1923. Although the *Report of the Royal Commission on Lunacy and Mental Disorder* advocated more dignified and liberal person-centred therapeutic approaches, its recommendations were not mandatory, and it did little to directly improve the wellbeing of inpatients. It is disturbing that much was known about what ought to be done, but little was implemented.

A round number of one hundred years is conducive to reflecting on change. The mental hospital system a century ago was far from perfect, but practice inside the institutions was also far from uniform. Some aspects of it were humane – we hear of compassionate staff who did their best despite many challenges, and of patients who benefited from the care they received. Other aspects were inhumane and shameful concerning the needs of individuals – both patients and staff. Flawed science led down dangerous lanes, lunacy law was out of date, funding was inadequate, the leadership was authoritarian and the system was inflexible. Today, mental healthcare in the NHS remains far from ideal. In many respects things have improved, while in others they have not. Psychiatrist Professor David Jolley wrote in 2023:

> The lack of meaningful activities for patients in those days matches the sad situation for many people with long-term and recurring [mental] illnesses now. The contrast between life with long admissions in a steady or static environment, same place, same staff can be contrasted with the turmoil of many short-term admissions, rotating between different wards and different hospitals punctuated by general hospital involvement via Accident and Emergency, the police or other agencies – and with staffing often reliant on 'agency' nurses and doctors.[2]

This view resonates with that of historian Peter Barham, who noted that since the closure of the institutions, people with long-term mental illness in the community 'may find themselves as structurally isolated as ever they were in the asylums, and in addition, their health needs may now be ignored. In equal measure they find themselves neglected both as patients and as citizens'.[3] In her oral history study of change at Mapperley Hospital, Nottingham in the second half of the twentieth century, Verusca Calabria cited a patient who referred to the new 'community care': 'There is an absence of community and an absence of care.'[4] The situation of many, reliant on welfare benefits, unemployed and living in impoverished circumstances,[5] provides an uncomfortable comparison between purported community care today and deprived wards in mental hospitals of the past. If not institutional deprivation, then perhaps today it is institutionalised deprivation, to which many turn a blind eye.

Since the 1920s, research has given us a greater understanding of the causes of mental disorders, and various biological, psychological and social therapeutic measures have become available. Arguably, the mid-twentieth century saw some relaxation of rules and regulations and a more flexible approach to treating people with mental illness, in parallel with other more liberal social attitudes. However, despite more knowledge and new treatments, an inflexible system of providing services has emerged in the twenty-first century which echoes the 1920s. Some might call it a return to petty tyranny and soulless discipline, with aspects of policy, prioritisation, leadership style and institutional culture resonating with those a century ago. The warning bells are disturbing.

Then and now, the mental healthcare landscape is overshadowed by, among other things, a bureaucratic red tape regulatory culture. Today it has rigid care pathways which are task- rather than compassion-driven, it appears to value process targets rather than patients' outcomes, and it shows a lack of focus on the wellbeing of individual patients and staff.[6] Both periods are associated with healthcare worker discontent and 40-year-old mental health legislation in need of reform.[7] The uncertainty of having to compete for NHS priority in policy, political and financial spaces echoes pauper lunatic un-deservingness. There are plenty of ideas, but unclear means for crossing the gap between actual practice and acknowledged best practice. In October 2023 a *Guardian* headline stated, 'Mental healthcare in England is a national emergency'; it has 'slipped down [the] priority list and patients are being forgotten'.[8] The material world has changed but the low status of mentally unwell people continues. Stigma is still very much alive and kicking, with a mismatch between recommendations, rhetoric and responses regarding mental healthcare and the social welfare provision integral to it. In 2024, according to Dr Shubulade Smith, president of the Royal College of Psychiatrists:

> People with severe mental illness are discriminated against every day. They face outdated and old-fashioned stereotypes and tropes, which are simply wrong. Discriminatory attitudes have us believe that [serious mental illness] is somehow a negative character flaw, intrinsic to who people are, that can never be changed, rather than an illness that can be treated.[9]

The *Lancet* also recently argued that:

> Despite increased spending on mental health services, few could credibly argue that the National Health Service Long Term Plan has met its ambition to 'expand access and deliver timely, high quality mental health support by 2023/24'. The reality is excessive bureaucracy, breakdown in continuity of care, and high-throughput targets at the expense of wellbeing … Patients often undergo a lonely and disjointed care journey, devoid of enduring empathic relationships. We have a system that incentivises indifference.[10]

The view that indifference is a systemic problem reverberates with perceptions a century ago. It implies that healthcare workers and management at all levels are complicit in it.[11]

In the current climate, when 'history and memorialisation are under sustained assault globally',[12] forgetting may merge with ignoring and denying, and failing to learn from the past. This epilogue cannot be comprehensive, but it will endeavour to reflect on some aspects of the history of the mental institutions in the 1920s and consider what can be learnt from them a century on.

Institutional culture: then and now

Healthcare systems need to be designed to allow for change influenced by the shifting world around us. Elements of this include a population's collective and individual health needs, culture and expectations. Adding to the mix are the science, technology, psychological and social understandings which shape and comprise dimensions of healthcare practices. No sooner is provision optimal than further shifts require consideration and action. The built environment of healthcare is inevitably slow to change. Buildings are vital but may lag behind their original objectives: as Dr Devine said in 1922, it is difficult to predict how they will need to be used in the future.[13] Like technology, buildings are tangible, quantifiable and valued by those who provide them and support them, as well as many who receive help in them. In the 1920s, some hospital leaders blamed the barrack-like mental hospitals for impeding improvements in care, although the proverb 'a bad workman blames his tools' might be apt. There was a need to consider how better to use the tools available, and to place principles of humanity, compassion, empathy, kindness and the needs of individual patients and staff at their forefront. When in 1922 Dr Turnbull yearned for a new, ideal hospital built on the 'villa pattern' of separate buildings for separate purposes, he recognised that these new buildings were likely to become like those already in existence, unless cultural and organisational changes also took place.[14]

In the 1920s, mental hospital leadership in central and local government and in professional and administrative groups was hierarchical and top-down, often existing in silos. Each group thought it did things the right way. Within each group there was an uneasy tolerance of diverse opinion, and too often self-righteous bickering between groups rather than constructive negotiation to create the best way forward.[15] Decision making on these leadership ladders impacted on the lives of patients, but none placed compassion and empathy for patients' wellbeing as their overarching objective. Those at the foot of the hierarchy – both patients and frontline staff – who experienced and witnessed unacceptable practices were expected to acclimatise, rather than offer potentially constructive criticism. This was typical of a 'total institution' as Erving Goffman described, with the majority of those inside lacking a voice, or, if heard, with lip-service paid to their words. There is little evidence that the leaders reflected on how they might be contributing to a harmful institutional culture.

Good intentions about practice emerged in pockets. Some institutions, and individuals inside and outside them, identified needs and demonstrated how to provide above and beyond what was then generally classed as adequate. However, the widespread rolling out of therapeutic and beneficial practices was an uphill struggle. The leadership resisted change, and since, from their perspective, the system worked, it did not need fixing.[16] Pairings of caution and haste, like care and control, created continuums which required understanding and balancing in different circumstances. Caution could protect patients, such as when considering the introduction of new biological treatments, given the limitations of scientific research and statistical methods underpinning them. Some who lacked caution and quickly cast aside or accepted new information uncritically and hastily, for whatever reasons, caused great harm, notably those who neglected rising death rates in the asylums in England at the end of WW1 and those who supported Henry Cotton's surgical methods in the USA.

Excessive caution about making change, however, could also be detrimental, such as when the system propagated standards of care which were inhumane, unkind or disrespectful. Stereotypes which undervalued mentally ill people as human beings and regarded them as generally irresponsible and potentially dangerous, as voiced by influential people across the social spectrum, did not fit with evidence but favoured a restrictive one-size-fits-all custodial approach. Moves to (re)introduce less restrictive and more therapeutic occupational, psychological and social approaches, in the light of evidence that patients benefitted from them, were perceived as hard to control and risky. They were also staff-intensive, and therefore more expensive, especially in the short term. In addition, they would require trust between the tiers of leadership, staff and patients – an ingredient too often absent. Overall, it was easier to maintain the status quo, with a tight grip on staff, patients and short-term expenditure. Proposals to make mental hospitals more like general hospitals would need to overcome these cumulative cultural hurdles.

Extreme wariness and blanket restrictive rules regarding maintaining patients' safety tied in with a defensive and punitive institutional culture. Fear of an individual patient catastrophe or allegations of neglect which would jeopardise personal and institutional reputation permeated the mental hospital system, from the Ministry of Health down to visiting committees and frontline staff. Leaders at the top of the hierarchy tended to abdicate responsibility and blame those lower down. In 2023, the *British Medical Journal* cited Rob Behrens, the Parliamentary and Health Service Ombudsman: 'A toxic culture of defensiveness and hostility pervades the NHS ... [which] leads to a perception that organisational reputation and professional reputation are more important than patient safety.' Patients and staff are both 'victims' in a climate where it is difficult to work and to tackle problems.[17] Rob Behrens also referred to an NHS culture of 'bunker-ism' – a state of mind especially among members of a group that is characterised by chauvinistic defensiveness and self-righteous intolerance of criticism – aligning with what critics of mental hospital provision a century ago called 'the system'.

Returning to the 1920s, outside the direct leadership, others had the potential to improve the mental hospitals. Their emphasis, however, contributed to distracting from the primacy of patients' needs: trades unions primarily supported staff; council and parliamentary representatives risked losing their seats if they sought more public funding; erroneous and negative stereotypes about patients passed unchallenged and lay visiting committees were among those who brought such assumptions into the mental hospitals. Innovation around patients' needs tended to come from voluntary organisations such as the Mental After Care Association (MACA), campaign groups, a handful of outspoken psychiatrists and other doctors in England; and psychiatrists, academia and psychiatric systems in Scotland and further afield. Concurrent with the Royal Commission, the Board of Control shifted its approach from low cost as a benchmark of successful institutional function to spending more to improve care, including giving patients more choice and freedom, to achieve better mental health outcomes. The Commission may not have added much to what was already known, but it opened the door to re-evaluating policy and practice, and paved the way for the implementation of more flexible and patient-focussed approaches.

Some county and borough mental hospitals successfully introduced more liberal treatment regimes, but elsewhere a deeply embedded rigid culture was slow to change – perhaps even slower than the buildings themselves. The culture was arguably more harmful to the people within than the bricks and mortar of the institution with its metaphorical as well as physical walls. The Royal Commission was the only body which had the authority, independence and detachment to see the defects and evaluate them credibly. It acted as the country's conscience for people with mental disorders. However, it could only make recommendations, not mandate change. It assisted in breaking down the metaphorical walls and offering designs for the future, but it was not within the Commission's remit to create something different or replace walls with transparent glass.

Medical knowledge and clinical directions

The aim of separating mental and physical disorders, treating one group in mental hospitals and the other in general, was unrealistic, especially when mental symptoms were frequently caused by physical diseases which could be severe and rapidly fatal. The overlap pointed to the need for a more medical approach in the mental hospitals, including access to general hospital standards of diagnostic technology and to the advice of medical colleagues across various disciplines to facilitate restoration of health. Sharing across the mental-physical conceptual divide also facilitated new approaches, such as treating GPI with malaria inoculation, and employing dentists to treat mental hospital patients. It is sobering to note that, just as rates of potentially preventable disorders of tuberculosis, dysentery and typhoid, and deaths from them, were higher in the mental hospitals than in the general population in the 1920s, people suffering severe chronic mental disorders and living in the community today continue to die prematurely from potentially preventable physical disorders, such as heart disease and cancer. Since 2020 they have also been more likely to die from Covid-19 than their mentally well peers. In both centuries, mental health services' neglect of their patients' physical wellbeing has contributed to this premature mortality.[18]

Some historians have aligned psychiatrists' motivation to treat patients in the general hospitals with their desire to gain greater power and professional status.[19] Although looking at the pinnacle of the profession can only partly reflect on its status, it is notable that a number of the psychiatrists mentioned in this study were knighted, including Charles Hubert Bond, Edward Marriott Cooke, Maurice Craig, James Crichton-Browne, David Kennedy Henderson and Frederick Mott – hardly an indication of a second-class profession. Rather than professional status, there is greater evidence that psychiatrists' motivation was primarily towards bringing people suffering from mental conditions into general hospitals to facilitate modern clinical investigation and treatment in the early stages of a disorder, based on medical principles accepted for treating physical conditions to improve chances of recovery.[20] It was a step on the path to what has become known as parity of esteem: equity of resources for providing treatment for both mental and physical disorders.[21]

In the 1920s, Adolph Meyer, Henderson and others recognised the importance of 'psychobiology': biological, psychological, social and environmental factors were integral to both the causes of, and treatments for, mental disorders. This was their 'medical model'. It was a far cry from how that term has since been used disparagingly and narrowly over many years, in the sense of referring solely to biological causes and treatments.[22] That might be a future ideal: hypothetically, biological discoveries may have the potential to eradicate debilitating mental disorders, while allowing the existence of often constructive, diverse individual psychological and emotional responses to help deal with life's challenges. Until that time, however, we act at our peril if we see the medical dimension of mental dysfunction as solely biological. Psychiatric disorders still need to be understood and treated in their real-world context.

Many steps towards understanding mental disorders and identifying scientifically based treatments emerged from the work of our predecessors, somewhere else and at some other time. Regarding inspiration for influential biological approaches affecting care in the 1920s, Karl Kahlbaum inspired Emil Kraepelin; William Hunter inspired Henry Cotton; and observations over many years that fevers might ameliorate mental disorders intrigued Julius Wagner-Jauregg. Understanding the pitfalls and successes our predecessors encountered may inform future generations when considering research directions and new treatments in psychiatry. Ann Harrington's book *Mind Fixers* is dedicated to exploring the prolonged and contested theme of biological treatments in psychiatry. She concludes with a warning that psychiatry 'will need to resist self-serving declarations of imminent breakthroughs and revolutions. In contrast with much that has gone before, it will need to make a virtue of modesty, continually acknowledging just how complex are the challenges that it faces.'[23] Likewise, historian Jack Pressman cautioned his readers about self-righteousness among leaders in the field of psychiatry:

> [I]t is all too easy to explain away their actions as the consequence of reckless judgment – no doubt something that right-minded persons (like us) can recognize and avoid when facing similar challenges,

now and in the future. It would be ironic indeed should it turn out that we have cultivated our own hubris in identifying theirs.[24]

In contrast to Harrington's and Pressman's cautions about psychiatrist-scientists' mindsets past and present, in the 1920s, some of them expressed a degree of humility and recognised their own limitations. Emil Kraepelin for one, referred to the need for every step of the way to be trodden with unwavering care and thoroughness.[25]

Debates between psychiatrists in the 1920s covered matters similar to those in the 'anti-psychiatry' debates of the 1960s and in 'critical psychiatry' in the 2020s, particularly related to the nature of psychiatric disorders and biological, psychological and social causes and treatments.[26] Other clinical debates recur, indicating the ongoing struggles to reach conclusive endpoints. Whether repressing painful thoughts caused mental disturbance, as Freud proposed, was debated in England in 1921, and stimulated research in 2023.[27] Focal sepsis theory, related to whether periodontal (gum) disease might be responsible for disorders in other parts of the body, has also been re-explored recently.[28] It is notable that the biological mechanisms of neither encephalitis lethargica nor long-Covid have been elucidated, in the context of post-pandemic chronic disorders affecting body and brain.[29] Terminology of diagnosis is more refined today but is still influenced by more than just biological fact, with repeated modifications of disease classification reflecting the many uncertainties. Our armamentarium of scientific knowledge, research ethics, methodology, technology and analytical statistics surpasses that of our predecessors a century ago, but we are still faced with the enormity of seeking to prevent and cure the most disabling mental illnesses. While medications today can alter the symptoms and course of disorders such as schizophrenia and bipolar disorder in ways undreamt of a century ago, curing them remains elusive.

Legal aspects

Outdated mental health-related legislation has repeatedly compounded the multiplicity of challenges facing people with severe mental disorders.[30] In the 1920s, use of the Lunacy Act was inevitable in the treatment of patients in the mental hospitals. Some organisations, such as MACA and the National Society for Lunacy Reform (NSLR), as well as psychiatrists and the Royal Commission, considered it outdated. Today, the Mental Health Act 1983 (amended 2007) is not automatically needed for treatment, as its predecessor of 1890 was, but nevertheless it shapes practices and processes, especially relating to the care of the most mentally disturbed patients. Today, it is regarded as being overly restrictive, and lacking scope for patient choice and autonomy.[31] Criticism of both the 1890 and 1983 Acts relates to their fitness for purpose, particularly in terms of patients' volition and decision making. Societal expectations are integral to understanding, shaping and valuing the sorts of decisions patients should be allowed to make, and the degree to which they should have autonomy and choice when making them. Neither the nearly 40-year-old Lunacy Act in the 1920s, nor the over 40-year-old Mental Health Act today, could or can be expected to be fit for purpose in a rapidly changing social context.

Regarding the process of introducing new legislation in the twenty-first century, the Government commissioned an independent review of the Mental Health Act 1983 in 2017, and the committee reported the following year. With more than fifty thousand people subject to the Act in 2022, the Government's decision in 2023 to shelve a bill proposing to reform it was a blow to the mental health community, including patients, professionals, and voluntary and campaigning organisations. Baroness Buscombe, former Chair of the Joint Committee on the draft Mental Health Bill, commented: 'I note the Minister's intention to bring forward a Bill when Parliamentary time allows, however she cannot but be aware that the clock is ticking.'[32] Her comment is uncannily similar to Percy Barter's in 1926 about 'the limitations of Parliamentary time', after which it took another four years before the Mental Treatment Act came into being.[33] Seven years have now passed since the independent review. Historical continuity into the present regarding providing the best possible mental healthcare appears not only to be associated with the practices of psychiatrists, whom Andrew Scull and other historians focus on in this regard,[34] but it also pervades priorities in political and policy discourse.

Staff and patients: kindness, compassion and care

Doctors John Lord, Montagu Lomax and Grafton Elliott Smith and psychologist Tom Hatherley Pear were among those who encouraged their colleagues in the 1920s to show kindness to patients. Reminders may be needed about that, but I would hope to find them stated informally. It was with dismay that I read the instruction by the GMC, the doctors' regulatory body, 'You must treat patients with kindness', in their

2024 guidance which sets out 'standards of patient care and professional behaviour expected of all doctors in the UK'.[35] One wonders how such essential ingredients of care can be neglected to the degree that official restatement is required.

Kindness has many dimensions, including respect for, and the dignity of, individuals. That includes the need for professionals to listen to, and respond to, the words of patients supportively and actively. In 2023, Rob Behrens stated that doctors' training and education may induce a degree of arrogance which may hinder communication between them and their patients.[36] His finding is disconcerting and echoes styles of listening in the 1920s, illustrated by Dr Cooke and Mr Trevor claiming to have achieved the impossible feat of interviewing 279 patients in two days.[37]

There are other basic problems of care which affect the wellbeing of individual patients on wards both today and in the 1920s. We hear of patients in the 1920s who were put in the humiliating position of being denied access to sanitary protection when menstruating; journalist Rachel Stonehouse reported that this was happening on NHS psychiatric wards in 2023.[38] Also in 2023, the Nuffield Trust reported on the practice of sending patients 'out of area', meaning admitting them to an inpatient unit which is not part of their usual local network of services, sometimes over a hundred miles from their home. This deprives patients of visits from their family, friends and care coordinator to provide the best possible continuity of support and care and effective discharge planning. These contemporary placements reflect resource provision and financial decisions taking priority over patients' care in the 1920s. In 2016 NHS England's *Five Year Forward View for Mental Health* stated that 'the practice of sending people out of area for acute inpatient care as a result of local acute bed pressures [will be] eliminated entirely by no later than 2020/21'.[39] It has not happened.[40] The *Manchester Guardian* informed us in 1929 that 'an evil does not mend' just because those with authority explain its nature.[41] The same applies today.

There was much staff discontent in the mental hospitals of the 1920s. There were high rates of turnover among nurses, in part associated with excessive workloads, long hours, little control over their work environment, and a state of exhaustion, probably something similar to what today would be called 'burnout'. Frontline staff were expected to obey orders, take a task-oriented approach which contributed to objectifying patients, and achieve minimum standards rather than being given opportunities to think and encouragement to excel.[42] They had little scope to question those in authority and little voice to shape their daily work. If someone lower in the hierarchy challenged or opposed someone more senior, rather than automatically following their orders, it was simplest to take a bad apple approach: throw out the one who was deemed incompatible with the existing culture. A punitive workplace culture also reinforced the tendency of staff to conceal unacceptable practices due to fear of reprisals. Rather than understanding those practices with a view to preventing or remedying them, the culture perpetuated them. If staff stayed in the hostile environment long enough, they tended to acclimatise to it and extend it. The lack of compassion and understanding shown towards frontline staff raises the question of how they were expected to show compassion to patients if no one showed it to them.

In 2023, a University of Cambridge study on compassion in mental health services found failings at the interpersonal level, underpinned by high-level systemic and institutional forces. It also found that staff disillusionment, emotional exhaustion and a risk-centric culture was associated with less compassion from staff, which, in inpatient settings, could give rise to institutional oppression. The study concluded that compassion requires a reflexive ethos, an environment that prioritises therapeutic relationships, and one that permits challenging of policies and cultures that normalise oppression.[43] The King's Fund, an independent charitable organisation working to improve health and care in England, also recently highlighted that a management culture which lacks compassion towards its staff is associated with staff discontent and high staff turnover, and that when staff are shown compassion, they are more able to treat patients in the same way. The King's Fund urged a more compassionate leadership, with a focus on relationships through careful listening and understanding, and empathising with and supporting staff. That approach should enable staff to feel more valued, respected and cared for, so that they can reach their potential, do their best work and act consistently with their values: 'Compassionate leaders don't have all the answers and don't simply tell people what to do, instead they engage with the people they work with to find shared solutions to problems.'[44] The King's Fund conclusions resonate disturbingly with the situation in the mental hospitals a century ago. Today, across the NHS, many nurses leave the profession early in their careers,[45] similar in degree to the rates reported in the 1920s mental hospitals.

Neither the Cobb Committee nor the Royal Commission appeared able or willing to contemplate, investigate or comprehend these leadership and management issues. To do so would have required the difficult task of believing the unbelievable and creating a degree of soul-searching and introspection within the leadership, across central and local government and the institutions, concerning their role in maintaining a status quo that was harmful to patients. Those at the top of the hierarchy seemed to flounder when it came to that vital component of showing compassion.

Complaints and inquiries

In the 1920s, the perspectives of patients, visitors and staff new to a mental hospital or on its fringes, such as the charitable bodies MACA, the NSLR and the National Council for Mental Hygiene, contrasted with those of officials within the system – the so-called experts in positions of authority. As reported in 1922, the experts did not experience the 'sense of horror which the layman feels'.[46] Rather, familiarity and habituation blinded the leadership to defective and deeply embedded, detrimental institutional cultures and practices. Although the asylums are now gone, the 'Lomax Affair' – the way Montagu Lomax was derided and his evidence rejected – continues to resonate, regarding both complaints about unacceptably low standards of care and attitudes towards those who bring them to public attention.[47]

Too often, the authorities alleged that informants exaggerated and were deceptive, and lacked qualification to comment. Little heed was paid to initial inquiry reports which made some recommendations but overall tended to reassure the public about the adequacy of provision and were self-congratulatory about the leadership. Over the years, the press has contributed to questioning the methods and outcomes of those inquiries. If the original inquiry was associated with an ardent band of reformers with the emotional energy to persist despite being publicly discredited, like Montagu Lomax and the NSLR and their supporters, eventually an independent investigation might materialise. Louise Hide pointed to at least 10 inquiries into mental hospital care of national significance in the 1960s and '70s.[48] The first of these, spearheaded by the work of Barbara Robb and her book *Sans Everything: A case to answer*, received the same sort of reception and consideration as Montagu Lomax and *The Experiences of an Asylum Doctor.*[49] John Martin emphasised the culture and pattern of defensive inquiries in *Hospitals in Trouble* in 1984. Martin referred to suppression of information and corrupt administration.[50] He argued against the bad apple theory, having found that it was rare. The perpetrator was rarely a cruel person, as the magistrate recognised in 1928 when he dismissed the case of a remorseful nurse probationer whom the mental hospital authorities had prosecuted for pulling a patient's hair. He asked the hospital to show more compassion.[51]

In 2007, Julie Bailey, the daughter of a former patient treated at Stafford Hospital, highlighted concerns about standards of care. The hospital authorities ignored her complaints and those of other patients and their families.[52] Statutory regulatory bodies also failed to detect warning signs aligning with poor standards and a rising mortality rate. Appointed in 2010, the Mid Staffordshire NHS Foundation Trust Public Inquiry reported in 2013 on the deficiencies of the care provided and made 290 wide-ranging recommendations.[53] The saga repeats: the outsider not being believed; the hospital authorities turning a blind eye; long delays before identifying the roots of the problems and proposing solutions; and even longer to implement them effectively.

The pattern of healthcare leadership rejecting unimaginable allegations continues.[54] Researchers Judith Smith and Ruth Thorlby reflected 10 years on from the Mid Staffordshire Inquiry Report:

> some progress has been made, but the diagnosis seems in many respects unchanged. Those leading and regulating the NHS at all levels must be able to hear, heed and speak up on behalf of the patients and families they serve. Without this, the NHS appears doomed to repeat many shameful failures of the past.[55]

Today, regarding speaking up, although the NHS has a legal duty of candour, whistleblowers are still victimised, likely not to be believed and at risk of losing their jobs in a cover-up culture. Just because there are legal obligations and guidelines about how to respond to whistleblowers, does not mean that self-protective institutional leadership and cultures change accordingly.

The media

Other challenges of the 1920s have echoes a century on. The media (and today social media) contribute to shaping public understanding of mental disorders, both positively and negatively. The public can benefit from knowledge of mental health matters, to inform their decision making about their own wellbeing and that of those close to them. But, as Dr Lord stated in 1927, dissemination of such knowledge should preferably avoid creating excessive preoccupation with mental symptoms.[56]

In both the 1920s and 2020s psychiatrists and others have raised concerns that sensationalist reporting may be unhelpful or dangerous, such as giving details of suicide methods which may trigger copycat suicides.[57] Inflammatory narratives around mental illness and crime may also be misleading: mentally ill people are disproportionately likely to be victims of crime, rather than perpetrators. Emphasis on mentally ill perpetrators may detract from systemic issues and prejudice public opinion regarding the elephant in the room: the cost of mental healthcare. Such reports may also increase stigma, making life harder for mentally unwell people generally and those who care for them. As the *Lancet* Commission on ending stigma and discrimination in mental health highlighted in 2022, demonising media portrayals of severe mental illness can be profoundly damaging.[58]

Sorting a wicked problem

Wicked problems are associated with confusing information; with individuals, groups and decision makers championing conflicting values; with baffling ramifications; and often, proposed solutions do not cure them.[59] Such are the challenges faced in providing holistic, humane therapeutic care for mentally unwell people, especially those suffering from the most severe disorders. Wicked problems are hard to solve and require a multi-faceted process spanning far wider than professional groupings. No one group is to blame. Stakeholders across society need to work collaboratively, creatively and honestly.

On a micro level, methods of 'radical collaboration' attempt to tackle complex societal problems. That starts with addressing the underlying psychological drives and emotional factors which perpetuate them and may hold clues to identifying solutions to them.[60] On a macro level, the Multiple Streams Framework identifies three basic streams to bring about public policy change: defining the problem, creating the policy, and achieving political will – all of which need to coincide to open a window of opportunity.[61] Such models provide insights and awareness of steps to help overcome problems and guide plans. Blame, scapegoating and punitive approaches do not help, and do not show compassion to staff or patients. Change requires the involvement and commitment of public, professionals, government, voluntary groups and others.

In 2023 the Institute for Government, the UK's leading independent think tank working to make government more effective, stated: 'Public services that have for years been creaking are now crumbling … [The] Government is stuck in a public service performance doom loop,' associated with short-sighted decisions which undermine longer-term planning by those further down the leadership hierarchy.[62] For people with severe, ongoing mental disorders the effects of short-termism undermine their wellbeing and that of their families and others who care for them. Those most in need of longer-term public services to maintain their health are typically neglected. It is a rumbling story, exemplified by good words but insufficient implementation. Many people with severe mental illnesses were and are trapped by inadequate public services which contribute to a socially, psychologically and economically deprived lifestyle, itself a risk to further ill health, both mental and physical.[63]

The material context of the former mental hospitals is long gone, but Rob Behrens' comments about a toxic and hostile NHS culture suggest that an ethos similar to that of past times permeates today. Constraints on public health and welfare spending, with competing agendas and priorities, disproportionally affect mental healthcare. Today, as in the past, provision does not match the needs of many severely mentally unwell people. *Plus ça change*, but what can we do about it? By probing the long 1920s, I hope this book has given insights into recurring challenges and patterns of response to them. In that way it may stimulate thought by clinicians, managers, policy and political leaders and others on how to overcome them. It may also prompt consideration about resource provision, and stimulate reflection on leadership styles and bureaucratic processes, with the potential to build a more humane healthcare culture. In those ways, it may help to provide more individualised, dignified, compassionate and flexible care for people suffering incapacitating mental disorders so that they can live the best lives possible.

Notes

1 Thane, *Divided Kingdom*, 108.
2 David Jolley, email, 2023.
3 Barham, *Closing the Asylum*, 62.
4 Calabria, An exploration of the function of nostalgia, 239.
5 Royal College of Psychiatrists, *National Clinical Audit of Psychosis*.
6 Smyth, Red tape.
7 Garratt, *Mental Health Policy and Services in England*.
8 Campbell, Mental healthcare in England is a national emergency.
9 Smith, 'Discrimination against people with severe mental illness is cutting lives short'.
10 *Lancet*, Editorial.
11 Anon., Asylum and lunacy law reform.
12 Wynter et al., Marking time, Abstract.
13 BoC, *Conference on Lunacy Administration*, 81.
14 BoC, *Conference on Lunacy Administration*, 79.
15 Anon., Our friends – the medical superintendents; Pierce, Some present-day problems, 198.
16 Morrison, Henderson and Meyer in correspondence, 83.
17 Rimmer, NHS culture change is difficult, not impossible.
18 Office for Health Improvement and Disparities, *Premature mortality*; Royal College of Psychiatrists, over 26,000 adults with severe mental illness die prematurely.

19 Takabayashi, Surviving the Lunacy Act of 1890, 266.
20 BoC, *Annual Report for 1929*, Part 1, 1.
21 Mitchell, Hardy and Shiers, Parity of esteem.
22 Shah and Mountain, The medical model is dead, 375; Chakravarty, Medicalisation of mental disorder, 266.
23 Harrington, *Mind Fixers*, 276.
24 Pressman, *Psychosurgery*, 17.
25 Kraepelin, Ends and means, 143.
26 Moncrieff, Why I don't like the idea that mental disorder is a disease; Craddock and Owen, The Kraepelinian dichotomy; Rybakowski, 120th anniversary of the Kraepelinian dichotomy.
27 Pierce, Medico-Psychological Association; Mamat and Anderson, Improving mental health.
28 Kumar, From focal sepsis to periodontal medicine.
29 Davis et al., Long COVID.
30 *Lancet*, Editorial.
31 Bunn and Ryland, Research briefing.
32 UK Parliament, Comment on Government Response to Joint Committee's report on the draft Mental Health Bill.
33 Percy Barter, memo, 24 Aug 1926, TNA MH 58/216.
34 Scull, *Museums of Madness*, 259.
35 General Medical Council, *Good Medical Practice*, 11, 12.
36 Rimmer, NHS culture change is difficult, not impossible.
37 BoC, *Annual Report for 1920*, 17; Hilton, 'I have to-day seen all the 671 patients'.
38 Stonehouse, NHS psych ward period provision criticised by patients.
39 Mental Health Task Force, *The Five Year Forward View*, 35.
40 Nuffield Trust, Mental health care outside local area.
41 *Manchester Guardian*, 13 Jun 1929. Reprinted and circulated by NSLR, WL SA/EUG/D.142.
42 Martin, *Hospitals in Trouble*, 244.
43 Liberati et al., Tackling the erosion of compassion.
44 Bailey and West, What is compassionate leadership?
45 Campbell, Growing numbers of NHS nurses quit; Campbell, Numbers of nurses and midwives leaving NHS highest for four years.
46 Anon., Asylums and mental hospitals.
47 Harding, 'Not worth powder and shot'.
48 Hide, Mental hospitals, social exclusion and public 'scandals'.
49 Hilton, *Improving Psychiatric Care*, 5, 147.
50 Martin, *Hospitals in Trouble*, 241.
51 Anon., Struggle with a mental patient.
52 Cure the NHS, https://www.curethenhs.co.uk.
53 *Mid Staffordshire NHS Foundation Trust Public Inquiry* (Francis Report).
54 Moritz et al., Hospital bosses ignored months of doctors' warnings about Lucy Letby.
55 Smith and Thorlby, Ten years after the Francis Inquiry Report.
56 Lord, *Mental Hospitals and the Public*, 18.
57 Anon., Imitative suicides; Anon., Publicity in cases of suicide; Royal College of Psychiatrists, *Self-Harm and Suicide*, 67.
58 Thornicroft et al., The *Lancet* Commission on ending stigma.
59 Churchman, Guest editorial: Wicked problems; Rittel and Webber, Dilemmas in a general theory of planning.
60 Kahane, Radical collaboration.
61 Kingdon, *Agendas, Alternatives and Public Policy*.
62 Institute for Government, *Performance Tracker 2023*.
63 Tudor-Hart, The inverse care law; Townsend and Davidson (eds), *Inequalities in Health*; Marmot et al., *Health Equity in England*.

References

A patient for five months. A living death. *Saturday Review of Politics, Literature, Science and Art* 1919, 128:3347, 586.

Ackerly, Samuel Spafford. Worcester State Hospital examples of patients, 1929. https://www.youtube.com/watch?v=s8znK7zDpOY (accessed Jan 2025).

Adler, Jeffrey S. Less crime, more punishment: Violence, race, and criminal justice in early twentieth-century America. *Journal of American History* 2015, 102:1, 34–46. https://doi.org/10.1093/jahist/jav173.

Allmond, Gillian. Liberty and the individual: The colony asylum in Scotland and England. *History of Psychiatry* 2017, 28:1, 29–43. https://doi.org/10.1177/0957154X16677510.

An ex-patient. The asylum environment. *British Journal of Medical Psychology* 1930, 10:4, 344–64.

Anderson, Edward W. Prognosis of the depressions of later life. *JMS* 1936, 82:340, 559–88. https://doi.org/10.1192/bjp.82.340.559.

Anderson, Edward W. The sedimentation velocity of erythrocytes in the psychoses: A study of seventy-three cases. *JMS* 1929, 75:308, 80–100. https://doi.org/10.1192/bjp.75.308.80.

Anon. 8-hour day for lunatics. *NAWU Magazine* 1919, 8:9, 12, citing *Manchester Evening News*, 27 Aug 1919.

Anon. 48-hour week. *NAWU Magazine* 1919, 8:1–3, 3.

Anon. 300,000 mental defectives. *NAWU Magazine* 1929, 18:5–6, 2.

Anon. Abstract of the Report of the Lord Chancellor's Committee on Insanity and Crime. *JMS* 1924, 70:288, 96–109.

Anon. The administration of public mental hospitals in England and Wales. *JMS* 1923, 69:284, 90–8.

Anon. Annual Conference. *NAWU Magazine* 1929, 18:8, 4.

Anon. Another attempt to dodge the Royal Commission? *NAWU Magazine* 1922, 11:3, 3.

Anon. Another book of asylum 'revelations'. Experiences of a female patient. *NAWU Magazine* 1922, 11:10, 11.

Anon. The asylum inquiry. *Medical Press and Circular*, 21 Sept 1921, 228.

Anon. The asylum and lunacy law reform. *Medical Press and Circular*, 19 Jan 1921, 44–45, 44.

Anon. Asylum and lunacy law reform. *Medical Press and Circular*, 2 Feb 1921, 95.

Anon. Asylum patients. *NAWU Magazine* 1919, 8:4–6, 1.

Anon. Asylums and mental hospitals. *Times*, 20 Jan 1922, 11.

Anon. The Board of Control and asylum administration. *Medical Press and Circular*, 31 Aug 1921, 162.

Anon. The Board of Control (England and Wales) and the malarial treatment of general paralysis. *JMS* 1924, 70:289, 337–41. https://doi.org/10.1192/bjp.70.289.337.

Anon. The causes of insanity. Glasgow asylum doctor's views. Drink and disease – environment's effect. *NAWU Magazine* 1923, 12:3, 3.

Anon. Cloud of suspicion lifted: Willerby Asylum officials and staff vindicated. *NAWU Magazine* 1923, 12:10, 8.

Anon. The collapse of the Miscellaneous Health Bill. *Medical Press and Circular*, 22 Dec 1920, 492.

Anon. County Mental Hospital: Users of front drive. *NAWU Magazine* 1921, 10:4, 6.

Anon. Court of Appeal. *Times*, 6 Mar 1924, 5.

Anon. Cushy jobs. *NAWU Magazine* 1919, 8:7–8, 23.

Anon. Dancing in asylums: Patients receiving better treatment. *NAWU Magazine* 1920, 9:6, 9, citing *Manchester Evening News*, 17 Jun 1920.

Anon. 'Death chamber' in an asylum. Ex-inspector's evidence. *Times*, 16 Mar 1922, 9.
Anon. Departmental Committee on Mental Nursing: NEC's resolution. *NAWU Magazine* 1924, 13:11–12, 11.
Anon. Disorders of the mind. Book review of *Mind and Medicine* by WHR Rivers. *Athenaeum* 1919, 4666, 979.
Anon. Double training for mental nurses. Very limited facilities. *NAWU Magazine* 1927, 16:6–7, 5.
Anon. Exeter Asylum strike terminated. *NAWU Magazine* 1919, 8:11–12, 1.
Anon. The Exeter strike. *NAWU Magazine* 1919, 8:7–8, 26.
Anon. Female nurses in male asylum wards. *NAWU Magazine* 1920, 9:9–10, 14.
Anon. Female nursing in asylum male wards must go! *NAWU Magazine* 1920, 9:5, 2.
Anon. Female nursing in male wards. *NAWU Magazine* 1927, 16:3, 2.
Anon. Female nursing in male wards of asylums. *NAWU Magazine* 1920, 9:1, 8.
Anon. The first international malaria congress. *BMJ* 1925, 2:3386, 970–1.
Anon. General Nursing Council (England and Wales): Interview with members of the Royal Medico-Psychological Association, May 23rd, 1929. *NAWU Magazine* 1929, 18:7, 4–5.
Anon. High Court of Justice, King's Bench Division. Alleged wrongful detention in an asylum, Harnett v. Bond and Another. *Times*, 7 Feb 1924, 5.
Anon. Hospitals for training male nurses. *NAWU Magazine* 1928, 17:8, 25.
Anon. Hours of work. *NAWU Magazine* 1923, 12:10, 6.
Anon. House of Lords. *Times*, 8 Mar 1921, 5.
Anon. Imitative suicides. *JMS* 1920, 66:272, 80.
Anon. Impressions of a probationer. *NAWU Magazine* 1923, 12:9, 7.
Anon. Insanity and its treatment: The expectation of reform. *NAWU Magazine* 1929, 18:7, 5.
Anon. John Bull, Female nurses in male wards 'The scandal must end'. *NAWU Magazine* 1920, 9:3, 2.
Anon. Joint Conciliation Committee for the Mental Hospital Service. *NAWU Magazine* 1928, 17:5, 2.
Anon. Lectures and demonstrations. *NAWU Magazine* 1928, 17:5, 3.
Anon. Local government reform. *Medical Press and Circular*, 31 Oct 1928, 362.
Anon. Lunacy Acts Amendment (London) Bill. *BMJ* 1903, 2:2219, 102.
Anon. Lunacy during the war. *Times*, 6 Sept 1919, 11.
Anon. Lunacy treatment (new style). *NAWU Magazine* 1921, 10:5, 7.
Anon. Macclesfield Asylum. An insane departure. *NAWU Magazine* 1918, 7:10–12, 21.
Anon. Medico-legal. *BMJ* 1924, 1:3302, 692–4.
Anon. Medico-legal. *BMJ* 1925, 1:3360, 989–92.
Anon. Medico-legal notes: Harnett v. Bond and Adam. *JMS* 1924, 70:289, 264–80.
Anon. Medico-Psychological Association. *JMS* 1906, 52:219, 809–38.
Anon. Medico-Psychological Association. *JMS* 1919, 65:268, 45–54.
Anon. Medico-Psychological Association. *JMS* 1923, 69:287, 528–80.
Anon. Medico-psychological examinations still to be carried on. *NAWU Magazine* 1925, 14:2–3, 1.
Anon. The Mental After-Care Association. *JMS* 1925, 71:293, 344–5.
Anon. Mental Hospital Matrons' Association. *NAWU Magazine* 1923, 12:10, 6.
Anon. Mental hospitals' administration. *NAWU Magazine* 1920, 9:12, 1.
Anon. Mental hygiene: National Council formed: hopes of world-wide league. *Times*, 5 May 1922, 18.
Anon. Montrose Asylum Board: Question of female nurses in male wards. *NAWU Magazine* 1920, 9:3, 6.
Anon. More applicants – but unsuitable. *NAWU Magazine* 1920, 9:11, 7.
Anon. Mr Harnett's death. 'Found drowned' in London. *NAWU Magazine* 1927, 16:11, 10.
Anon. My impressions at Exminster. *NAWU Magazine* 1923, 12:10, iii.
Anon. National Conference of Labour Women. Preliminary agenda. *NAWU Magazine* 1928, 17:4, 1.
Anon. National Council for Mental Hygiene. *BMJ* 1922, 1:3202, 766–7.
Anon. National Council for Mental Hygiene. *JMS* 1922, 68:282, 278–81.
Anon. National Council for Mental Hygiene. *JMS* 1923, 69:286, 404–7.
Anon. National Programme. Adopted by special delegate meeting held in London, on September 28th, 1918. *NAWU Magazine* 1918, 7:10–12, ii.
Anon. New training school for male nurses. A Stepney scheme. *NAWU Magazine* 1927, 16:9, 5.
Anon. The ninth and tenth annual reports of the Board of Control for the years 1922 and 1923. *JMS* 1925, 71:294, 558–70.
Anon. No Harley-Street law. Judge on insanity. *Times*, 9 Dec 1920, 9.

Anon. Northumberland County Asylum, Morpeth. Making the patients objects of public ridicule. Board of Control's apathetic attitude. *NAWU Magazine* 1925, 14:2–3, 2.
Anon. Nurse famine in the country. Dunfermline doctor's remedy. *NAWU Magazine* 1920, 9:4, 9.
Anon. Nursing of mental patients: Suggestions for reform. *BMJ* 1924, 2:3334, 964–5.
Anon. The nursing service in county and borough mental hospitals. *British Journal of Nursing* 1924, 72, 274–5.
Anon. Obituary: Montagu Lomax, MRCS Eng. LRCP Edin. *Lancet* 1933, 221:5717, 668.
Anon. Obituary notices, TC Graves, BSc MD FRCS MRCVS. *BMJ* 1964, 1:5399, 1,711.
Anon. Our friends – the medical superintendents. *NAWU Magazine* 1920, 9:6, 4.
Anon. Oxford County and City Mental Hospital reciprocal training scheme with Radcliffe Infirmary. *NAWU Magazine* 1925, 14:12, 2.
Anon. Parliamentary news. *JMS* 1921, 67:279, 571–2.
Anon. Patients' dietary scales at Winwick Mental Hospital. *NAWU Magazine* 1925, 14:6–7, 1.
Anon. Pauper asylum patients (property). 17 Dec 1924. *NAWU Magazine* 1925, 14:1, 7.
Anon. Personalities of the week: People in the public eye. *Illustrated London News*, 8 Mar 1924, 393.
Anon. Poverty and insanity. Board of Control (Scotland) Report. *NAWU Magazine* 1919, 8:11–12, 14.
Anon. Prussian practices at Powick: Locking out the lasses-O. *NAWU Magazine* 1923, 12:1–2, 1, citing *Worcestershire Advertiser*, 16 Dec 1922.
Anon. Publicity in cases of suicide. *Medical Press and Circular*, 21 Oct 1925, 334.
Anon. The question of asylum administration. *Medical Press and Circular*, 3 Aug 1921, 82.
Anon. The question of asylum and lunacy law reform. *Medical Press and Circular*, 16 Feb 1921, 128.
Anon. Reform in asylum administration. *Medical Press and Circular*, 16 Mar 1921, 208.
Anon. Report of proceedings. *NAWU Magazine* 1928, 17:8, 4.
Anon. The reproach of psychiatry in England. *JMS* 1920, 66:273, 189–90, reprinted from *Lancet*, 6 Mar 1920.
Anon. Retirement of Prestwich superintendent. *NAWU Magazine* 1923, 12:10, 6.
Anon. Royal Medico-Psychological Association. *JMS* 1927, 73:303, 691–728.
Anon. Royal Medico-Psychological Association, the annual dinner. *JMS* 1927, 73:303, 729–64.
Anon. Seconding of mental nurses to general hospitals. *NAWU Magazine* 1926, 15:12, 8.
Anon. Seventeen lunatics to a bath. Woman councillor's allegation. *NAWU Magazine* 1923, 12:3, 3.
Anon. Sir Cyril Cobb. *Times*, 9 Mar 1938, 16.
Anon. Stafford Branch, NAWU 8 Mar 1921 to *Staffordshire Chronicle* (Letter). *NAWU Magazine* 1921, 10:4, 3.
Anon. The strike at Exeter Asylum. *NAWU Magazine* 1919, 8:4–6, 10.
Anon. Struggle with a mental patient. Nurse accused of ill-treatment. Summons dismissed. *NAWU Magazine* 1928, 17:6–7, 4.
Anon. Trade union membership. Intimidation of mental hospital employees. *NAWU Magazine* 1929, 18:1, 2.
Anon. Visits to patients in mental hospitals. *NAWU Magazine* 1928, 17:4, 3.
Anon. What makes a lunatic? *Times*, 1 Mar 1924, 11.
Anon. What patients like: Cinema and newspapers, but not radio. *NAWU Magazine* 1925, 14:5, 7.
Anon. Willerby Asylum Inquiry: Lady councillor's sensational charges. Attack upon nurse's character. *NAWU Magazine* 1923, 12:4, iii.
Anon. Willerby Asylum inquiry committee breaks up. General refusal any longer to put up with insults. Mrs. Hatfield's amazing letter. Request for Board of Control to investigate. *NAWU Magazine* 1923, 12:5, 18–19.
Anon. The wrong bottle: Asylum patients poisoned. *Times*, 16 Sept 1921, 5.
Anon. Wrongful detention in an asylum: £25,000 damages. *Harnett v. Bond and Another. Times*, 28 Feb 1924, 5.
Argyle, John Michael. *Psychology and Social Problems*. London: Methuen, 1964.
Arie, Tom. Discussion. In *Brain Failure in Old Age: Proceedings of a conference held December 1975, Jersey, Channel Islands*, edited by William Ferguson Anderson and JR Carlton-Ashton. *Age and Ageing*, 1977 (supplement), 115.
Arnold-Forster, Agnes. *Cold, Hard Steel: The myth of the modern surgeon*. Manchester: Manchester University Press, 2023.
Arton, Michael. The professionalisation of mental nursing in Great Britain, 1850–1950. PhD thesis, UCL, 1998. https://discovery.ucl.ac.uk/id/eprint/1317913/1/299873.pdf (accessed Jan 2025).

Auden, GA. Encephalitis lethargica – its psychological implications. *JMS* 1925, 71:295, 647–58. https://doi.org/10.1192/bjp.71.295.647.

Barham, Peter. *Closing the Asylum: The mental patient in modern society*. London: Process Press, 2020.

Barham, Peter. *Forgotten Lunatics of the Great War*. New Haven, Ct: Yale University Press, 2004.

Barton, Russell. *Institutional Neurosis*. Bristol: John Wright and Sons, 1959.

Beauchamp, Tom L. Informed consent: Its history, meaning, and present challenges. *Cambridge Quarterly of Healthcare Ethics* 2011, 20:4, 515–23. https://doi.org/10.1017/S0963180111000259.

Beers, Clifford. *A Mind that Found Itself*. New York: Longmans, Green and Co, 1908.

Belloc, Hilaire. *Cautionary Tales for Children: Designed for the admonition of children between the ages of eight and fourteen years*. London: Eveleigh Nash, 1907.

Bennet, Edward. *What Jung Really Said*. London: Macdonald, 1966.

Berrios, German. British psychopathology since the early 20th century. In *150 Years of British Psychiatry 1841–1991*, edited by German Berrios and Hugh Freeman. London: Gaskell, 1991, 232–44.

Beveridge, Allan. Life in the asylum: Patients' letters from Morningside, 1873–1908. *History of Psychiatry* 1998, 9:4, 431–69. https://doi.org/10.1177/0957154X9800903602.

Bewley, Thomas. *Madness to Mental Illness: A history of the Royal College of Psychiatrists*. London: Royal College of Psychiatrists, 2008.

Bewley, Thomas. Online archive 34: Honorary members and fellows. https://www.rcpsych.ac.uk/docs/default-source/about-us/library-archives/archives/madness-to-mental-illness-online-archive/honorary-members-and-fellows.pdf?sfvrsn=3a948c26_6 (accessed Jan 2025).

Bewley, Thomas. Online archive 36: Prizes and prize winners. https://www.rcpsych.ac.uk/docs/default-source/about-us/library-archives/archives/madness-to-mental-illness-online-archive/prizes-and-prize-winners.pdf?sfvrsn=4c736a4e_6 (accessed Jan 2025).

Binding, Karl and Alfred Hoche. *Allowing the Destruction of Life Unworthy of Life: Its measure and form* (trans. C Modak). Greenwood, WI: Suzeteo Enterprises, 2012.

Bishop, TF. Our asylums. *Saturday Review of Politics, Literature, Science and Art* 1920, 129:3351, 59.

Black, Gerry. Health and medical care of the Jewish poor in the East End of London, 1880–1914. *Jewish Historical Studies* 1999, 36, 93–111. https://www.jstor.org/stable/29780014 (accessed Jan 2025).

Blythe, Hannah. Mental recovery, citizenship roles, and the Mental After-Care Association, 1879–1928. *History of the Human Sciences* 2023, online ahead of print. https://doi.org/10.1177/09526951231164266.

BoC [Board of Control]. *Annual Reports of the Board of Control* (series, for the years 1914–1930). London: HMSO, 1915–31.

BoC [Board of Control]. *Conference on Lunacy Administration*. London: HMSO, 1922.

BoC [Board of Control]. *Report of the Departmental Committee Appointed to Inquire into the Nursing Service in County and Borough Mental Hospitals*. London: HMSO, 1924.

Bolton, Joseph Shaw. The myth of the unconscious mind. *JMS* 1926, 72:296, 25–38. https://doi.org/10.1192/bjp.72.296.25.

Bond, Charles Hubert. The position of psychological medicine in medical and allied services: The presidential address at the annual meeting of the Medico-Psychological Association of Great Britain and Ireland, held in London on July 11th–15th, 1921. *JMS* 1921, 67:279, 404–49. https://doi.org/10.1192/bjp.67.279.404.

Bottome, Phyllis. *Private Worlds*. Harmondsworth: Penguin, 1937.

Bourke, Joanna. *Fear: A cultural history*. London: Virago, 2005.

Bower, David. In Medico-Psychological Association of Great Britain and Ireland: Seventy-Ninth Annual Meeting, held at Buxton. *JMS* 1921, 67:276, 97–123, 111. https://doi.org/10.1192/bjp.67.276.97.

Brabin, Bernard J. Malaria's contribution to World War One – The unexpected adversary. *Malaria Journal* 2014, 13:497, 1–22. https://doi.org/10.1186/1475-2875-13-497.

Braslow, Joel T and Stephen R Marder. History of Psychopharmacology. *Annual Review of Clinical Psychology* 2019, 15, 25–50. https://doi.org/10.1146/annurev-clinpsy-050718-095514.

Broderick, Frederick. Dental sepsis as a factor in the aetiology of disease. *British Dental Journal* 1926, 47:24, 1,385–95.

Brown, Haydn. Asylums: What are the basic facts? *Medical Press and Circular*, 24 Aug 1921, 147–9.

Brumby, Alice. 'A painful and disagreeable position': Rediscovering patient narratives. *First World War Studies* 2015, 6:1, 37–55. https://doi.org/10.1080/19475020.2015.1047891.
Bullough, Vern. Merchandising the sanitary napkin: Lillian Gilbreth's 1927 survey. *Signs* 1985, 10:3, 615–27. https://doi.org/10.1086/494174.
Bulwer-Lytton, Rosina. *A Blighted Life*. London: London Publishing Office, 1880.
Bunn, Sarah and Howard Ryland. Reforming the Mental Health Act – Approaches to improve patient choice. UK Parliament (research briefing), 11 May 2023. https://post.parliament.uk/research-briefings/post-pn-0695 (accessed Jan 2025).
Burns, Patricia B, Rod J Rohrich and Kevin C Chung. The levels of evidence and their role in evidence-based medicine. *Plastic and Reconstructive Surgery* 2011, 128:1, 305–10. https://doi.org/10.1097/PRS.0b013e318219c171.
Butler, Jessica. Representations of paternal child killing in English national newspapers, 1900 to 1939. PhD thesis, Liverpool, 2018. https://livrepository.liverpool.ac.uk/3035338/1/200627993_December2018.pdf (accessed Jan 2025).
Calabria, Verusca. An exploration of the function of nostalgia in oral histories of institutional care. In *Memory, Anniversaries and Mental Health in International Historical Perspective*, edited by Rebecca Wynter, Jennifer Wallis and Rob Ellis. London: Palgrave Macmillan, 2023, 231–55.
Campbell, Denis. Growing numbers of NHS nurses quit within three years, study finds. *Guardian*, 23 Sept 2020. https://www.theguardian.com/society/2020/sep/23/growing-numbers-of-nhs-nurses-quit-within-three-years-study-finds (accessed Jan 2025).
Campbell, Denis. Mental healthcare in England is a national emergency, say hospital bosses. *Guardian*, 9 Oct 2023. https://www.theguardian.com/society/2023/oct/09/mental-healthcare-in-england-is-a-national-emergency-say-hospital-bosses (accessed Jan 2025).
Campbell, Denis. Numbers of nurses and midwives leaving NHS highest for four years. *Guardian*, 18 May 2022. https://www.theguardian.com/society/2022/may/18/numbers-of-nurses-and-midwives-leaving-nhs-highest-for-four-years (accessed Jan 2025).
Chakravarty, Tina. Medicalisation of mental disorder: Shifting epistemologies and beyond. *Sociological Bulletin* 2011, 60:2, 266–86. https://doi.org/10.1177/0038022920110204.
Chaney, Sarah. 'No "sane" person would have any idea': Patients' involvement in late nineteenth-century British asylum psychiatry. *Medical History* 2016, 60:1, 37–53. https://doi.org/10.1017/mdh.2015.67.
Cherry, Steven. *Mental Health Care in Modern England: The Norfolk Lunatic Asylum/St Andrew's Hospital c. 1810–1998*. Suffolk: Boydell Press, 2003.
Cherry, Steven and Roger Munting. 'Exercise is the thing'? Sport and the asylum c.1850–1950. *International Journal of the History of Sport* 2005, 22:1, 42–58. https://doi.org/10.1080/0952336052000314629.
Christie, Agatha. *The Murder of Roger Ackroyd*. Glasgow: Collins/Fontana, 1926/1990.
Churchman, C West. Guest editorial: Wicked problems. *Management Science* 1967, 14:4 (Application Series), B141–B142.
Civis. Our 'mad' asylums. *English Review*, Sept 1921, 212–5.
Cole, Robert. Presidential address, Section of Psychiatry, Royal Society of Medicine, 10 Nov 1925. Cited in Anon. Psychiatry and the public. *JMS* 1926, 72:296, 97–8.
Committee on Dietaries in Mental Hospitals. *Report of the Departmental Committee Appointed to Inquire into Certain Matters Relating to the Diet of Patients in County and Borough Mental Hospitals*. London: HMSO, 1924.
Committee on Insanity and Crime. *Report*, Cmd 2005. London: HMSO, 1923.
Cooke, E Marriott and C Hubert Bond. *History of the Asylum War Hospitals in England and Wales*. London: HMSO, 1920.
Coombs, Carey F. Mental disorder in cardiac disease. *JMS* 1928, 74:305, 250–9. https://doi.org/10.1192/bjp.74.305.250.
Cotton, Henry A. The relation of chronic sepsis to the so-called functional mental disorders. *JMS* 1923, 69:287, 434–65. https://doi.org/10.1192/bjp.69.287.434.
Cowan, Colin. Mental observation wards: An alternative provision for emergency psychiatric care in England in the first half of the twentieth century. *History of Psychiatry* 2021, 32:4, 419–35. https://doi.org/10.1177/0957154X211034981.
Craddock, Nick and Michael J Owen. The Kraepelinian dichotomy – Going, going ... but still not gone. *British Journal of Psychiatry* 2010, 196:2, 92–5. https://doi.org/10.1192/bjp.bp.109.073429.
Craig, Maurice. *Psychological Medicine: A manual on mental diseases*. London: Churchill, 1917.

Crammer, John. Extraordinary deaths of asylum inpatients during the 1914–1918 war. *Medical History* 1992, 36:4, 430–41. https://doi.org/10.1017/S0025727300055708.

Crichton-Browne, James. *The Doctor's Second Thoughts*. London: Ernst Benn, 1931.

Cronin, AJ. *The Citadel*. London: Victor Gollancz, 1937.

Crookshank, Francis G. The frequency, causation, prevention, and treatment of phthisis pulmonalis in asylums for the insane. *JMS* 1899, 45:191, 657–83. https://doi.org/10.1192/bjp.45.191.657.

County and City of Worcester Lunatic Asylum. *Sixty-Sixth Annual Report for 1918–19*. Worcester, 1919.

da Costa, John Chalmers. *Modern Surgery, General and Operative*. London: WB Saunders, 1925.

Davidson, D. *Remembrances of a Religio-Maniac*. Stratford-upon-Avon: Shakespeare Press, 1912.

Davis, Hannah E, Lisa McCorkell, Julia Moore Vogel and Eric J Topol. Long COVID: Major findings, mechanisms and recommendations. *Nature Reviews Microbiology* 2023, 21, 133–46. https://doi.org/10.1038/s41579-022-00846-2.

Day, Gerald Langston. *Rivers of Damascus*. London: Rider and Co, 1939.

Departmental Committee on Sterilisation. *Report*, Cmd 4485. London: HMSO, 1934. https://pmc.ncbi.nlm.nih.gov/articles/PMC5096091 (accessed Jan 2025).

Dickson, Melissa. Experiments in life: Literature's contribution to the history of psychiatry. In *Sources in the History of Psychiatry, from 1800 to the Present*, edited by Chris Millard and Jennifer Wallis. Abingdon: Routledge, 2022, 101–15.

Diefendorf, Allen Ross. *Clinical Psychiatry: A text-book for students and physicians, abstracted and adapted from the sixth German edition of Kraepelin's Lehrbuch der Psychiatrie*. New York and London: Macmillan, 1902.

Drolet, Godias J. World War I and tuberculosis: A statistical summary and review. *American Journal of Public Health and the Nation's Health* 1945, 35:7, 689–97. https://ajph.aphapublications.org/doi/pdf/10.2105/AJPH.35.7.689 (accessed Jan 2025).

Dwyer-Hemmings, Louis. 'A wicked operation'? Tonsillectomy in twentieth-century Britain. *Medical History* 2018, 62:2, 217–41. https://doi.org/10.1017/mdh.2018.5.

Editor. At the periphery. *Medical Press and Circular*, 8 Mar 1922, 188–9.

Editor. At the periphery: The Harnett case. *Medical Press and Circular*, 12 Mar 1924, 205.

Elgood, Paul. The asylum as it should be. *English Review*, Mar 1922, 292–5.

EM. T Saxty Good, OBE MRCS. *BMJ* 1945, 2:4429, 747.

Ernst, Waltraud. Therapy and empowerment, coercion and punishment: Historical and contemporary perspectives on work, psychiatry and society. In *Work, Psychiatry and Society, c. 1750–2015*, edited by Waltraud Ernst. Manchester: Manchester University Press, 2016, 1–30.

Fairfield, Letitia. Mental observation wards in London. *Mental Welfare* 1937, 18:4, 107–12. https://pmc.ncbi.nlm.nih.gov/articles/PMC5105458 (accessed Jan 2025).

Farquharson, Jennifer. Health and hierarchy: Soldiers, civilians and mental healthcare in Scotland, 1914–34. *History of Psychiatry* 2018, 29:1, 79–95. https://doi.org/10.1177/0957154X17745262.

Fennell, Phil. *Treatment without Consent: Law, psychiatry and the treatment of mentally disordered people since 1845*. Abingdon: Routledge, 1996.

Ferrier, Ian Nicol. Mortality in Victorian asylums, ca. 1870–1910: The causes, processes and monitoring of lunatic death, with a focus on post-mortems. PhD thesis, Newcastle, 2022. https://theses.ncl.ac.uk/jspui/handle/10443/5834 (accessed Jan 2025).

Fielding, Jonathan E. Smoking and women. *New England Journal of Medicine* 1987, 317:21, 1,343–5. https://doi.org/10.1056/NEJM198711193172108.

Foley, Paul. *Encephalitis Lethargica: The mind and brain virus*. New York: Springer, 2018.

Foucault, Michel. *Madness and Civilization: A history of insanity in the age of reason* (abr. and trans. Richard Howard). London: Tavistock, 1965.

Freebody, Jane. *Work and Occupation in French and English Mental Hospitals, c.1918–1939*. Cham: Palgrave Macmillan, 2023.

Freud, Sigmund. *The Interpretation of Dreams* (trans. AA Brill). New York: Macmillan, 1913.

Freud, Sigmund. *The Psychopathology of Everyday Life* (trans. AA Brill). London: T Fisher Unwin, 1914.

Garratt, Katherine. *Mental Health Policy and Services in England*. House of Commons Library, 4 Oct 2024. https://researchbriefings.files.parliament.uk/documents/CBP-7547/CBP-7547.pdf (accessed Jan 2025).

Gelder, Michael. Adolph Meyer and his influence on British psychiatry. In *150 Years of British Psychiatry 1841–1991*, edited by German Berrios and Hugh Freeman. London: Gaskell, 1991, 419–35.

General BoC [Board of Control] for Scotland. *Sixteenth Annual Report. For the year 1929*. Edinburgh: HMSO, 1930.

General BoC [Board of Control] for Scotland. *Twelfth Annual Report. For the year 1925*. Edinburgh: HMSO, 1926.

General Medical Council. *BMJ* 1929, 1:3570 (supplement), 225–6.

General Medical Council. *Good Medical Practice*, 2024. https://www.gmc-uk.org/professional-standards/good-medical-practice-2024 (accessed Jan 2025).

General Medical Council. *Medical Register* (series), 1859–current.

Gillespie, Isabella A. Treatment of post-encephalitis. *JMS* 1928, 74:306, 410–15. https://doi.org/10.1192/bjp.74.306.410.

Glew, Liana. Documenting insanity: Paperwork and patient narratives in psychiatric history. *History of the Human Sciences* 2022, 35:3–4, 3–31. https://doi.org/10.1177/09526951211068975.

Goffman, Erving. *Asylums: Essays in the social situations of mental patients and other inmates.* New York: Anchor, 1961.

Gordon, Harvey. *Broadmoor.* London: Psychology News Press, 2012.

Grant, Alastair R. The treatment of general paralysis by malaria. *BMJ* 1923, 2:3277, 698–700. https://doi.org/10.1136/bmj.2.3277.698.

Grant, Alastair R and JD Silverston. Malaria therapy in general paralysis: Being observations on fifty cases treated at the County Mental Hospital, Whittingham. *JMS* 1924, 70:288, 81–9. https://doi.org/10.1192/bjp.70.288.81.

Grant-Smith, Rachel. *The Experiences of an Asylum Patient*. London: Allen and Unwin, 1922.

Graves, Thomas C. The relation of unresolved infective processes following acute infective diseases to the causation of mental disorder. *JMS* 1929, 75:308, 31–44 (abridged from paper read at Trenton State Hospital, 1928). https://doi.org/10.1192/bjp.75.308.31.

Grzybowski, Stefan and Edward A Allen. History and importance of scrofula. *Lancet* 1995, 346:8988, 1,472–4. https://archives.sochara.org/files/original/314/RF-TB-1.15.pdf (accessed Jan 2025).

Gwynn, Denis. Our asylums. *Saturday Review of Politics, Literature, Science and Art* 1920, 129:3351, 59.

Hall, John. From work and occupation to occupational therapy: The policies of professionalisation in English mental hospitals from 1919 to 1959. In *Work, Psychiatry and Society, c. 1750–2015*, edited by Ernst Waltraud. Manchester: Manchester University Press, 2016, 314–33.

Hamlett, Jane and Lesley Hoskins. Comfort in small things? Clothing, control and agency in county lunatic asylums in nineteenth- and early twentieth-century England. *Journal of Victorian Culture* 2013, 18, 93–114. https://doi.org/10.1080/13555502.2012.744241.

Hansard: debates and answers to questions:

Asylum Inmates (Property). HC Deb vol 182 cols 1,520–1 (2 Apr 1925).

Asylums Visiting Committees (Women). HC Deb vol 123 col 1,067w (22 Dec 1919).

County Lunatic Asylums. HC Deb vol 128 col 391 (21 Apr 1920).

Date of Adjournment. HC Deb vol 167 cols 230–5 (24 Jul 1923).

Harnett v. Bond and Adam. HC Deb vol 170 cols 968–70 (3 Mar 1924).

London County Council (Parks, etc.) Bill. HC Deb vol 72 cols 1,419–25 (24 Jun 1915).

Lunacy. HC Deb vol 199 cols 1,556–7 (15 Nov 1926).

Lunacy Act. HC Deb vol 177 cols 505–6 (8 Oct 1924).

Lunacy Act Amendment (London) Bill. HC Deb vol 144 col 477 (5 Apr 1905).

Lunacy Act (Private Patients). HC Deb vol 149 cols 417–8w (19 Dec 1921).

Lunacy Acts. HC Deb vol 135 col 431 (24 Nov 1920).

Lunacy Acts. HC Deb vol 143 cols 444–5w (15 Jun 1921).

Lunacy Law. HC Deb vol 217 col 1,195 (17 May 1928).

Lunacy Laws. HC Deb vol 170 cols 1,142–6 (3 Mar 1924).

Lunacy Laws. HC Deb vol 170 cols 1,904–5 (10 Mar 1924).

Lunacy and Mental Disorder. HL Deb vol 66 cols 232–57 (24 Feb 1927).

Lunacy (Visiting Committees). HC Deb vol 155 cols 1,314–5 (21 Jun 1922).

Lunacy (Visiting Committees) Bill. HC Deb vol 157 cols 14–15 (24 Jul 1922).

Lunacy (Visiting Committees) Bill. HC Deb vol 157 col 1,917w (4 Aug 1922).

Lunatic Asylums (Administration). HC Deb vol 150 cols 996–1,000 (15 Feb 1922).

Lunatic Asylums (Women Visitors). HC Deb vol 157 cols 1,440–1 (2 Aug 1922).
Lunatic Patients. HC Deb vol 126 col 1,524 (11 Mar 1920).
Lunatics (Detention in workhouses). HC Deb vol 187 cols 1,155–6 (4 Aug 1925).
Mental Cases. HC Deb vol 143 col 636w (16 Jun 1921).
Mental Cases. HC Deb vol 159 cols 1,228–30w (4 Dec 1922).
Mental Cases. HC Deb vol 166 cols 1,539–40 (12 Jul 1923).
Mental Cases (Detention). HC Deb vol 157 cols 1,905–6w (4 Aug 1922).
Mental Patients (Detention and Discharge). HC Deb vol 216 cols 1,884–5 (3 May 1928).
Mental Treatment Bill. HC Deb vol 71 col 2,102 (17 May 1915).
Mental Treatment Bill. HL Deb vol 53 cols 1,060–76 (3 May 1923).
Mental Treatment Bill. HL Deb vol 54 cols 277–89 (30 May 1923).
Mental Treatment Bill. HL Deb vol 54 cols 455–8 (12 Jun 1923).
Mental Treatment Bill. HL Deb vol 75 cols 724–67 (28 Nov 1929).
Mental Treatment Bill. HL Deb vol 75 cols 1,050–119 (10 Dec 1929).
Mental Treatment Bill [Lords]. HC Deb vol 235 cols 957–1,009 (17 Feb 1930).
Ministry of Health (Miscellaneous Provisions) Bill. HC Deb vol 134 cols 1,029–148 (9 Nov 1920).
Ministry of Health (Miscellaneous Provisions) Bill. HL Deb vol 39 cols 119–49 (14 Dec 1920).
Mr WS Harnett. HC Deb vol 187 cols 237–8 (28 Jul 1925).
National minimum wage. HC Deb vol 161 cols 627–75 (7 Mar 1923).
New Ministries Bill. HL Deb vol 26 cols 238–58 (8 Aug 1917).
Pauper Lunatics. HC Deb vol 126 cols 36–7 (1 Mar 1920).
Pauper Lunatics. HC Deb vol 134 cols 372–3 (3 Nov 1920).
Pauper Lunatics (Maintenance). HC Deb vol 126 cols 952–3w (8 Mar 1920).
Pauper Lunatics (Maintenance). HC Deb vol 126 col 1,827w (15 Mar 1920).
Pauper Lunatics (Maintenance). HC Deb vol 131 col 268w (29 Jun 1920).
Sterilization. HC Deb vol 255 cols 1,249–57 (21 Jul 1931).
Voluntary Boarders at Public Asylums. HL Deb vol 72 cols 375–82 (4 Dec 1928).
Voluntary Mental Treatment Bill. HL Deb vol 17 cols 89–92 (22 Jul 1914).

Harding, Timothy W. 'Not worth powder and shot'. A reappraisal of Montagu Lomax's contribution to mental health reform. *British Journal of Psychiatry* 1990, 156:2, 180–7. https://doi.org/10.1192/bjp.156.2.180.

Hare, Edward. Old familiar faces: Some aspects of the asylum era in Britain. In *Lectures in the History of Psychiatry*, edited by Robin Murray and Trevor Turner. London: Gaskell, 1990, 82–100.

Harrington, Anne. *Mind Fixers: Psychiatry's troubled search for the biology of mental illness*. New York: Norton, 2019.

Heaton, Matthew M. Contingencies of colonial psychiatry: Migration, mental illness, and the repatriation of Nigerian 'lunatics'. *Social History of Medicine* 2013, 27:1, 41–63. https://doi.org/10.1093/shm/hkt070.

Henderson, David K. In Occupational therapy. A series of papers read at a meeting of the Scottish Division held at the Glasgow Royal Mental Hospital on Friday, May 2, 1924. *JMS* 1925, 71:292, 59–80. https://doi.org/10.1192/bjp.71.292.59.

Henderson, David K and Robert Gillespie. *A Text-book of Psychiatry for Students and Practitioners*. Oxford: Oxford University Press, 1927; 10th edn ed. Ivor Batchelor, 1969.

Hervey, Nicholas. Advocacy or folly: The Alleged Lunatics' Friend Society, 1845–63. *Medical History* 1986, 30:3, 245–75. https://doi.org/10.1017/S0025727300045701.

Hess, Volker and Benoît Majerus. Writing the history of psychiatry in the 20th century. *History of Psychiatry* 2011, 22:2, 139–45. https://doi.org/10.1177/0957154X11404791.

Hide, Louise. *Gender and Class in English Asylums 1890–1914*. London: Palgrave, 2014.

Hide, Louise. Mental hospitals, social exclusion and public 'scandals'. In *Mind, State and Society: Psychiatry and mental health in Britain 1960–2010*, edited by George Ikkos and Nick Bouras. Cambridge: Cambridge University Press, 2022, 60–68.

Hide, Louise and Joanna Bourke. Cultures of harm in institutions of care: Introduction. *Social History of Medicine* 2018, 31:4, 679–87. https://doi.org/10.1093/shm/hky103.

Hilton, Claire. *Civilian Lunatic Asylums during the First World War: A study of austerity on London's fringe*. London: Palgrave Macmillan, 2021.

Hilton, Claire. George Stephen Penny (1885–1964): His life and medical encounters, before, during and after admission to Broadmoor Criminal Lunatic Asylum (1923–25). *History of Psychiatry* 2023, 34:2, 196–208. https://doi.org/10.1177/0957154X221146399.

Hilton, Claire. 'I have to-day seen all the 671 patients in residence in this institution': Not listening to patients in the long 1920s. *History of Psychiatry* 2022, 33:4, 394–411. https://doi.org/10.1177/0957154X221119105.
Hilton, Claire. *Improving Psychiatric Care for Older People: Barbara Robb's campaign 1965–1975*. London: Palgrave Macmillan, 2017.
Hilton, Claire. A mysterious diagnosis in 1920. Royal College of Psychiatrists, 4 Oct 2023. https://www.rcpsych.ac.uk/news-and-features/blogs/detail/history-archives-and-library-blog/2023/10/04/a-mysterious-diagnosis-in-1920 (accessed Jan 2025).
Hilton, Claire. Our values and our historical understanding of psychiatrists. *BJPsych Bulletin* 2024, 48:2, 117–20. https://doi.org/10.1192/bjb.2023.16.
Hoffman, Leslie A and Joel A Vilensky. Encephalitis lethargica: 100 years after the epidemic. *Brain* 2017, 140:8, 2,246–51. https://doi.org/10.1093/brain/awx177.
Holocaust Memorial Day Trust. 23 June 1944: The Red Cross visits Terezin Concentration Camp. https://www.hmd.org.uk/resource/23-june-1944-the-red-cross-visits-terezin-concentration-camp (accessed Jan 2025).
Hornstein, Gail A. *Bibliography of First-Person Narratives of Madness in English,* 2011. http://www.gailhornstein.com/attachments/Bibliography_of_First_Person_Narratives_of_Madness_5th_edition.pdf (accessed Jan 2025).
House of Commons. *Standing Committee A. Mental Treatment Bill [Lords]. Official Report.* London: HMSO, 1930.
Hubbard, Andrew. Risk and confinement: Geographies of mental illness. PhD thesis, Griffith School of Environment, 2009. https://research-repository.griffith.edu.au/bitstream/handle/10072/367560/Hubbard_2009_02Thesis.pdf?sequence=1&isAllowed=y (accessed Jan 2025).
Hunter, Richard and Ida Macalpine. *Psychiatry for the Poor: 1851 Colney Hatch Asylum – Friern Hospital 1973*. London: Dawson's Pall Mall, 1974.
Hunter, William. Chronic sepsis as a cause of mental disorder. *JMS* 1927, 73:303, 549–63. https://doi.org/10.1192/bjp.73.303.549.
Hunter, William. Oral sepsis as a cause of disease. *BMJ* 1900, 2:2065, 215–16. https://doi.org/10.1136/bmj.2.2065.215.
Hurren, Elizabeth T. 'Abnormalities and deformities': The dissection and interment of the insane poor, 1832–1929. *History of Psychiatry* 2012, 23:1, 65–77. https://doi.org/10.1177/0957154X11428907.
Hwang, Hye Jean. Women and depression in interwar Britain: Case notes, narratives and experiences. PhD thesis, Warwick, 2018. http://wrap.warwick.ac.uk/109478 (accessed Jan 2025).
Hyslop, Theophilus. *The Borderland: Some of the problems of insanity.* New York: George Doran, 1925.
Imperial War Museum. Lives of the First World War. https://livesofthefirstworldwar.iwm.org.uk (accessed Jan 2025).
Imperial War Museum. Voices of the First World War: Arrival of the American Troops. https://www.iwm.org.uk/history/voices-of-the-first-world-war-arrival-of-the-american-troops (accessed Jan 2025).
Institute for Government. *Performance Tracker 2023*. https://www.instituteforgovernment.org.uk/publication/performance-tracker-2023 (accessed Jan 2025).
Jalland, Pat. *Death in War and Peace: Loss and grief in England.* Oxford: Oxford University Press, 2010.
Jalland, Patricia. Bereavement and mourning (Great Britain). In *1914–1918 Online International Encyclopedia of the First World War*, edited by Ute Daniel, Peter Gatrell, Oliver Janz, Heather Jones, Jennifer Keene, Alan Kramer and Bill Nasson, issued by Freie Universität Berlin, 2014. https://doi.org/10.15463/ie1418.10178.
Janowitz, Hans and Carl Mayer. *The Cabinet of Dr Caligari* (film). Berlin: Decla-Bioscop, 1920.
Jones, Edgar. 'An atmosphere of cure': Frederick Mott, shell shock and the Maudsley. *History of Psychiatry* 2014, 25:4, 412–21. https://doi.org/10.1177/0957154X14544262.
Jones, Edgar and Shahina Rahman. Framing mental illness, 1923–1939: The Maudsley Hospital and its patients. *Social History of Medicine* 2008, 21:1, 107–25. https://doi.org/10.1093/shm/hkm115.
Jones, Edgar, Shahina Rahman and Robin Woolven. The Maudsley Hospital: Design and strategic direction, 1923–1939. *Medical History* 2007, 51:3, 357–78. https://doi.org/10.1017/S0025727300001484.

Jones, Kathleen. *Asylums and After: A revised history of the mental health services. From the early 18th century to the 1990s.* London: Athlone Press, 1993.

Jones, Kathleen. *Mental Health and Social Policy 1845–1959.* Abingdon: Routledge and Kegan Paul, 1960.

Jordanova, Ludmilla. The social construction of medical knowledge. *Social History of Medicine* 1995, 8:3, 361–81. https://doi.org/10.1093/shm/8.3.361.

JSC (former patient). The mental patient as he feels himself. *JMS* 1925, 71:293, 346–7.

Kahane, Adam. Radical collaboration to transform social systems: Moving forward together with love, power, and justice. *Journal of Awareness-Based Systems Change* 2023, 3:2, 23–40. https://doi.org/10.47061/jasc.v3i2.6709.

Kahlbaum, Karl. The clinico-diagnostic perspective in psychopathology (trans. and introduced by GE Berrios). *History of Psychiatry* 2007, 18:2, 231–45. https://doi.org/10.1177/0957154X070180020602.

Keane, Anne. Mental health policy in Scotland, 1908–1960. PhD thesis, Edinburgh, 1987. https://era.ed.ac.uk/handle/1842/6956 (accessed Jan 2025).

Kearin, Madeline Bourque. Dirty bread, forced feeding, and tea parties: The uses and abuses of food in nineteenth-century insane asylums. *Journal of Medical Humanities* 2022, 43:1, 95–116. https://doi.org/10.1007/s10912-019-09603-8.

Kingdon, John. *Agendas, Alternatives and Public Policy.* New York: Pearson, 2010.

Kopeloff, Nicholas and Clarence O Cheney. Studies in focal infection: Its presence and elimination in the functional psychoses. *American Journal of Psychiatry* 1922, 79:2, 139–56. https://doi.org/10.1176/ajp.79.2.139.

Kopeloff, Nicholas and George H Kirby. Focal infection and mental disease. *American Journal of Psychiatry* 1923, 80:2, 149–97. https://doi.org/10.1176/ajp.80.2.149.

Kraepelin, Emil. Ends and means of psychiatric research (trans. Sydney Cole). *JMS* 1922, 68:281, 115–43. https://doi.org/10.1192/bjp.68.281.115.

Krakauer, Siegfried. *From Caligari to Hitler: A psychological history of the German film.* Princeton, NJ: Princeton University Press, 1947/2019.

Kumar, Purnima S. From focal sepsis to periodontal medicine: A century of exploring the role of the oral microbiome in systemic disease. *Journal of Physiology* 2017, 595:2, 465–76. https://doi.org/10.1113/JP272427.

Lamb, Susan. Social skills: Adolf Meyer's revision of clinical skill for the new psychiatry of the twentieth century. *Medical History* 2015, 59:3, 443–64. https://doi.org/10.1017/mdh.2015.29.

Lancet. Editorial: Severe mental illness in the UK: A crisis of compassion. *Lancet* 2024, 403:10427, 587. https://doi.org/10.1016/S0140-6736(24)00308-8.

Lehmann, Heinz E. Before they called it psychopharmacology. *Neuropsychopharmacology* 1993, 8:4, 291–303. https://doi.org/10.1038/npp.1993.69.

Lewis, Aubrey. Fertility and mental illness. *Eugenics Review* 1958, 50:2, 91–106. https://pmc.ncbi.nlm.nih.gov/articles/PMC2973172 (accessed Jan 2025).

Liberati, Elisa, Natalie Richards, Sahanika Ratnayake, John Gibson and Graham Martin. Tackling the erosion of compassion in acute mental health services. *BMJ* 2023;382:e073055. https://doi.org/10.1136/bmj-2022-073055.

Lloyd George, David. Speech, 23 Nov 1918. In Jordan Reynolds, 'A fit country for heroes': 100 years since Lloyd George made legendary speech in Wolverhampton. *Express and Star*, 23 Nov 2018. https://www.expressandstar.com/news/politics/2018/11/23/a-fit-country-for-heroes-100-years-since-lloyd-georges-legendary-wolverhampton-speech (accessed Jan 2025).

Lomax, Montagu. The asylum inquiry. *Medical Press and Circular*, 22 Feb 1922, 148.

Lomax, Montagu. The asylum report and asylum reform. *Fortnightly Review* 1922, 112:671, 850–9.

Lomax, Montagu. *The Experiences of an Asylum Doctor: With suggestions for asylum and lunacy law reform.* London: Allen and Unwin, 1921.

Lomax, Montagu. Lunacy reform. *Times*, 3 Feb 1922, 11.

Lomax, Montagu. *A Reply to the 'Report of the Committee on the Administration of Mental Hospitals'*, 1922 (no publisher stated).

Lomax, Montagu. Searchlight on asylums. *NAWU Magazine* 1921, 10:12, 2.

Long, Vicky. Changing public representations of mental illness in Britain 1870–1970. PhD thesis, Warwick, 2004. http://wrap.warwick.ac.uk/1217/1/WRAP_THESIS_Long_2004.pdf (accessed Jan 2025).

Long, Vicky. *Destigmatising Mental Illness? Professional politics and public education in Britain, 1870–1970*. Manchester: Manchester University Press, 2014.
Lord, John R. American psychiatry and its practical bearings on the application of recent local government and mental treatment legislation, including a description of the author's participation in the First International Congress on Mental Hygiene, Washington, D.C., May 5–10, 1930. *JMS* 1930, 76:314, 456–95. https://doi.org/10.1192/bjp.76.314.456.
Lord, John R. The clinical study of mental disorders: The presidential address at the 85th annual meeting of the Royal Medico-Psychological Association, held in London, July 13–16, 1926. *JMS* 1926, 72(S298), 1–79. https://doi.org/10.1192/bjp.72.298_Supplement.1.
Lord, John R. Lunacy law and institutional and home treatment of the insane: Being the final of a course of lectures on psychiatry for local secretaries of Mental Welfare Associations delivered at Horton Mental Hospital, Epsom, October, 1922. *JMS* 1923, 69:285, 155–62. https://doi.org/10.1192/bjp.69.285.155.
Lord, John R. *Mental Hospitals and the Public: The need for closer co-operation*. London: Adlard and Son, 1927.
Loughran, Tracy. Shell shock, trauma, and the First World War: The making of a diagnosis and its histories. *Journal of the History of Medicine and Allied Sciences* 2012, 67:1, 94–119. https://doi.org/10.1093/jhmas/jrq052.
MACA [Mental After Care Association]. *Mental After Care Association, 1925*. London: MACA, 1926.
MacArthur, John. *Mental Hospital Manual*. London: Frowde Hodder and Stoughton, 1921.
MacGuire, William and RFC Hull (eds). *CG Jung Speaking: Interviews and encounters*. Princeton, NJ: Princeton University Press, 1977.
Mackenzie, Ivy. Epidemic encephalitis. *JMS* 1927, 73:303, 567–75. https://doi.org/10.1192/bjp.73.303.567.
Macmillan, Hugh Pattison. Mental hygiene: An address. *JMS* 1927, 73:300, 181–5. https://doi.org/10.1192/bjp.73.300.181.
Macpherson, John. The ninth Maudsley lecture: The new psychiatry and the influences which are forming it. *JMS* 1928, 74:306, 386–99. https://doi.org/10.1192/bjp.74.306.386.
Magnello, Eileen. The introduction of mathematical statistics into medical research: The roles of Karl Pearson, Major Greenwood and Austin Bradford Hill. In *The Road to Medical Statistics*, edited by Eileen Magnello and Anne Hardy. Amsterdam: Rodopi, 2002, 94–124.
Mamat, Zulkayda and Michael C Anderson. Improving mental health by training the suppression of unwanted thoughts. *Science Advances* 2023, 9:38. https://doi.org/10.1126/sciadv.adh5292.
Mandziuk, Roseann M. 'Ending women's greatest hygienic mistake': Modernity and the mortification of menstruation in Kotex advertising, 1921–1926. *Women's Studies Quarterly* 2010, 38:3–4, 42–62. https://www.jstor.org/stable/20799363 (accessed Jan 2025).
Mapother, Edward. Emil Kraepelin: Psychiatrist. *JMS* 1927, 73:303, 509–34. https://doi.org/10.1192/bjp.73.303.510.
Marmot, Michael, Jessica Allen, Tammy Boyce, Peter Goldblatt and Joana Morrison. *Health Equity in England: The Marmot Review 10 years on*. Institute for Health Equity, 2020. http://www.health.org.uk/publications/reports/the-marmot-review-10-years-on (accessed Jan 2025).
Marshall, CF and EG Ffrench. *Syphilis and Venereal Diseases*. London: Ballière, Tindall and Cox, 1921.
Marshall, Robert Macnab. The mental aspects of epidemic encephalitis. *JMS* 1927, 73:303, 589–95. https://doi.org/10.1192/bjp.73.303.589.
Martin, John. *Hospitals in Trouble*. Oxford: Blackwell, 1984.
Mathew, Theobald (rev. Hugh Mooney). Lush, Sir (Charles) Montague (1853–1930). *Oxford Dictionary of National Biography*. https://doi.org/10.1093/ref:odnb/34635.
McCowan, PK and JH Quastel. Blood-sugar studies in abnormal mental states. *Lancet* 1931, 218:5640, 731–6. https://doi.org/10.1192/bjp.77.318.525.
McCrae, Niall and Peter Nolan. *The Story of Nursing in British Mental Hospitals: Echoes from the corridors*. Abingdon: Routledge, 2016.
McCrae, Niall and Maureen Wright. Work, rest and play: Professional and social progress of nurses at a British mental hospital in the early 20th century. *Journal of Psychiatric and Mental Health Nursing* 2016, 23:9–10, 614–23.
Meagher, Edward. *General Paralysis and its Treatment by Induced Malaria*. London: HMSO, 1929.
Medical Directory. London: J and A Churchill, 1925.
Medico-Psychological Association. *Handbook for Attendants on the Insane*. London: Baillière, Tindall and Cox, 1911 (6th edn).

Medico-Psychological Association. *Handbook for the Instruction of Attendants on the Insane: Prepared by a Sub-Committee of the Medico-Psychological Association appointed at a branch meeting held in Glasgow on the 21st February, 1884.* London: Baillière, Tindall, and Cox, 1885.

Medico-Psychological Association. *Handbook for Mental Nurses*. London: Baillière, Tindall and Cox, 1923 (7th edn).

Medico-Psychological Association. Members of the Association. *JMS* 1920, 66:272, vii–xxix.

Medico-Psychological Association. Memorandum of the evidence given on May 4 and 5, 1925, on behalf of the Association to the Royal Commission on Lunacy and Mental Disorder. *JMS* 1925, 71:294, 494–558.

Medico-Psychological Association. Report of the Committee on the Status of British Psychiatry and of Medical Officers. *JMS* 1914, 60:251, 667–74.

Medico-Psychological Association. Report of English Lunacy Legislation Sub-Committee. *JMS* 1919, 65:268, 36–44.

Mental Health Task Force. *The Five Year Forward View for Mental Health.* NHS England, 2016. https://www.england.nhs.uk/wp-content/uploads/2016/02/Mental-Health-Taskforce-FYFV-final.pdf (accessed Jan 2025).

Menzies, William F. The mechanism of involutionary melancholia: The presidential address at the annual meeting of the Medico-Psychological Association of Great Britain and Ireland, held at Buxton on July 26th–28th, 1920. *JMS* 1920, 66:275, 355–414. https://doi.org/10.1017/S0368315X00013645.

Menzies, William F. Some points connected with tuberculosis in asylums. *JMS* 1905, 51:214, 548–60. https://doi.org/10.1192/bjp.51.214.548.

Mercier, Charles. *The Attendant's Companion: A manual of the duties of attendants in lunatic asylums*. London: J and A Churchill, 1898.

Mercier, Charles. *Lunatic Asylums: Their organisation and management.* London: C Griffin, 1894.

Mercier, Charles. Psycho-analysis. *BMJ* 1916, 2:2922, 897–900. https://doi.org/10.1136/bmj.2.2922.897.

Mercier, Charles. *A Textbook of Insanity.* London: George Allen and Unwin, 1914.

Michael, Pamela and David Hirst. Recording the many faces of death at the Denbigh Asylum, 1848–1938. *History of Psychiatry* 2012, 23:1, 40–51. https://doi.org/10.1177/0957154X11430032.

Mid Staffordshire NHS Foundation Trust Public Inquiry (Francis Report), HC 947. London: Stationery Office, 2013. https://www.gov.uk/government/publications/report-of-the-mid-staffordshire-nhs-foundation-trust-public-inquiry (accessed Jan 2025).

Millard, Chris and Jennifer Wallis (eds). *Sources in the History of Psychiatry, from 1800 to the Present*. Abingdon: Routledge, 2022.

Miller, Edgar. Twentieth century British clinical psychology and psychiatry: Their historic relationship. In *150 Years of British Psychiatry 1841–1991: The aftermath*, edited by Hugh Freeman and German Berrios. London: Athlone Press, 1996, 156–68.

Mitchell, Alex J, Sheila Hardy and David Shiers. Parity of esteem: Addressing the inequalities between mental and physical healthcare. *BJPsych Advances* 2017, 23:3, 196–205. https://doi.org/10.1192/apt.bp.114.014266.

MoH [Ministry of Health]. *Report of the Committee on Administration of Public Mental Hospitals* (Cobb Report), Cmnd 1730. London: HMSO, 1922. https://wellcomecollection.org/works/d3yspugy/items (accessed Jan 2025).

Monbiot, George. Covid deaths are on the rise again, so what happens? Mask-wearing in hospitals is scrapped. *Guardian*, 16 Oct 2023. https://www.theguardian.com/commentisfree/2023/oct/16/covid-deaths-rise-scrap-mask-wearing-hospitals (accessed Jan 2025).

Moncrieff, Joanna. Why I don't like the idea that mental disorder is a disease. Critical Psychiatry Network blog, 18 Apr 2021. http://www.criticalpsychiatry.co.uk/news/why-i-dont-like-the-idea-that-mental-disorder-is-a-disease (accessed Jan 2025).

Mond, Alfred. Lunacy reform. *Times*, 4 Feb 1922, 11.

Monrad-Krohn, GH. Regarding the treatment of general paralysis. *JMS* 1920, 66:272, 46–8. https://doi.org/10.1192/S0368315X00013050.

Moritz, Judith, Jonathan Coffey and Michael Buchanan. Hospital bosses ignored months of doctors' warnings about Lucy Letby. BBC News, 18 Aug 2023. https://www.bbc.co.uk/news/uk-66120934 (accessed Jan 2025).

Morrison, Hazel. Conversing with the psychiatrist. *Journal of Literature and Science* 2013, 6:1, 18–37. https://www.literatureandscience.org/wp-content/uploads/2013/09/JLS-6.1-Complete-Issue.pdf#page=25 (accessed Jan 2025).

Morrison, Hazel. Henderson and Meyer in correspondence: A transatlantic history of dynamic psychiatry, 1908–29. *History of Psychiatry* 2017, 28:1, 72–86. https://doi.org/10.1177/0957154X16674656.
Mott, Frederick W. The investigation of some of the causes of insanity. *JMS* 1925, 71:295, 631–47. https://doi.org/10.1192/bjp.71.295.631.
Mould, Gilbert. Our asylums. *Saturday Review of Politics, Literature, Science and Art* 1920, 129:3351, 58–9.
Mueller, Thomas and Thomas Beddies. 'The destruction of life unworthy of living' in National Socialist Germany. *International Journal of Mental Health* 2006, 35:3, 94–104. https://doi.org/10.2753/IMH0020-7411350311.
Murray, John F. Tuberculosis and World War I. *American Journal of Respiratory and Critical Care Medicine* 2015, 192:4, 411–14. https://doi.org/10.1164/rccm.201501-0135OE.
National Society for Lunacy Reform. *Annual Report 1925*. London: NSLR, 1926.
National Survivor User Network. Our mission, vision and values. https://www.nsun.org.uk/about-us/our-mission (accessed Jan 2025).
NHS England. Bed availability and occupancy data – overnight. https://www.england.nhs.uk/statistics/statistical-work-areas/bed-availability-and-occupancy/bed-data-overnight (accessed Jan 2025).
Nicol, WD. The care and management of induced malaria. *JMS* 1927, 73:301, 209–17. https://doi.org/10.1192/bjp.73.301.209.
Nicolaou, Claire. Countering the narrative on international interventions: Paternalism as a constant of British interventionary discourse and practice from the 19th century onwards. PhD thesis, Sheffield, 2018. https://etheses.whiterose.ac.uk/21543/1/thesis%20final%20CNicolaou.pdf (accessed Jan 2025).
Noble, Helen and Roberta Heale. Triangulation in research, with examples. *Evidence-Based Nursing* 2019, 22:3, 67–8. https://doi.org/10.1136/ebnurs-2019-103145.
Nuffield Trust. Mental health care outside local area. https://www.nuffieldtrust.org.uk/resource/out-of-area-placements (constantly updated; last accessed Jan 2024).
Office for Health Improvement and Disparities. *Premature Mortality during COVID-19 in Adults with Severe Mental Illness*, 19 Oct 2023. https://www.gov.uk/government/publications/premature-mortality-during-covid-19-in-adults-with-severe-mental-illness (accessed Jan 2025).
Olshansky, Simon. Stigma: Its meaning and some of its problems for vocational rehabilitation agencies. *Rehabilitation Literature* 1965, 26: 71–4. https://doi.org/10.1177/0145482X6505900804.
Olszynko-Gryn, Jesse and Caroline Rusterholz. Reproductive politics in twentieth-century France and Britain. *Medical History* 2019, 63:2, 117–33. https://doi.org/10.1017/mdh.2019.1.
Oosterhuis, Harry. Between institutional psychiatry and mental health care: Social psychiatry in the Netherlands, 1916–2000. *Medical History* 2004, 48:4, 413–28. https://doi.org/10.1017/S0025727300007948.
Oram, Gerard. *Military Executions during World War I*. Basingstoke: Palgrave Macmillan, 2003.
Oswald, Ute. 'Distraction from hurtful thoughts': Recreational activities as agents of healing in nineteenth-century British asylums. *Medizinhistorisches Journal* 2021, 56:1–2, 30–57. https://www.jstor.org/stable/48636493 (accessed Jan 2025).
Oswald, Ute. Entertaining the insane: Recreation in nineteenth-century British asylums. PhD thesis, Warwick, 2022. https://wrap.warwick.ac.uk/175177 (accessed Jan 2025).
Our Medical Correspondent. Asylum horrors. *Times*, 23 Jul 1921, 7.
Our Medical Correspondent. Disease as cure: A new study of malaria fever. *Times*, 17 May 1924, 9.
Oxonian. Confined as a lunatic. *English Review*, Jun 1920, 528–37.
Oxonian. Confined as a lunatic ii. *English Review*, Jul 1920, 42–50.
Oxonian. Confined as a lunatic iii. *English Review*, Aug 1920, 138–46.
Parfitt, David. A mental hospital in 1929. In *150 Years of British Psychiatry 1841–1991: The aftermath*, edited by Hugh Freeman and German Berrios. London: Athlone Press, 1996, 465–76.
Parley, Ernest. *Life in a Madhouse*. London: Independent Labour Party, 1920.
Pereira, José Morgado. Psychiatry in Portugal: Key actors and conceptual history (1884–1924). *History of Psychiatry* 2018, 29:2, 147–64. https://doi.org/10.1177/0957154X18756525.
Philo, Chris. Troubled proximities: Asylums and cemeteries in nineteenth-century England. *History of Psychiatry* 2012, 23:1, 91–103. https://doi.org/10.1177/0957154X11428931.

Pierce, Bedford. In Medico-Psychological Association: Seventy-ninth annual meeting, held at Buxton. *JMS* 1921, 67:276, 97–123, 111. https://doi.org/10.1192/bjp.67.276.97.

Pierce, Bedford. Psychiatry a hundred years ago: with comments on the problems of to-day. The presidential address at the annual meeting of the Medico-Psychological Association of Great Britain and Ireland, held at York, July 22nd, 1919. *JMS* 1919, 65:271, 219–35. https://doi.org/10.1192/bjp.65.271.219.

Pierce, Bedford. Some present-day problems connected with the administration of asylums. *JMS* 1919, 65:270, 198–201. https://doi.org/10.1192/bjp.65.270.198.

Porter, Roy (ed.). *The Faber Book of Madness*. London: Faber and Faber, 1991.

Porter, Roy. The patient's view: Doing medical history from below. *Theory and Society* 1985, 14, 175–98. https://doi.org/10.1007/BF00157532.

Pressman, Jack. *Psychosurgery and the Limits of Medicine*. Cambridge: Cambridge University Press, 1998.

RCF. KA Anklesaria MRCS LRCP. *BMJ* 1970, 1:5689, 179–80.

Read, Charles Stanford. Familial care of the insane. *JMS* 1921, 67:277, 186–95. https://doi.org/10.1192/bjp.67.277.186.

Reade, Charles. *Hard Cash: A matter-of-fact romance*. London: Sampson Low, 1863.

Richards, Graham. Britain on the couch: The popularization of psychoanalysis in Britain 1918–1940. *Science in Context* 2000, 13:2, 183–230. https://doi.org/10.1017/S0269889700003793.

Rickard, Mrs Victor (Jessie Louisa). *Cathy Rossiter*. New York: George Doran, 1919.

Riggall, Mary. *Reminiscences of a Stay in a Mental Hospital.* London: Arthur Stockwell, 1929.

Rimmer, Abi. NHS culture change is difficult, not impossible – but essential, says health ombudsman. *BMJ* 2023, 383, 2,742. https://doi.org/10.1136/bmj.p2742.

Rittel, Horst WJ and Melvin M Webber. Dilemmas in a general theory of planning. *Policy Sciences* 1973, 4, 155–69. https://doi.org/10.1007/BF01405730.

Robb, Barbara. *Sans Everything: A case to answer*. London: Thomas Nelson and Sons, 1967.

Robbins, Richard. Profiles in medical courage: Evidence-based medicine and Archie Cochrane. *Southwest Journal of Pulmonary and Critical Care Medicine* 2012, 5, 65–73. https://static1.1.sqspcdn.com/static/f/654826/19697558/1343923149940/SWJPCC+059-12.pdf?token=tLAmFuFEmsy4z5jhorteBE2osgc%3D (accessed Jan 2025).

Robertson, Dorothea. In Occupational therapy. A series of papers read at a meeting of the Scottish Division held at the Glasgow Royal Mental Hospital on Friday, May 2, 1924. *JMS* 1925, 71:292, 75–80. https://doi.org/10.1192/bjp.71.292.59.

Robertson, George M. Is dementia præcox a definite clinical entity? *JMS* 1924, 70:291, 529–36. https://doi.org/10.1192/bjp.70.291.529.

Robertson, George M. The employment of female nurses in the male wards of mental hospitals in Scotland. *JMS* 1916, 62:257, 351–62. https://doi.org/10.1192/bjp.62.257.351

Robertson, George M. The hospitalisation of the Scottish asylum system: The presidential address at the annual meeting of the Medico-Psychological Association of Great Britain and Ireland, held in Edinburgh, July 19–21, 1922. *JMS* 1922, 68:283, 321–33. https://doi.org/10.1192/bjp.68.283.321.

Robertson, George M. Mental disorders. *Times*, 12 Feb 1920, 15.

Robertson, George M. The seventh Maudsley lecture: The prevention of insanity – a preliminary survey of the problem. *JMS* 1926, 72:299, 454–91. https://doi.org/10.1192/bjp.72.299.454.

Robinson, Michael. 'Definitely wrong'? The Ministry of Pensions' treatment of mentally ill Great War veterans in interwar British and Irish society. *War in History* 2021, 28:1, 71–92. https://doi.org/10.1177/0968344519827034.

Roelcke, Volker. Eugenic concerns, scientific practices: International relations in the establishment of psychiatric genetics in Germany, Britain, the USA and Scandinavia, c.1910–60. *History of Psychiatry* 2019, 30:1, 19–37. https://doi.org/10.1177/0957154X18808666.

Rolleston, Humphry. Discussion on prophylaxis of mental disorder. *BMJ* 1925, 2:3383, 781–8. https://www.jstor.org/stable/25446676 (accessed Jan 2025).

Royal College of Psychiatrists. *National Clinical Audit of Psychosis: Employment spotlight audit report 2021*. London: Healthcare Quality Improvement Partnership. https://www.hqip.org.uk/resource/national-clinical-audit-of-psychosis-employment-spotlight-audit-report-2021 (accessed Jan 2025).

Royal College of Psychiatrists. Over 26,000 adults with severe mental illness die prematurely from preventable illness each year. Royal College of Psychiatrists (press release), 17 May 2023.

https://www.rcpsych.ac.uk/news-and-features/latest-news/detail/2023/05/17/over-26-000-adults-with-severe-mental-illness-die-prematurely-from-preventable-illness-each-year (accessed Jan 2025).

Royal College of Psychiatrists. *Self-Harm and Suicide in Adults: Final report of the Patient Safety Group*. CR229, Jul 2020. https://www.rcpsych.ac.uk/improving-care/campaigning-for-better-mental-health-policy/college-reports/2020-college-reports/cr229 (accessed Jan 2025).

Royal Commission on Lunacy and Mental Disorder. *Minutes of Evidence Taken before the Royal Commission on Lunacy and Mental Disorder*. London: HMSO, 1926. https://wellcomecollection.org/works/y57vqy99/items?canvas=7 (accessed Jan 2025).

Royal Commission on Lunacy and Mental Disorder. *Report of the Royal Commission on Lunacy and Mental Disorder*, Cmd 2700. London: HMSO, 1926.

Royal Medico-Psychological Association. Year Book. *JMS* 1930, 76:312, f1–f50.

Rybakowski, Janusz. 120th anniversary of the Kraepelinian dichotomy of psychiatric disorders. *Current Psychiatry Reports* 2019, 21, art. 65. https://doi.org/10.1007/s11920-019-1048-6.

Sacks, Oliver. *Awakenings*. London: Pan Macmillan, 1991.

Sakula, Alex. A hundred years of lumbar puncture: 1891–1991. *Journal of the Royal College of Physicians of London* 1991, 25:2, 171–5. https://pmc.ncbi.nlm.nih.gov/articles/PMC5377212 (accessed Jan 2025).

Salaman, Redcliffe. Mental Health. *Times*, 23 Sept 1930, 8.

Scambler, Graham. Liberal ideology, the mixed economy and the British welfare state. In *Mind, State and Society: Social history of psychiatry and mental health in Britain 1960–2010*, edited by George Ikkos and Nick Bouras. Cambridge: Cambridge University Press, 2021, 23–31.

Sclare, AB. John Carswell: A pioneer in Scottish psychiatry. *Scottish Medical Journal* 1981, 26:3, 265–70. https://doi.org/10.1177/003693308102600317.

Scott, James. *Sane in Asylum Walls*. London: Fowler Wright, 1931.

Scott, Peter and Anna Spadavecchia. Did the 48-hour week damage Britain's industrial competitiveness? *Economic History Review* 2011, 64:4, 1,266–88. https://doi.org/10.1111/j.1468-0289.2010.00590.x.

Scripture, EW. The treatment of general paralysis by malaria: The use of speech inscriptions for early diagnosis. *JMS* 1923, 69:284, 77–83. https://doi.org/10.1192/bjp.69.284.77.

Scrutator. Asylum whitewash. *Truth*, 16 Aug 1922, 274–6.

Scull, Andrew. Creating a new psychiatry: On the origins of non-institutional psychiatry in the USA, 1900–50. *History of Psychiatry* 2018, 29:4, 389–408. https://doi.org/10.1177/0957154X18793596.

Scull, Andrew. *Desperate Remedies: Psychiatry and the mysteries of mental illness*. Harmondsworth: Penguin, 2022.

Scull, Andrew. *Madhouse: A tragic tale of megalomania and modern medicine*. New Haven, Ct: Yale University Press, 2005.

Scull, Andrew. *Museums of Madness: Social organization of insanity in 19th century England*. London: Allen Lane, 1979.

Shah, Premal and Deborah Mountain. The medical model is dead – long live the medical model. *British Journal of Psychiatry* 2007, 191:5, 375–7. https://doi.org/10.1192/bjp.bp.107.037242.

Sharot, Tali and Jennifer Gledhill. 'Just because we are used to something, doesn't make it OK'. British Psychological Society (blog), 5 Feb 2024. https://www.bps.org.uk/psychologist/just-because-we-are-used-something-doesnt-make-it-ok (accessed Jan 2025).

Shaw, B Henry. Infection in mental hospitals, with special reference to floor treatment. *JMS* 1923, 69:284, 24–45. https://doi.org/10.1192/bjp.69.284.24.

Shorter, Edward. The history of nosology and the rise of the *Diagnostic and Statistical Manual of Mental Disorders*. *Dialogues in Clinical Neuroscience* 2015, 17:1, 59–67. https://doi.org/10.31887/dcns.2015.17.1/eshorter.

Shorter, Edward. *A History of Psychiatry: From the era of the asylum to the age of Prozac*. New York: Wiley, 1997.

Slater, Eliot. Mapother memorial: The psychiatrist. *Bethlem Maudsley Hospital Gazette* 1960, 3, 7–10.

Smith, Grafton Elliot and Tom Hatherley Pear. *Shell Shock and its Lessons*. Manchester: Manchester University Press, 1917.

Smith, Judith and Ruth Thorlby. Ten years after the Francis Inquiry Report: Will we ever learn? University of Birmingham (news item), 6 Feb 2023. https://www.birmingham.ac.uk/news/2023/ten-years-after-the-francis-inquiry-report-will-we-ever-learn (accessed Jan 2025).

Smith, Lade. 'Discrimination against people with severe mental illness is cutting lives short' – UK's top psychiatrist. Royal College of Psychiatrists (press release), 21 May 2024. https://www.rcpsych.ac.uk/news-and-features/latest-news/detail/2024/05/21/discrimination-against-people-with-severe-mental-illness-is-cutting-lives-short----uk-s-top-psychiatrist (accessed Jan 2025).

Smyth, Chris. Red tape has cost the UK £143bn, says Liz Truss's team. *Times*, 29 Sept 2023. https://www.thetimes.com/article/red-tape-has-cost-the-uk-143bn-says-liz-trusss-team-xpw2nbs5s (accessed Jan 2025).

Soanes, Stephen. Reforming asylums, reforming public attitudes: JR Lord and Montagu Lomax's representations of mental hospitals and the community, 1921–1931. *Family and Community History* 2009, 12:2, 117–29. https://doi.org/10.1179/146311809X12520565987250.

Soanes, Stephen. Rest and restitution: Convalescence and the public mental hospital in England, 1919–39. PhD thesis, Warwick, 2011. https://wrap.warwick.ac.uk/54604/1/WRAP_THESIS_Soanes_2011.pdf (accessed Jan 2025).

Sommer, Robert and Humphry Osmond. Autobiographies of former mental patients. *JMS* 1960, 106:443, 648–62. https://doi.org/10.1192/bjp.106.443.648.

Steen, Robert. *The Modern Mental Hospital*. London: Methuen, 1927.

Steinberg, Holger. The sin in the aetiological concept of Johann Christian August Heinroth (1773–1843). Part 2: Self-guilt as turning away from reason in the framework of Heinroth's concept of the interrelationships between body and soul. Citing JCA Heinroth, *Anweisung für angehende Irrenärzte zu richtiger Behandlung ihrer Kranken*. Leipzig: Vogel, 1825, 4. *History of Psychiatry* 2004, 15:4, 437–54. https://doi.org/10.1177/0957154X04043742.

Stilitz, Ivor. A token economy of the early 19th century. *Journal of Applied Behavior Analysis* 2009, 42:4: 925–6. https://doi.org/10.1901/jaba.2009.42-925.

Stoddart, William. A brief résumé of Freud's psychology. *JMS* 1921, 67:276, 1–8. https://doi.org/10.1192/bjp.67.276.1.

Stonehouse, Rachel. NHS psych ward period provision criticised by patients. *BBC Newsbeat*, 16 Oct 2023. https://www.bbc.co.uk/news/newsbeat-66988651 (accessed Jan 2025).

Sturdy, Steve. Scientific method for medical practitioners: The case method of teaching pathology in early twentieth-century Edinburgh. *Bulletin of the History of Medicine* 2007, 81:4, 760–92. https://dx.doi.org/10.1353/bhm.2007.0093.

Szasz, Thomas. *The Myth of Mental Illness*. New York: Harper and Row, 1961.

Takabayashi, Akinobu. Surviving the Lunacy Act of 1890: English psychiatrists and professional development during the early twentieth century. *Medical History* 2017, 61:2, 246–69. https://doi.org/10.1017/mdh.2017.4.

Thane, Pat. *Divided Kingdom: A history of Britain, 1900 to the present*. Cambridge: Cambridge University Press, 2018.

Thompson, Stanley and Everett Howard. Ex-service mental patients. *Times*, 30 Nov 1923, 8.

Thomson, David G. A descriptive record of the conversion of a county asylum into a war hospital for sick and wounded soldiers in 1915. *JMS* 1916, 62:256, 109–35. https://doi.org/10.1192/bjp.62.256.109.

Thomson, Mathew. Mental hygiene in Britain during the first half of the twentieth century: The limits of international influence. In *International Relations in Psychiatry: Britain, Germany, and the United States to World War II*, edited by Volker Roelcke, Paul Weindling and Louise Westwood. Rochester, NY: University of Rochester Press, 2010, 134–55.

Thomson, Mathew. Mental hygiene as an international movement. In *International Health Organisations and Movements 1918–1939*, edited by Paul Weindling. Cambridge: Cambridge University Press, 1995, 283–304.

Thomson, Mathew. *The Problem of Mental Deficiency: Eugenics, democracy, and social policy in Britain, c.1870–1959*. Oxford: Clarendon Press, 1998.

Thornicroft, Graham, Charlene Sunkel, Akmal Alikhon Aliev et al. (another 41 authors). The *Lancet* Commission on ending stigma and discrimination in mental health. *Lancet* 2022, 400:10361, 1,438–80. https://doi.org/10.1016/S0140-6736(22)01470-2.

Tiemersma, Edine, Marieke van der Werf, Martien Borgdorff, Brian Williams and Nico Nagelkerke. Natural history of tuberculosis: Duration and fatality of untreated pulmonary tuberculosis in HIV negative patients: A systematic review. *PloS One*, 6(4), 4 Apr 2011. https://doi.org/10.1371/journal.pone.0017601.

Todd, Selina. Young women, work, and leisure in interwar England. *Historical Journal* 2005, 48:3, 789–809. https://doi.org/10.1017/S0018246X05004668.

Towers, Bridget A. The management and politics of a public exposé: The Prestwich Inquiry 1922. *Journal of Social Policy* 1984, 13:1, 41–61. https://doi.org/10.1017/S0047279400022819.
Townsend, Peter and Nick Davidson (eds). *Inequalities in Health: The Black Report*. Harmondsworth: Penguin, 1982.
Trades Union Congress and the Labour Party. *The Labour Movement and the Hospital Crisis: Statement of policy with regard to hospitals.* London: Trades Union Congress and the Labour Party, c.1922.
Tudor-Hart, Julian. The inverse care law. *Lancet* 1971, 297:7696, 405–12.
Turda, Marius. Legacies of eugenics: Confronting the past, forging a future. *Ethnic and Racial Studies* 2022, 45:13, 2,470–7. https://doi.org/10.1080/01419870.2022.2095222.
Turner, John, Rhodri Hayward, Katherine Angel, Bill Fulford, John Hall, Christopher Millard and Mathew Thomson. The history of mental health services in modern England: Practitioner memories and the direction of future research. *Medical History* 2015, 59:4, 599–624. https://doi.org/10.1017/mdh.2015.48.
Turner, Trevor. 'Not worth powder and shot': The public profile of the Medico-Psychological Association, c.1851–1914. In *150 Years of British Psychiatry 1841–1991*, edited by German Berrios and Hugh Freeman. London: Gaskell, 1991, 3–16.
UK Government, Population data tables for England and Wales. https://assets.publishing.service.gov.uk/government/uploads/system/uploads/attachment_data/file/879057/population-data-tables.xlsx (accessed Jan 2025).
UK Parliament, Comment on Government Response to Joint Committee's report on the draft Mental Health Bill, 25 Mar 2024. https://committees.parliament.uk/committee/605/joint-committee-on-the-draft-mental-health-bill/news/200628/comment-on-government-response-to-joint-committees-report-on-the-draft-mental-health-bill (accessed Jan 2025).
Wallace, James. Making a healthy change: A historical analysis of workplace wellbeing. *Management and Organizational History* 2022, 17:1–2, 20–42. https://doi.org/10.1080/17449359.2022.2068152.
Wallis, Jennifer. *Investigating the Body in the Victorian Asylum: Doctors, patients, and practices*. London: Palgrave Macmillan, 2017.
Walter, B. Hermann Simon – Psychiatriereformer, Sozialdarwinist, Nationalsozialist? [Hermann Simon – reformer of psychiatry, social Darwinist, and National Socialist?]. *Nervenarzt* 2002, 73:11, 1,047–54. https://doi.org/10.1007/s00115-002-1431-z.
Ward, Tony. Law, common sense and the authority of science: Expert witnesses and criminal insanity in England, ca.1840–1940. *Social and Legal Studies* 1997, 6:3: 343–62. https://doi.org/10.1177/096466399700600302.
Ward, Tony. A terrible responsibility: Murder and the insanity defence in England, 1908–1939. *International Journal of Law and Psychiatry* 2002, 25:4, 361–77. https://doi.org/10.1016/S0160-2527(02)00128-0.
Warmark (George Stephen Penny). *Guilty but Insane: A Broadmoor autobiography*. London: Chapman and Hall, 1931.
Warner, Christopher H, George N Appenzeller, Thomas Grieger, Slava Belenkiy, Jill Breitbach, Jessica Parker, Carolynn M Warner and Charles Hoge. Importance of anonymity to encourage honest reporting in mental health screening after combat deployment. *Archives of General Psychiatry* 2011, 68:10, 1,065–71. https://doi.org/10.1001/archgenpsychiatry.2011.112.
Weatherly, Lionel. Asylum administration. *Medical Press and Circular*, 10 Aug 1921, 113–14.
Weatherly, Lionel. Asylum and lunacy law reform. *Medical Press and Circular*, 26 Jan 1921, 74.
Weatherly, Lionel. Lunacy reform. *Medical Press and Circular*, 28 Sept 1921, 261–2.
Weatherly, Lionel. *A Plea for the Insane*. London: Grant Richards, 1918.
Weatherly, Lionel. 'A plea for the insane' *Medical Press and Circular*, 8 Jan 1919, 31–2.
Weatherly, Lionel. The treatment of incipient and unconfirmed insanity. *Lancet* 1914, 183:4720, 497. https://ia800607.us.archive.org/view_archive.php?archive=/8/items/crossref-pre-1923-scholarly-works/10.1016%252Fs0140-6736%252800%252954367-0.zip&file=10.1016%252Fs0140-6736%252800%252954574-7.pdf (accessed Jan 2025).
Wells, HG. *Christina Alberta's Father*. New York: Macmillan, 1925.
Weston, Janet. *Looking after Miss Alexander: Care, mental capacity, and the Court of Protection in mid-twentieth-century England.* Montreal: McGill-Queen's University Press, 2023.
Westwood, Louise. A quiet revolution in Brighton: Dr Helen Boyle's pioneering approach to mental health care, 1899–1939. *Social History of Medicine* 2001, 14:3, 439–57. https://doi.org/10.1093/shm/14.3.439.
WG. Re: Impressions of a probationer. *NAWU Magazine* 1924, 13:1, 10–11.

Whitrow, Magda. Wagner-Jauregg and fever therapy. *Medical History* 1990, 34:3, 294–310. https://doi.org/10.1017/S0025727300052431.

Wilberforce, Octavia. *The Autobiography of a Pioneer Woman Doctor* (ed. Patricia Jalland). London: Cassell and Co, 1989.

Winslow, Lyttleton. *Manual of Lunacy: A handbook relating to the legal care and treatment of the insane in the public and private asylums of Great Britain, Ireland, United States of America and the continent*. London: Smith, Elder and Co, 1874.

Wolseley-Lewis, Herbert. Ministry of Health (Miscellaneous Provisions) Bill. *JMS* 1921, 67:277, 255.

Woolf, Virginia. *Mrs Dalloway.* London: Hogarth Press, 1925 / London: Penguin, 2019.

Woolnough, Sarah. Challenge and change: What does 2024 hold for the health and care system? King's Fund blog, 10 Jan 2024. https://www.kingsfund.org.uk/insight-and-analysis/blogs/challenge-change-what-does-2024-hold-for-the-health-and-care-system (accessed Jan 2025).

Wynter, Rebecca, Rob Ellis and Jennifer Wallis. Marking time: Memory, mental health, and making minds. In *Memory, Anniversaries and Mental Health in International Historical Perspective*, edited by Rebecca Wynter, Jennifer Wallis and Rob Ellis. London: Palgrave Macmillan, 2023, 1–35.

Younger, Edward. *Insanity in Everyday Practice* (rev. and ed. GW Smith). London: Baillière, Tindall and Cox, 1924.

Zaniletti, Isabella, Dirk R Larson, David G Lewallen, Daniel J Berry and Hilal Maradit Kremers. How to distinguish correlation from causation in orthopaedic research. *Journal of Arthroplasty* 2023, 38:4, 634–7. https://doi.org/10.1016/j.arth.2022.11.019.

Index

References to figures are in *italics* and references to tables are in **bold**